The Mammoth Book of
BRIDGE

MARK HORTON is an established International player and the editor of *Bridge Magazine*. He has won tournaments in Australia, Canada, Egypt, Germany, Malta, Romania and the Netherlands. He has crossed swords with World Champions from every corner of the planet.

He is the Editor of the Batsford Bridge series and is ever present at World and European Championships in his capacity as Editor of the Daily Bulletins. His previous books include *Step by Step Signalling* and *Learn from the Stars*.

He is married to Vera Nesterovitsh and lives in Romford.

Also available

The Mammoth Book of Armchair Detectives & Screen Crimes
The Mammoth Book of Arthurian Legends
The Mammoth Book of Battles
The Mammoth Book of Best New Horror 99
The Mammoth Book of New Science Fiction 12
The Mammoth Book of Cats
The Mammoth Book of Chess
The Mammoth Book of Comic Fantasy
The Mammoth Book of Dogs
The Mammoth Book of Erotica
The Mammoth Book of Gay Erotica
The Mammoth Book of Gay Short Stories
The Mammoth Book of Heroic and Outrageous Women
The Mammoth Book of Historical Detectives
The Mammoth Book of Historical Erotica
The Mammoth Book of Historical Whodunnits
The Mammoth Book of How It Happened
The Mammoth Book of International Erotica
The Mammoth Book of Jack the Ripper
The Mammoth Book of British Kings & Queens
The Mammoth Book of Lesbian Short Stories
The Mammoth Book of Men O'War
The Mammoth Book of New Erotica
The Mammoth Book of New Sherlock Holmes Adventures
The Mammoth Book of Nostradamus and Other Prophets
The Mammoth Book of Puzzles
The Mammoth Book of Seriously Comic Fantasy
The Mammoth Book of Tasteless Lists
The Mammoth Book of the Third Reich at War
The Mammoth Book of True Crime (new edition)
The Mammoth Book of True War Stories
The Mammoth Book of 20th Century Ghost Stories
The Mammoth Book of Unsolved Crimes
The Mammoth Book of War Diaries and Letters
The Mammoth Book of the Western
The Mammoth Book of the World's Greatest Chess Games

The Mammoth Book of

BRIDGE

MARK HORTON

ROBINSON
London

Robinson Publishing Ltd
7 Kensington Church Court
London W8 4SP

First published in the UK by Robinson Publishing 1999

A copy of the British Library Cataloguing in
Publication data is available from the British Library

ISBN 1-84119-009-8

Printed and bound in the EC

CONTENTS

INTRODUCTION

While this book is designed to be read as a guide to the game of bridge, it is not a beginner's book in the traditional sense. By the same token it contains a lot of high-level material but is not specifically aimed at experts. My idea is to have produced a book that will provide both inspiration and information in equal measure for everyone who is interested in bridge: from those who are taking their first tentative steps to seasoned campaigners at every level.

If I have succeeded, you will find here a book that you will return to again and again in the new millennium, a book you will enjoy all the more as you develop into an accomplished player.

WHY PLAY BRIDGE?

Everyone who plays bridge will happily provide an answer to this question and given that you have got as far as turning to this page the game clearly has some attraction for you.

Make no mistake about it bridge is without doubt one of the finest card games, perhaps the best ever invented. Once learnt it provides satisfaction at many levels.

As a social game it has no equals. Wherever you go in the world you will never be alone if you can play bridge, for every city in the world contains at least one club and the door is always open, especially to visitors.

Because the game involves four people it automatically brings you together with those who have a common interest.

The challenge of bridge is never ending. Every few minutes you are involved in a new hand with different problems to solve almost every time.

In the first part of the book I will introduce you to the game of bridge in a way that is easy to understand.

The second part of the book is designed to take you on from the knowledge you have gained earlier.

Part three introduces you to the competitive side of the game.

The final part of the book provides you with some essential information.

PART ONE

Mastering Bridge

The Basics

GETTING STARTED

Bridge is a game for four players. They sit round a table occupying four points of the compass: West, North, East and South. North and South face each other as partners. They play against East and West.

At the start of the game thirteen cards are dealt face down to each player and the first task is for each player to arrange their hand into suits. If you inspect a deck of cards you will discover that there are four suits each containing thirteen cards. (Thirteen is a cardinal number in bridge). These suits are spades (♠), hearts (♡), diamonds (♢) and clubs (♣). Spades and hearts are the *major suits*, diamonds and clubs the *minor suits*. Each player picks up his thirteen cards and generally sorts them into suits. The cards rank in this order:

Ace (highest) King Queen Jack 10 9 8 7 6 5 4 3 2 (lowest)

The top five cards are known as *honours*, the remainder as *spot cards*.

The standard method of sorting your hand is to place the cards in descending order of rank from left to right, whilst alternating the suits. A typical hand would look like this:

♠ A J 7 4   ♡ 8 4 2   ♢ K 9   ♣ K Q 8 5

As you become more experienced and start to encounter other players you will doubtless hear hands described verbally. That can be done in several ways: "ace jack fourth, three low, king small and king queen fourth" is one possibility, while another is "ace jack to four, three small, king doubleton and king queen to four".

When an individual hand is being set out in a book, magazine or newspaper it is usually done like this:

♠ A J 7 4
♡ 8 4 2
◇ K 9
♣ K Q 8 5

Once the hands have been sorted the players get involved in the first phase of the game, the bidding. I will come back to that later. The idea is for the two partnerships to try and determine how many of the thirteen "tricks" they will make when the cards are played out.

If I want to describe the bidding in detail it will be set out like this:

West	North	East	South
1♠	2♡	Pass	Pass

When this first phase of the game is over the cards can be played out. The partnership that made the highest bid must try to make at least the number of tricks they said they could. Once all thirteen tricks have been completed the score can be calculated and a fresh hand is dealt to all the players.

In addition to the essentials of four players, a table and chairs and a pack of cards (although two packs are usual so each side has its own for the purposes of dealing, you can get by with one) you need something to keep the score with and on: any old piece of paper and a writing implement will do or you can get fancy and buy a bridge scoring set from your local department store.

Although you can learn the basics of bridge in around twenty minutes, it will take you rather longer to master it! World Champion Benito Garozzo maintains that he still learns something new every time he plays – and he has been hard at it for over 40 years!

If you are still with me you will remember that the four players sit North, East, South and West. In this book you are going to be South quite a lot of the time as in bridge books South always becomes *declarer*. That will make your partner, North, the *dummy*. The meaning of these terms will become clear in due course.

You are going to see a lot of hands in this book so it's time to show you how a full deal is represented:

```
                          ♠ A J 7
                          ♡ K 9 4 2
                          ◇ Q 7 3
                          ♣ A 8 2
        ♠ Q 10 6      ┌──────────┐      ♠ 8 4 2
        ♡ 8 7 3       │    N     │      ♡ J 10 6 5
        ◇ K 9 2       │  W   E   │      ◇ A 8 4
        ♣ Q 7 5 3     │    S     │      ♣ K J 4
                      └──────────┘
                          ♠ K 9 5 3
                          ♡ A Q
                          ◇ J 10 6 5
                          ♣ 10 9 6
```

There are four distinct phases to every deal:

Dealing
Bidding
Playing
Scoring

Let's take a brief look at each of them.

Dealing

This is one aspect of bridge that I really enjoy. Practically all my partners claim it's the best part of my game!

You are all sitting comfortably at the table facing your respective partners. Someone shuffles the deck of cards and puts them face down on the table. You all take one card and the one who selects the highest deals the first hand. Guess what? This player is the *dealer*. At the end of each hand the onus of dealing rotates clockwise, so each player deals once every four hands.

The mechanics of dealing are easy. The dealer starts with the player on his left and distributes the cards one at a time in a clockwise direction until all the cards have been dealt. This will result in all four players having thirteen cards.

When all the cards have been dealt you can pick your thirteen up and take a look at them. It's a good idea to count your cards before you look at them. Try to resist the temptation to start picking your cards up before the deal is finished!

Now you can sort your cards. You can use any method you prefer but for the time being you will probably find it easiest to adopt the one I described earlier. By the way, when you take a look at your hand make sure that only you can see it! Part of the fun of bridge is trying to work out what the other players have and showing the other players your hand defeats the object!

Bidding

Armed with your thirteen cards, you and your partner (and your opponents!) use this phase of the game to try to estimate how many *tricks* you can take.

What's that I hear you say? It's not difficult.

Each player has thirteen cards and in turn he plays a card face up on the table. The highest card in the suit that has been led wins the trick. This happens thirteen times on every hand. So there are thirteen tricks.

This is fundamental, as the key feature of every hand at bridge is how many tricks each side wins.

The dealer is always the first person to bid and, like during the dealing phase of the game, continues in a clockwise direction. All four players get a chance to *bid*. If you don't want to make a positive bid then you say "Pass".

If you want to make a positive bid you must, as a minimum, try for seven of the thirteen tricks. As the bidding goes around the table the number of tricks that one or both sides try for can be increased, sometimes going all the way to thirteen.

The bidding finishes when three players in turn say "Pass". The last positive bid is called the *final contract*. That determines the number of tricks that each side is going to try to take.

This whole procedure can be over in just a few seconds, or it can last for a few minutes as each of the players in turn consider his possible bids. This phase is frequently referred to as the *auction*.

Playing

Once the auction has finished the play can begin. Let's imagine that your side has made the highest bid, trying for eight tricks. If you succeed your side will score points. If you fail then points will go to your opponents.

It will often be the case that the person making the last positive bid will end up being the declarer. His partner becomes the dummy. For this deal the opponents are now the *defenders*. The player on declarer's left plays a card to the first trick. This is called *leading* and the first lead is called the *opening lead*.

At this point something unusual happens. The next player, dummy, doesn't play a card! Instead he puts his hand face up on the table! The correct way is to do it is in four vertical rows, one for each of the four suits with the high cards at the top. It would look like this:

♠	♡	◇	♣
A	K	Q	A
J	9	7	8
7	4	3	2
	2		

From this point on dummy can pretty much say or do nothing – no wonder the French call dummy *le mort*!

Can you remember what the cards that have been placed on the table are called? You've got it – the dummy!

It is declarer's responsibility to play a card from the dummy to each trick, as well as a card from his own hand. Sounds like hard work! Remember, though, you have a big advantage; you can see all twenty-six of your side's cards while the two defenders still have to try to figure out what their partner has. Being able to see all your partner's cards allows you to plan how you will arrive at the required number of tricks.

So far we have seen the opening lead and the dummy. Declarer, playing on behalf of himself and the dummy, and the remaining opponent must play a card in the same suit as the one that has been led. This is called *following suit*. So, if the opening lead is a diamond, that suit must be played from all three remaining hands. The cards that each player selects are put face up on the table. These four cards are a trick. The highest card played wins the trick. The player who wins the trick leads to the next one. If a card played from the dummy wins the trick then declarer leads to the next trick from dummy. A quick calculation will tell you that there are going to be thirteen leads on every hand.

If you don't have a card in the suit that has been led you can select any of the cards in your hand from one of the remaining suits and play it to that trick. This is called *discarding*. Don't ask me why!

The important thing to remember is that you can never win the trick with a discard. Most of the time if you have to discard you will select a card that would be unlikely to win a trick later – you are more likely to throw away a two than an ace!

You have to follow suit if you can. If you discard when you could have followed suit you have *revoked*. This will get you into trouble if the opponents find out, but not to worry as everyone does it sooner or later – the first time I played in a bridge club, I revoked while playing against the owner!

You need to keep a record of the tricks that have been won by either side. This is simple. If you win the trick, you collect the four cards together and place them neatly in front of you face down on the table. As dummy plays no part in the play of the cards declarer collects all the tricks taken by his side. The first defender to win a trick will do the same for his side.

When all the cards have been played you can add up the tricks and move on to the next deal. If South dealt the first hand West will deal the next one. Before you do that only one thing remains.

Scoring

Each side will make a note of the score achieved on each deal. I'll explain it in detail later, but for the moment the only thing you need to know is that each side is trying to make two game contracts or their equivalent. Once you have done that you have won a rubber. You will always win a rubber by 2-0 or 2-1 in games but as you will see later you may not necessarily end up with more points than your opponents!

TRUMPS

We are getting near to the point where you could start playing, but there is one more important thing for you to learn. The difference between *trumps* and *no-trumps*. This is another fundamental point that you need to master.

I have a sneaking feeling that many of you will know what a trump is already. If you have played games like German Whist, Oh Hell, Sevens and the like you will be aware that whilst all the suits are equal, one of them, the *trump suit* ends up being more equal than the others – sort of "primus inter pares".

You already know there are four suits: spades, hearts, diamonds and clubs.

On every hand of bridge you play it is possible for one of these suits to end up as trumps. By the same token it is possible for every hand to be played without a trump suit – in no-trumps.

I can hear you asking, "How do I know if there will be a trump suit?" The bidding provides the answer. If the last positive bid includes a suit then they will be the trumps for the purposes of that hand. So if you bid Four Hearts then hearts will be trumps. If the last bid is, for example, Two No-Trumps then the hand is played without trumps and the highest card played in the suit that has been led wins each trick.

As you delve further into this book you will discover that so far I have given you only a brief insight into how to play bridge. Indeed I have deliberately withheld some information that you will find easier to absorb later on. However, you should now have a grasp of the basic mechanics of the game so it's time to move on.

TRICKS WITHOUT TRUMPS

When books on how to play bridge first started to appear it was fairly standard for the author to start off with an explanation about the bidding. I know this because in the book that I learnt from, *The Game of Bridge* by the late Terence Reese, he makes that very point. He, followed by many subsequent authors, realized that the bidding can have little meaning until a player has an idea of how tricks are won and lost and what cards are needed to make the number of tricks you have bid for.

Before we examine the process of winning tricks I want to take time out to make another fundamental point.

No mathematical genius is required in order to be able to play bridge. I was absolutely hopeless at maths at school! The ability to *count* is all that is required. That and a few calculations that will become automatic with practice.

Now let's see how we can win tricks.

You may have guessed from the chapter heading that we are going to play without trumps. So in every situation we are in a no-trump contract.

There are two ways in which we can win tricks at no-trumps; either with high cards such as aces and kings, or with *long cards* that are left when all the high cards are gone. Here we go.

♠ A 6 5

♠ K Q 4

In a bridge book South gets to play all the hands and North is always the dummy. So here you are South and you can see the six spades that you and your partner hold. This is quite an easy combination of cards. If you have remembered the order in which the cards rank you will realize that you have the three highest spades between the two hands. When spades are led you will be able to win three tricks in the suit.

Imagine West leads the jack of spades. You can put on dummy's ace, making sure you play the four of spades from your hand, or you could play either the five or six of spades from the dummy and win the trick in your hand with either the king or queen of spades. If you win the trick you can either carry on with spades or move on to another suit.

That was easy because you had all the top cards in spades. This situation is different:

♠ 7 4 2

♠ A K 5

West makes the same opening lead of the jack of spades.

The first thing you should notice is that you no longer have the queen of spades. Your spot cards are very small so you can count on only two tricks this time, the ace and the king. An additional point, worth noting for the future, is that you can't win a trick in the dummy this time as both the high cards are in your hand. When you are lucky enough to hold the highest cards in a suit and are playing no-trumps you are certain to take tricks with them. You can decide when to take those tricks, so here you are entitled, if you wish, to play one of dummy's small spades to the trick and contribute the five of spades from your hand. Of course, you will have to win the next round of spades, as you will have only the ace and king left.

In these two examples each hand has contained three cards. That will not always be the case.

♡ A Q 8

♡ K 6 5 3

Here you, South, have four cards facing dummy's three. Once again you have the three top cards in the suit. Once you have taken tricks with the ace, king and queen you will be left with the six of hearts in your hand. Could that by any chance take a trick?

The answer will depend on how the opponents' cards are distributed. Before we take a look at the possibilities, ask yourself this simple question: "How many hearts do the opponents have between their two hands?"

You and dummy have seven cards in hearts and as each suit contains thirteen cards that leaves six for East and West.

The layout of the heart suit around the table might look like this:

♡ A Q 8

♡ J 10 9   [   ]   ♡ 7 4 2

♡ K 6 5 3

Remember, the opponents have to follow suit if they can, so when you have played out the ace, king and queen of hearts the remaining heart in your hand will be the only card left in the suit. At no-trumps it is a winner. You are going to make a trick with a long card.

Let's change the situation slightly:

♡ A Q 8

♡ J 10 9 7   [   ]   ♡ 4 2

♡ K 6 5 3

You will see that now, after the three top hearts have been taken, West's remaining heart will be higher than South's. The distribution of the cards has changed. This is one of the areas where a little bit of counting will help you to work out if your remaining heart is a winner. There are thirteen cards in each suit and if all the players follow suit to a trick then four of them have gone. If this happens three times in a suit, then twelve cards are accounted for and only one remains. This may seem a little difficult to understand now but, as you become experienced, this type of calculation and many others will become second nature. In our example you should be able to work out that after three heart tricks have been completed, only two cards will be left in the suit. You should try to get used to recognizing the trick-taking potential of various combinations as this will help you enormously when you have to start thinking about a complete hand.

Here is an important illustration:

◇ 7 6 3

◇ A K Q 5 2

You have been dealt eight diamonds between the two hands, leaving only five for your opponents. If those remaining cards are distributed between their two hands with, say, three for West and two for East, in bridge terms a 3-2 break, then, after you have cashed your top cards in diamonds, both the five and two of diamonds will be winners. They will be *established*.

You may not be so lucky, as the complete distribution of the diamond suit may look like this:

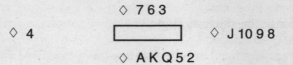

◇ 7 6 3

◇ 4   ◇ J 10 9 8

◇ A K Q 5 2

Now, after you cash the top diamonds, East will still have a winner in the suit – the *master* diamond. However, once you have lost a trick to that card your remaining diamond will be established as a winner.

In the examples so far you have been able to make tricks quite easily as you have held the all-important high cards. Sometimes you will find that a poor distribution will affect the number of tricks you can take in a particular suit.

♣ K J

♣ A Q

Here you have the top four cards in the club suit, but they stand alone, unaccompanied by any of the spot cards. As a result you can win only two tricks in clubs. The technical way to describe this is to say you have *duplicated values*.

♠ A K Q 7 6 3

♠ 5 4 2

This looks fantastic. You have nine spades and the top three cards in the suit. This is surely going to produce six tricks. Indeed it will unless one of your opponents holds all of the remaining spades, the ♠J-10-9-8, when you will have to lose one trick if you want to make five tricks in spades.

♡ K 8 3

♡ A 7 5 4 2

This is something new. You have eight cards between the two hands, but only the ace and king of hearts. How many tricks do you expect to take in this suit?

The answer depends on how the remaining cards are distributed. This might be the layout:

♡ K 8 3

♡ Q J 10   ♡ 9 6

♡ A 7 5 4 2

Now, after you cash the ace and king of hearts, West will be left with the master heart, the queen. After you concede a trick to that card you will be left with two established winners in the suit. If you want to be mischievous you can arrange for one of them to be the two; after all, anyone can win a trick with an ace!

This type of combination is another important one, worthy of careful study.

The first important thing to realize is that in the absence of the queen of hearts you must lose at least one trick in the suit.

The second is to be aware that you can decide when you lose that trick.

You can begin by playing off your top cards and then giving up a trick but as you become more accomplished you will realize that a more subtle approach may be better. You can begin by playing a low card from both your hand and the dummy! This manoeuvre is very common in bridge and is called *ducking*. Notice that even after you have ducked a round of hearts you can still choose where you would like to win the next trick in the suit as you have a high card in both hands. You have retained *communications* between your two hands.

We are nearly ready to have a stab at a full pair of hands, but before we do let's consider another aspect of establishing tricks.

Take a look at this combination in the diamond suit:

♢ K Q J

♢ 8 4 2

Dummy has an impressive holding in the suit, but the ace is missing. This means that sooner or later a trick must be lost to the ace of diamonds. You will always make two diamond tricks, no more, no less.

♣ Q 10 9 5 3

♣ J 8 2

This time you have more cards, but both the ace and king of clubs are absent. You will have to lose two tricks in this suit. That's the bad news. The good news is that once they have been played you will be left with three tricks in clubs.

Just one more example and then we'll try looking at 26 cards in combination.

♠ 8 7 6 2

♠ 5 4 3

You will probably be distressed by the absence of any high cards between your two hands and at first glance it seems impossible for your side to win a trick. However, if the layout of the suit is like this:

♠ 8 7 6 2

♠ A K Q   ♠ J 10 9

♠ 5 4 3

Once three rounds of the suit have been completed then one of dummy's lowly spades will have become "top dog!"

All right, let's try to plan the play with a sight of two complete hands.

♠ A J 5 4
♡ K J
◇ A Q 8 2
♣ K 8 3

```
      N
  W       E
      S
```

♠ K Q 6
♡ A Q 2
◇ K J
♣ A Q J 4 2

Hold on! That's really too easy. I hope you can see that you and your partner have every high card in the pack and taking all thirteen tricks will present no problem.

I can still remember the first hand I played in an International match. My partner Richard Winter and I bid and made Seven No-trumps! As you are not quite ready to represent your country just yet I'll be generous and on the next hand your task is just to make twelve of the thirteen tricks. Your contract is Six No-Trumps.

♠ A 9 5 4
♡ K 7
◇ A Q 8 2
♣ K 8 3

```
       N
  W        E
       S
```

♠ K Q 6
♡ A 4 2
◇ K 6
♣ A 7 5 4 2

West starts off by leading the queen of hearts.

The first thing to do on every hand that you play as declarer is to formulate a plan. When you are in a no-trump contract the initial step is to count your certain winners. Let's do that here.

In spades you have the ace, king and queen – three tricks.

In hearts you have only the ace and king – two tricks.

In diamonds you again have the ace, king and queen – three tricks.

In clubs you possess the ace and king – two tricks.

That's a total of ten tricks and to fulfil the contract of Six No-Trumps you need twelve. Where are the two extra tricks to come from?

The place to look for extra tricks is in the suits where you have honours supported by spot cards. You have seven spades, so if the remaining six cards in that suit are divided 3-3 you can make an extra trick in that suit which will bring you total up to eleven. That will not be enough as your target is twelve. I hope you are ahead of me here, for the suit you should be looking at is clubs.

You have eight cards in the suit, leaving only five for your opponents. If they split 3-2 then you will be able to take four tricks in the suit. Now three spade tricks, two heart tricks, three diamond tricks and four club tricks bring your total up to twelve.

Eureka! Well, not quite, as we still have a long way to go.

I hope you realize that after you have won the opening lead of the queen of hearts with either the ace or king you must immediately tackle the club suit. It would be disastrous simply to play off your high cards before setting up those all-important long cards in clubs.

Now for a real treat. I am going to let you play a hand where you can see all 52 cards! As slam hands are not very frequent I'll make your task more mundane by making the contract Three No-Trumps. So, you need nine tricks to be a winner.

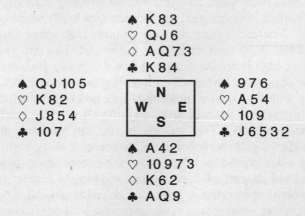

```
                    ♠ K 8 3
                    ♡ Q J 6
                    ◇ A Q 7 3
                    ♣ K 8 4
  ♠ Q J 10 5                          ♠ 9 7 6
  ♡ K 8 2           N                 ♡ A 5 4
  ◇ J 8 5 4      W     E              ◇ 10 9
  ♣ 10 7            S                 ♣ J 6 5 3 2
                    ♠ A 4 2
                    ♡ 10 9 7 3
                    ◇ K 6 2
                    ♣ A Q 9
```

As ever, you, South, are the declarer, so West is going to make the opening lead.

You will discover later that no-trump contracts are basically a race between the two sides. The winner will be the one who can establish its tricks the fastest.

Since West wants to try to set up some tricks for the defence he should logically lead his strongest suit. Unless either North or South had bid spades at some point he should select the queen of spades.

OK. What do you do now?

Right!

Count up your certain winners.

In spades you have the ace and king – two tricks.

In hearts you have no immediate winners – no tricks

In diamonds the ace, king and queen represent – three tricks.

In clubs you have a similar situation to diamonds – three tricks.

That makes a total of eight and you need nine. You are just one shy, so where is the extra trick to come from?

One possibility is in the diamond suit. You have all the top honours and a seven-card fit. If the outstanding cards divide 3-3 you will be able to score a fourth trick in the suit, all you need for your contract. You can't hope for any extra tricks in spades or clubs but there are some prospects in hearts. True, you are missing the ace and king, but once they have been dislodged your remaining cards will be winners. Two extra tricks will bring your total up to ten, one more than you need!

So, for the moment it looks as if you should rely on the heart suit. Let's go through the play. Say you win the opening lead with one of your side's spade honours and play the queen of hearts, forcing out the ace or king. A defender wins and plays another high spade, forcing out your remaining high card or *stopper* in the suit. You win and knock out the other high heart. At this point you will make your contract as long as the opponents cannot take more than two spade tricks. If West started life with five spades rather than four and he now has the lead, then he will cash his winning spades giving his side five tricks, three spades and two hearts. That will mean you can take only the eight tricks you started with, so you will fail by one trick and go one down.

Clearly a lot will depend on how the outstanding spades are distributed and also on who has the ace and king of hearts.

This is another important aspect of declarer play at no-trumps. Having counted your certain winners and looked around to see where extra tricks might come from you need to consider what dangers may lie ahead.

On this hand the danger is obvious, it lies in the spade suit.

I hope you will remember that in a previous example I described the possibility of declarer giving up a trick that he had to lose on purpose, a ducking play. One of the cornerstones of no-trump play is the *hold-up*. It was not, as you might have supposed, invented by Jesse James, but it will frequently have a similar effect as it deprives the defenders of something they would like to have – communications and the ability to cash long cards in the suit they have led.

Without going into a detailed explanation at this stage, imagine that, rather than winning the queen of spades, you let West take the trick, playing a low spade from both your hand and the dummy. West will undoubtedly continue with a second spade, not least because it is always possible that his partner has the ace sitting poised to behead dummy's king. You have to win this spade so let's imagine you take the trick with dummy's king and lead the queen of hearts. East wins with the ace of hearts and plays yet another spade, forcing out your remaining stopper in the suit.

At this point it would be very easy to panic and go after the diamond suit, hoping it breaks 3-3. But wait! Have you been counting?

We have had three rounds of spades and everyone has followed. How many spades are left?

Of course! Only one spade remains, so it is completely safe to carry on with your original plan and knock out the king of hearts. West will be able to win and cash his long card in spades but that will be only the fourth trick for the defence and you must win all the remaining tricks, thereby arriving at the nine you need.

Notice that it would have been a fatal mistake to go for the diamonds as West would be left with the master card in that suit.

You should also make a note of the fact that as a result of ducking the spade you knew more about the distribution of the suit when it mattered. If you had simply taken your ace and king of spades on the first two rounds of the suit you would have been in the dark as to how the suit was divided. West could have started with either four spades or five. How important that is can be shown by this illustration:

```
                  ♠ K 8 3
                  ♡ Q J 6
  ♠ Q J 10 7 5  ┌─────────┐   ♠ 9 6
  ♡ K 8 2       │         │   ♡ A 5 4
                └─────────┘
                  ♠ A 4 2
                  ♡ 10 9 7 3
```

If you win the first spade and play a heart, East can win and play a second spade. I hope you can see that this will force out your remaining stopper in the suit, either on this round or the next, as if you duck West will overtake his partner's card and continue spades. When he regains the lead with the king of hearts he will be able cash his spades.

The situation I have just described will repay careful study, particularly if you remember the hold-up play. It is of fundamental importance in no-trump play and you will encounter it over and over again.

Just to make sure you are familiar with the idea I will give you one more example.

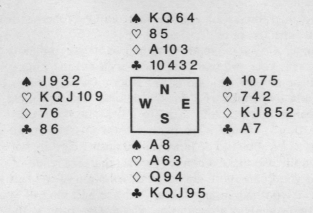

You are trying to make Three No-Trumps so you need nine tricks. West is bound to lead the king of hearts and if you count your certain winners you will see that you have three in spades, one in hearts and one in diamonds. A total of five leaves you well short of your target. You have a good five-card club suit but because the ace is missing you cannot count any tricks there for the moment. Once a trick has been lost to the ace you will have four winners and that just happens to the number of extra tricks you are looking for. You are still new to this game and I can imagine that you are sorely tempted to grab your ace of hearts and play the king of clubs. If you do, East will win and play a heart, returning his partner's suit. West will be able to win four more tricks with the ♡Q-J-10-9 and you will make only eight of the nine tricks you need. Of course, if East is out of hearts at the point where the ace of clubs wins a trick, he will not be able to reach the West hand. You can make that happen! Not by magic but simply by refusing to part with your ace of hearts for a while. Let West win the first trick with the king of hearts. The queen of hearts is sure to come next but the situation hasn't changed. Keep that ace in your hand! You will have to win the next heart but now, when you play clubs and East wins, he is out of hearts and you will take the nine tricks you need. I'll return to this subject later.

So far, winning tricks has not been too complicated as I have given you plenty of high cards in sequence. Clearly if your holding in a suit is:

♡ A K Q J

♡ 7 4 3

You will win four tricks.
 If you have:

♡ K Q J 10

♡ 7 4 3

You will win three tricks once you have dislodged the ace.
 Of course, you have already seen similar examples and are now becoming familiar with the theme. I think you are ready to move on to something that is more complicated but also more interesting.

BRIDGE PLAYERS DO IT WITH FINESSE

That's a title I have been saving up for a long time! If you ever see it as a car sticker then remember you read it here first! A finesse is an attempt to win a trick by hoping that one or more of the opponents' cards will be in the right place. This is the simplest example:

```
                 ◇ A Q
  ◇ K 9       [            ]       ◇ 8 4
                 ◇ 3 2
```

You lead one of your little diamonds and when West plays the nine you try dummy's queen, finessing against the king. Hurrah!

Of course, the situation may be different:

```
                 ◇ A Q
  ◇ 10 9      [            ]       ◇ K 8
                 ◇ 3 2
```

Now the queen will lose to the king and you will make only one trick.

Before we move on I offer a cautionary tale about this position. A relative newcomer to the game was faced by the situation I have just described. He played a card towards the ace-queen, intending to finesse. When West unexpectedly contributed the king he forgot to revise his plan and played the queen! That's what I call a *Fingerfehler*!

In the two previous examples North's holding of ◇ A-Q is called a *tenace*. They feature a lot in the play of a hand so keep the word in mind for later on.

You will remember this situation I described a little earlier:

♡ K Q J 10

♡ 7 4 3

Once the ace is dislodged you will win three tricks. It doesn't matter where the ace is located. That is not the situation where a finesse is involved.

Here is a typical scenario where, although no tenace is involved, the location of the missing high cards is all-important:

♣ K Q 8 4

♣ A 10 9   ♣ J 6 2

♣ 7 5 3

By leading towards the honours in the North hand twice you can ensure that the defenders take only one trick in the suit. Suppose I simply swap the East-West cards to give this diagram:

♣ K Q 8 4

♣ J 6 2   ♣ A 10 9

♣ 7 5 3

Now you can see that either the queen or king will fall to the ace. The result will be that you make only two tricks instead of three.

In both examples you should realize the importance of leading towards the honours in the North hand. If you start by playing one of North's cards then you can never make more than two tricks whoever has the ace.

In the next example you have even less to work with:

♡ Q J 8 4

♡ A 7 6   ♡ K 10 9

♡ 5 3 2

By leading towards the honours in combination you will eventually arrive at two tricks.

You can frequently repeat a finesse if you have the right sort of holding.

♠ A Q J

♠ K 8 2   [   ]   ♠ 10 7 6 4

♠ 9 5 3

If West has the king you can score three tricks in this suit by finessing twice.

♠ K J 10

♠ Q 9 5   [   ]   ♠ A 7 3 2

♠ 8 6 4

In this situation you will have to lose a trick to the ace sooner or later but as long as the queen is in the West hand you will arrive at two tricks by leading twice towards the North hand, playing first the ten and next time the jack.

So far it has been the location of just one of the defenders' cards that has been important but sometimes more can be involved.

◇ A Q 10

◇ K J 6   [   ]   ◇ 7 5 4 3

◇ 9 8 2

By starting with a small card to the ten you can ensure three tricks when West is kind enough to have both the king and jack. If East has the jack then you will still be able to try for two tricks by finessing the queen on the next round.

♠ K J 5

♠ A Q 8 2   [   ]   ♠ 10 7 3

♠ 9 6 4

Once again you are hoping West has both the missing honours as that will allow you to score two tricks by leading twice towards the

North hand. If East has either of them you will have to be content with just one.

This type of play is frequently referred to as a *double finesse*.

Honour cards in combination can be very useful, frequently offering the declarer opportunities to develop tricks. These are everyday situations:

```
                    ♡ A J 10
                  ┌───────────┐
   ♡ Q 8 2        │           │        ♡ K 7 5 3
                  └───────────┘
                    ♡ 9 6 4
```

South starts with a finesse, playing a low card to the ten. East wins the trick but the second finesse against the remaining high card will give declarer two tricks in the suit as long as West has the missing honour. If you are a gambler at heart you will realize that it would be unlucky and well against the odds to find East with both the king and queen.

The next situation illustrates what is usually described as a *deep finesse*.

```
                    ♣ A J 9 5
                  ┌───────────┐
   ♣ K 10 6       │           │        ♣ Q 8 4
                  └───────────┘
                    ♣ 7 3 2
```

Your initial reaction might be to hope that West has both the king and queen and start with a low card to the jack. That is not the best way to tackle this combination! Try playing a small card to the nine. East wins with the queen, but next time you try a club to the jack, thanks to the favourable location of the king and the 3-3 split, you will make three tricks.

You don't have to be a genius to realize that the chance of West holding either ♣K-10 or ♣ Q-10 is greater than ♣K-Q.

As an aside, in a few hundred pages time you will realize it would be a great play for West to put up the king of clubs on the first round of the suit. Why? You'll just have to be patient!

So far, every example of the finesse has featured the potentially favourable location of the defenders' honour cards. In this next illustration of the deep finesse I go one further, introducing the concept of a finesse against a spot card.

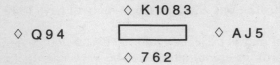

◊ K 10 8 3

◊ Q 9 4

◊ A J 5

◊ 7 6 2

Hoping West has the nine of diamonds,, you begin by running the diamond seven. East wins with the jack and when you try the suit again West produces the nine on the second round. It may seem to you that it is now just a guess as to whether you should play the ten or the king, but the former is a better choice – and not just because it happens to work here! It is only wrong to play the ten when East has ◊ Q-J but it works when East started with ◊ A-J or ◊ A-Q. Another way of looking at it is to realize that playing the ten works when West was dealt either the queen or the jack and playing the king works only when West was dealt the ace.

I recommend you take one suit and deal it out a few times, giving North four cards and the other three hands three each. You should get to see lots of potential finesse positions.

It's a while since we saw a full deal, but just before we take a look at one let's just recap on one important point. Small cards can win tricks too.

Every player can win tricks with aces and kings but on many of the hands you play or defend you will find yourself needing your little cards to come home to roost. How many tricks would this combination be likely to produce:

♣ A K Q 2

♣ 8 6 4

I hope you would answer, "It depends on how the clubs break."

If the remaining clubs are 3-3 then after you have cashed the ♣A-K-Q, the two of clubs will have been promoted to glory.

I think it's time to look at a hand that embodies several of the principles we have already discussed and also introduces some new variations and ideas.

♠ A 7 5
♡ A 10 9 5
♢ Q 7
♣ Q 10 9 4

♠ J 10 9 3
♡ K 8 2
♢ A 6 3
♣ K J 5

Remember, you are playing in no-trumps and this time you have reached a game contract of Three No-Trumps which requires you to make nine tricks.

Following the recommended strategy West attacks with his longest suit and leads the five of diamonds. Do you remember the advice I gave you earlier?

I'll repeat it – no extra charge!

The first thing to do on every hand that you play as declarer is to formulate a plan. When you are in a no-trump contract the initial step is to count your certain winners. Let's do that here.

In spades you have one trick.

In hearts you have two.

In diamonds you have one.

In clubs you have none.

That's a total of only four certain tricks and you need nine so there is plenty of work to do. Let's take a closer look at each suit.

In spades the king and queen are missing but you have a good-looking sequence in your hand – remember you are South – and can take finesses against West. If one of the missing honours is with West you will make at least two tricks, three if the suit divides 3-3.

Your spot cards in hearts are very good and this time the queen and jack are missing. You should be able to make one extra trick from this combination.

Your weakest suit is diamonds, the one the opponents have attacked. If West has led away from the king you will get a second trick by putting up dummy's queen.

In clubs the only important card that is missing is the ace. Once that has been dislodged you will be sure of three tricks in the suit.

Between them these possibilities may add up to the nine tricks you need. Before we play the hand out here is the full deal.

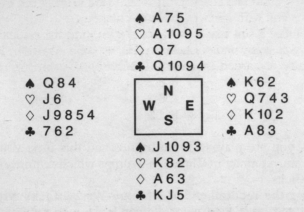

```
                    ♠ A 7 5
                    ♡ A 10 9 5
                    ◇ Q 7
                    ♣ Q 10 9 4
   ♠ Q 8 4                          ♠ K 6 2
   ♡ J 6          N                 ♡ Q 7 4 3
   ◇ J 9 8 5 4   W   E              ◇ K 10 2
   ♣ 7 6 2          S               ♣ A 8 3
                    ♠ J 10 9 3
                    ♡ K 8 2
                    ◇ A 6 3
                    ♣ K J 5
```

Remember, the opening lead is the five of diamonds. You go up with the queen but East covers it with the king. That's a blow but it may not be fatal provided you recall the idea of the hold up. If you win this trick with the ace of diamonds then as soon as the opponents gain the lead they will be in a position to cash at least three tricks in the suit. If, as in this case, the outstanding diamonds are divided 5-3 then they will take four tricks and the contract will have failed.

The correct play is to withhold your ace both on this round of diamonds and the next. You will have to win the third round but you are hoping that West will not have the ace of clubs.

You will have to discard something from dummy on the third round of diamonds and the obvious card to part with is the five of hearts. Now it's time to try to develop some of the tricks you need. The best way to start is by running the jack of spades. East wins with the king and, having no diamonds left, will probably try a club. You should try to win this in hand by playing the jack. When that works you continue your attack on the spade suit by running the ten. When it holds you cross your fingers and cash the ace of spades, hoping the defenders' cards divide 3-3. When that proves to be the case you can turn to the club suit, driving out the ace of clubs to ensure the nine tricks you need: three in spades, two in hearts, one in diamonds and three in clubs.

This hand contained three important elements that are nearly always present when the contract is some number of no-trumps: the hold-up play designed to prevent the opponents from running a long suit against you, the finesse (relying on the favourable location of the opponent' cards) and suit establishment (the driving out of high cards to leave you with winners in a particular suit).

It also featured a suit that was never played until the critical part of the hand was over, namely hearts. This was the situation, North having already discarded the five of hearts on the third round of clubs:

$$\heartsuit \text{ A } 10\ 9$$

$$\heartsuit \text{ J } 6 \qquad \boxed{} \qquad \heartsuit \text{ Q } 7\ 4\ 3$$

$$\heartsuit \text{ K } 8\ 2$$

When East gained the lead with the king of spades he might have switched to a heart. Can you see what happens if he does?

Say he plays the three of hearts. South plays the two and, in order to prevent dummy winning with the nine, West has to play the jack. North wins with the ace and is left with a finesse position against East's queen.

Declarer can make three tricks in this suit without losing any. If he has to tackle the suit he is bound to lose a trick unless the $\heartsuit$Q-J are doubleton in either hand.

The point of this is that it can be a real bonus to make your opponents lead a suit for you. In the previous example you were in possession of the ace and king. In the following one the roles are reversed.

$$\spadesuit \text{ J } 8\ 3$$

$$\spadesuit \text{ A } 9\ 5 \qquad \boxed{} \qquad \spadesuit \text{ K } 10\ 7\ 5$$

$$\spadesuit \text{ Q } 6\ 2$$

Whichever side has to play this suit will lose a trick. If West starts by leading the five you play low from the North hand and sooner or later you will score a trick. If you have to play the suit first and are sure one player does not hold both the ace and the king then your best chance is to lead a high honour from whichever hand you are in and hope it is not covered. Then later on you can lead towards the remaining honour and eventually score one trick.

This is another situation you will encounter:

♣ A 10 5

♣ J 5 2

If West leads this suit you will play low and doubtless lose the trick to East who will play either the queen or king. That will leave you in a position to take a finesse against the remaining honour the next time the suit is played. If East is the one to play first you will be bound to take two tricks even if West produces one of the missing high cards. You will win with the ace and still be left with the jack and ten, one of which will score a trick once the remaining high card has gone.

If you have to play the suit first yourself then it should be clear that you will take only two tricks when the king and queen are both in the West hand.

As you become more experienced you will encounter many similar combinations, but the principle is exactly the same in virtually every case – it can pay to make your opponents lead a suit first.

Before I leave the subject of the finesse I want to take a look at some slightly more complicated examples that you are bound to encounter over and over again.

♠ A K J 8 7 4

♠ 9 5 3

You have nine spades between the two hands and you have a choice of plays. You can cash the ace and king of spades. That will be fine if the queen is a singleton or doubleton. Alternatively you can take just one of your top spades and then finesse against West. That will be the winning play if West has started with three spades that include the queen. How do you decide between these two alternatives?

If you ask one of your bridge-playing friends they may suggest you rely on the advice contained in the old saying, "Eight ever, nine never". It simply means that if you have eight cards missing the queen between the two hands you should finesse while with nine you should play for the queen to drop. While this is not 100% accurate it is usually correct to play for the drop with nine cards. However, sometimes you will be in possession of information that will cause you to assume the suit is not breaking 2-2.

An eight-card fit such as the next one is very common.

♠ A J 7 3

♠ K 8 4 2

This actually came up in one of my classes recently and most of my students realized that with only eight cards in combination the best chance of making all four tricks would be to play West for the queen and finesse the jack. The correct technique is to cash the king first in case East started with a singleton queen and then finesse. Everyone did this and West followed with the five and East with the ten.

On the next round of the suit West played the six. Should declarer finesse or play the ace, hoping East started with just the ♠Q-10?

This is pretty close, but remember you are not obliged to play your cards in a particular order and East might have started with ♠10-9 or even just the ten. If West's second card had been the nine, a tricky East might be trying to fool you with the ♠10-6! Sometimes you will have a clue from something else that has happened, sometimes you will have to guess. Most of the class felt it was right to finesse but one lady stuck to her guns and played the ace. This time she was a big winner as East had been dealt the ♠Q-10!

The point of this story is simply to show you that in some situations you may be right to follow your instincts. I would have finessed and lost to the queen!

Some combinations offer a 100% way for you to arrive at the number of tricks you are after. This is a classic example:

♣ K 10 6 4

♣ A Q 9 7 3

The four missing cards are the ♣J-8-5-2. Most of the time they will be distributed between the East and West hands, either 2-2 or 3-1. When that is the case you will have no problem in making all the tricks. Now and then all four missing cards will be dealt to one hand and that is the possibility that you must guard against. Suppose you start by playing the king of clubs from the North hand and East unkindly discards? Now you will have to lose a trick to West who started with all the missing cards. If East has all four cards then West will discard on the first round and now it will be easy for you to collect all the tricks by finessing against the jack.

When you have to tackle a suit like this you may have some clue as to who is more likely to hold the missing cards, but when you have this much power it doesn't matter, for if you play correctly you can avoid losing a trick however they are located. The secret is to start by playing the ace or queen. If both opponents follow, you clearly have no problem but, if either player shows out, you will still be able to collect all the tricks by finessing against the jack.

The situation changes if I remove the ten.

◊ K 8 6 4

◊ A Q 9 7 3

Now the missing cards are the ◊J-10-5-2. If West has all of them you cannot avoid losing a trick but if East is the guilty party then you can, as long as you start by leading the king first.

In both the above examples your aim was to take as many tricks as possible. As you develop your playing skills you will discover that sometimes you can afford to set your sights a little lower. Imagine you have a combination like this:

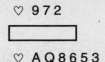

♡ 9 7 2

♡ A Q 8 6 5 3

Only four cards are missing, the ♡K-J-10-4. If you need to take all six tricks your only hope is that East was dealt only two cards in the suit and that one of them was the king. In that case a finesse of the queen will bring home the bacon. However, imagine that your target was only five tricks. Now it would be a big mistake to finesse the queen as you will see if you compare these two diagrams:

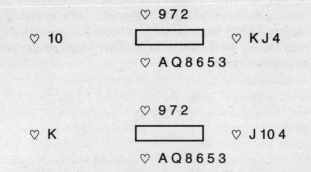

♡ 9 7 2

♡ 10   ♡ K J 4

♡ A Q 8 6 5 3

♡ 9 7 2

♡ K   ♡ J 10 4

♡ A Q 8 6 5 3

In the first example you will survive if you finesse the queen but in the second you lose to the singleton king and must allow East a second trick. The solution is to start by playing the ace! On the next round of the suit you lead towards the queen. Now you make five tricks in either situation.

I hope you realize that you cannot guarantee five tricks: for instance, West might have ♡K-J-4. However, playing the ace first is your best shot.

UNDERSTANDING TRUMPS

Having spent some time learning how to win tricks in a trump-free world it's now time to redress the balance! Once a suit has been selected as trumps it automatically acquires a great deal of power. All the cards in the trump suit rank above all the remaining cards – the two of trumps will beat an ace every day of the week! That sounds great, and it is, but remember that your first duty is to follow suit. Only when you can no longer follow suit, can you start using your trumps to ruff. Just as in all the other suits, the highest trump played to a particular trick will win it. This single-trick example will show you what I mean:

♠ A

♠ K   ♡ 2

♡ 3

Hearts are trumps and West leads the king of spades. You play the ace expecting to win the trick but East has no spades and ruffs with the two of hearts. That would be good enough to win the trick even though you have played the highest card in spades. Luckily you also don't have any spades so you are able to overruff with the three of hearts and win the trick.

I hope this simple example gives you an idea of how powerful a trump suit can be. Remember that if you are playing in no-trumps the trick is always taken by the highest card in the suit led but if there is a trump suit and you are void of the suit being played you can win the trick by ruffing.

During the phase of the game devoted to the bidding you and your partner will get the chance to nominate the suit that you prefer – but so will your opponents! One of the key issues in the bidding is deciding between playing in no-trumps or a suit. If you and your partner have one suit that is very weak it will usually be best to avoid no-trumps.

This illustrates what I mean:

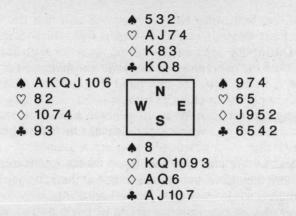

```
            ♠ 5 3 2
            ♡ A J 7 4
            ◇ K 8 3
            ♣ K Q 8
♠ A K Q J 10 6        ┌─────────┐        ♠ 9 7 4
♡ 8 2                 │    N    │        ♡ 6 5
◇ 10 7 4            W │         │ E       ◇ J 9 5 2
♣ 9 3                 │    S    │        ♣ 6 5 4 2
                      └─────────┘
            ♠ 8
            ♡ K Q 10 9 3
            ◇ A Q 6
            ♣ A J 10 7
```

If the hand is played in no-trumps and the defenders start by leading
spades then North-South will lose the first six tricks. If hearts are
trumps then South can ruff the second round of spades and will
easily make all the remaining tricks. That's twelve instead of seven
– quite a difference.

Whichever suit ends up as trumps it is extremely unlikely that
you and your partner will have all of them. That means that the
defenders will have some as well. One of your tasks is to try to
make sure that they don't get the chance to use them to ruff any of
your high cards in the other suits. To avoid the danger you have to
draw trumps. The problem is that sometimes you have to wait a
while before you can do that. It's time to look at some examples of
how tricks are made when there is a trump suit.

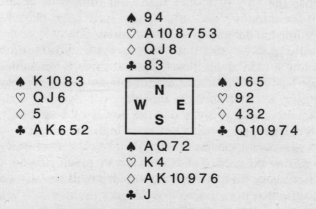

```
            ♠ 9 4
            ♡ A 10 8 7 5 3
            ◇ Q J 8
            ♣ 8 3
♠ K 10 8 3        ┌─────────┐        ♠ J 6 5
♡ Q J 6           │    N    │        ♡ 9 2
◇ 5             W │         │ E       ◇ 4 3 2
♣ A K 6 5 2       │    S    │        ♣ Q 10 9 7 4
                  └─────────┘
            ♠ A Q 7 2
            ♡ K 4
            ◇ A K 10 9 7 6
            ♣ J
```

As you can see, both sides have at least one suit that fits well for them. For East-West it is clubs, while for North-South it is diamonds. During the bidding one of the aims for both sides is to try to determine the denomination that will suit them best if there is going to be a trump suit. On this hand it would be dreadful for North-South to play with clubs as trumps – they have only three of them, leaving ten for East-West. In general terms you should be looking for a trump suit where your side has at least eight of the thirteen cards.

On the deal we are currently looking at North-South might play in hearts where they have an eight-card fit, but their strongest suit is clearly diamonds where they have all the high cards.

Notice that playing in no-trumps would be terrible. East-West will take the first five tricks in clubs, the suit where there is no stopper.

We'll assume that North-South have located their diamond fit and are trying for twelve tricks in a contract of Six Diamonds.

I hope you can remember that when you play a no-trump contract one of the things you have to do is count your winners. When there is a trump suit this is also a good idea, but just as important is to count your losers. On this deal when West leads the ace of clubs you should be able to see that your only obvious loser is in that suit. You will be able to trump the second round of clubs and the question now is how you can arrive at the twelve tricks you need.

If you try counting your sure tricks you will discover there are six in the trump suit, two in hearts and one in spades. That is only nine, well short of your target. You have a finesse position in spades and if East has the king of spades then your total goes up to ten. Of course, once dummy's two little spades have been played you can use the trumps in dummy to ruff those losers.

It would not be awful to try to make your contract by constructing a plan along those lines but there is something better. Your side has eight of the cards in the heart suit. That leaves only five for East-West. Most of the time they will divide 3-2 and if that is the situation here you can use the power of your trump suit to establish the three extra tricks you need in the heart suit.

Let's see how you can do it.

After ruffing the second club you start by playing one of the high trumps from your hand. That is a good idea because you would like to make sure that the missing ones are not divided 4-0. When East and West both follow to the first round of trumps it is safe to take a second round. On this occasion that will leave just one trump outstanding. It would be a big mistake to draw that trump now. What you must do is work on the heart suit.

An important aspect of declarer play is to use your entries wisely. You want to turn your little hearts into winners by ruffing one of them so it would be an error to play the ace first and then come back to your hand with the king. That would leave you in the wrong place at the wrong time.

Start with the king of hearts. You will play a second round of the suit winning with dummy's ace. Now you play another heart. West still has the queen but you don't care. You use one of your trumps to ruff the heart and you now return to the dummy by playing one of your smaller trumps so that the queen of diamonds wins the trick. That will take care of the outstanding trump – I trust you didn't forget about it! Although dummy has nothing left in the way of high cards it still contains three jewels beyond price. The only hearts left are the ones you can see and you can play them one after the other, discarding the two, seven and queen of spades. That will leave you with just the ace of spades and a trump and they are both winners.

In this example you used the power of your trump suit to establish a side suit.

Another common way to make tricks when there is a trump suit is to use dummy's trumps to ruff losers.

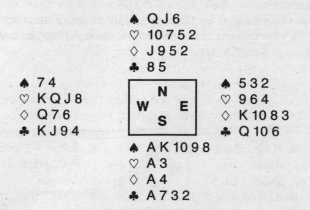

North-South's best suit is spades and they may try for ten tricks in a contract of Four Spades. West is likely to lead from his powerful sequence in hearts and the king would be the normal card. South can see eight tricks, having the five top trumps and three outside aces and need to find two more. There is no prospect of establishing any tricks in one of dummy's side suits so the only hope is to ruff losers in the North hand. Since dummy's shortest suit is clubs that is the obvious place to look. The South hand has only one winning club and three losers.

We talked about the hold-up or duck in relation to no-trump contracts and it can sometimes be correct to do that in a suit contract. However, this would not be the right moment as West might see the danger and switch to a trump, aiming to get rid of dummy's only real asset.

So you win the ace of hearts and start to tackle the club suit. In some situations, especially when you are worried about entries, it might be essential to start with a low club from your hand but here you don't need to worry and simply play the ace of clubs and follow with a second round of the suit. West will probably allow his partner to win the trick and East is likely to switch to a trump. You will win that in hand and ruff a club. You return to your hand with the ace of diamonds and ruff your last club with dummy's remaining trump. You have to lose a trick in each red suit but then all your remaining cards are high trumps.

Apart from using your trumps to set up a side suit and to ruff losers in the dummy you will occasionally encounter a hand where the best plan is not to draw trumps at all!

Don't be discouraged by this apparently contradictory scenario – you wouldn't be reading this book if you thought bridge was going to be that easy, would you?

```
                    ♠ 7
                    ♡ A 9 6 4 2
                    ◇ K Q 10 5
                    ♣ A K 9
♠ K Q J 9 8 2                        ♠ 6 4
♡ 10 5            ┌─────────┐        ♡ K Q J 8 3
◇ 7 3 2          │    N    │        ◇ 4
♣ Q 5            │ W     E │        ♣ J 10 7 6 3
                 │    S    │
                 └─────────┘
                    ♠ A 10 5 3
                    ♡ 7
                    ◇ A J 9 8 6
                    ♣ 8 4 2
```

Although West has a good holding in the highest suit, North-South have the majority of the high cards and an excellent fit in diamonds. Let's imagine they are trying to make twelve tricks in a contract of Six Diamonds.

West's natural lead is the king of spades and the declarer, South, wins the ace. There are no immediate losers and it probably looks tempting to get rid of the opponents' trumps. Resist the temptation!

If you do that you cannot possibly arrive at the number of tricks you need. The best plan is to try to ruff your losing spades in the dummy, rather like the previous example. However, you will need to keep getting back to your hand in order to play spades. You will need lots of entries and, looking at the South hand, it is clear they must come from the trump suit. However, it would be a bad mistake to try to get back to your hand by playing trumps as you will soon exhaust dummy's trumps and be unable to ruff your losing spades. The correct technique, known as a *cross-ruff*, is to ruff dummy's losing hearts in your hand, utilizing the power of your trumps to the full. Let's see how the play might go.

After winning with the ace of spades you immediately ruff a spade with the five of diamonds. Then you cash the ace of hearts and ruff a heart in your hand. You ruff another spade in dummy and a further heart in hand. That will leave the situation looking like this:

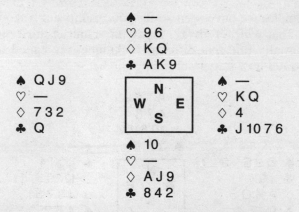

While you have been gaily ruffing, each of your opponents has had to make a discard. East has got rid of a harmless club but West's discard in that suit will be fatal to your contract as now you will never be able to collect two winners in that suit.

This is an important lesson to learn: when you are planning a cross-ruff make sure you cash your side-suit winners early on.

Let's try playing the hand again. After winning with the ace of spades cash the two winning clubs at once, take the ace of hearts and ruff a heart and proceed as before, ruffing spades in dummy and hearts in hand. At the point when you are about to ruff dummy's remaining heart East still has three trumps left but they will score only one trick. When you ruff the nine of hearts with the jack of diamonds East has to underruff.

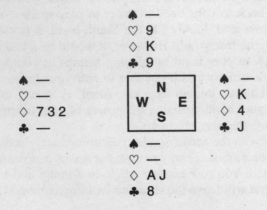

```
              ♠ —
              ♡ 9
              ◊ K
              ♣ 9
  ♠ —                      ♠ —
  ♡ —          N           ♡ K
  ◊ 7 3 2   W     E        ◊ 4
  ♣ —          S           ♣ J
              ♠ —
              ♡ —
              ◊ A J
              ♣ 8
```

In the examples we have seen so far your trump suit has been very powerful. That will not always be the case and in those situations you will usually find that different techniques are called for. This hand illustrates how important timing can be:

```
              ♠ A 7 6 2
              ♡ A 7 3
              ◊ 10 6 4 2
              ♣ J 7
  ♠ Q 9 5                  ♠ J 10 4
  ♡ J 9         N          ♡ Q 10 5
  ◊ A K Q 3   W     E      ◊ J 9 7 5
  ♣ 9 6 5 4     S          ♣ A 8 2
              ♠ K 8 3
              ♡ K 8 6 4 2
              ◊ 8
              ♣ K Q 10 3
```

Despite the lack of high cards North-South have eight cards in hearts and their hands fit well together. Let's see if we can find a way to make ten tricks in a contract of Four Hearts.

West has an obvious opening lead in the shape of the ace of diamonds and, when that wins the trick, the king of diamonds is sure to follow. An inspection of your combined assets reveals that you appear to have a loser in each of the four suits. A player taking his first steps in the game would probably tackle the hand like this: ruff the second diamond and play on trumps, cashing the ace and king in no particular order and then, realizing that a trump was still outstanding, play another round. East would win and play another diamond, forcing declarer to ruff with the last trump. Now when East wins a trick with the ace of clubs he will play his remaining diamond and declarer will have no trumps left to deal with it and the contract will be defeated.

A more thoughtful player would start in the same way but realize that a third round of trumps would be a waste of time. They would switch their attention to the club suit where only the ace is missing. Unfortunately East has that card and can win and cash the master trump, drawing two trumps for one, always a good bargain for the defence.

Once again, a diamond will result in declarer's remaining trump being used up and the contract will fail. Is there no way in which the contract can be made?

The secret is to postpone the attack on the trump suit. After ruffing the second round of diamonds declarer should attack the club suit at once. East will win and continue the forcing defence by playing another diamond. Declarer ruffs and only now plays off the top hearts. There is still a trump outstanding but it no longer matters. Declarer plays his winning clubs discarding two spades from the dummy. This will be the position when the second spade is discarded:

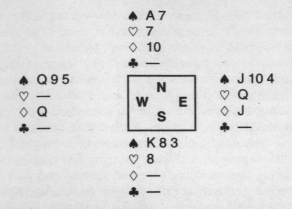

East still has to play to this trick and he can ruff with the queen of hearts. However, declarer will then be able to score his remaining trumps separately, ruffing a spade in dummy and a diamond in hand. Look closely and you will see it makes no difference if East refuses to ruff. Declarer simply carries on with the plan of ruffing a spade in dummy and a diamond in hand. East can score the master trump but that is all.

The key to this and many similar hands is not to allow the defence to draw a round of trumps with the master.

You may have noticed a theme that is common to all the preceding examples. Your trump suit has always contained least eight cards between the two hands. Before I leave the topic of playing with trumps there is one important principle you need to take on board. That is the idea of the 4-4 trump fit.

Perhaps your first instinct is that you should strive to make your longest suit trumps? In that case you would prefer a 5-3 fit to a 4-4 one, wouldn't you? Let's see how that works out on this deal.

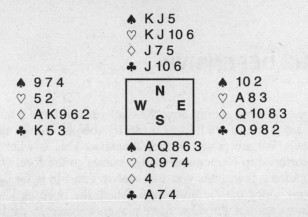

Although the high cards are evenly split between the four players once again North-South have a much better fit and they could easily try for ten tricks in either Four Spades or Four Hearts.

Against Four Spades West will lead the ace of diamonds and continue the suit, forcing South to ruff. After drawing trumps South will knock out the ace of hearts but East will win and continue to attack in diamonds. Declarer's last trump will disappear and unless the defenders make a bad mistake the contract will fail. Declarer will take five trump tricks, three hearts and one club – one short of the required number.

If the contract is Four Hearts West will start as before with two top diamonds. Declarer ruffs, this time with a heart and now plays a trump to dummy's ten. East may try the effect of ducking but declarer can now ruff his remaining diamond and play another trump. This will result in no less than eleven tricks made up of five spades, five trumps (two by ruffing in hand) and the ace of clubs.

I hope you can see where the two extra tricks have come from. With hearts as trumps each diamond ruff was worth another trick. With spades as trumps the ruffs were taken in the long trump hand and nothing was gained.

In due course you will realize – if you haven't done so already – that the 4-4 fit is worth looking for. That type of trump fit will usually produce an extra trick or two.

You will discover when we come to the bidding that a lot of thought has been put into how to locate a 4-4 fit – bridge's answer to the "magic bullet".

ON THE DEFENSIVE

So far we have been seeing how the declarer can have a lot of fun. Now we are going to see how you can try to spoil things and make life difficult. We are going on the defensive! This is where one of the two partnership elements of bridge comes to the fore. Once you have defended a few times you will realize that life is far easier for the declarer. Once the bidding has finished, the opening lead made and dummy exposed, the other three players can see 26 cards – their own and dummy's. However, it is clearly easier for declarer to make the best of his cards for he can see all his side's assets. You and your partner cannot see each other's cards. Therefore the defenders must rely on their ability to exchange information as the play develops. They can do this in a number of ways. As you will discover later, it is possible for the defenders to use their cards to give information to each other – they can signal.

However, the first opportunity for the defence to put the declarer under pressure comes with the opening lead. The defenders can exchange a lot of information at this stage depending upon the card that is led. I can promise you that if you find the best opening lead every time you will end up being one of the greatest players of all time!

Don't forget that you are allowed to use all the clues at your disposal when making your selection. Your partner may have bid a suit or you may have a strong holding of your own. The opponents' bidding may have pinpointed a potential weakness that you can take exploit. Never stop concentrating just because you have a poor hand – you may still have a vital part to play.

When you are faced with having to make the opening lead you will be defending against one of two types of contract, either in no-trumps or one of the four suits. We'll start by looking at the former.

Leading against no-trumps

The card you lead will tell your partner something about your hand even if you have made no positive contribution to the bidding. There are two things for you to decide on; the suit to lead and the card to choose.

When there are no trumps the hand usually turns into a race between the defenders and the declarer. You and your partner will be trying to establish enough tricks to defeat the contract before declarer can reach the required number. The outcome will frequently be decided by who is first to establish their long suit.

By now you must be itching to see an example but first we need to put in place a few ground rules that will help you select the right card. If you have a good suit that is headed by a strong sequence such as A-K-Q, K-Q-J, Q-J-10 or even J-10-9 then you can start with your highest card. A lot of the time you won't have that type of holding and in those cases you start by leading your fourth highest card from your chosen suit. For example, if you were going to lead from, ♡K-J-8-6-3, then the correct card would be the six of hearts. If you start a suit with a low card partner will expect you to have an honour.

Opening leads against no-trumps have become standardized and can be summarized in tabular form. These are the most common where you have a four-card suit:

From K Q J 5	lead the king
From K Q 10 5	lead the king
From K J 10 5	lead the jack
From Q J 10 5	lead the queen
From Q J 9 5	lead the queen
From J 10 9 5	lead the jack
From J 10 8 5	lead the jack
From 10 9 8 5	lead the ten

You would make the same lead in each case if you had five cards in the suit.

The more cards you have in your suit the greater the chance that you will be able to establish it. Let's examine some more holdings.

From A K 10 6 5	lead the six
From A K 8 6 5	lead the six

You are leading fourth best for good reasons. Firstly the suit may be distributed round the table like this:

$\heartsuit$ Q J 2

$\heartsuit$ A K 10 6 5   ☐ $\heartsuit$ 7 3

$\heartsuit$ 9 8 4

Unless you have an entry, if you start by leading the ace of hearts you will never be able to make all your long cards in the suit once you have given up a trick to the queen. When your partner gets the lead he will have no heart left to play back to you. By starting with your fourth-best card you preserve communications between your hand and your partner's. If he gains the lead he can play his remaining heart enabling you to cash four tricks in the suit.

$\heartsuit$ 9 7 3

$\heartsuit$ A K 8 6 5   ☐ $\heartsuit$ Q 4

$\heartsuit$ J 10 4

Here the situation is even worse! If you start with a top heart the suit will be blocked even if you subsequently play a low one. By starting with your fourth-best you will be able to take the first five tricks.

$\heartsuit$ Q 10 4

$\heartsuit$ A K 8 6 5   ☐ $\heartsuit$ J 9

$\heartsuit$ 7 3 2

This time leading the ace will tell declarer that you have the king and as a result the queen will certainly score a trick. If you start with the six of hearts declarer will have to guess what to do. Since $\heartsuit$ A-J-8-6-5 and $\heartsuit$ K-J-8-6-5 are twice as likely as $\heartsuit$ A-K-8-6-5 declarer will probably try the ten and your partner will be able to win with the jack and return the suit, allowing you to cash four more tricks.

From A J 10 6 5   lead the jack

That may look a little odd but there is a method in your madness! The situations you have to worry about are these:

If you lead fourth-best you will allow declarer to take two tricks in the suit, as the first one will be won cheaply by the nine. If you lead the jack and declarer wins with the king or queen, a subsequent lead by your partner through declarer's hand will give you four tricks.

♠ K 3

♠ A J 10 6 5   ♠ 8 7 4

♠ Q 9 2

Again, the lead of the six of spades will cost your side a trick and give declarer a nice bonus via the nine of spades.

A holding such as A-J-10-6-5 is known as an interior sequence. There are many others, and in general the right lead is the second-highest card.

From A 10 9 6 5	lead the ten
From K 10 9 6 5	lead the ten
From Q 10 9 6 5	lead the ten

There will be many occasions when you don't have any of the holdings mentioned above. More often than not you may have to select from a couple of four-card suits. Although the golden rule is "fourth best of your longest and strongest" there are some exceptions. If your choice lay between ◇ Q-8-5-3 and ♣ J-8-5-3 then the diamond three would be a better choice as you need less support for the suit in partner's hand to make that work. If I make the combinations a little stronger the choice becomes harder. With ◇ K-8-5-3 and ♣ Q-8-5-3 either suit could turn out to be the winner. The king of diamonds is more likely to be an entry to your hand later on but if partner has ◇ A-9-7-6-4 they will not be amused if you lead a club! Looking at ◇ A-8-5-3 and ♣ K-8-5-3 there is a lot to be said for leading a club. The ace of diamonds represents a sure entry to any tricks you may be able to set up.

If the two suits you are considering are a major and a minor then, assuming neither of them has been bid, there is a slight case for going with the major suit. The reason is that most of the time everyone bids a major suit if they have one so when they don't get mentioned it is more likely that your partner will have a reasonable holding.

There will be times when you have to think twice about leading your best or longest suit.

If your partner has bid a suit then you need a good reason not to lead it. At a major championship multiple World Champions Sandra Landy and the then Sally Horton were playing together. On one hand Sandra bid a suit but Sally did not lead it with disastrous consequences. The following day I was partnering Sandra and the same thing happened. Sandra's reaction was to make a polite enquiry: "Doesn't anyone from Nottingham lead their partner's suit?"

Even if you might have done better by leading something else, you will keep your partner happy, and that is a vital element of the game.

I have noticed that beginners tend almost automatically to play high cards. That is especially true when they are leading partner's suit.

Don't!

It's fine to lead your top card from a doubleton, even if it's an honour, but in other situations it will frequently cost your side a trick. Here are two examples:

```
                        ♣ J
    ♣ 10 7 4    [              ]    ♣ K Q 8 5 2
                     ♣ A 9 4 3
```

If you lead the ten then declarer's nine becomes an important card. He may not end up winning a trick with it but it will stop your side running the suit.

```
                        ♣ 6 2
    ♣ Q 9 3    [              ]    ♣ K 10 8 5 4
                     ♣ A J 7
```

Starting with the queen turns the jack into a trick. Declarer will win with the ace and, even if your side abandons the suit, declarer can always set up the jack by leading towards it from the dummy.

If your opponents have bid your best suit you will have to think twice about leading it. Imagine declarer has bid hearts on the way to a no-trump contract. Your best suit is ♡K-J-9-5-2. It would clearly be dangerous to lead round to a known suit that could easily be headed by ♡A-Q-10-8.

You may have the type of hand where your longest suits are not attractive and you simply want to let declarer find his own tricks. Then you will look for a safe lead. This would be typical:

    ♠ Q 7
    ♡ 10 9 8
    ◇ A Q 7 2
    ♣ J 7 5 3

Neither of your four-card suits is especially powerful and there is much to be said for leading the ten of hearts.

With a very weak hand you may have to try to guess where your partner's strength lies. Of course, you will try to be intelligent about it. Look at this example:

    ♠ 9 3
    ♡ 6 4 2
    ◇ 10 8 5 3 2
    ♣ J 8 5

It would be a minor miracle if your partner had enough strength in diamonds to make the lead of that suit a success. Any of the other three suits could be right but in the absence of a clue from the bidding you should probably go with the suit that contains an honour and lead the five of clubs.

I hope you are beginning to realize how difficult it can be to decide on your opening lead. Don't worry about it, simply remember that when you are declarer the boot will be on the other foot!

Now it's time to see how the defence might develop after the opening lead has been made. By the way, it's a good habit always to make your opening lead face down. That will give your partner a chance to ask any questions about the bidding, but more importantly it will save you if you happen to have led when it was really your partner's turn. Yes, I know you will be concentrating like mad but some day you will lead out of turn. OK, back to business.

Once the opening lead has been made, dummy will be displayed and everyone will be able to see those thirteen cards. In general terms you should try to play your cards to each trick at an even tempo, but when the dummy appears you should always take a little time to think about how the defence might go. It's especially true at trick one, as many a contract has been won or lost right at the start as a result of a careless play from either the declarer or a defender.

Once declarer has formed a plan, a card will be played from the dummy. Now it will be your turn. What should you do?

The answer will depend on a number of factors: the card partner has led, the card played from dummy and your own holding in the suit.

For the moment we'll concentrate on the suit that has been led but never forget that the whole hand is important when it comes to defending; you won't make much progress as a bridge player if you defend in a vacuum. Let's check out some everyday situations.

$$\clubsuit \ 8\ 6\ 5$$

$$\clubsuit \ K\ Q\ 10\ 9\ 3 \qquad \boxed{} \qquad \clubsuit \ A\ 7$$

$$\clubsuit \ J\ 4\ 2$$

When your partner leads the king of clubs you know that he has struck gold because it must be from a sequence. You must overtake it with the ace and return the suit, giving your side the first five tricks.

$$\clubsuit \ J\ 4\ 2$$

$$\clubsuit \ K\ Q\ 10\ 9\ 3 \qquad \boxed{} \qquad \clubsuit \ A\ 7$$

$$\clubsuit \ 8\ 6\ 5$$

I have swapped the North-South holdings. Now overtaking the king will cost your side a trick. You will have to play the seven. Your partner will realize you have the ace as declarer would certainly win the trick if he had that card. Partner will continue with a small card hoping the suit is distributed round the table like this:

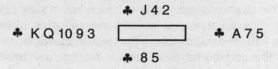

♣ J 4 2

♣ K Q 10 9 3   ♣ A 7 5

♣ 8 5

In this situation you will be able to win with your ace and return the suit. When you don't have a third club you will have to hope your partner has an entry.

This is a variation on the same theme:

♡ 9 6 2

♡ Q J 10 8 4   ♡ K 7

♡ A 5 3

When your partner leads the queen of hearts you must overtake it with the king and return the suit. If you play your low card declarer will duck. When your king appears on the next round declarer withholds the ace again. The heart suit will be well and truly blocked. Your partner now needs two entries to make anything of the heart suit. One is needed to set up two winners and the other to cash them.

When partner's lead is an honour you will have a lot of information to work with but it is still all too easy to make a mistake. This would be a common error:

♠ 8 2

♠ K J 10 9 3   ♠ A 7 5

♠ Q 6 4

When the jack of spades settles on the table you should make sure you play the ace and return the suit, catering for this layout. Failing to play the ace gives declarer an undeserved bonus trick. If declarer has the king and queen of spades little has been lost by your play of the ace.

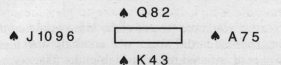

♠ Q 8 2

♠ J 10 9 6   ♠ A 7 5

♠ K 4 3

Once again the first card played is the jack of spades. If declarer plays dummy's queen then you should win the trick with the ace and return the suit. If declarer plays the two of spades from dummy, then playing the ace would be a serious mistake as now declarer would be guaranteed two tricks instead of one. The correct play is the seven of spades, encouraging partner to continue with the suit the next time that he gains the lead.

Try to get into the habit of making this and similar types of play in tempo. If you think for a while and then play the seven of spades everyone will know you have either the ace or king. It's far better to let your cards do the talking!

We have already seen how a suit can be blocked. This is another example:

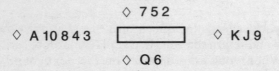

$\diamond$ 7 5 2

$\diamond$ A 10 8 4 3 $\diamond$ K J 9

$\diamond$ Q 6

This time the opening lead is the four of diamonds. I hope you have remembered that it is likely to be partner's fourth best card in the suit. There is nothing threatening in the dummy and you should play the king. When that wins the trick you are clearly going to continue the suit. If you play the nine of diamonds partner will be able to captures declarer's queen with the ace but then your jack will be in the way. The correct card to return is the jack. After winning with the ace your partner will be able to play the ten of diamonds and your side will be off to a good start.

In the previous example you were in the happy position of having two honours in the suit partner led. In such situations it is important to play them in the right order.

$\clubsuit$ 8 6

$\clubsuit$ J 9 4 2 $\clubsuit$ K Q 5

$\clubsuit$ A 10 7 3

When your partner leads the two of clubs you know that it must be from at best a four-card suit. When declarer calls for dummy's six of clubs you should play one of your high clubs. The correct card is the queen, the lower of the two touching honours. You intend to play the king on the next round of the suit. I can almost hear you thinking, "What difference does it make?"

Consider things from your partner's point of view. If you play the king of clubs and declarer wins with the ace he will assume that declarer has the queen as well. If you play the queen of clubs and declarer wins with the ace then the location of the king of clubs will still be in question but your partner will know that it is still possible for you to have that card. On the other hand, if you play the king and partner is first to regain the lead, he will never try a second club, and that may have fatal consequences for the defence.

It's important to realize that you may have an important holding even if you are devoid of high cards. For instance:

$$\heartsuit \; A \; 3$$

$\heartsuit \; Q \; J \; 9 \; 7 \; 4$ ☐ $\heartsuit \; 10 \; 8 \; 5$

$$\heartsuit \; K \; 6 \; 2$$

When your partner leads the queen of hearts you know that it must be from a suit headed by the ♡Q-J. That makes your ten very important and you should let your partner in on the good news by playing the eight of hearts.

$$\diamondsuit \; 9 \; 4$$

$\diamondsuit \; K \; Q \; J \; 6$ ☐ $\diamondsuit \; 8 \; 7 \; 5 \; 2$

$$\diamondsuit \; A \; 10 \; 3$$

The king of diamonds proclaims a powerful sequence. Your length is important and you should let partner know by playing the seven of diamonds. You plan to play one of your lower diamonds on the next round of the suit. This high-low play is usually referred to as an *echo* or *peter*.

The next example is quite tricky:

$$\spadesuit \; 7 \; 3$$

$\spadesuit \; K \; J \; 9 \; 4$ ☐ $\spadesuit \; A \; 10 \; 5 \; 2$

$$\spadesuit \; Q \; 8 \; 6$$

When your partner leads the four of spades you naturally win the trick with the ace. You are going to carry on with the suit and the only question is which card should you play at trick two?

The general rule is to return your fourth-best card and play the two of spades. If declarer plays the six then the eight of spades, your partner might be tempted to place him with ♠Q-10-8-6. However, that would leave you with ♠A-5-2 and with that holding you should return the five of spades.

The principle is that if you win the first trick and then have two cards left you should return the highest one. Here is another illustration:

```
                    ♣ 9 5
  ♣ K 10 7 4 3   ┌──────────┐   ♣ A 8 2
                 └──────────┘
                    ♣ Q J 6
```

West leads the four of clubs and you win with the ace. The correct return is the eight of clubs. A wide-awake West will realize that the two is missing and duck when declarer plays the queen or jack. Then the defenders will have retained communications and be ready to cash three more tricks in the suit as soon as one of them regains the lead.

We'll finish with something a little more complicated. I like this example for a couple of reasons. Firstly, it demonstrates what an infinitely fascinating game bridge is and, secondly, I can still remember the first time I made this play in a tournament!

```
                    ◇ 10 2
  ◇ J 9 6 4 3    ┌──────────┐   ◇ A Q 7
                 └──────────┘
                    ◇ K 8 5
```

When your partner leads the four of diamonds it looks obvious to play the ace and continue with the queen. However, declarer can withhold his king until you play a third round of the suit. Then if your partner has no entry you will make only two tricks in the suit instead of four. The correct card to play to the first trick is the queen of diamonds. If your partner has led from a holding including the king of diamonds it will make no difference. When he has led from his actual holding declarer will be put in an impossible situation when you play the queen. Since the opening lead may be from $\diamond$A-J-9-4-3 he can hardly afford to duck, for then a second diamond from you will mean declarer scores no trick in the suit.

Getting this sort of combination right will always give you a little buzz and keep you coming back for more!

The Rule of Eleven

Way back in 1890 Robert F Foster was putting together his *Whist Manual*. He realized that, when a defender led a low card in a suit and it was fourth-best, a formula could be applied that would provide information about the suit. By subtracting the value of the card led from eleven you would automatically know the number of cards that were higher than the one led that were contained in the other three hands.

This was one of the many ideas that temporarily turned whist into a craze and made the game easier to play. Its application is just as valid for bridge and can help both declarer and defenders alike. These examples will show you how it works:

$$\diamond \text{ A Q 9 4 2}$$

$\diamond$ K J 8 6   [   ] $\diamond$ 3

$$\diamond \text{ 10 7 5}$$

If West leads the six of diamonds then, by subtracting that from eleven, the declarer arrives at five. His hand and dummy contain all those cards and by taking repeated finesses against West declarer can make five tricks in the suit.

$$\heartsuit \text{ Q 9 7}$$

$\heartsuit$ 5 3   [   ] $\heartsuit$ 10 8 6

$$\heartsuit \text{ A K J 4 2}$$

If West leads the five of hearts then the key number is six. East can see six cards higher than the five between his hand and dummy but he knows his partner cannot have a high card because with a suit headed by $\heartsuit$A-K-J he would have led an honour.

```
                    ♠ K 6 3
  ♠ Q 10 8 7      ┌──────────┐      ♠ A J 9 2
                  └──────────┘
                    ♠ 5 4
```

West leads the seven of spades. East can see all four of the higher cards and if declarer plays low from the dummy it is safe to play the two of spades, allowing partner to retain the lead and continue the suit.

This rule can be applied every time you think the lead of a small card is from a four-card or longer suit.

We are nearly ready to leave the world of no-trumps but before we go there is just one more point to make. Remember that no-trump contracts are usually a race between the two sides as to who can establish their long suits and tricks first. You can sometimes stop the declarer from reaching all his tricks by making sure you take your high cards at the right moment. Suppose your partner leads the jack of spades against a no-trump contract and this is what you can see:

```
                    ♠ 8 7
                    ♡ 6 4
                    ◇ 7 4 2
                    ♣ K Q J 10 8 6
              ┌──────────┐     ♠ Q 6 5
              │    N     │     ♡ J 5 3 2
              │ W     E  │     ◇ 8 6 3
              │    S     │     ♣ A 7 3
              └──────────┘
```

It will almost certainly be vital for you to withhold your ace of clubs on the first round of the suit. Your aim should be to win a trick with that card when you are sure declarer can no longer reach dummy with a club.

How can you tell?

We'll find out later on. Meanwhile it's time for a change of emphasis.

Leading against suits

It's a whole new ball game when there is a trump suit. Unless you think declarer is going to run out of trumps – and that is not an everyday occurrence – there is little point in trying to establish a long suit. Remember that once declarer or dummy is void of a suit then that hand will be able to ruff your winning cards.

In general terms your aim should be to set up some fast winners – the tortoise will definitely not beat the hare in this contest!

Do you remember the table of leads from the no-trump section? A lot of them can still be applied here:

From K Q J 5	lead the king
From K Q 10 5	lead the king
From K J 10 5	lead the jack
From Q J 10 5	lead the queen
From Q J 9 5	lead the queen
From J 10 9 5	lead the jack
From J 10 8 5	lead the jack
From 10 9 8 5	lead the ten

However, in these two examples:

From A K 10 6 5
From A K 8 6 5

The situation changes completely. At no-trumps the recommended lead was the six. Against a suit contract that would be very silly as you could easily allow the declarer to score a trick to which he is not entitled, perhaps even with a singleton queen. The correct strategy is to start with the ace, giving you a chance to look at the dummy and formulate a plan based on what you see there. Add that to the information you have from the bidding and partner's play to the first trick and you are almost certainly off to a good start.

It won't always be so simple!

You should usually lead the top card from two touching honours: ace from A-K, king from K-Q, queen from Q-J and so on.

The opening lead is the one edge you have over declarer. The subject is so complex that several books have been devoted to this single topic. When it comes to a suit contract I have two pieces of general advice to offer. Opposite a silent partner you will have only the opponent's bidding to act as a guide and that may not tell you much. If you have an awkward choice then never underlead an ace and think twice before you lead away from a king.

Faced with a choice between these two holdings:

♡ Q 7 4
◇ K 7 4

I would go for the four of hearts. Neither lead is completely safe but leading from the queen is less likely to be a disaster.

If you are leading from a four-card suit that does not contain a sequence then fourth-highest is still correct. So from suits like ◇ K-8-7-2 or ♣ Q-9-6-2 the two would be the card to lead.

When there is a trump suit it can be attractive to lead from a short suit as you may be able to score a ruff. My advice is that leading a singleton or doubleton can work well but it helps if you have a degree of control in the trump suit. This is what I mean:

♠ A 8 4
♡ 5
◇ Q 9 6 5
♣ K 8 5 4 2

If the opponents are in a spade contract a heart lead may enable you to collect one or more ruffs, because your ace of spades prevents all your trumps from being drawn immediately.

It has become an established custom to avoid a short-suit lead when you have a good holding in the trump suit. The idea is to start with your longest side suit in the hope that repeated leads in it will make the declarer use up too many of his trumps. The so-called *forcing defence*. This would be a typical hand:

♠ A 8 4
♡ K 10 6 3
◇ 9
♣ Q 10 7 4 2

If hearts are trumps the suggestion is that you should lead the four of clubs. I have never been entirely convinced that this is correct! Because declarer almost always has more trumps at his disposal than your side, you may have to wait a long time before you find a hand where this is better than going for the simple shot of leading your singleton diamond.

I thought this was pretty heretical stuff, but just as I was finishing this book an article entitled "The Macho Lead" by Swedish International Anders Wirgren supporting this theory appeared in *Bridge Today*.

When you lead a singleton your partner may have the ace and be able to give you a ruff at once. That is less likely to happen if you start with a doubleton as your partner will need more in the way of high cards. Nevertheless it can still be a good idea to start with such a lead. The normal lead from two cards is the highest one, so from ♠10-5 you would lead the ten. You will sometimes be tempted to lead from a doubleton honour, say, ♡A-4, ♡K-4, ♡Q-4, ♡J-4 or the like.

Oscar Wilde once remarked that he could "resist everything except temptation" but my advice is to try to avoid starting your defensive campaign with a lead from one of these combinations. You may score the odd triumph when partner has a decent holding in the suit, particularly when you have the ace or king, but more often than not you will concede a tempo and maybe a trick.

The situation changes if your partner has bid a suit. Now it is usually going to be right to start by leading it. With a doubleton you start with your highest card. With three or four cards in the suit you should lead your lowest unless you have the ace or two touching honours. Holding, say, ♠A-7-5 or ♠A-7-5-3 in partner's suit, the right card to lead would be the ace. With a lesser honour it becomes correct to lead a small card. This example shows you why:

```
                    ♣ 9 6 5
  ♣ K 7 4        ┌──────────┐        ♣ A J 10 2
                 └──────────┘
                    ♣ Q 8 3
```

If you start with the king of clubs it will cost your side a trick. By leading the four of clubs you allow your partner to win with the ace and return the jack, collecting declarer's queen.

I broach the next topic with a degree of trepidation – when should you lead a trump?

The reason is simply that the risk factor is very high. You are sacrificing a tempo by starting on declarer's best suit rather than one of your own. The main reason for leading a trump is in an attempt to prevent declarer from making a lot of trump tricks separately. This will usually be when you have a powerful holding in another suit bid by declarer. Imagine that declarer has bid hearts and diamonds and ends up in hearts. If your hand is:

♠ 8 5 3
♡ 8 6 2
◇ A Q 10 9
♣ 7 5 2

Then, by leading a trump – the two is the right card from this type of holding – then you may prevent declarer from ruffing losing diamonds in the dummy.

If your hand is so bad that you face a choice of leads from poor suits such as ◇9-7-5-3 or ◇9-6-3 then you are in trouble! Whatever you lead, partner is likely to be fooled. A high card will look like it is from a doubleton, while a low one will make parner think you have an honour. My personal preference is to lead the second highest from four cards and the middle one from three. This latter rejoices in the wonderful name of "MUD", standing for "Middle, Up, Down". the idea being to play the higher card on the second round of the suit to let partner know you didn't start with a doubleton.

If your opponents bid a slam against you, then your priorities change a little as time may not be on your side. Like so many areas of the game, the subject is complex and there are lots of ideas on the subject. One distinguished magazine devoted an entire series of articles to the question of whether or not you should lead an ace against a slam contract. I don't recall the conclusion, but it is certainly a double-edged sword as this hand illustrates:

```
                    ♠ K Q 9 8
                    ♡ K Q 6
                    ◇ J 8 3 2
                    ♣ 10 8
   ♠ 7                                    ♠ 10 4
   ♡ J 5 4 3         ┌─────────┐          ♡ 9 8
   ◇ A 7 5 4         │    N    │          ◇ Q 10 9
   ♣ Q 4 3 2       W │ W   E   │ E        ♣ K J 9 7 6 5
                     │    S    │
                    └─────────┘
                    ♠ A J 6 5 3 2
                    ♡ A 10 7 2
                    ◇ K 6
                    ♣ A
```

North-South bid simply and aggressively to a slam via the sequence
1♠ – 3♠ – 6♠.

With nothing to go on West led the ace of diamonds – the only
card to allow the slam to make. Let's change the North-South hands:

♠ J 10 9 8
♡ K Q 6
◇ J 8 3 2
♣ K 8

♠ A K 6 5 3 2
♡ A 10 7 2
◇ Q 6
♣ A

Now, anything other than a diamond lead allows declarer to get rid
of a loser on dummy's king of clubs. If you have an ace your choice
will usually be between leading it or trying to establish a trick in
another suit, hoping to get in with the ace to cash it.

OK, the bidding has finished and you have made your opening
lead. Time for dummy to make an appearance and for you to see
how your opening lead pans out.

By examining a full deal we can also take a brief look at some of
the signals the defenders can employ:

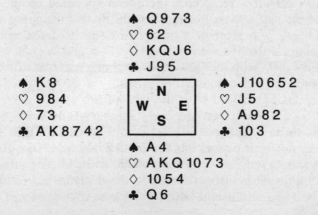

♠ Q 9 7 3
♡ 6 2
◇ K Q J 6
♣ J 9 5

♠ K 8
♡ 9 8 4
◇ 7 3
♣ A K 8 7 4 2

♠ J 10 6 5 2
♡ J 5
◇ A 9 8 2
♣ 10 3

♠ A 4
♡ A K Q 10 7 3
◇ 10 5 4
♣ Q 6

South is trying to make ten tricks in a contract of Four Hearts.

Your honour combination is the obvious place to start so you lead the ace of clubs. Your partner should play the ten, the top card from a doubleton, just as if he was leading rather than following suit. When declarer plays the six of clubs you know partner has one of three possible holdings:

♣ 10
♣ 10 3
♣ Q 10 3

With the last of these three it is correct for partner to play the ten because he wants to encourage you to continue clubs. When you play the king of clubs partner produces the three and declarer the queen. I know you were hoping your partner had a singleton so that at this point you could give him a ruff, but at least declarer didn't have one thus restricting you to a single trick in the suit.

Now that the top three cards in the club suit have gone, dummy's jack is the master. You know that your partner has no clubs left but you also know that declarer is now void of the suit so at this point you may be tempted to switch to another suit. However, if you do, then declarer will probably be able to get rid of a loser on the jack of clubs at a later stage in the play. The correct strategy is for you to play another club. When declarer plays the jack your partner can ruff.

On this occasion it does not matter which card your partner chooses to ruff with, but in this type of situation it is usually correct to play the higher card. Even if he suspects that declarer may be going to overruff – remember the queen appeared on the second round of the suit – there is a real possibility that trumping with the jack of hearts will promote a trump trick for the defence. Imagine that declarer's trumps were ♡A-K-Q-9-7-3 and West's ♡10-8-4. When East ruffs with the jack of hearts South can overruff but now the ten of hearts is bound to score a trick.

After East has ruffed with the jack of hearts and declarer has overruffed with the queen, the ace, king and ten of hearts will take the next three tricks as declarer draws trumps. While you are following suit your partner has to find two discards. That gives him two chances to tell you something about his hand. The information that he transmits is also available to the declarer but most of the time it will be more useful to the defenders. Here East will start by discarding the two of spades, suggesting that he has no significant high card in the suit. The second discard will be the nine of diamonds indicating that he has a useful holding in that suit.

Having drawn trumps, declarer will turn his attention to the diamond suit, playing a small card from his hand to dummy's king. This is a critical moment for the defence. If East makes the mistake of taking his ace of diamonds, either on this trick or the next one, the contract of four hearts will make. Declarer will be able to enjoy three diamond tricks and on the last round of the suit the losing four of spades will be discarded. Ten tricks will have been accumulated via one spade, six hearts and three diamonds.

East must keep his ace of diamonds, playing it only on the third round of the suit. Now, if declarer started life with only two diamonds, this would be a big mistake because the ace would then hit thin air. Being out of diamonds declarer would be able to ruff. East needs to know how many cards in diamonds declarer started with. The answer comes from the cards you play in the diamond suit. With a doubleton you starts by playing your highest card. With three cards the lowest is played first.

If you had played the three of diamonds on the first round of the suit your partner would place you with three cards leaving declarer with two and take his ace on the second round. When you play the seven of diamonds, a glance at the spot cards tells East that it cannot be the lowest card. This time it is declarer who has three cards so East must keep his ace for the third round of the suit.

This type of defensive play, where you withhold your winner until the right moment, is important so study this hand carefully.

After winning with the ace of diamonds you switch to a spade and sooner or later your partner will take the setting trick with the king of spades.

There are many signals that the defenders can make and, although declarer also receives the information,, it is undoubtedly more important to give guidance to your partner than try to keep declarer in the dark. Without some form of signalling, defence would be even more difficult – some might say impossible.

I will tell you later about some of the methods you and your partner can employ but now it's time for you to get your bidding boots on.

BASIC BIDDING

After the cards have been dealt and before the play can begin the two partnerships try to describe the nature of their hands to each other during the bidding phase of the game. The more accurate the bidding, the more likely it is that a sensible contract will be reached. The final contract reached will determine the number of tricks each side is trying to take. If declarer is successful, then his side will score points, but if declarer fails to collect the right number of tricks, then his side will concede penalty points.

This phase of the game is important for several reasons. It determines who will be the declarer and dummy for each individual deal and it also indicates how many tricks each side is trying to win and the denomination that the deal will be played in. I hope you remember that every deal will be played either in a trump suit or without one in no-trumps.

I like to think of the bidding as a conversation. The more sensible the discussion, the more likely it is that the final outcome will be successful. The partners use the bidding to give each other important information about the number of high cards they hold and any long suits they possess. Using this information the partners decide how many of the thirteen tricks they think they can win. Most of the time the side with the majority of the high cards will end up playing the hand, leaving the other partnership to defend.

The information that the partners transmit to each other is done via a bidding system. From time to time you and your partner may use a special type of bid called a *convention*. Obviously it's important that you and your partner are using the same system and that you can understand each other's conventional bids.

Just as you and your partner try to convey information to each other, so will your opponents. Because you are all able to hear every bid that is made, both sides can frequently form an impression of where the high cards and long suits are located. That information may turn out to be very useful both in the play and defence of the hand once the bidding has finished.

If you consistently bid to the right contract your partnership will be both a happy one – and a winning one!

Before you can start bidding you have to have a means of evaluating your hand. The thirteen cards you pick up following completion of the deal will be different on every single hand but you will soon start to recognize some familiar patterns. You will see hands that are balanced and contain nothing longer than a four-card suit; hands that contain a lot of high cards – sometimes so many that you think you are visiting a picture gallery; hands with one or more long suits – you can often have a lot of fun with those; hands that are very weak with hardly any high cards – don't worry you'll get used to them.

The classic way to evaluate your hand is by allocating a value to the four highest cards in each suit using the method introduced by Bryant McCampbell in 1915 and popularized by the man whose name is now permanently linked to it, Milton Work.

It is simplicity itself, the cards being allocated the following values:

Ace	4
King	3
Queen	2
Jack	1

With every suit containing one of these cards, there are evidently 10 points in each suit and therefore the average number of points you can expect to hold on each hand is 10. This would represent an average hand:

♠ A 8 5 3
♡ K 6 4
◇ Q 7 3
♣ J 9 6

Just as important as the number of high-card points you hold is the way in which your cards are distributed. By changing the number of cards you have in each suit I can turn a hand with only an average number of points into something much more powerful:

♠ A J 9 8 5 3
♥ K Q 9 6 4 3
♦ —
♣ 7

You still have only 10 points but your distribution is tremendous. As you become more experienced you will realize that the potential of the second hand is far greater than the first. Even so, you can only establish the true worth of your hand by combining it with that of your partner. If you can establish that you have a fit, then hands with long suits can become very powerful even when you have a modest number of high cards.

The initial evaluation of your hand will be based on a combination of these two factors: the number of points you have and the length of your suits. You are almost ready to see how this works but first you need to understand two more things.

When you make a bid at the one level you are indicating that you are prepared to take a minimum of seven tricks in that denomination, be it a suit or no-trumps. Bidding at the two level shows a willingness to try for eight tricks and at the three level nine. This applies all the way up to a bid at the seven level and if you get that high it means you will be trying to make all thirteen tricks – a grand slam. You are not necessarily saying you always have the requisite number of tricks in your own hand but you are initially hoping that you will get some support from your partner. As the auction develops you will be able to gauge how high to bid.

You also need to understand the mechanics of the auction.

The first person to have the opportunity to bid is the dealer. If the dealer's hand is good enough he will open the bidding. That will immediately tell everyone else something about the dealer's hand, the exact information depending on the bid that is made. If the dealer's hand is not good enough to make a positive bid then he will announce the fact by passing.

After the dealer has bid, the auction continues round the table in a clockwise direction. Each bid must be higher than the previous one. If the dealer bids One Spade, the next player can't bid One Diamond because diamonds is a lower-ranking suit. If you make a bid of, say, Two Clubs over an opponent's opening bid of One Heart, you are *overcalling*.

If you make a bid and your partner replies, he is said to be making a *response* to your bid. With a very poor hand he is allowed to pass.

When a bid is followed by three passes – usually described in a bidding diagram as "All Pass" – the auction has finished. The partnership that made the last positive bid will play the hand and that will be the contract. The player who bid the final denomination first will be the declarer.

Every once in a while none of the players will have the values to open the bidding. Then the auction will go like this:

West	North	East	South
Pass	Pass	Pass	Pass

This is no great disaster and you simply shuffle the cards and deal again. By the way, most people don't shuffle half well enough. I recommend seven riffles and a cut.

The only time the rank of the suits is important is during the bidding. They have no significance during the play other than that one of them may be the trump suit. Before you can complete an auction you have to understand the way the suits are ranked.

Topping the list is no-trumps. Yes, I know it's not really a suit at all but, since playing in a no-trump contract usually suggests you have values in all the suits, it's logical that this denomination should outrank everything else.

The four suits you find in the pack go in this order:

Spades
Hearts
Diamonds
Clubs

So if you open the bidding with One Club the next player can for example bid One Diamond. Your partner might then respond One Heart and the next player might join in the fun by bidding One Spade. As long as the next bid is higher than the previous one anything goes. Exactly how high you bid will be governed by what you and your partner see and hear as the auction develops. This might be your auction:

West	North	East	South
1♢	Pass	1♡	1♠
2♣	2♠	Pass	Pass
3♣	Pass	Pass	Pass

West will be the declarer in a contract of Three Clubs. The target for declarer is nine tricks while the defenders will be trying for at least five. Clubs are trumps.

That's enough preamble. Let's find out what you need to start the bidding.

Opening bids at the one level

The requirements for an opening bid at the one level have never suffered from inflation and as you become more experienced you will start to judge for yourself what constitutes an opening bid. In general terms, you need 12 high-card points to make an opening bid. This is not an absolute rule! Recently one of my students was reluctant to open One Heart with this hand:

    ♠ 9
    ♡ A Q J 10 9 7 4
    ♢ 4
    ♣ A 10 6 3

She pointed out that it contained only 11 high-card points. While that is true, the heart suit is so powerful that it would be silly not to let partner in on the news. Some learned authorities suggest you add on a point for each extra card above four that you have in a suit. There is nothing wrong with that, but you need to get used to recognizing when a hand is improved by its distribution.

Your initial aim is to find a fit with your partner. If you are going to end up with a trump suit your optimum requirement is an eight-card fit. Once you have established that one exists you can re-evaluate your hand.

These hands would all qualify for an opening bid at the one level:

    ♠ J 7 2
    ♡ A Q 5
    ♢ K 9 3
    ♣ A 10 8 5

You have 14 points but nothing good in the way of distribution. You should normally start with your best suit so the correct opening bid is One Club.

♠ A 7
♡ K Q 9 7 5
◇ J 10 8 4
♣ Q 6

There is nothing exceptional about this hand but you have the right number of points and a reasonable suit. You can happily open One Heart.

♠ A K J 9 3
♡ Q J 7 5 2
◇ 8
♣ K 9

This hand is promising because it is a two-suiter, the more so because you have both major suits. You can happily open One Spade. If your holdings in the major suits were reversed it would still be correct to open One Spade even though hearts would now be your strongest suit. The main reason is that if you open One Heart you may run into difficulties in the subsequent part of the auction. Say your partner responds Two Diamonds and you now bid Two Spades. If responder prefers hearts to spades, he has to go to the three level. By opening One Spade you allow the bidding to develop more easily. When partner bids Two Diamonds you bid Two Hearts and now if your partner prefers spades to hearts he can simply bid Two Spades.

♠ 8
♡ K Q J 10 8 5
◇ 5 2
♣ A J 7 4

You have only 11 points but your distribution and the quality of your heart suit give you an easy opening bid of One Heart. Even if I replaced the jack of clubs with a small card, leaving you with only 10 points, it would be reasonable to open the bidding.

♠ A K 10 6 2
♡ 8
◊ 9 3
♣ K Q 9 5 3

This is clearly worth an opening bid and the only question is which one of your two suits you should bid first. Various authorities hold different views. Mine is that you should open One Spade.

♠ A K 7 4 2
♡ 5
◊ 6
♣ K Q 10 6 5 2

You have the same suits as in the previous example but this time your choice is simple. You will never go far wrong if you always start with your longest suit and here you would open One Club.

Have you noticed that in all the examples where the opening bid is in a major suit you always have five of them? That is because I am suggesting you start your bridge bidding life with a system based around five-card major-suit opening bids.

Here are a couple of tips to help you deal with two-suited hands:

- When your suits are equal in length start with the higher-ranking intending to bid your other suit next time.
- If one suit is longer than the other, bid the longer one first.

You will sometimes have a close decision about whether or not your hand qualifies for an opening bid. In those situations my advice is to look at the quality of the suit you are thinking of bidding and the location of your high cards. You should also examine the ratio of your offensive/defensive potential. Take a look at this hand:

♠ A Q
♡ K 9
◊ Q 7 5 4 3 2
♣ 8 4 3

This hand is one shy of the minimum number of points for an opening bid but you do have a six-card suit. However, your diamond intermediates are poor and your other honours are in short suits, unsupported by small cards. I would be inclined to pass.

Here is another example:

♠ Q J 7
♡ Q J 5
◊ Q J 10 6
♣ Q J 4

You have 12 points but your hand has no offensive potential. I wouldn't open this hand if you paid me!

The lesson to be learned from hands such as the above is that in order to become a good bidder you have to learn to judge the value of your hand. Even the greatest champions don't get it right 100% of the time but the closer you get to perfection the better your results will be.

A two-suited hand is not too difficult to handle but a three-suiter can sometimes give you a headache. What would you open with this hand?

♠ A J 8 4
♡ 6
◊ A J 7 3
♣ K Q 10 4

You can't open One Spade because I am going to make it a rule that you need five cards in a major before you can open it. So the choice is between One Club and One Diamond. The general rule is that with three four-card suits you should start with the one below the singleton. That means you should open this hand One Diamond.

It would not be a crime to open One Club and you should certainly exercise your judgement from time to time. If I change the hand to:

♠ A J 8 4
♡ 6
◊ 8 7 4 2
♣ A K Q 10

I would open One Club every day of the week.

That would also be the correct bid on this hand:

♠ A J 8 4
♡ K J 7 6
♢ 5
♣ K Q 10 4

If all this is gradually sinking in, I hope you are asking yourself a question. If you are not allowed to open the bidding on a four-card major suit, then what do you do when you have this kind of hand?

♠ A J 8 4
♡ K 10 9 4
♢ Q 5
♣ A 7 3

As Sherlock Holmes once remarked, "Once you have eliminated the obvious only the impossible remains." You have to pretend you have an extra card in one of your minor suits and open One Club or One Diamond. Because you and your partner will be playing the same system, he will be alive to this possibility and keep it in mind as the bidding develops.

I will change the rank of the suits in the previous example so the hand looks like this:

♠ A 7 3
♡ Q 5
♢ K 10 9 4
♣ A J 8 4

You can pretty much toss a coin as to which minor suit you should open. Nothing bad will happen to you in either event but assuming the two suits are similar in nature then you may find life easier while you are gaining experience always to open One Diamond.

The majority of the hands I have shown you in this section so far have been unbalanced. What do you do when you pick up a hand like this one?

♠ K J 3
♡ A Q 7 4
◇ K 10 2
♣ Q 9 5

With the previous example in mind, perhaps you think it's a trick question and the answer is One Club. Remove the jack of spades and you would be correct. However, when you have a balanced hand and between 15 and 17 points you can start with the highest ranking bid at the one level, One No-Trump.

Before I consider this in more detail you need to be clear as to what constitutes a balanced hand. There are three possible distributions:

4-3-3-3	You only have one four-card suit
4-4-3-2	You have two four-card suits
5-3-3-2	You have a five-card suit, usually not a major

You depart from them at your peril, not because it would be ridiculous to open One No-Trump with, say, a 5-4-4-2 distribution, but because your partner will not be expecting it.

Here are examples of a One No-Trump opening bid containing the other distributions:

♠ K 9 6 4   ♠ A J 6
♡ A 10 9 4   ♡ A 7
◇ K Q 5   ◇ K Q 9 6 5
♣ A 3   ♣ K 8 2

What would you open with this hand?

♠ K 8 3
♡ A Q J 7 4
◇ A 9
♣ A 10 5

With 18 points it is too strong for One No-Trump. The answer is to open One Heart. You will show your extra values on the next round. The same principle applies to all balanced hands that fall outside the range – remember it's 15 to 17 points – whether they contain more or less than the required number of points. With this hand for example:

♠ A J 8 4
♡ K J 9 4
♢ K 5
♣ A K 3

You open the bidding with One Club.

It's important that you practise opening the bidding. If you are "Home Alone" I suggest you deal out four hands and check them out for points and distribution. That way you will soon be able to recognize the hands that should be opened and the correct opening bid.

I am going to tell you how to respond to a low-level opening bid later on but now I want to move on to hands that are too strong to be opened at the one level. These are the hands you are just going to love to pick up!

Strong opening bids

When you are lucky enough to pick up a very powerful hand with lots of high-card points you need a way to let partner in on the secret. Alas, standing on your chair and waving a flag is not allowed, so you must find an alternative. The solution comes in two parts.

STRONG BALANCED HANDS

By strong I mean at least 20 high-card points. By balanced I mean one of the three hand patterns that are associated with the One No-Trump opening bid, 4-3-3-3, 4-4-3-2 or 5-3-3-2.

Keeping these two factors in mind, when you have a hand with 20 to 21 high-card points you open the bidding with Two No-Trumps.

If you have a more powerful balanced hand you open with a conventional bid of Two Clubs. This is an artificial bid that may well have nothing to do with the club suit. It is the first move on all very strong hands. It is a forcing bid and your partner has to reply. We will deal with that aspect in a moment but for now all you need to know is that after your partner's response you describe a strong balanced hand of between 22 and 24 points with a rebid of Two No-Trumps.

If you have an even better balanced hand with 25 or 26 points, you plan to jump to Three No-Trumps over your partner's reply.

These hands would qualify for an opening bid of Two No-Trumps:

♠ K 8	♠ K Q 7 4	♠ A 10 3
♡ K 6 2	♡ A Q	♡ K Q J 6
◇ A Q 4	◇ K J 10 5	◇ K 9 5
♣ A K Q 10 5	♣ A J 7	♣ A K J

Making them all stronger means they qualify for an opening bid of Two Clubs.

♠ K 8	♠ K Q 7 4	♠ A K 3
♡ K Q 2	♡ A Q	♡ A K Q J
◇ A Q 4	◇ A J 10 5	◇ Q 10 5
♣ A K Q 10 5	♣ A K 7	♣ A K 6

On the first two hands you plan to rebid Two No-Trumps while on the third you hope to be able to jump to Three No-Trumps.

There are two good reasons why you should bid strong balanced hands in this way. One is that it is always a good idea for the opening lead to come round to your hand rather than through it. On the first two example hands you would hate it if your hand was dummy and the opening lead was a spade through your ♠K-8 or a heart through the ♡A-Q. The other is that the more points you have, the less are left for the other three players including your partner. If you open with a bid at the one level your partner may pass, not knowing that his few modest assets may be enough to produce a game for your side.

The other type of powerhouse you will pick up from time to time falls into a different category.

STRONG UNBALANCED HANDS

I promise you it will be a great feeling when you pick up your first really powerful hand. I can still recall mine. I had more than 30 points and ten certain winners. Not knowing any better, I opened with the only strong bid I knew at the time, Two No-Trumps. My partner, with only a solitary queen, passed and raised an eyebrow when I proceeded to win trick after trick. You can avoid a similar fate by remembering to open Two Clubs when you have a really powerful hand. Most of the time your hand will be very strong in high cards but once in a while you will have such a fantastic distribution that you simply have to use the strongest of all the opening bids.

Here are some examples of unbalanced hands that should be opened Two Clubs.

♠ A 8
♡ A K Q 10 7 6 4 2
◇ A K Q
♣ —

This is a breathtaking hand. If partner has the king of spades you are a big favourite to make a grand slam in hearts.

♠ A K Q 7 6 4
♡ A Q
◇ A J 10 5
♣ A

This is a very good hand – it has more high-card points than the previous example – but you need a little bit of help from your partner. It will help you to understand why hands this strong are opened Two Clubs if you imagine that your partner has no points at all. He would certainly pass an opening bid of One Spade when as little as ♠J-5 would mean you could collect nine virtually certain trick in no-trumps.

♠ A K Q J 6 4 3
♡ A K 10 8 4 2
◇ —
♣ —

You may never get a hand like this but if you do it is a 100% Two Club opening bid even though you have only 17 points.

The Two Club opening bid is 100% forcing! If you are the responder you are not allowed to pass – never – ever – on pain of death! Most of the time you will have a rotten hand with less than 7 points and you will give your partner the news – he will be expecting it anyhow – by making a conventional bid of your own. Your reply will be Two Diamonds. It has nothing to do with the diamond suit; it simply says you have a poor hand. Now your partner gets a chance to describe his hand. Remember that with a balanced hand he will rebid in no-trumps. With an unbalanced hand he will bid a suit.

You are permitted to pass only in one special set of circumstances. If your partner rebids Two No-Trumps, promising 22 to 24 points, and you have a completely worthless hand then, and only then, are you allowed to pass. With as little as 3 points you should scrape up a raise to game and bid Three No-Trumps.

I have now covered all the opening bids at the one level and those at either end of the two level. All the bids I have discussed so far have been constructive in the sense that they all promise certain values and are made in the hope that your side will be able to bid to its best contract. In the best traditions of Monty Python's Flying Circus, "Now for something completely different."

WEAK TWO BIDS

Howard Schenken was considered by a lot of people to be the best player ever. He was a member of the winning American team in the first recognized World Championship in 1935 and he subsequently won three Bermuda Bowls. In the Vanderbilt and Spingold Trophy events he was on the winning team 20 times, recording ten victories in each competition.

Arguably his greatest contribution to the game was the development of the Weak Two-bid a convention that is now played the world over.

In the early days of bridge a lot of attention was lavished on the use of opening bids at the two level to describe strong hands. Although "Strong Twos" can be very effective when the right hand comes along, Schenken realized that they simply didn't occur often enough to devote a whole range of bids to them. By including strong hands in an opening bid of Two Clubs, the remaining suit bids at the two level are available to describe a different type of hand that appears with much greater frequency.

Schenken's original idea was to use the opening bids of Two Hearts and Two Spades to show a weak hand with a six-card suit. It was quickly realized that Two Diamonds could also be used in the same way.

Being able to start the bidding more often inevitably presents your opponents with additional problems they would rather do without. It is no wonder that Schenken's suggestion has been almost universally adopted.

The Weak Two has become a fearsome weapon in the hands of modern players who pay little regard to suit quality and quite often have only a five-card suit.

The range for a Weak Two can vary depending on style and vulnerability but 5–9 or 6–10 points is a reasonable guide. When you have fewer than 10 points it is quite like your side has less than its fair share of the high cards. If your partner is a passed hand it becomes even more probable. By making a pre-emptive bid you take the risk that your side will incur a penalty but you hope it will save you points when compared with whatever contract your opponents might make.

You are prepared to sacrifice some points in an attempt to stop your opponents bidding a game, or perhaps even a slam. By starting the bidding at a high level you make it more difficult for the opponents to exchange information and they will sometimes have to guess what to do. Nobody guesses right all the time!

Every now and then you will catch your partner with a good hand and he will have the problem. At least he will have a good idea about the nature of your hand.

To make a pre-emptive bid you ideally need a reasonable number of tricks in your suit. That will afford you some protection against a big loss if you get doubled. However, since part of your strategy is to make life difficult for your opponents, you may sometimes take a calculated risk.

Now let's look at some examples.

♠ 7 4
♡ A Q J 8 5 3
♢ 8 2
♣ 10 6 4

This would be a perfect Two-Heart bid at any vulnerability. All your points are concentrated in your suit and you are likely to make five tricks all on your own.

♠ K Q 9 6 5 3
♡ 8 5
◇ K 7
♣ 9 5 4

The suit is not quite so strong this time so bidding carries more risk. In the interests of trying to make life difficult for your opponents you should take a chance and open Two Spades.

♠ 7 5 3
♡ A 6 3
◇ Q 10 9 8 7 3
♣ 7

Your suit gets worse still in terms of high cards but the intermediates make Two Diamonds a reasonable choice.

♠ 6 3
♡ Q 8 7 6 4 2
◇ 8
♣ K 7 5 3

Now your suit is dreadful but at favourable vulnerability many players would still try Two Hearts.

♠ Q 8 7 4
♡ A Q J 8 5 3
◇ 8
♣ 4 2

You have a good suit and the right values, but holding four cards in the other major is a considerable flaw because your partner won't expect it. It usually works better to pass this type of hand.

♠ Q 8 7 4
♡ A Q J 8 5 3
◇ —
♣ 8 4 2

Just a slight change, turning the eight of diamonds into a club, and

it is even more clear not to open Two Hearts. This time you have
two "flaws": the four-card spade suit and the diamond void.
Experience has taught me that two flaws are definitely one too
many. Mind you I might open One Heart!

Obviously if you are facing a passed hand you can afford to be
less critical.

> ♠ Q 8 7 4
> ♡ A Q J 8 5 3
> ◊ 8
> ♣ 4 2

Now this earlier example would now be a routine third in hand
Two Hearts.

Third in hand is also the position where the five-card suit is likely
to put in an appearance.

> ♠ 8
> ♡ 7 5 3
> ◊ K Q J 7 4
> ♣ K 8 4 2

This would now be a perfectly acceptable Two Diamonds.

Some players would regard the presence of the king of clubs in
the previous example as something of a luxury! Take a look at this
full deal:

Love All
Dealer South

	♠ A K 9 8 6	
	♡ Q 10	
	◊ A 7 6 3	
	♣ 8 4	
♠ Q 10 3	N	♠ J 7
♡ A J 6 3 2	W E	♡ K 5 4
◊ —	S	◊ 10 9 8 5
♣ A K 7 5 2		♣ Q J 6 3
	♠ 5 4 2	
	♡ 9 8 7	
	◊ K Q J 4 2	
	♣ 10 9	

West	North	East	South
Vd Porten	*Horton*	*Hamman*	*Landy*
—	—	—	2◇
Double	2♠	All Pass	

World Champion Sandra Landy did not hesitate to open with a
weak Two Diamonds and that gave the American pair a problem
they were unable to solve. Two Spades can be defeated if the
defenders find their diamond ruffs but declarer was allowed to get
in a couple of rounds of trumps and so recorded eight tricks.

In the other room South passed, allowing West to open One Heart
which made it easy for his side to reach Four Hearts.

Responses to Weak Two bids

When it comes to responding to a Weak Two bid the experts all
agree that a Two No-Trump reply should be forcing, asking the
opener to describe his hand. Unfortunately, that is about all they do
agree on! There are many opinions as to how the bidding should
develop from there.

Before addressing that question there are several other responses
to consider. The first is straightforward: raising partner with
support. Two examples will suffice:

West	North	East	South
2♡	Pass	?	

♠ 8 5 3	♠ 7 5 2
♡ A J 10 6	♡ J 9 4
◇ 8 4	◇ 8 6
♣ K 9 4 2	♣ A Q 10 7 3

You can put your opponents under pressure by jumping to Four
Hearts on the first hand while on the second you should content
yourself with a gentle raise to Three Hearts.

The basic principles relating to responding to pre-emptive bids
that we are about to discuss in more detail apply.

    ♠ K J 7 4
    ♡ 5
    ◇ A K J 6
    ♣ K 7 4 2

With this hand you should calmly pass partner's opening bid of
Two Hearts.

Then there is the question as to whether a change of suit should
be forcing, for example:

West	North	East	South
Pass	2♡	Pass	2♠
Pass	?		

Does North have to bid or not?

I suggest that a new suit at the two level is regarded as
constructive but not forcing. The opener should be prepared to raise
with suitable non-minimum hands.

    ♠ 7 5 3
    ♡ A 6 3
    ◇ Q 10 9 8 7 3
    ♣ 7

Here, opener would be delighted to raise either major.

Let's use this hand as an example:

    ♠ Q 8 7 4
    ♡ A Q J 8 5 3
    ◇ 8
    ♣ 4 2

If responder replies to an opening bid of Two Hearts with Two
Spades then it would be in order to jump to Four Spades.

A new suit at the three level should be forcing and will not
usually have much of a fit for opener's suit – as you will see in a
moment, hands with a fit are best dealt with by using the artificial
response of Two No-Trumps.

This would be a typical hand for a three-level response:

West	North	East	South
2♡	Pass	?	

♠ A K Q J 7 3
♡ 8
♢ A Q 4
♣ A 10 7

East bids Three Spades.

As I mentioned earlier, a response of Two No-Trumps is forcing and asks the opener to describe his hand. There is no universally accepted way of replying but here is a reasonable scheme that is similar to the responses originally proposed by Harold Ogust who represented the USA in two world championships.

3♣	bad hand and bad suit
3♢	bad hand but good suit
3♡	good hand but bad suit
3♠	good hand and good suit
3NT	AKQxxx (!)

When I am partnering the well-known British player and writer Brian Senior we use the response of Three Clubs to indicate a hand so poor that we wish we had not opened the bidding!

It's worth pointing out that a response of Three No-Trumps is very rare and that bid might be better employed to show a maximum hand with a suit headed by two of the top three honours.

This is one of the areas in bidding where new ideas are still emerging – perhaps you will develop an idea that appears in a book on conventions!

WEAK THREE BIDS

If opening at the two level with a weak hand can give your opponents a headache, imagine what it is like if you go even higher!

You can use all the suits at this level to tell partner you have a poor hand with less than 10 points and a seven-card suit.

If it was difficult for your opponents to exchange information at the two level after a weak opening bid, think how much more awkward it will be when they have to start at the three level.

Here are a couple of typical examples:

♠ 8
♡ K Q J 10 8 5 2
◇ 8 3
♣ 10 6 4

With hearts as trumps you can hardly fail to take six tricks and you should open Three Hearts.

♠ 6 4
♡ 9 5
◇ 8 5
♣ A Q J 10 7 6 3

Hands that are distributed 7-2-2-2 are not ideal for a pre-emptive bid but you should still open Three Clubs with such a good suit.

Responding to Weak Three bids
You will not have much of a problem if you are dealt a weak hand and your partner opens with a pre-emptive bid. Unless you happen to have a good fit and can increase the defensive barrage by raising partner's suit, you will pass and hope the pre-empt has done its work.

When you do have support for your partner's suit and raise it, you may have a good hand, especially when the suit is one of the majors. Both of these hands would raise an opening bid of Three Hearts to Four Hearts.

♠ 9	♠ A K 10 3
♡ A 8 5 3	♡ A 9 5
◇ 10 7 4	◇ 7 5
♣ K J 8 5 2	♣ A Q 7 4

In the first example your raise is defensive, trying to make it difficult for your opponents to locate their spade fit. In the second you are on to a sure thing and if the opponents are kind enough to bid you will collect a substantial penalty.

When your partner opens with a pre-emptive bid you will often find that the most likely game for your side is Three No-Trumps. That is especially true when the pre-empt is in a minor. Imagine that your partner has opened Three Diamonds and the next player passes. You could happily respond Three No Trumps with either of these hands:

♠ K Q 7 4 2	♠ K 9
♡ A 7	♡ A 8 5
◇ A 10 5	◇ 7
♣ A 8 4	♣ A K Q J 7 4 2

In the first case Three No-Trumps is odds on whatever the lead. In the second a non-spade lead may give you a problem but you may find partner with something useful, perhaps the ace of diamonds or the king of hearts.

It would be wrong to try for the nine-trick game without a good fit for partner or a running suit of your own.

♠ A K Q 7
♡ K Q 7
◇ J 8
♣ A J 10 5

It would be wrong to bid Three No-Trumps in reply to an opening bid of Three Diamonds. The correct bid is Five Diamonds. If you imagine partner's hand to be something like:

♠ 6
♡ 9 5
◇ K Q 10 9 7 5 2
♣ 8 5 2

You will see that nine tricks in no-trumps will be almost impossible unless the ace of diamonds is singleton, while eleven in diamonds will be a breeze.

With a very good suit of your own you can bid it, forcing partner to respond. Consider the following:

♠ K Q J 8 4 2
♡ A K 7
◇ A 6
♣ 8 3

It would be reasonable to respond Three Spades to an opening bid of Three of a Minor. With a suitable hand for spades, i.e. at least a doubleton in the suit, your partner should raise you to game.

WEAK FOUR BIDS

Opening the bidding at the four level really puts it to your opponents. You are still going to be short on high cards, usually having no more than 10 points, but you will have an eight-card suit or perhaps a concentrated 7-4-2-0 or 7-4-1-1 distribution.

Here are a few examples:

♠ 7
♡ A K Q 10 9 7 5 2
♢ 6
♣ 10 6 4

With eight almost certain tricks, you can open Four Hearts. If your partner produces just a couple of tricks you will make it. If he has a worthless hand, you may make it too difficult for your opponents to reach their best contract.

♠ A Q J 9 6 5 3
♡ 8 4
♢ —
♣ Q 10 9 7

By opening Four Spades you may really make life awkward for your opponents.

♠ 6
♡ 3
♢ 10 4
♣ K Q J 10 7 6 5 3 2

This is ideal for an opening bid of Four Clubs. At favourable vulnerability you might even try Five Clubs.

Responding to a Weak Four bid

Since Four Spades and Four Hearts are game bids you should disturb them only if you are looking for a slam. You may want to

raise an opening bid of Four Diamonds or Four Clubs to game if
you have the right sort of hand. With a very good hand you will
probably wish partner had not pre-empted, but that's life. In the
long run pre-empts will give you more gains than losses.

Now you know how to make the first positive move on a variety
of hands. That is all well and good but you also have to know what
happens next. As I said earlier, bidding is a conversation. You may
have made the opening address but now it is up to your partner to
reply. We are about to enter the world of responses.

Responding to an opening bid

When your partner opens the bidding the player on your right has a
chance to bid before you do. After he has made either a positive bid
or passed, it is your turn. It is up to you to describe the type of hand
you have.

An opening bid at the one level can be made on quite a strong
hand but does not usually contain more than 19 high-card points.
You are therefore allowed to pass with a poor hand unless you have
support for your partner. For example:

♠ Q J 8 6 4
♡ 7 5
♢ 9 8 4
♣ J 6 3

Raise One Spade to Two Spades but otherwise you should pass.

♠ 7 2
♡ K J 10 7 4
♢ 8 4
♣ J 9 5 3

Here you have just enough to bid One Heart over One Club or
One Diamond. You have an easy raise to the two level if your
partner opens One Heart. If he opens One Spade you should
probably pass.

In general you need 6 points to respond to an opening bid. If you
have a fit for the suit your partner has bid you can re-evaluate your
hand by adding on extra points for distribution. I suggest you use
the following table:

For a doubleton add on   1 extra point
For a singleton add on   3 extra points
For a void add on   5 extra points
Using the previous example:

    ♠ 7 2
    ♡ K J 10 7 4
    ♢ 8 4
    ♣ J 9 5 3

This hand is worth 7 points in support of hearts or clubs because
you have two doubletons. Remember, these extra points should be
added on only when you have a good fit, and that means at least
four cards in support of your partner's suit. This hand is worth only
5 points if it is facing an opening bid of One Spade or One
Diamond, but the quality of the heart suit allows you to make a
response at the one level.

When you have 6 or more points you will have a number of
options depending on the nature of your hand. You will have to
choose between introducing a new suit, responding in no-trumps
and raising your partner's suit.

Let's take a look at what you should do when your partner starts
with one of the minor suits.

RESPONDING TO ONE CLUB OR ONE DIAMOND
Introducing a new suit

If you reply in a new suit at the one level you are promising at least
6 points and at least four cards in the suit that you bid. You may
have a lot more than 6 points and for that reason your partner is not
allowed to pass if you respond in a new suit. Your bid is forcing for
one round. These hands would respond One Heart to an opening bid
of One Club or One Diamond:

    ♠ A J 3
    ♡ Q J 10 8
    ♢ 10 7 3
    ♣ 9 7 4

You are hoping your partner may be able to support your suit and at
the same time keeping the bidding alive in case he has a strong hand.

```
♠ Q J 6
♡ A K 7 4 2
◇ K 8 3
♣ J 7
```

A simple but effective rule to follow is that, if your partner opens the bidding and you have an opening bid, make sure you get to game. Here, you have more than enough points and you want to discover the best denomination, which could be either your suit or partner's or no-trumps.

If you have two reasonable suits of the same length, then you bid them in ascending order unless they are five or six cards long. In those cases you should bid the higher-ranking suit first, planning to bid the other one on the next round. Here are some examples.

```
♠ K J 8 5
♡ A Q 7 4
◇ J 6 2
♣ 9 5
```

Here you would respond One Heart hoping your partner can support you or introduce a four-card spade suit of his own. If he doesn't do either then you probably don't want to play this hand in a major suit.

```
♠ K J 8 5
♡ 9 5
◇ A Q 7 4
♣ J 6 2
```

Here you would respond One Spade to an opening bid of One Club. If your partner opens One Diamond then you should resist the temptation to support him at once and bid One Spade. The major suits are more important because only ten tricks are needed there to make a game. You can show your diamond support later.

```
♠ A J 7 4 3
♡ K Q 9 6 4
◇ K 7
♣ 8
```

You should start by replying One Spade. If your partner rebids his suit you can continue with Two Hearts.

Perhaps the trickiest situation to cope with is when the opening bid is One Diamond and your best suit is clubs. The rules don't allow you to respond One Club – remember each bid must be higher than the last one – so you have to bid Two Clubs. However, because you are now committing your side to the two level, you need a reasonable hand with around 11 high-card points. This would be a typical hand:

    ♠ 9 5
    ♡ A J 3
    ♢ K 6 3
    ♣ A J 10 7 4

If you are not strong enough to respond at the two level then you can bid a four-card major suit at the one level. If you don't have one then you will find yourself having to respond One No-Trump. Here are a couple of examples:

    ♠ 10 5
    ♡ K J 6 4
    ♢ 8 3
    ♣ A J 9 3 2

When partner opens One Diamond you don't have enough points to bid Two Clubs, but you can introduce your heart suit by bidding One Heart. If your partner then bids One Spade your best move will be to bid One No-Trump, suggesting that you can look after the club suit.

    ♠ Q 7 4
    ♡ 8 5 3
    ♢ J 5
    ♣ A J 9 3 2

This time you have no major suit to bid but too many points to pass. You have to respond One No-Trump. Your partner will assume you have around 6-10 points.

Responding with a balanced hand

If you find yourself looking at a balanced hand without a four- or five-card major suit then you can consider an immediate response in no-trumps.

I suggest you adopt the following scale:

Respond One No-Trump with	6–10	points
Respond Two No-Trumps with	11–12	points
Respond Three No-Trumps with	13–15	points

Here is an example of each type of response:

♠ K J 7
♡ K 6 5
◇ J 8 4
♣ Q 9 7 3

If your partner opens One Club then a response of One No-Trump describes your hand perfectly.

♠ K J 7
♡ K Q 4
◇ Q 9 7 3
♣ J 8 4

This time you can happily respond with Two No-Trumps.

♠ A J 7
♡ A Q 4
◇ Q 9 7 3
♣ J 8 4

Now you have enough to reply Three No-Trumps.

You can use a similar scale when you have a balanced hand facing an opening bid in one of the major suits. Mentioning the major suits leads us neatly on to our next topic.

RESPONDING TO ONE SPADE OR ONE HEART

An opening bid in one of the majors promises a minimum of five cards in the suit bid. Because a lot of your bidding is going to centre around the location of an eight-card trump fit, the way you respond to an opening bid in one of the major suits will be influenced by the number of cards you have in the suit your partner opens.

Before I look at what you should do when you know you have a fit, let's check out what to do when you don't.

Remember that you have to keep the bidding going with as few as 6 points. Also, to respond at the two level you need around 11 points. If the opening bid is One Heart and you a have a hand that is too weak to respond at the two level but has more than 5 points you will have only two choices: to introduce a spade suit or to bid One No-Trump. These hands illustrate the point:

     ♠ K Q 7 4
     ♡ 8 2
     ◇ Q J 9 7
     ♣ 10 6 4

When your partner opens One Heart you have an easy response of One Spade.

     ♠ Q 10 4
     ♡ 7 3
     ◇ K 8 3
     ♣ K 10 6 4 2

You don't have enough points to introduce your club suit so you respond One No-Trump.

With a hand that is strong enough you can reply at the two level. For instance:

     ♠ A Q 3
     ♡ 10 4
     ◇ A Q J 7 6 5
     ♣ 8 5

Now you can happily respond Two Diamonds to One Heart.

When the opening bid is One Spade you have no way to show a suit at the one level. That means you will have to include hands with many different shapes in a response of One No-Trump. All these hands would qualify for a response of One No-Trump facing an opening bid of One Spade:

♠ 9 3	♠ 5	♠ —
♡ K J 5 4	♡ Q J 9 3	♡ K J 10 7 3
◊ Q 6 3 2	◊ K 8 4 3 2	◊ J 9 3
♣ K 7 4	♣ J 10 6	♣ K 9 6 4 2

If you have the right number of points – yes 11 is still the magic number – you can respond at the two level. Five-card suits take priority, especially hearts, but if you have two five-card suits you should almost always bid your highest suit first.

♠ 6 4
♡ A K J 7 2
◊ A J 10 6 3
♣ 10

You respond Two Hearts to One Spade. If your partner rebids Two Spades you can continue to describe your hand by bidding Three Diamonds.

♠ 7
♡ K 8 6 4 2
◊ K 6
♣ A K Q 8 3

Even though the club suit is the stronger of the two you should still start with Two Hearts. When you bid Two Hearts over One Spade your partner knows you have at least five of them. If you start by bidding Two Clubs and then introduce your hearts you will mislead your partner about the shape of your hand. That may cause all sorts of problems as the auction develops.

When your longest suit is a four-carder the picture changes. Now you should start at the bottom and work your way up. Pretty good advice for the aspiring player now I come to think of it! You still need those 11 points I keep mentioning. These hands would all qualify for a response at the two level:

♠ 7 3
♡ A Q 8 4
♢ 6 5 2
♣ A K J 9

You have an easy response of Two Clubs.

♠ J 5
♡ A K Q 6
♢ K 8 4 2
♣ 7 5 3

This time you can reply Two Diamonds.

♠ 10 6
♡ A J 9
♢ K J 7 4
♣ Q 8 5 3

It would not be a mistake to respond Two Clubs to One Spade but remember you are allowed to bid no-trumps when you have a balanced hand with stoppers in the unbid suits. Here your point count indicates a response of Two No-Trumps.

When you have exactly three-card support for your partner's major suit you know that you have found that potentially all-important eight-card fit right at the start of the bidding. You will have to let partner in on this piece of good news but exactly when you do so will depend on the distribution and strength of your hand.

With around 6 to 10 points you should usually give partner a simple raise to the two level. This hand would qualify over a One Heart opening bid:

♠ 9 5
♡ Q 7 4
♢ A 10 5 2
♣ Q 8 6 3

Your doubleton spade is useful if your partner has some length in that suit as your trumps might then be used to ruff partner's losers.

It would not be wrong to upgrade your hand because of that but you are still only worth a raise to Two Hearts.

When you have a completely balanced hand the right bid is less clear. Suppose you are looking at:

- ♠ K84
- ♡ K75
- ◇ Q852
- ♣ Q95

It would not be wrong simply to raise One Heart to Two, but a response of One No-Trump is attractive, especially when you have no ruffing value and something in every suit. There is no "right" answer to this kind of question. However, if you tend to think in terms of no-trumps when you are balanced and a suit contract when you are not then nothing bad is likely to happen to you.

When you have four-card support for your partner's suit you need look no further for a fit. Your reply will be based on the strength of your hand; don't forget you are allowed to add on extra points for distributional features. Taking them in combination you should raise your partner to the two level with up to 8 points. With around 9 to 12 points you should advance to the three level. When you have an even better hand you can sometimes afford to show a new suit before supporting your partner's major at the four level. Let's take a look at examples of the different responses.

- ♠ J863
- ♡ 84
- ◇ A1052
- ♣ Q83

This hand is worth 8 points in support of spades and you can happily raise to the two level. It would be OK to do that even if you didn't have the queen of clubs.

- ♠ QJ74
- ♡ 1094
- ◇ K95
- ♣ AJ7

You can't add on any points for distribution but you are worth a raise to Three Spades.

♠ 10 4
♡ K 10 7 2
◊ A 6
♣ A K 10 5 2

This is a powerful hand in support of hearts. You can respond Two Clubs to an opening bid of One Heart intending to jump to Four Hearts at your next turn.

With a very weak highly distributional hand it is a good idea to make a pre-emptive raise. Apart from the fact that every now and then partner's hand will be good enough to allow you to make the contract you make it more difficult for your opponents to get into the bidding.

♠ 8
♡ Q 10 9 7 6
◊ A 10 8 5 4 2
♣ 6

You would be more than happy to raise your partner's opening bid of One Heart to game by bidding Four Hearts.

On the rare occasions that you find yourself with five-card support for your partner's suit you should strain to let partner know.

♠ Q 9 7 4 2
♡ J 7 4
◊ 5
♣ 10 8 5 3

Not much of a hand, but when partner opens One Spade you can justify a raise to Two Spades. You don't even need the jack of hearts.

A lot of thought has been put into the best way to respond to an opening bid in one of the majors and I will be exploring some more sophisticated methods later on. Now it is time to look at an area of bidding that has been under the spotlight ever since bridge was invented.

RESPONDING TO AN OPENING BID OF ONE NO-TRUMP

Of all the opening bids in bridge One No-Trump presents one of the clearest pictures. It promises a balanced hand containing between 15 and 17 points. The responder knows that any long suit in his hand will be facing at least a doubleton – remember you don't open One No-Trump with a singleton. Any long suit with a couple of honours in it is likely to produce a fair number of tricks because partner's holding in the suit usually includes an honour.

When your hand is balanced the responses to One No-Trump are very easy to understand.

With 0 to 7 points you should pass.
With 8 or 9 points you should make an invitational raise to Two No-Trumps.
With 10 to 15 points you should bid Three No-Trumps.

When your hand is unbalanced or very weak or you want to explore the possibility of playing the contract in a major suit you can resort to the use of a little bit of applied science. I am going to introduce you to a couple of conventions that are just about indispensable.

Stayman

'Stayman and Blackwood partner?'

Enter any rubber bridge club and you are sure to hear those words at one of the tables. They have both become an integral part of the game.

Samuel (Sam) Stayman explained the convention that carries his name in an article in the June 1945 issue of the *Bridge World*. He modestly gave the credit to his partner George Rapee but it has forever been known as the Stayman convention.

One of my predecessors as Editor of *Bridge Magazine*, Ewart Kempson, was collaborating with Stayman on a British version of one of his books and was rather impressed by the luxurious penthouse that the great man occupied in the heart of New York.

"Terribly expensive?" ventured Kempson.

"Not really," Stayman replied. Detecting Kempson's surprise he added, "I happen to own the block."

The principle idea of the convention is the use of a bid of Two Clubs in response to an opening bid of One No-Trump to locate a fit in a major suit.

It can be applied when the responder has a variety of hands:

- When the responder has the values for game and at least one four-card major.
- When the responder has the values to invite game and at least one four-card major.
- With a weak hand, either 4-4-5-0 or 4-4-4-1 where the idea is to find a better resting place than One No-Trump.

Here is a typical example of each:

North	South	♠ K 8 4
1NT	2♣	♡ A J 7 3
		◇ J 9 4 2
		♣ Q 7

You have enough points to bid game but want to explore the possibility of a 4-4 fit in hearts.

North	South	♠ A K 6 2
1NT	2♣	♡ 6 3
		◇ 8 5 2
		♣ Q 9 4 2

This time you have the values for an invitational bid. You will raise a reply of Two Spades to Three Spades, or bid Two No-Trumps over a response of Two Diamonds or Two Hearts.

North	South	♠ J 7 6 3
1NT	2♣	♡ 9 8 5 2
		◇ 9 8 7 4
		♣ 5

You have a dreadful hand but by responding Two Clubs you give yourself a chance of locating an eight-card fit. You plan to pass your partner's response.

It may have dawned on you from these examples that after the bidding has started 1NT – Pass – 2♣, the opener has three possible replies:

2◇	simply denies a four-card major suit.
2♡	promises a four-card heart suit.
2♠	promises a four-card spade suit.

If you are responding to Two Clubs and find yourself with both four hearts and four spades then I suggest you always start by responding Two Hearts.

Let's take a look at an example of each possible reply.

North	South		
1NT	2♣	♠	A J 5
?		♡	K Q 5 4
		◇	K 8
		♣	A 9 7 5

You show your four-card major by bidding Two Hearts.

North	South		
1NT	2♣	♠	Q 10 3
?		♡	A K 7
		◇	K J 10 9
		♣	A 7 3

With no four-card major you have to reply to your partner's enquiry with Two Diamonds.

North	South		
1NT	2♣	♠	A Q 7 2
?		♡	K J 6 3
		◇	J 6
		♣	A 8 4

You have both major suits but start by showing the lower, by bidding Two Hearts.

We can see how things would work out when we use the convention by putting these hands opposite each other.

♠ A J 5
♡ K Q 6 4
◇ A 10 8 3
♣ Q 5

♠ K 8 4
♡ A J 7 3
◇ J 9 6 2
♣ K 6

If you play these hands in a contract of Three No-Trumps and the
opponents lead a club you will succeed only when a finesse for the
queen of spades works. In Four Hearts you have many more
chances because the control the trump suit gives you ensures there
will be time to play on diamonds.

♠ Q 10 3
♡ A K 7
◇ K 8 3
♣ A J 10 9

♠ A K 6 2
♡ 6 3
◇ Q 9 4 2
♣ 8 5 2

After South's Stayman enquiry North, with no four-card major,
replies Two Diamonds. South then bids Two No-Trumps, inviting
North to go on to game with a maximum. With 17 good points and
two tens it is clear for North to bid Three No-Trumps. A heart lead
would have been testing but if North's hand had been:

♠ Q 10 8 3
♡ A K 7
◇ K 8
♣ A J 10 9

Then the Two Club bid would have located the spade fit and the almost laydown Four Spades would have been reached.

♠ A Q 8 2
♡ K J 7 3
◇ J 5
♣ A 7 4

♠ J 7 5 3
♡ 10 8 6 4
◇ 10 8 7 4
♣ 5

Here South intends to pass whatever North bids, which in this case will be Two Hearts. Remember that if North has no four-card major he must respond Two Diamonds and in the vast majority of cases that will mean he has at least three diamonds. Only when North has a 3-3-2-5 distribution will you be in danger of going "out of the frying pan" and "into the fire".

Not everyone knows that if the responding hand is 4-4 in the majors you will have a 4-4 fit 58.28% of the time. If the combined honour strength of the two hands is around 22 high-card points then, if you have a fit, a suit contract will usually play a trick better than One No-Trump. That's an important consideration for a tournament player to keep in mind.

Now I want to take a look at what happens after the opening bidder has replied to the Stayman enquiry.

Responder bids a major suit.
This promises 8 or 9 points and at least a five-card suit. If you play the convention I describe after this one, Jacoby Transfers, this implies you have four cards in the other major.

North	South	
1NT	2♣	♠ Q J 7 2
2♢	2♡	♡ A J 9 5 2
		♢ 9 4
		♣ 6 3

With a minimum North will pass your Two Heart bid. With a maximum he will bid game in hearts with three-card support (remember, he has already denied four cards in either major) or Three No-Trumps with only two hearts. With something in the middle his choice will rest with either Two No-Trumps or Three Hearts.

Responder bids 2NT
This shows 8 or 9 points and implies you have an unbid four-card major.

North	South	
1NT	2♣	♠ K 9 6 4
2♡	2NT	♡ 9 6
		♢ J 7 3
		♣ A 9 6 2

You will remember that it is still possible for North to have four spades so with a minimum hand he will either pass or bid Three Spades. With a maximum he bids Three No-Trumps or Four Spades.

Three of a minor
This promises at least 10 high-card points, so it is forcing to game. It may sometimes be based on a much stronger hand that has visions of a slam.

North	South	
1NT	2♣	♠ K J 7
2♠	3♢	♡ A 8
		♢ K J 7 5 3 2
		♣ 8 4

If North now bids Three No-Trumps you should pass. If he makes a more encouraging bid then you will be on the way to a slam.

Three of an unbid major
This time you promise at least 10 points and a five-card suit. Once again the bidding cannot stop below game and if you are using

Jacoby Transfers partner will know you have four cards in the other major.

North	South	
1NT	2♣	♠ K Q 9 6 2
2♦	3♠	♡ A J 8 3
		♦ 6
		♣ Q 7 4

North has three possible courses of action. He can raise to Four Spades, bid Three No-Trumps or, with a maximum and good spade support, make a cuebid. Suppose he has the following hand:

♠ A J 6
♡ K Q 7
♦ 10 8 4 2
♣ A K 6

He would bid Four Clubs and that would put you well on the way to bidding Six Spades.

Raising a major to the three level
This promises 8 or 9 points and invites partner to bid game.

North	South	
1NT	2♣	♠ J 8 4
2♡	3♡	♡ K J 8 7
		♦ K 9 7 4
		♣ 7 3

North raises to game with a maximum and passes with a minimum.

Bidding 3NT
This shows a raise to game and guarantees a four-card major.

North	South	
1NT	2♣	♠ A 10 6 2
2♡	3NT	♡ 9 4
		♦ K 7 6
		♣ K 9 3 2

Your partner will pass unless he also has four spades in which case he will convert to Four Spades.

Four of a major
As you might imagine, this is a natural sign-off.

North	South	♠ K 10 7 5 4 2
1NT	2♣	♡ A Q 6 3
2◊	4♠	◊ 6
		♣ 7 4

You used Stayman in case partner had four hearts but now you bid
Four Spades because that is where you want to play.

Four No-Trumps
This is a quantitative raise, inviting partner to bid Six No-Trumps
with a maximum.

North	South	♠ A 7 4
1NT	2♣	♡ K 8 2
2♠	4NT	◊ K Q 10 5
		♣ A 6 4

You may have noticed that two situations have not been covered.

One involves the use of the bid Four Clubs after partner's reply to
Stayman. That is a convention called Gerber.

The other is an immediate bid of Three of a Minor after partner
has opened One No-Trump. This can be used to describe a weak
hand with no interest in game. A typical example would be:

North	South	♠ 7
1NT	3♣	♡ 9 4 2
		◊ J 5 3
		♣ Q 8 7 5 3 2

Reverse the minor suits and the response would be Three
Diamonds.

In order to play Stayman you have to give up the idea of using a
bid of Two Clubs as a natural response to One No-Trump. It is a
small price to pay.

Now I want to introduce you to another important convention.

Jacoby Transfer

If the eternal cry of the rubber bridge player is "Stayman and Blackwood", that of his tournament-playing counterpart is undoubtedly "Stayman and Transfers".

It was Oswald (Ozzie) Jacoby who introduced transfers into the game and they have become one of the cornerstones of modern bidding.

Jacoby realized that a natural response to an opening bid of One No-Trump meant that the opening lead would be made through the strong hand. It would be much better if the hand could be played from the other side because (a) the lead would run around to the strong hand, and (b) the strong hand would be concealed, making life harder for the defenders.

His solution, the Jacoby Transfer, has had a far-reaching effect on the way hands have been bid ever since.

The basic idea is as follows:

After an opening bid of One No-Trump the responder bids either Two Diamonds, asking opener to bid Two Hearts, or Two Hearts, asking opener to reply Two Spades. In either case the responder will have a five-card or longer suit in the major opener has been asked to bid.

The obvious advantage of this method is that it allows the no-trump bidder to play the hand, thereby protecting his high cards from the opening lead. Less obviously, it gives you room to investigate the best game contract and it also permits you to explore for a possible slam, usually without going past the all-important Three No-Trumps.

The only concession you have to make is the loss of a natural bid of Two Diamonds.

Because you are forcing your partner to respond in a particular way you have no information about the quality of the support that you will find for your suit. The only certainty you have is that partner, having opened One No-Trump, will have at least a doubleton in support for your five-card suit .

Let's take a look at a few examples of the convention in action.

North	South
1NT	?

♠ Q 9 7 4 3
♡ 6 5 2
♢ 7 6 4 2
♣ 5

Your bid is Two Hearts promising at least five spades. When your partner bids Two Spades you intend to pass.

North	South	
1NT	?	♠ A 8
		♡ A Q J 8 2
		◇ 9 5
		♣ K Q 10 4

This time you bid Two Diamonds to show at least five hearts. You do not intend to pass at your next turn!

That leads us on to the next question; what does the responder do after making the transfer?

Here are some examples.

North	South	
1NT	2◇	♠ 7 4
2♡	?	♡ J 10 7 5 3
		◇ 7
		♣ Q J 8 6 2

You are sure that your combined hands do not contain the values for game so you can happily pass.

North	South	
1NT	2◇	♠ Q J 9 7 2
2♡	?	♡ A 10 8 5 3
		◇ 6
		♣ 7 3

Having shown five hearts with your first bid you can now introduce your other major by bidding Two Spades. This promises at least 5-5 and gives partner two options. With a minimum he may pass if he prefers spades or else bid Three Hearts; with a maximum he should jump to game in his better major. Remember that with a four-card major in your hand you should use the Stayman convention!

North	South	
1NT	2♡	♠ A J 8 5 3
2♠	?	♡ K Q 9 6 2
		◇ 4
		♣ 6 3

Once again you have two five-card majors. However, this time your hand is strong enough for you to insist on playing in a game contract. By showing your spades first you are telling partner that your hand is good enough to force to game. Now you can bid Three Hearts.

North	South
1NT	2♡
2♠	?

♠ A 10 8 6 2
♡ 7 4 2
♢ J 8 3
♣ K 9

You don't have enough points to insist on game, but if partner has a maximum you would like him to try Three No-Trumps or Four Spades. By bidding Two No-Trumps you tell partner that you have an invitational hand with five spades and leave the final decision to him.

North	South
1NT	2♢
2♡	?

♠ A 8
♡ A Q J 8 2
♢ 9 5
♣ K Q 10 4

This was an earlier example. Having shown your heart suit you now continue with Three Clubs. Bidding Three of a Minor after the transfer promises at least four cards in the suit and, as here, may well indicate the possibility of a slam.

Partner can show support for one of your suits by raising clubs or going back to hearts, or he can deny any support by bidding Three No-Trumps.

North	South
1NT	2♡
2♠	?

♠ K 10 7 6 4 2
♡ 4
♢ 9 6 5
♣ A 8 2

With a six-card suit and invitational values you want to consult partner as to the best contract. Here you bid Three Spades to let partner know about your sixth spade. He will raise you to game with a maximum and pass with a minimum.

North	South	♠ K 8
1NT	2◇	♡ A J 9 4 2
2♡	?	◇ 10 6 5
		♣ Q 7 4

You know your side has enough points for game so the correct action is to jump to Three No-Trumps. Partner knows you have five hearts and a balanced hand and can choose between game in no-trumps or hearts. He will usually prefer the major-suit game when he has three or more hearts.

North	South	♠ 8
1NT	2◇	♡ K J 9 8 6 3
2♡	?	◇ 9 6 4
		♣ A 10 4

With a good six-card suit and reasonable values you should go to game without bothering to issue an invitation. Bid Four Hearts.

North	South	♠ A Q 9 8 4
1NT	2♡	♡ K 8
2♠	?	◇ Q 6 2
		♣ K J 7

If partner has a maximum you are likely to have a good chance of making twelve tricks. Having seen how the bids of Two No-Trumps and Three No-Trumps are used after a transfer you may have worked out that the correct thing to do is bid Four No-Trumps.

Partner can reject your overture by passing or correcting to Five Spades. Otherwise your side will be in a slam.

Intervention
Once in a while you and your partner will not be left to your own devices. The situations that I am interested in are those where the opponents bid after responder has had the chance to make the transfer bid. This is a common scenario:

West	North	East	South
—	1NT	Pass	2♡
Double			

South is promising at least five spades and West's double shows a reasonable heart suit. As an aside, if West had a fair hand with short spades he could bid Two Spades, the suit South is known to hold, as a take-out bid, asking East for his best suit.

Returning to my main theme, North is no longer compelled to bid and with a doubleton spade the correct action is to pass. This would be a typical hand:

♠ Q 7
♡ J 6 2
♢ A Q 7 3
♣ A Q J 4

That means the auction can continue along the following lines:

West	North	East	South
—	1NT	Pass	2♡
Double	Pass	Pass	?

When North passes East will quite often do the same. If South has the type of hand I used in an earlier example he might well take his chances in the doubled partscore:

♠ A J 8 5 3
♡ K Q 9 6 2
♢ 4
♣ 6 3

Otherwise he is obliged to bid. Of course, he can always fall back on Two Spades if he has no ambitions for game, but then one of the advantages of the transfer bid, that of letting the lead run up to the strong hand, will have been lost. The answer is for South to redouble, which asks North to go ahead and complete the transfer.

As a general rule, once an auction becomes competitive you should let partner know if you have a fit.

West	North	East	South
—	1NT	Pass	2♡
Double			

You have this hand:

♠ K 8 2
♥ 8 4
♦ A Q 7 2
♣ A K 6 2

Bid Two Spades to let partner know you have support for his suit.

With a maximum and three-card support you can redouble. This would be a typical example:

♠ K 10 3
♥ 9 4
♦ A J 10 3
♣ A K Q 4

If you have four-card support then you may consider jumping to Three Spades.

In general terms, it is not too difficult to cope if the transfer bid is doubled. It is not quite so simple if the opponents overcall. This is a standard situation:

West	North	East	South
—	1NT	Pass	2◇
2♠	?		

At this stage you have no idea about partner's strength, so you can't rely on him for any defensive tricks. With an average hand you should pass:

♠ Q 7 3
♥ K 6 2
♦ A J 5
♣ K Q J 6

Of course, you are allowed to bid, but you should have a good hand in support of partner, something like:

♠ A 8 2	or	♠ A 8 2
♡ K J 4		♡ K 10 7 4
◇ A 9		◇ A Q J 6
♣ A J 10 7 3		♣ K 7

Remember that partner may be very weak, so you would need a
remarkable hand to be able to double West's bid for penalties,
perhaps something like:

♠ A Q 10 8
♡ Q 6
◇ A 10 7 2
♣ A J 6

Here you can hope to take six tricks all on your own!

There is one aspect that I have not yet mentioned: the reaction of
opener to partner's transfer bid. Take a look at this situation.

North	South		♠ A 5
1NT	2◇		♡ K 10 5 2
?			◇ A 7 2
			♣ A Q 8 6

Partner has asked you to bid Two Hearts but has no idea that you
have such a suitable hand in support of his suit. You can let partner
in on the secret by jumping to Three Hearts, promising a maximum
in points, four-card support and a ruffing value.

Of course, responder must now re-adjust to this news. If game is
still out of the question he will pass. He may sign off by bidding
Four Hearts. With greater ambitions he can cuebid or resort to Four
No-Trumps, which in this case would be another conventional bid,
Blackwood.

It is perfectly possible to use the same kind of responses to an
opening bid of Two No-Trumps. So the sequence 2NT – 3◇ is a
request for the opener to bid Three Hearts whilst 2NT – 3♡ asks
him to bid Three Spades.

There is one area where the experts do not always agree. It is
when the bidding goes like this:

West	North	East	South
—	2NT	Pass	3◇
Pass	3♡	Pass	4♣ or 4◇

South has shown at least five hearts with the transfer bid of Three Diamonds. The question is what does the next bid show? Mike Lawrence thinks this kind of sequence should show a singleton in the minor bid, while Bill Root and Richard Pavlicek think it should be natural. Both methods are playable – I happen to prefer the latter. Make sure you and your partner are in agreement!

The idea of playing Stayman and Transfers may seem complicated but with a little practice they will become second nature.

Every now and then I have given you an insight into how the auction continues after an opening bid and a response. It is now time to look at the subject in a little more detail.

Opener's rebid

Earlier on I asked you to think of the bidding as a conversation. Of course, it shouldn't go on forever! The secret is knowing when to stop. At the outset you are hoping you and your partner will have enough points to get you to a game or slam contract. As soon as it becomes clear that you have the right values for that kind of enterprise, fine, keep on bidding until you achieve your aim. Once it becomes clear you don't have enough values then your objective should be to reach a sensible partscore.

You will need to get the hang of when a bid is forcing and when you are allowed to pass. Actually, you know quite a lot about this already although you may not have realized it yet!

You are allowed to pass an opening bid at the one level with less than 6 points so clearly that is not a forcing bid. You are not allowed to pass an opening bid of Two Clubs so that is a forcing bid. You are not obliged to bid if your partner opens One or Two No-Trumps. See, you know a lot about this topic already.

When you have the values to respond to an opening bid it's up to your partner to try to describe what kind of hand he has in terms of high cards and distribution. He will take into account your response to the opening bid, particularly if you have made an unlimited bid. One thing is for sure, he is not allowed to pass after that kind of response.

A bid in a new suit is an example of an unlimited response so in the following sequences opener is not allowed to pass.

North	South
1♣	1♡

North	South
1♡	2◇

North	South
1♡	1♠

Broadly speaking, a hand that has opened the bidding at the one level falls into one of three categories:

A minimum hand with around 11–14 points
An intermediate hand with about 15–18 points
A strong hand with either 19 or 20 points

In terms of distribution you will always have a one-, two- or three-suited hand. When you are selecting your rebid you must consider two factors: is your hand balanced and do you have a fit for your partner?

Let's look at some examples.

♠ 10 7
♡ K J 4
◇ A 9
♣ A J 10 9 7 3

This hand is clearly worth an opening bid of One Club. You intend to rebid Two Clubs on the next round.

♠ 10 7
♡ K J 4
◇ A 9
♣ A K J 10 7 3

You are still going to open One Club but you plan to rebid Three Clubs to tell partner you are better than minimum.

♠ K 7
♡ K J 4
◇ A 9
♣ A K J 10 7 3

Now you are too strong to consider rebidding Three Clubs. A jump to Three No-Trumps will tell your partner you started with a strong hand.

When you are two suited – that means at least one five-card suit and one four-card suit – you will often be able to show them both.

♠ 8 5
♡ A J 7 4 2
◇ A 6
♣ K 9 7 3

Obviously you open One Heart. If your partner responds One Spade you must bid and the right rebid is Two Clubs, telling your partner about your second suit and implying you have a minimum hand. You could make the same bid if partner responded One No-Trump, even though that is a limited, and therefore non-forcing, response.

If your partner responds Two Diamonds you might imagine that you could still show your second suit by bidding Three Clubs. Sorry, you would be out of line!

You need a much stronger hand to commit your side to the three level, usually around 17 points. Repeating your hearts would promise a six-card suit so you would be stuck with bidding Two No-Trumps. That tells your partner you have around 11–14 points. It's the best you can do on this particular hand.

The situation can be different when your four-card suit is higher ranking.

♠ A J 8 5
♡ 8 7
◇ A K 9 6 3
♣ J 5

You have an easy opening bid of One Diamond. If your partner responds One Heart you have the chance to show your second suit by bidding One Spade. However, if your partner replies One

No-Trump or Two Clubs, forget all about that spade suit. In neither case do you have a good enough hand for what would be a *reverse* bid; you should also appreciate that if the response is One No-Trump then your partner will not have a four-card spade suit. Also, if partner bids Two Clubs he won't have four spades unless he is going to bid them later.

When your second suit is higher ranking than your first, you need extra values to bid it at the two or three level. This is because you are forcing your partner, with a minimum hand and preference for your first suit, to go to the three level.

♠ A J 8 5
♡ K 7
♦ A K 9 6 3
♣ J 5

When your partner responds Two Clubs to your opening bid of One Diamond you have the values to bid Two Spades. If your partner had responded One No-Trump then there would be no point in mentioning spades and you should simply raise to Two No-Trumps, inviting your partner to go on to game with 8–10 points.

When you have a three-suited hand, either 5-4-4-0 or 4-4-4-1, your aim should be to try to be as economical as possible. That way you will have more chance of discovering a fit. Suppose you have this hand:

♠ A K J 6
♡ Q 8 5 2
♦ 5
♣ A 10 7 4

You open One Club and your partner responds One Diamond. You should now bid One Heart. Yes, your spades are much stronger but your partner may have a four-card heart suit and if you bid One Spade the heart fit may get lost.

You should always keep in mind that your partner may respond in a suit that you can support. While you would always prefer to have four-card trump support, you are allowed to raise with only three provided you are not completely balanced.

♠ A J 8 5
♡ J 6
◇ K 8 4
♣ K J 10 7

When you open One Club you are delighted to hear your partner respond One Spade. You have an easy raise to Two Spades which tells your partner you have support and a minimum hand.

♠ A J 8
♡ J 10 6
◇ K 8 4
♣ K J 10 7

You still have reasonable support for spades but your hand is too balanced for an immediate raise. It's better to rebid One No-Trump intending to support spades if there is more bidding.

When you have a balanced hand you will usually find yourself contemplating a rebid in no-trumps. Remember, with 15-17 points and the right distribution you open One No-Trump, so a rebid in this denomination will either be in the range of 12-14 or 18-19 points. No, partner does not have to guess how many points you have!

A minimum rebid in no-trumps shows the weaker of the two ranges. A jump bid promises the stronger. Let's look at some illustrations.

♠ A 6
♡ K J 7 3
◇ A 10 4 2
♣ J 8 4

After you open One Diamond your partner responds One Spade. You have an easy rebid of One No-Trump.

♠ A 6
♡ A K 7 3
◇ A 10 4 2
♣ K 8 4

This time you jump to Two No-Trumps to show your extra values.

Of course, you may have a hand that is strong in high cards and distribution and therefore unsuitable for a rebid in no-trumps. In those situations the answer is usually to bid your second suit at an unnecessarily high level, a *jump rebid*.

```
♠ A K J 4
♡ 10 4
♢ A Q J 7 2
♣ A 9
```

If your opening bid of One Diamond attracts a response of One Heart, then you can jump to Two Spades to tell partner the good news.

```
♠ 9
♡ A K Q 7 2
♢ K 5
♣ A Q J 8 4
```

Your partner replies One Spade to your opening bid of One Heart. Let him know you have a great hand by jumping to Three Clubs.

When your partner responds to your opening bid at the two level you know that he has at least 11 points and is going to bid again. Your duty is to try to describe your hand. You may be able to introduce a second suit, rebid a long suit, support partner or bid no-trumps. The level at which you bid will be governed by the strength of your hand.

Don't forget that a rebid of Two No-Trumps in this situation says you have a minimum and a jump to Three No-Trumps shows a powerful hand.

As I mentioned earlier, it's great to have four-card support for the suit partner replies in. You are allowed to raise with only three cards, particularly in this situation.

North	South	
1♠	2♡	♠ A J 10 6 3
?		♡ K 8 4
		♢ A 6 5
		♣ 10 7

Whereas a response at the two level may be made on only four cards in one of the minor suits your partner needs at least five hearts in order to reply in that suit.

You have a minimum hand but it is quite good in support of hearts and you should let your partner know that by bidding Three Hearts.

You can go on studying the theoretical side of bidding for a long time – I can't count the number of books that have been written on the subject. I once came across a player who claimed to have invented the best bidding convention in the world. He called it KISS. It stood for Keep it Simple Stupid! By no means bad advice.

Another player adorned his card with the letters BHL. That stood for Bloody Hard Luck! My favourite story about these strange conventions relates to the player who always displays the letters YOURS in a prominent place. When an opponent innocently asks, "What's Yours?" our hero flashes out the reply, "I'll have a beer thanks!"

OK, enough, noses back to the grindstone. One way to keep things simple is to bid to the limit of your hand as quickly as possible. This is especially true when your partner is kind enough to support your suit.

The moment your partner raises your suit your hand gets better because you have just located that all important eight-card fit. If your partner supports a suit in which you have five cards, your hand is almost worth an extra trick. As the size and quality of your trump fit improve, doubletons, singletons and voids tend to become assets rather than liabilities as you will have plenty of small trumps to take care of potential losers.

Let's check out a few scenarios.

♠ 8 4
♡ A J 10 6 4
◇ A 7
♣ K 10 9 5

When you open One Heart, your partner raises you to Two Hearts. He is not promising more than 10 points and your hand is nothing special. You pass.

♠ A K 9 7 3
♡ K J 10 5
◇ —
♣ A J 7 4

Your opening bid of One Spade is raised to Two Spades. Don't mess around; go directly to Four Spades.

```
♠ A K J 7 3
♡ 5
◇ A Q 7
♣ 10 6 4 2
```

The first two examples were straightforward. That will not always be the case, simply because your hand will sometimes be too good to pass a raise to the two level but not quite strong enough to go straight to game. This hand illustrates the problem. When you open One Spade, your partner raises you to Two Spades. You may be facing a hand where Four Spades is trivial, needs a lot of luck or simply hopeless.

♠ Q 10 6 4	♠ 10 9 6 4	♠ 10 9 6 4
♡ 9 6 3 2	♡ K J 8 2	♡ K Q J
◇ K J 8 2	◇ 9 3	◇ K 5 3
♣ 5	♣ K J 7	♣ J 7 3

Facing the first hand you will probably make eleven tricks. Notice that although it's the weakest in terms of high cards it has the best distribution. Opposite the second hand you will need plenty of luck in the finessing and guessing departments and ten tricks are by no means guaranteed. On the last hand your partner has a maximum in terms of high cards but you will probably be beaten before you start in Four Spades, losing a heart and three clubs.

The solution to the problem is to make a trial bid at the three level. The message you are conveying to partner is that you have a hand that is close to game but need more information before proceeding. The bridge universe is full of trial bids – long-suit bids, short-suit bids, fake trial bids, Romex trial bids, etc – in your bridge career you will encounter all these and more. One common sense approach is to make your bid in the suit where you need some help.

Imagine that on our three example hands the bidding goes:

North	South
1♠	2♠
3♣	?

On the first hand South has no support for clubs but the singleton will help to cut down partner's losers and, despite the paucity of points, a jump to Four Spades is in order.

On the second one the club support is good and the high cards justify a bid of Four Spades. It is not guaranteed to make!

On the final hand South has plenty of high cards but the worst possible holding in clubs. The high-card points justify a game bid but there are four top losers in a spade contract. The balanced nature of the hand argues for a bid of Three No-Trumps. If North is brave enough to pass, nine tricks may prove to be possible.

This area of bidding is not an exact science and you will not always come up with the right answer. It is worth remembering that there is a premium for bidding game so you can, and should, be aggressive in this area.

When Michelangelo was painting the Sistine Chapel the Pope kept on asking him: "When will you make an end?" The artist's reply was always the same: "When I've finished." We haven't finished with the development of the auction yet but there are four players around the table and there is no law that says anyone has to go quietly. It's time to look at another important area in the bidding arena.

DEFENSIVE AND COMPETITIVE BIDDING

Being able to open the bidding confers a definite advantage. It puts you in contact with your partner and he may already have an idea whether your side belongs in a part-score, game or slam contract.

In absolute terms, it is far easier to bid to the right contract when your opponents leave you to your own devices. If you want to acquire a reputation as a difficult opponent then this section is definitely for you!

While it is still entirely possible that your side has a majority of the high cards and may be able to make something if an opponent has opened, your side is definitely starting on the back foot. Obviously you and your partner want to investigate how high the partnership should bid as best you can but one of your main aims is to make life difficult for the opposition. There are several ways to achieve this. I'll start with one of the most common actions, the overcall.

Overcalling

An overcall happens when you bid a new suit after an opponent has opened the bidding. To make a simple overcall at the one level you need a decent suit containing at least five cards. To overcall at the two level you need a six-card suit or an exceptional five-card one. You don't have to have an opening bid to overcall at the one level but you need at least something close to an opening bid to enter the auction at the two level. In general you will have around 9–16 points but the quality of your suit is a more important factor.

You have a number of aims; the deal may belong to your side and you hope to reach a makable contract or push the opponents too high; to suggest a reasonable lead to your partner; to make things awkward for your opponents; to pave the way for a profitable sacrifice.

Here are some examples.

♠ A K J 7 3
♡ 6 3
♢ 9 4
♣ J 8 4 2

This would be a perfect hand to overcall One Spade, whatever suit is opened.

♠ 9 4
♡ A 3
♢ K Q J 7 6 3
♣ 10 7 3

You have an excellent diamond suit that you should overcall at the one level if the opening bid is One Club or at the two level if the opening bid is One Heart or One Spade.

♠ 8 4 2
♡ A K 9 8 3
♢ 6 3
♣ K 7 4

You could overcall after an opening bid of One Club or One Diamond but if the opening bid were One Spade you would be unwise to overcall because you have only a five-card suit.

♠ 9 5
♡ A 7 4
♢ Q 6 2
♣ A Q 10 8 3

I hope you would not be tempted to overcall Two Clubs. Your suit is broken and if the next player has a good hand you may concede a large penalty. This was a hand I used in a training weekend for the German Women's team. One of their stars Daniela von Arnim overcalled on this hand and lost 800 points when she was doubled. She wasn't sure it was so bad to overcall on this type of hand and later on she tried a similar tactic. That cost her 1,100 points and she had got the message. Two years later she was winning the World Championship! Don't overcall at the two level on hands like this and you might wind up winning one as well!

♠ A Q J 7 4
♡ 8 4
◇ K J 9 4
♣ A 5

Your overcall does not always have to be based on a hand that might not have opened the bidding. This is close to the maximum for an overcall of One Spade.

Let's return to a hand I mentioned earlier:

♠ 9 4
♡ A 3
◇ K Q J 7 6 3
♣ 10 7 3

You have overcalled the opening bid of One Spade with Two Diamonds. Imagine the next player bids Four Spades and your partner has the following hand:

♠ —
♡ 9 7 2
◇ A 10 4 2
♣ Q J 9 6 5 2

It will be clear to your partner that Five Diamonds is unlikely to be expensive – turn your ace of hearts into the ace of clubs and it might even be a make. Even if the contract is defeated your side is bound to show a profit as Four Spades cannot possibly be defeated.

The idea of sacrificing is based on three sound precepts:

* The penalty you concede will be less than the value of your opponents' contract.
* Your opponents may be tempted to bid on – and discover they cannot make their contract.
* You may sometimes make your contract.

There are bound to be times when you have a hand where you would like to get into the bidding but either have too many points to overcall or don't have a suit that is long enough or strong enough. Then you have to put your faith in one of the oldest conventions

around. You may also have a less powerful hand with support for all
the unbid suits. To be able to cope with those hands you need a
bidding tool. There just happens to be one.

Take-out double

Two names are associated with the development of this essential aid
to bidding: Bryan McCampbell of St Louis was a top-class auction
bridge player; Major Charles Lee Patton was a leading
administrator of his day. It is one of the easiest conventions to
understand and an absolute must for the aspiring player.

An immediate double of an opening bid of One of a suit is for
take-out, asking partner to make a bid. As a minimum it usually
promises an opening bid with support for the three unbid suits. This
would be typical:

West	North	
1♡	?	♠ K Q J 8
		♡ 7 2
		◇ Q 10 7 3
		♣ A J 5

By doubling One Heart you indicate that you can support any suit
your partner bids. Notice that if West had opened with any of the
other suits the correct action is to pass as you have no support for
hearts.

The ideal shape for a take-out double is 5-4-4-0 or 4-4-4-1, with
the shortage being in the suit that has been bid in front of you. With
that distribution you can bid with a slightly weaker hand.

West	North	
1♡	?	♠ A Q 5 2
		♡ —
		◇ K 9 6 3
		♣ J 10 8 6 4

This would be perfect for a double of One Heart, but you could also
do it if the four of clubs was a heart.

There are a lot of players who think it's a good idea to make a
take-out double on this type of hand:

```
          ♠ A Q J 4
          ♡ J 8 4
          ◇ K 10 9
          ♣ Q 5 2
```

They will happily double an opening bid of One Club, One Diamond or One Heart, arguing that they have reasonable support for all the unbid suits. My advice is to reserve your take-out doubles for the hands where you are short in the opponents' suit. That means having a doubleton, singleton or void.

The concept of the take-out double is easy to understand but players often struggle with the responses. The basic replies are as follows:

1 A MINIMUM SUIT BID

West	North	East	South	
1♠	Double	Pass	?	♠ 10 7 5 3
				♡ J 5 2
				◇ Q 9 6 4
				♣ 8 3

Your partner has asked you to bid your best suit so you should respond Two Diamonds. You are promising nothing more than 0–8 points.

2 1NT

West	North	East	South	
1♠	Double	Pass	?	♠ K J 9
				♡ 9 5 2
				◇ Q 6 4
				♣ K 7 5 3

You show a stopper in the enemy suit and around 6–9 points. This value-showing bid is better than a response of Two Diamonds, which you might have to make with no points at all!

3 2NT

West	North	East	South	
1♣	Double	Pass	?	♠ Q 8 4
				♡ K 9 3
				◇ J 8 4 2
				♣ A J 10

When you reply Two No-Trumps you are showing a balanced hand of around 10–12 points.

4 A JUMP IN A NEW SUIT

West	North	East	South	
1◇	Double	Pass	?	♠ K 10 7 3
				♡ A 6
				◇ Q 8 7 4
				♣ J 7 6 2

By bidding Two Spades you promise around 9–12 points and at least four spades.

5 PASS

West	North	East	South	
1♠	Double	Pass	?	♠ K Q 10 9 7
				♡ J 8 4
				◇ 7 4 3
				♣ 8 3

You have to have a very special type of hand to consider passing your partner's take-out double. You need very good trumps! In this example you hope your trumps will be worth four tricks and that your partner will provide at least three more.

West	North	East	South	
1♠	Double	Pass	?	♠ Q J 7 5 3
				♡ 9 5 2
				◇ 6 3
				♣ J 9 3

Now your spades are too weak to risk passing the double. You don't have enough points to bid One No-Trump so you have to bid your best "suit" and try Two Clubs.

6 STRONGER HANDS

West	North	East	South	
1◇	Double	Pass	?	♠ K 10 8 5
				♡ A J 7 4
				◇ A 8 6
				♣ 7 2

You have an excellent hand but you can't be sure which major you would like to play in. The answer is to cuebid the enemy suit with Two Diamonds. That can't be a natural bid as with very good diamonds you would pass for penalties as in my earlier example. You are asking partner to bid a suit, intending to raise a major to game.

With a balanced hand of 13–16 points you can simply bid Three No-Trumps and with the right sort of hand you can bid game in a major suit.

The take-out double is an equally effective weapon against higher-level opening bids. It is very much the preferred method when it comes to dealing with the often-awkward pre-emptive actions of the opponents.

You can make a take-out double at other stages of the auction as well. For instance, after both opponents have bid or on the second round of the auction as in these examples:

West	North	East	South	
1♡	Pass	1♠	?	♠ 10 9 6 3
				♡ 5
				◇ A J 10 2
				♣ A K J 8

By doubling you tell partner that you have values in the two unbid suits, diamonds and clubs.

West	North	East	South	
1♡	Pass	1♠	Pass	♠ A J 10 2
2♡	Pass	Pass	?	♡ 5
				◇ 10 9 6 3
				♣ A K J 8

Influenced by your spade holding and weak diamonds you decided not to double on the first round but now you can double for take-out. When partner's hand proves to be:

♠ 9 3
♡ K Q J 10
◇ A 8 4 2
♣ 10 9 5

you will collect a substantial penalty.

Very strong hands can be started with a take-out double.

West	North	East	South	♠ A Q 4
1♦	?			♡ K Q J 9 6 4
				♦ 10 6
				♣ A Q

You are far too strong to make a simple overcall of One Heart so you start with a double, planning to introduce your suit on the next round.

West	North	East	South	♠ A 10 4
1♦	?			♡ K J 9 6
				♦ A Q 4
				♣ A 8 7

An overcall of One No-Trump would show 15–17 points and you have 18. The solution is to start with a double. On the next round you will rebid in no-trumps and partner will know you have around 18–19 points.

When you begin your side's bidding campaign with a take-out double you have to know what you are going to do at your next turn and what information this will convey to your partner. There are two situations to keep in mind.

West	North	East	South
1♦	Double	Pass	1♡
Pass	?		

If North now bids a new suit, either spades or clubs, it shows a good hand but, facing what could be a very weak South hand, it isn't forcing.

West	North	East	South
1♦	Double	1♡	1♠
Pass	?		

This time your partner has made a free bid so he will not have a completely worthless hand. If you bid a new suit at this point then it should be forcing for one round – your partner is not allowed to pass.

Overcalling One No-Trump

It should be clear to you by now that balanced hands tend to belong in no-trumps while unbalanced ones are generally best played in a suit contract. When you have a strong balanced hand and the player in front of you opens then, provided you have a stopper in the enemy suit, you can overcall One No-Trump. It promises a similar type of hand to one that you would have opened One No-Trump given the chance.

    ♠ K7
    ♡ QJ6
    ◊ J94
    ♣ AKQ85

If the opening bid is One Heart or One Spade then One No-Trump is a perfect description of your hand. You could consider bidding it even after an opening bid of One Diamond but the absence of a diamond stopper is a defect.

When your partner overcalls One No-Trump you can respond in exactly the same way as if he had opened One No-Trump, using both Stayman and Jacoby Transfers. A tournament player has a quaint phrase for this arrangement, calling it "system on".

With the right type of hand you can still get into the bidding even when you have little in the way of high cards. If you enjoyed the earlier discussions about Weak Two bids and pre-empts then the next section is just what you have been waiting for!

Weak jump overcalls

In the good old days if one of your opponents opened the bidding and you made a jump overcall you were promising a very strong hand with lots of high cards and plenty of distribution. Unfortunately, that type of hand does not come up all that often and it was eventually realized that it was more efficient – and more fun! – to use a jump bid to describe a weak hand.

Your main aim in making one of these bids is to try to make life difficult for your opponents. Believe me, it will! By taking away one or two rounds of bidding you will make it very difficult, if not impossible, for your opponents to describe their hands accurately.

To make a weak jump overcall at the two level you need a six-card suit and around 6–9 points. If the vulnerability is in your favour you may be able to get away with murder. The same principles apply to an overcall at the three and four levels but you need a correspondingly longer suit.

Let's see how things work.

♠ K Q J 9 7 4
♡ 5
◇ 8 7 4 2
♣ 10 5

This is an ideal hand for a weak jump overcall of Two Spades.

♠ K 9 7 4 3 2
♡ 5
◇ K 7 4 2
♣ Q 7

You have more points than in the previous example but your suit is much weaker. Non-vulnerable some players would still risk Two Spades but a simple One Spade overcall is safer.

♠ 7
♡ A J 10 9 7 4 3
◇ 8 2
♣ 9 4 3

You have a great suit in an otherwise worthless hand. If the opening bid is One Club, One Diamond or One Spade then you can happily bid Three Hearts.

♠ 6 2
♡ 5
◇ 7 4
♣ A Q J 10 8 6 4 2

This time you have an eight-card suit that will surely produce seven tricks even if partner has nothing useful. Go the whole hog and jump to Four Clubs over the opponent's opening bid.

Weak jump overcalls will not work on every hand but provided you have a reasonable suit I predict you will come out way ahead in the long run. Good hunting!

Landy

When one of your opponents opens the bidding with One No-Trump you are at quite a disadvantage. When a strong balanced hand has already been announced, the opponents will be quick to deal with any ill-judged intervention. Nevertheless, you should not be afraid to get involved in the bidding, provided you have the right type of hand. Experience has taught us that some kind of conventional defence is best. One of the easiest to understand was devised by Alvin Landy. He was a prominent administrator, an ACBL tournament director and became the League's business manager. He was one of the original officers of the World Bridge Federation.

Landy was one of the first players to appreciate that it was difficult for a player to enter the bidding after an opponent had opened One No-Trump. The possession of a two-suited hand, especially if those two suits were the majors, would make life easier. His concept was to use a bid of Two Clubs to show both majors. The perfect distribution would be 5-5, but 5-4 or 4-5 is OK and, with concentrated values, even 4-4 is permissible. With the right shape you don't need many points for the bid, but your partner is entitled to expect around 11–12 as a minimum.

These would be acceptable hands for the Two Club bid:

♠ K 10 5 3	♠ Q J 9 6 3	♠ K Q J 8
♡ A Q J 7 4	♡ K Q 10 8 5	♡ A K J 6
◇ 6	◇ A 6	◇ 10 8 4 2
♣ K 7 3	♣ 7	♣ 7

When your partner makes a Landy overcall of Two Clubs the responses are easy to understand:

Pass	A weak hand with a long club suit
2◇	A weak hand with a long diamond suit
2♡	Natural limited preference for hearts
2♠	Natural limited preference for spades
2NT	Natural but non-forcing

3♣   A forcing relay simply asking partner to describe
                 his hand in more detail. It has nothing to do with
                 clubs.
3◇   Natural, encouraging but non-forcing
3♡   Natural, inviting partner to bid game
3♠   Natural, inviting partner to bid game

Of course with the right kind of hand the responder is allowed to
jump to game! For example with:

♠ K 10 8 6 4
♡ J 7 3
◇ K 7 4 2
♣ 3

You could consider a direct jump to Four Spades.

Overcalling in fourth seat

This is a complex subject, so much so that more than one entire
book has been devoted to it!

In general terms you are in quite a good position because there is
a reasonable inference that your partner will have some values. You
can make a take out double on quite a weak hand for instance with

♠ K J 10 5
♡ K 7 4
◇ Q 10 9 3
♣ 8

It would be perfectly reasonable to double an opening bid of One
Club.

There are lots of views as to how you should reply to a fourth in
hand or "protective" double. It won't matter too much as long as
you and your partner are on the same wavelength but one area that
can catch even experienced players out is in the strength of a bid in
no-trumps. I suggest that a reply of One No-Trump should show
10–12 points and that a jump to Two No-Trumps should promise
13–14 points.

In fourth position an overcall of One No-Trump can be made
with around 11–14 points, for example, with:

♠ Q 10 5
♡ A 10 6 3
◇ K J 6
♣ K 8 5

You could happily bid One No-Trump over an opening bid in any of the four suits.

The negative double

In the early days of bridge all doubles were for penalties. Then along came the take-out double. Nowadays we would be lost without it. Then along came "Son of Take-out Double".

Alvin Roth is recognized as one of the most original bidding theorists in bridge. His many contributions to the language of bidding include the Weak Two Bid, the Unusual No-Trump, the Forcing No-Trump response and even an entire system, Roth-Stone.

Perhaps his greatest discovery was the Negative Double, a convention that is probably used more than a million times a day in bridge tournaments all over the world. At the time of its invention the Russians were starting their space satellite programme and the name Sputnik became linked to the new idea.

Before the advent of the negative double if an opponent overcalled the opening bid a double was for penalties. Roth realized that it would be much better to use the bid as a take-out device. Here is an example of the convention in action:

West	North	East	
1♣	1♠	?	♠ 8 7 2
			♡ K J 8 5
			◇ A 9 7 2
			♣ 6 4

You have excellent support for the unbid suits but can hardly bid either of them. By using a negative double you promise at least the values to respond at the one level. If the overcall is in a major the double promises at least four cards in the other one.

It's important to understand that if you wanted to double the overcall for penalties you have to pass! Your partner is then expected to reopen the bidding with a double. Here is an illustration:

West	North	East	South	♠ A K 9 8 3
1♠	2♡	Pass	Pass	♡ 6
?				◇ 9 7 4
				♣ A J 6 4

Rather than rebid the spades, West should double, hoping to find East with a hand like:

> ♠ 6 2
> ♡ K J 9 8 4
> ◇ A 10 3
> ♣ Q 10 7

Even if you have excellent support for partner's suit it may be correct to start with a negative double.

West	North	East	♠ 9 5
1♣	1♠	?	♡ K Q 8 3
			◇ 6 4
			♣ K J 8 4 2

Of course, you could support clubs at once but then you would risk losing the heart suit. By starting with a double you inform partner that you have at least four hearts. If he bids Two Diamonds you will reveal the nature of your hand by bidding Three Clubs.

The negative double is a bit like an automobile – an essential luxury you can't afford to be without.

Let's take a look at some everyday auctions involving the use of doubles.

West	North	East	South
1♠	Double	2♠	Pass
Pass	Double		

North's second double carries the same message as the first one – please bid something partner.

West	North	East	South
1♣	Pass	2♣	Pass
Pass	Double		

Although North did not double on the first round, this is a take-out double. It is clear that East-West have limited values and North wants to compete for the partscore.

West	North	East	South
1◇	Pass	3◇	Double

This is a take-out double. In general when your opponents bid and support a suit thereby indicating that they have a fit, a double is for take-out.

West	North	East	South
1♡	Pass	Pass	Double
Pass	Pass	2♣	Double

When North passed the take-out double of One Heart he showed the nature of his hand so South's second double is for penalties.

West	North	East	South
1NT	Pass	Pass	2♡
Double			

There are two ways of playing this double: either for take-out with a weak doubleton in hearts or as a penalty double. I once had the misfortune to remove such a double, thinking it was for take-out. Since my partner's heart holding was K-Q-J-10-9 he was not amused!

You won't go wrong as long as you have an agreement.

West	North	East	South
1♣	1♡	Pass	2◇
Double			

This is another situation where there are two schools of thought. One suggests this should be a take-out double promising a good hand with four spades. The other is that it promises a powerful balanced hand with at least 18 points.

West	North	East	South
1♡	Pass	1♠	Pass
2♡	Double		

West can hardly be making a take-out double at this stage so this is a penalty double. I can recall a situation where the auction went:

West	North	East	South
1♣	Pass	1◇	Pass
1♡	Double	Pass	?

West's One Club was part of a system called the Roman Club and the reply of One Diamond was a negative. My hand was something like:

```
♠ 8 7 4
♡ 5 2
◇ 8 6 4 2
♣ 9 6 5 3
```

Would you pass or bid?

Well, your partner has a monstrous 23-point hand and can defeat single-handed any contract the opponents care to bid, including One Heart!

Penalty doubles

I have mentioned the phrase penalty double more than once. If you or your partner think the opponents' contract is going down you are allowed to double it. It can be very tempting to double a contract because you have lots of points but what you really need are tricks, particularly trump tricks if the contract is not in no-trumps. When your opponents bid freely to a contract it will usually be bad breaks that defeat them, not merely a collection of points.

Here is an example:

West	North	East	South	
1♣	1♠	2♡	Pass	♠ 8 4
3♡	Pass	4♡	?	♡ Q J 10 7
				◇ K Q J 4
				♣ 7 5 3

You know the trumps are breaking badly and you have an excellent lead in the shape of the king of diamonds. You should double for penalties.

When the auction is competitive it is generally a good idea to support your partner at the earliest opportunity. There is a very useful gadget you can use when an opponent makes a take-out double and you are considering an immediate raise of your partner's suit.

Truscott

Alan Truscott is English by birth but took up residence in the USA in 1962. Several conventions bear his name. He is recognized as one of the best bridge writers, his books including *The Great Bridge Scandal,* a vivid account of the darker side of the game following the Buenos Aires affair. He is married to Dorothy Hayden Truscott, regarded by many as the finest women player of all time. In 1968, at the age of 61, he completed the New York Marathon!

The Truscott Two No-Trumps is one of his most widely recognized contributions to theory.

It is used after a take-out double of partner's opening bid of one of a suit. The otherwise redundant bid of Two No-Trumps is used to show a good raise of partner's suit.

This would be typical:

North	East	South	
1♠	Double	?	♠ Q J 8 5
			♡ 7 3
			◇ Q 9 5
			♣ A J 8 2

By bidding Two No-Trumps you show 10–12 points and four-card trump support.

It follows that a raise to Three of partner's suit can be used in a different way:

North	East	South	
1♡	Double	?	♠ 9 5 2
			♡ K 8 5 4
			◇ Q 8 7 5 3
			♣ 9

You bid Three Hearts, promising around 5–9 points and four-card support. Take away the queen of diamonds and the right bid would be Two Hearts.

It's time to return to our main theme, the development of the auction.

BIDDING GAMES AND SLAMS

When you open the bidding you will be hoping that your side's combined assets will be sufficient for you to make a game or slam. One guideline you can use is the number of points you have between the two hands. You already know that there are 40 high-card points on every deal. To make a game in no-trumps you generally need around 25–26 points if the two hands are balanced. Obviously you may get away with less if you have a long suit that is a source of tricks. In a suit contract the number of points you require for game is about the same as in no-trumps but once again the distributional factor can reduce the figure. A point to keep in mind that it is almost impossible for both sides to be able to make a game in no-trumps on the same hand but perfectly possible that each can make a game in a different suit.

To be in with a chance of making a slam you need more points. To have a reasonable play for a small slam in no-trumps you tend to need around 33–34 points. You must also be sure that the opponents cannot cash two quick tricks against you. It will sometimes be easy to add up the number of points that your side possesses – for example, if partner opens One No-Trump – but most of the time you will have to work harder to uncover the information you need.

You can see that you need a lot of power to bid a slam in no-trumps. In a suit contract you may get away with less because of the power of your trump suit. A void may not be much use in a no-trump contract but it can be worth its weight in gold when there is a trump suit.

There are many devices that have been designed to help you bid slams. One of the most famous bears the name of its inventor.

Blackwood

Easley Blackwood probably invented the best-known convention in the world. His ace-asking Blackwood is now a firm part of bridge nomenclature. He was also an outstanding writer, his *Complete Book of Opening Leads* being one of the finest works ever penned on that subject.

A measure of his greatness can be gauged by the fact that Indianapolis proclaimed 28 October 1977 Easley Blackwood Day.

In the early days of bridge it was relatively easy for players to ascertain that their combined assets would be enough for a slam. However, it was all too often the case that the twelve or thirteen tricks that had been contracted for could only be gathered in after the opponents had cashed an ace or two!

Easley came up with the idea that the bid of Four No-Trumps was of little use as a natural call and so he suggested that instead it be used to ask partner a simple question: "How many aces do you have?"

The answers are equally straightforward:

5♣	Zero or four aces
5♢	One ace
5♡	Two aces
5♠	Three aces

After getting a response to the Four No-Trump bid, if your side has all the aces and you want to investigate the possibility of a grand slam, you can continue your detective work with a bid of Five No-Trumps, which asks partner: "How many kings do you have?"

Once again the responses are easy:

6♣	Zero kings
6♢	One king
6♡	Two kings
6♠	Three kings
6NT	Four kings

If you want to be fancy you can include the four kings reply in the Six Club response just as when asking for aces.

Very easy to understand, but for all that Blackwood is one of the most misused of all conventions. The key point to remember is that Blackwood is a question, nothing more. All you want to know is how many aces partner has. Before you ask that question you must be sure that when you have the answer you will be able to bid the final contract – and know it's the right one!

Let's look at a few examples:

North	South	
1♡	3♡	♠ A K Q 8
?		♡ K 10 8 7 5 3 2
		◊ 9
		♣ A

This is the perfect type of hand for Blackwood. At the very worst partner's hearts should be J-9-6-4 so if he has one ace you can bid Six Hearts. If in response to your Four No-Trump bid partner replies with Five Hearts, promising two aces, you can bid Seven Hearts.

North	South	
1♡	3♡	♠ A K Q 8 7
?		♡ A K Q 9 3
		◊ —
		♣ J 10 6

If you resort to Blackwood and discover that partner has one ace you will have no idea what to do, as clearly it might be in either minor suit. The right approach on this type of hand is to rely on a series of cuebids, hoping that partner will be able to come up with something useful in clubs.

West	North	East	South	
1♡	3◊	4♡	Pass	♠ A K 8 5 2
?				♡ Q J 10 9 7 6
				◊ —
				♣ K 7

After North's weak jump overcall a slam is a distinct possibility. Once again, Blackwood would be the wrong way to set about the problem. You should start with Four Spades, hoping partner can cuebid the ace of clubs.

North	South	
1♣	2♠	♠ K Q J 8 7 4
3♠	?	♡ A K
		◊ 5
		♣ K Q J 6

This is the perfect hand for Blackwood. In the unlikely event of partner having only one ace you will sign off in Five Spades. If he has two aces you will bid Six Spades and if he has three you can bid a grand slam with confidence – Seven No-Trumps being safest.

The answer to your question will provide you with all the information you need to know.

Before moving on it's worth making a note of what to do if an opponent bids over the Blackwood enquiry. The simplest solution is to resort to another convention.

DOPI

The responses to Blackwood are amended as follows:

Double	Zero aces
Pass	One ace
Cheapest bid	Two aces
Next cheapest	Three aces

This is easily remembered by thinking "Double = 0, Pass = 1".

Cuebids

A cuebid occurs most frequently after a suit has been agreed and usually happens at the four level or higher, although some partnerships allow them to be used at a lower level. The idea behind them is to show a control, either the ace, king, void or singleton. The information that is exchanged will enable a partnership to establish that the right suits are controlled before they bid to a slam. If the necessary controls are missing it should be possible to stop at a safe level.

Let's take a look a couple of examples that illustrate both sides of the coin:

```
    ♠ A K J 8 4          N          ♠ Q 9 7 3
    ♡ 7 5           W         E      ♡ A K 9 4
    ◊ 5                  S          ◊ 9 4 2
    ♣ A K Q 8 4                     ♣ J 5
```

West	East
1♠	3♠
4♣	4♡
5♣	5♡
6♠	

East's bid of Four Hearts is a cuebid. By not bidding Five Diamonds East denies any kind of control in that suit. It would not be ridiculous for West to take an immediate chance on Six Spades, but by bidding Five Clubs he gives East a chance to cuebid the king of hearts. Now West can be sure Six Spades is a good contract.

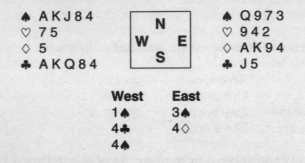

```
♠ AKJ84              N          ♠ Q973
♡ 75             W       E      ♡ 942
◇ 5                  S          ◇ AK94
♣ AKQ84                         ♣ J5
```

West	East
1♠	3♠
4♣	4◇
4♠	

The West hand is the same but when East makes a cuebid in diamonds West is not interested in looking for a slam because of the obvious weakness in hearts.

Bidding slams is very exciting, especially when they make! However, be very wary about bidding a grand slam. There is nothing worse than bidding a grand slam that goes down when twelve tricks and a small slam were certain. So, you should be pretty sure you can make all thirteen tricks before you take the risk of contracting for them.

We have come quite a long way and now it's time to find out what happens when we make or defeat a contract.

SCORING

There is nothing complicated about the scoring at bridge. If you make your contract you score points below the line. If you go down, or you defeat your opponents' contract then the appropriate side scores points above the line. You are contesting a rubber and the first side to score two games wins the rubber. You get extra points for winning the rubber, so it's worth taking the odd risk in pursuit of a game. Only points scored below the line count towards a game.

You can play as many rubbers as you wish, and if there are just four of you playing it is perfectly OK to change partners at the end of each completed rubber. In that case you will have to remember to keep individual scores.

Tricks
This table shows you how many points you score for tricks if you make your contract.

Tricks won	7	8	9	10	11	12	13
No-Trumps	40	70	100	130	160	190	220
Spades	30	60	90	120	150	180	210
Hearts	30	60	90	120	150	180	210
Diamonds	20	40	60	80	100	120	140
Clubs	20	40	60	80	100	120	140

Apart from the "odd" trick in no-trumps, which is worth 40 points, all the tricks in that denomination and spades and hearts are worth 30 points. In the two minor suits each trick is worth only 20 points.

Keep in mind that you need 100 points to record a game. You can do that in one hand by bidding and making one of the five game contracts. They are Three No-Trumps, Four Spades, Four Hearts, Five Diamonds and Five Clubs.

You can get your 100 points more slowly. If you bid and make Two Spades you score 60 points below the line (any overtricks you make at any time in any contract are scored above the line.) Now you need only 40 points to score a total of 100 and record a game. Your 60 points are called a partscore. If your opponents reach 100 points before you add the 40 points you need you have to go back to square one – you will need 100 to score a game.

A side that has made a game is said to be vulnerable.

If you haven't made a game you are non-vulnerable.

Undertricks and overtricks

If you bid a contact and fail to make the right number of tricks then you concede a penalty. 50 points per undertrick when you are non-vulnerable, 100 points per undertrick when you are vulnerable. If you are doubled, the penalties increase in accordance with the following tables:

	Non-Vulnerable	Vulnerable
Down 1	–100	–200
Down 2	–300	–500
Down 3	–500	–800
Down 4	–800	–1,100
Down 5	–1,100	–1,400

And so on all the way to down 13, although it's rare for a player to lose all the tricks, having contracted for a grand slam!

If you make your doubled contract you double the score for the tricks you make below the line. So making Four Spades doubled now becomes worth 240 points rather than 120. If you are lucky enough to make any overtricks then you score bonus points above the line, 100 for each extra trick if non-vulnerable, 200 when vulnerable.

You also get a special bonus of 50 points because your opponents "insulted" you by doubling – but only if you make the contract!

A contract that is doubled can be redoubled and that increases the potential plus and minus scores. For example:

	Non-Vulnerable	Vulnerable
Down 1	–200	–400
Down 2	–600	–1,000
Down 3	–1,000	–1,600

If you make your redoubled contract you redouble the score for the tricks you make below the line. So making Four Spades doubled now becomes worth 480 points rather than 120. If you are lucky enough to make any overtricks then you score bonus points above the line, 200 for each extra trick if non-vulnerable, 400 when vulnerable.

You also get a special bonus of 100 points because your opponents "insulted" you by doubling in the first place – provided you make the contract!

There is one thing you have to be very wary of when doubling. If you double your opponents in Four Spades and they make it you have not lost too much, for they were going to record a game anyway. If you double your opponents in Two Spades and they make it you have just increased their score below the line from 60 points to 120 and given them a game.

Slam bonuses

You get extra points above the line if you bid and make a slam. For a small slam – twelve tricks – non-vulnerable it is 500, vulnerable it is 750.

For a grand slam – thirteen tricks – it is 1,000 not vulnerable, 1,500 vulnerable.

Game and rubber bonuses

If you win a rubber by two games to nil you score an extra 700 points. If you win two games but lose one then you collect an extra 500. If you fail to finish a rubber, a side that is a game ahead is awarded 300 points. A side with a partscore towards an unfinished game picks up an extra 50 points.

Honours

If any player (including dummy or a defender) holds all four aces in a no-trump contract his side scores an extra 150 points. A player who has any four of the five honours in the trump suit (A-K-Q-J-10) collects 100 bonus points for his side. Holding all five is worth 150 points.

You should usually claim your bonus points for honours when the deal has been played out.

Because of the possibility of conceding penalty points it is perfectly possible for a partnership to "win" the rubber and end up losing. Here is an illustration of rubber bridge score chart.

We	They
500	
1100	
	700
	120
	100

Your opponents won the rubber by two games to nil, making Four Hearts and Three No-Trumps, giving them a 700-point bonus. However, while they were vulnerable they went two down doubled in Three Spades and four down doubled in Five Clubs. Your total of 1,600 points means you win by 680 points.

It is perfectly in order to play rubber bridge for money. The presence of a small stake will keep everyone on his or her toes. If you are playing with friends, one idea is for the money that changes hands at the end of the evening to go into a communal pot. When there is enough inside it for a good night out, the four of you can splash out and it won't cost you a penny!

PART TWO

Mastering Bridge:

The Knowledge

In this section I explain a range of techniques in bidding, play and defence. I have deliberately allowed a certain amount of overlapping, as what happens in one area can easily affect a decision that has to be made in another. I have also avoided grouping all the illustrations of each type of play together – that never happens at the table! The vast majority of the examples are taken from "real life" situations.

CONCENTRATION

Anyone wanting to drive a taxi in London has to pass an exam to prove they can locate any street within the capital. This awesome task is called "The Knowledge". Becoming a good bridge player also involves a lot of effort. After more than 40 years the legendary World Champion Benito Garozzo claims that he still learns something new every day!

To become a good player you have to acquire the ability to think about all 52 cards, not merely the ones you can see in your own hand. It is possible to become quite a good player without bothering, but if you want to make real progress then you simply have to make the effort.

You don't have to be a genius to count a hand. The bidding and the play to the first few tricks will often establish the distribution of the cards around the table. It will sometimes be easier for the defenders to make this calculation than for declarer.

While the skill required to do this is negligible, the effort of doing it over and over again on every hand is considerable.

Even top-class players find it difficult to maintain their concentration and that is when mistakes are likely to be made. Terence Reese claimed that a player who could count was one in a thousand. I suggest that a player who can count *and* concentrate is perhaps one in ten thousand.

Let me show you what I mean by a loss of concentration. The deal was played in the Prokom Software European Pairs Championship in Warsaw 1999.

North-South Game
Dealer North

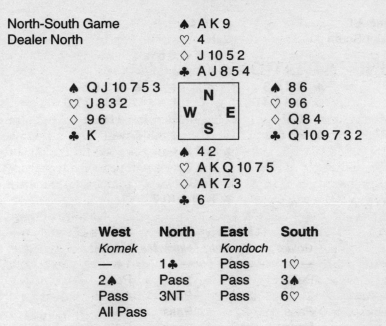

```
                        ♠ A K 9
                        ♡ 4
                        ◇ J 10 5 2
                        ♣ A J 8 5 4

  ♠ Q J 10 7 5 3           N           ♠ 8 6
  ♡ J 8 3 2                            ♡ 9 6
  ◇ 9 6              W         E       ◇ Q 8 4
  ♣ K                     S           ♣ Q 10 9 7 3 2

                        ♠ 4 2
                        ♡ A K Q 10 7 5
                        ◇ A K 7 3
                        ♣ 6
```

West	North	East	South
Kornek		*Kondoch*	
—	1♣	Pass	1♡
2♠	Pass	Pass	3♠
Pass	3NT	Pass	6♡
All Pass			

This was not the most instructive auction you will ever see, but the
final contract was perfectly reasonable. Looking at all four hands, it
is hard to see how declarer can go down, but where there's a will
there's a way.

West led the queen of spades. Declarer won with the ace and was
persuaded by the bidding to finesse the ten of hearts. No harm done
and West won and played the jack of spades. Declarer won with the
king and now had to get back to hand in order to draw trumps. The
obvious thing to do is to cross to a top diamond. Having drawn
trumps, then declarer can go back to dummy with the ace of clubs
and take the diamond finesse. Missing a simple point, South elected
to play dummy's remaining spade. East was not hard pressed to ruff
with the nine of hearts ensuring that West's eight became the setting
trick.

Of course, a defender, or for that matter a declarer, has to be wide
awake to punish a lapse in concentration. This classic example
comes from the Rhodes Olympiad in 1996.

Game All
Dealer South

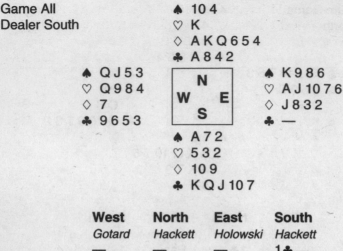

```
                    ♠ 10 4
                    ♡ K
                    ◇ A K Q 6 5 4
                    ♣ A 8 4 2
  ♠ Q J 5 3                          ♠ K 9 8 6
  ♡ Q 9 8 4         N                ♡ A J 10 7 6
  ◇ 7           W       E            ◇ J 8 3 2
  ♣ 9 6 5 3         S                ♣ —
                    ♠ A 7 2
                    ♡ 5 3 2
                    ◇ 10 9
                    ♣ K Q J 10 7
```

West	North	East	South
Gotard	*Hackett*	*Holowski*	*Hackett*
—	—	—	1♣
Pass	1◇	1♡	Pass
2♡	3♡	Pass	4♣
Pass	4♡	Pass	4♠
Pass	4NT	Pass	5♣
All Pass			

A minor-suit slam is a decent proposition on the North-South cards, but the bad breaks doom you to failure.

Five Diamonds should go down provided the defenders set up their spade trick, but Five Clubs looks straightforward – and that is the time to be especially careful.

The opening lead was the four of hearts taken by the ace. East switched to a spade. Declarer should duck this, win the next spade and ruff a heart. A trump to hand reveals the 4-0 split but declarer simply ruffs a major-suit loser with the ace of clubs and draws trumps. His remaining loser goes on the third round of diamonds.

Seeing no danger, declarer won with the ace of spades and cashed the king of clubs. Now he ruffed a heart and exited with the ten of spades. Andreas Holowski went up with the king of spades and found the devastating and brilliant return of the jack of diamonds! That ruined declarer's communications. He could win, return to hand with a trump and ruff a heart or a spade but then had no way back to hand to draw trumps.

Many players would have fallen into the trap that ensnared the declarer in my next example. It was played in the 1997 Brighton Summer Festival.

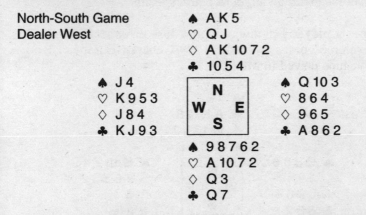

North-South Game
Dealer West

♠ A K 5
♡ Q J
♢ A K 10 7 2
♣ 10 5 4

♠ J 4
♡ K 9 5 3
♢ J 8 4
♣ K J 9 3

♠ Q 10 3
♡ 8 6 4
♢ 9 6 5
♣ A 8 6 2

♠ 9 8 7 6 2
♡ A 10 7 2
♢ Q 3
♣ Q 7

Both Souths played in Four Spades on this hand from the Swiss teams event. Both Wests found the club lead and the defence started with three rounds of the suit.

One declarer ruffed with the two of spades and cashed the ace and king of trumps. He then started on the diamonds and was pleased to find they were 3-3. However, he was less pleased when East ruffed the fourth round and played a heart. The precious two of spades had been wasted at trick three and there was no entry to the dummy.

At the other table, World Champion Pat Davies made no mistake, ruffing with six of spades and thereby retaining an entry to the winning diamonds.

When I originally reported this hand, I revealed that one of Victor Mollo's immortal characters had also defeated the contract. This is how I described the play.

Chatting to the Rueful Rabbit in the bar he revealed that his partnership had also managed to defeat the contract.

"So your declarer failed to ruff with the six of spades?" I enquired.

"Well no, er, that is I … er … didn't, I mean we didn't play three rounds of clubs'.

"You mean your partner switched to a heart at trick two and declarer got it wrong by finessing rather than relying on the 3-3 diamond break?"

"No. You see I had intended to lead the four of diamonds but the king of clubs was next to it and I led it by mistake. When it held I played another club and the Toucan won and switched to a heart."

The Rabbit's guardian angel had struck again.

Sometimes a player gets away with a loss of concentration. This recent example comes from the 1999 Generali European Bridge Championships played in Malta.

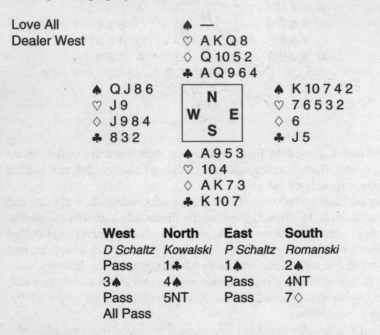

Love All
Dealer West

```
              ♠ —
              ♡ A K Q 8
              ◇ Q 10 5 2
              ♣ A Q 9 6 4
♠ Q J 8 6            N            ♠ K 10 7 4 2
♡ J 9                             ♡ 7 6 5 3 2
◇ J 9 8 4       W       E         ◇ 6
♣ 8 3 2              S            ♣ J 5
              ♠ A 9 5 3
              ♡ 10 4
              ◇ A K 7 3
              ♣ K 10 7
```

West	North	East	South
D Schaltz	Kowalski	P Schaltz	Romanski
Pass	1♣	1♠	2♠
3♠	4♠	Pass	4NT
Pass	5NT	Pass	7◇
All Pass			

In the face of the intervention, this was a great effort. However, Romanski had found it difficult to arrive at the winning decision and there was almost a dramatic conclusion.

West led the queen of spades and declarer won with the ace, discarding the eight of hearts. He cashed the ace and king of diamonds and now made a ridiculous play, continuing with the king of clubs and a club to the ace.

The correct approach is to draw trumps via the marked finesse and then play on clubs, unblocking the ten on an honour and then returning to the king of clubs, thereby picking up any four clubs in the West hand.

Luckily, the appearance of the jack offered a choice of routes back to hand. Eventually Romanski took East's card at face value and returned with the ten of clubs.

The relief on his face when West had to follow was visible to the audience.

These examples make it clear that the ability to concentrate plays a significant role on the road to bridge mastery.

What technical skills are required?

One question I am repeatedly asked is: "How much do I need to know about such things as squeezes, safety plays and the like?"

The answer is not as much as you think you do. Giorgio Belladonna, probably the finest player the game has ever seen, is on record as saying that you could get away with no knowledge of squeeze play at all.

What do you need to know to move up the bridge ladder?

Certainly you must be familiar with some of the simple probabilities.

PROBABILITIES

The figures here show how the missing cards in a suit are likely to be distributed.

When your side has an eleven-card fit – it won't happen very often – you can expect the two outstanding cards to divide 1-1 52 times in 100. You can expect them to be 2-0 the remaining 48 times. If you like to think in terms of percentages they are 52% and 48%.

When you have ten cards the chance of a 3-0 break is 22%. The rest of the time, the suit will break 2-1, a 78% chance.

The situation where your side has nine cards in a suit is one of the most interesting. The most likely distribution of the remaining four cards is 3-1, happening 52% of the time. The 2-2 break occurs 40% of the time and the most extreme 4-0 distribution ten times in a hundred.

When one of the four missing cards is the queen, it may therefore seem that you should decide upon a finesse rather than playing for the drop. However, appearances can be deceptive, and as each card is played, the odds change. When you reach the critical point at which there is only one card missing, it is slightly better to play for the drop.

You will play a huge number of hands in a 4-4 fit. The five missing cards will break 3-2 68% of the time. A 4-1 division happens 28% of the time and the remaining 4% is covered by the possible 5-0 split.

Every now and then you will be interested in how six missing cards are likely to divide. The 4-2 split is the most likely, happening 48% of the time, while the next best is the 3-3 break, which occurs 36% of the time. That leaves 16% and of the two remaining distributions 5-1 will happen 15 times compared to just once for the 6-0.

Why is it important to know how these missing cards are likely to divide?

There are a number of reasons.

Imagine that you have two possible ways to make your contract but can try only one of them. Your choice is between a finesse, which by now I hope you realize is an even money chance, or a 3-3 break. Clearly the former is a better bet.

Keep in mind that as you obtain clues from the bidding and play the odds may change. If a player makes a pre-emptive bid then he is known to have length in that suit and is therefore likely to be short in the other suits.

Let's take a look at how these and other factors influence the play and defence of each hand.

CONCENTRATING ON DECLARER

There are a number of ways in which the fate of a hand can be determined. Sometimes everything will be over after the opening lead but, more often than not, the play will feature a struggle between the declarer and the defenders.

Elimination
One of declarer's strongest weapons is the use of elimination play. In its purest form, a defender ends up having to choose between opening up an important suit or conceding a ruff and discard.

This illustration comes from the rubber bridge table.

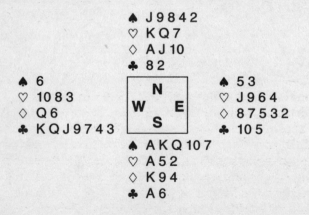

After West opened Three Clubs, South becomes declarer in a contract of Six Spades. When West leads the king of clubs it may look as if you need to locate the queen of diamonds to arrive at twelve tricks. It would not be too difficult to establish that West had one spade, at least three hearts and presumably seven clubs, thereby making East a heavy favourite to have the all-important queen.

However, there is a better approach.

You win the opening lead and draw trumps. After cashing three winning hearts you simply exit with a club. It does not matter which defender wins. If a heart or club is played you can ruff in one hand

and discard a losing diamond from the other. If either defender plays a diamond he will have located the missing queen for you.

When I use this hand in the classroom I give both East and West a queen of diamonds to ensure that any player who finesses goes down. Even with two diamond queens in the pack the contract cannot be defeated if you follow the elimination!

This deal comes from the 1997 Summer Festival in Brighton.

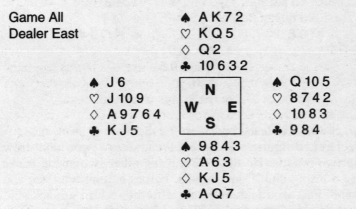

Game All   ♠ A K 7 2
Dealer East   ♡ K Q 5
         ◇ Q 2
         ♣ 10 6 3 2

♠ J 6   ♠ Q 10 5
♡ J 10 9   N   ♡ 8 7 4 2
◇ A 9 7 6 4   W   E   ◇ 10 8 3
♣ K J 5   S   ♣ 9 8 4

         ♠ 9 8 4 3
         ♡ A 6 3
         ◇ K J 5
         ♣ A Q 7

The contract at both tables was Four Spades by South.

One declarer won the opening heart lead and cashed the top trumps before playing on diamonds. West won with the ace and returned the suit. Declarer was able to eliminate the red suits ending in dummy and play a club to the eight, queen and king. When a club was returned declarer guessed wrong by playing the three and the nine forced the ace for one down.

This is how World Champion Pat Davies played the hand.

She won the heart lead and attacked diamonds at once. West won and played a second heart. Pat could win, cash the ace and king of spades and eliminate the red suits before exiting with a trump. East won and played a club but Pat simply ducked and West was endplayed.

This example comes from the 1999 Egyptian Festival played in Cairo.

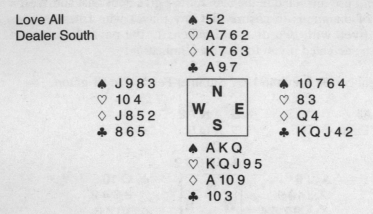

Love All
Dealer South

```
              ♠ 5 2
              ♡ A 7 6 2
              ◊ K 7 6 3
              ♣ A 9 7
♠ J 9 8 3                      ♠ 10 7 6 4
♡ 10 4           N            ♡ 8 3
◊ J 8 5 2     W     E         ◊ Q 4
♣ 8 6 5          S            ♣ K Q J 4 2
              ♠ A K Q
              ♡ K Q J 9 5
              ◊ A 10 9
              ♣ 10 3
```

The contract was Six Hearts and West led the three of spades.

The declarer, Bulgaria's Roumen Trendafizov, won and drew trumps in two rounds. He then cashed his other two spade tricks discarding a losing club from dummy, before exiting with ace and another club. East won and could not afford to return a black suit. In practice, he played the five of diamonds covered by the ten jack and king. When declarer played a diamond from the dummy the appearance of the queen allowed him to claim.

A stronger defence in this type of endgame is for the player to return an honour. If East plays the queen of diamonds then declarer has to decide who has the jack.

Good card-play has a timeless quality to it. This deal comes from the 1979 European Championships played in Lausanne.

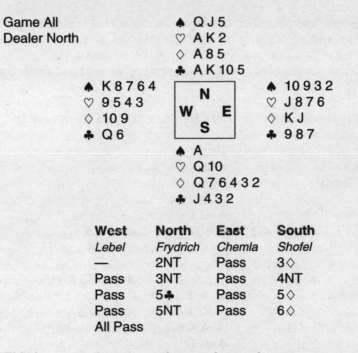

Game All
Dealer North

	North		
♠	Q J 5		
♡	A K 2		
◇	A 8 5		
♣	A K 10 5		

West: ♠ K 8 7 6 4 ♡ 9 5 4 3 ◇ 10 9 ♣ Q 6

East: ♠ 10 9 3 2 ♡ J 8 7 6 ◇ K J ♣ 9 8 7

South: ♠ A ♡ Q 10 ◇ Q 7 6 4 3 2 ♣ J 4 3 2

West	North	East	South
Lebel	*Frydrich*	*Chemla*	*Shofel*
—	2NT	Pass	3◇
Pass	3NT	Pass	4NT
Pass	5♣	Pass	5◇
Pass	5NT	Pass	6◇
All Pass			

This is a poor slam as you have to lose at least one trump trick and you have a possible outside loser as well.

Lebel led the ten of diamonds.

Let's take a look at the various possibilities on the hand:

A beginner would let East's king win the trick and later would finesse the queen of clubs and hope for the best.

A more experienced player would concede a trick to the king of trumps and play on two chances, first cashing the ace and king of clubs, hoping for the queen to drop and then if it did not would take a ruffing finesse in spades.

Shofel, however, took a much better line of play. He played the ace of diamonds at trick one dropping the jack from East. Then he played the ace of spades and three rounds of hearts discarding a club. Shofel then ruffed a spade in hand, led a club to the ace and ruffed dummy's last spade. The elimination was now complete and he played a small diamond from hand.

That left East on play with the king of diamonds and he had to play a club or concede a ruff and discard, the slam coming home in either event.

The Israeli had played on two assumptions: Lebel was unlikely to have led a singleton ten of trumps; Chemla had no reason to false-card with the jack of diamonds holding K-J-9 of diamonds.

Of course, as the cards lie even a beginner would have made the contract!

This deal comes from the 1997 European Pairs Championship in The Hague.

Game All
Dealer South

```
                    ♠ K 8 7
                    ♡ K 10 2
                    ◇ 8 6 5 4
                    ♣ Q 9 5
  ♠ 10 6 4 3 2            N            ♠ Q J 5
  ♡ 8 5              W         E       ♡ A 9 4
  ◇ J 10 7 3             S            ◇ Q
  ♣ 6 2                               ♣ K J 10 8 4 3
                    ♠ A 9
                    ♡ Q J 7 6 3
                    ◇ A K 9 2
                    ♣ A 7
```

West	North	East	South
v d Neut	Willard	Maas	Cronier
—	—	—	1♡
Pass	2♡	3♣	4♡
All Pass			

Jaap van der Neut led a club to the eight and ace, and Benedicte Cronier led a trump to the king and ace. Anton Maas switched to his diamond and declarer won and drew trumps, West pitching a spade, and played a club to the nine and ten. Maas played the king of clubs and Cronier ruffed while West again discarded a spade.

East's willingness to switch to the queen of diamonds but not to continue the suit, coupled with West's discards, convinced declarer that diamonds were 4-1.

She played ace, king and ruffed a spade to eliminate West's exit cards then led a low diamond from hand at trick eleven. Van der Neut was endplayed to give the tenth trick, a fine piece of card-reading from declarer to bring home her game.

As I mentioned earlier, when there is a trump suit the elimination will usually leave the defender choosing between opening up a vital suit or conceding a ruff and discard. When the contract is in no-trumps the elimination involves removing the defenders' exit cards and then throwing him in to lead into a tenace.

This deal was played at the 1999 Generali European Championships in Malta.

```
North-South Game        ♠ A 2
Dealer East             ♡ 9 3 2
                        ◇ A Q J 4
                        ♣ A J 7 5
        ♠ 10 9 5 3      ┌─────────┐      ♠ 6 4
        ♡ K 10 5        │    N    │      ♡ J 7 4
        ◇ 10 7 5 2      │ W     E │      ◇ 9 6
        ♣ Q 8           │    S    │      ♣ K 10 9 4 3 2
                        └─────────┘
                        ♠ K Q J 8 7
                        ♡ A Q 8 6
                        ◇ K 8 3
                        ♣ 6
```

The popular contract was Three No-Trumps. The commentators, of whom I was one, observed that a slam was not impossible on the North-South cards.

Six Diamonds was reached by several pairs. They all made the contract by taking a club ruff with a small diamond.

If East starts with a pre-emptive bid in clubs declarer, fearing an overruff, will probably ruff a club high, setting up a trump trick for West. When three rounds of diamonds reveal that fact declarer plays on spades, keeping just one heart in North. If West ruffs the last spade he will be endplayed to lead into the heart tenace. If he discards, declarer will dispose of his remaining heart and play ace and another heart, ensuring that the four of diamonds scores a trick even though West has the master trump. This neat little play goes by the name of the coup *en passant*.

Six Spades can be made by drawing trumps, ruffing a club, cashing the diamonds and playing a heart, covering East's card. If East started with a pre-emptive bid in clubs, that would be entirely reasonable.

Six No-Trumps can't be made on a club lead but was made when East had opened Three Clubs and, not unreasonably, didn't lead his suit or a heart. Declarer cashed five spades and four diamonds and, in order to prevent declarer from simply ducking a heart, West was forced to part with a club. Now declarer extracted West's remaining club by cashing the ace and endplayed him by playing a heart and simply covering East's card.

Bien joué!

The elimination has a close relative that we can consider next.

Endplay

Here is a complicated example from the 1998 Macallan played in London.

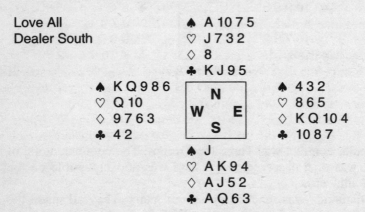

Love All
Dealer South

```
                 ♠ A 10 7 5
                 ♡ J 7 3 2
                 ◇ 8
                 ♣ K J 9 5
   ♠ K Q 9 8 6        N        ♠ 4 3 2
   ♡ Q 10                      ♡ 8 6 5
   ◇ 9 7 6 3     W       E     ◇ K Q 10 4
   ♣ 4 2              S        ♣ 10 8 7
                 ♠ J
                 ♡ A K 9 4
                 ◇ A J 5 2
                 ♣ A Q 6 3
```

Hamman & Wolff faced Auken & Blakset. South (Bobby Wolff) had to try to make Six Clubs after West had made a weak jump overcall of Two Spades.

The opening lead was the king of spades. Wolff won and Auken signalled as if he had a doubleton!

Using a heart and a spade ruff as entries to his hand declarer ruffed his losing diamonds to produce this ending:

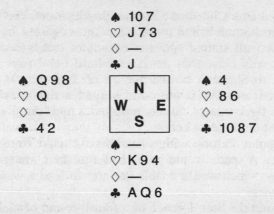

Having seen West play the ten of hearts on the first round of the suit it looked to declarer as if East was down to three heart and three clubs.

Seeing the chance for an endplay, Wolff overtook the jack of clubs with the queen and cashed the ace. He threw East in to lead away from Q-8-6 of hearts. Alas, he was two down when East found the spade he had said he didn't have!

Developing the side suit

It will often be the case that declarer needs to develop a side suit in order to arrive at the right number of tricks. This may well involve postponing the drawing of trumps.

Robert Sheehan, bridge correspondent of the London *Times,* writes one of the better bridge columns and has an eye for an instructive hand. This will repay close study.

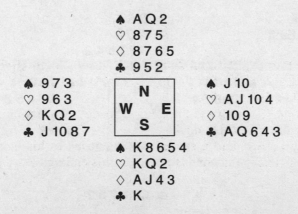

East opened One Club and Sheehan, South, overcalled One Spade. In due course South had to try to make Three Spades.

The opponents started with two rounds of clubs, forcing declarer to ruff. It was clear that declarer would need two tricks from diamonds, so Sheehan cashed the ace of diamonds and continued with a small one. West won and played a third club, reducing declarer to three trumps. Sheehan played a third diamond and West won as East discarded a heart.

At this point, exiting with a heart would make things very easy for declarer. A spade would be no better as there are two entries in the dummy, which would enable declarer to lead towards the heart honours twice.

West found the best defence of a fourth round of clubs, giving a ruff and discard. Declarer ruffed with dummy's two of spades and discarded the winning diamond from his hand. He now led a heart to the king and, when that held, he returned to dummy with a trump and played another heart. East went in with the ace but had no winning play. A final club can be ruffed low in hand and if West overruffs so can dummy.

The secret lay in the timing.

If declarer draws even one round of trumps then East can win the second heart and lead the last club promoting a trump trick for West.

The technique is to develop the side suit before dealing with trumps.

Take a look at this deal from the 1996 Olympiad in Rhodes.

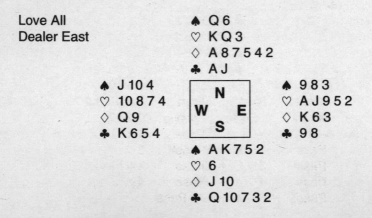

```
Love All              ♠ Q 6
Dealer East           ♡ K Q 3
                      ◇ A 8 7 5 4 2
                      ♣ A J

        ♠ J 10 4            N            ♠ 9 8 3
        ♡ 10 8 7 4                       ♡ A J 9 5 2
        ◇ Q 9         W         E        ◇ K 6 3
        ♣ K 6 5 4           S            ♣ 9 8

                      ♠ A K 7 5 2
                      ♡ 6
                      ◇ J 10
                      ♣ Q 10 7 3 2
```

West	North	East	South
Wu	*Robson*	*Kuo*	*Forrester*
—	—	Pass	1♠
Pass	2◇	Pass	2♠
Pass	3♠	Pass	4♠
All Pass			

The opening lead was a heart taken by the ace. Forrester won the second heart discarding a diamond and following the sound policy of getting the side-suit going before touching trumps played ace and another club. As the cards lay he was in control for +420.

There is a stronger line!

If either defender had just two cards in each black suit, a third round of clubs would have been fatal for declarer.

The correct play is rather neat. At trick three, declarer should play the jack of clubs! He can then win any return, cash the ace of clubs, and set about the trump suit.

This hand was played in the 1988 IOC Grand Prix in Lausanne.

North-South Game
Dealer East

```
              ♠ —
              ♡ A Q 9 6
              ◇ A J 9 5 2
              ♣ K 5 4 2
  ♠ J 10 7 4              ♠ A Q 8 3
  ♡ 7           N         ♡ J 10 5
  ◇ Q 10 7 6  W   E       ◇ K 3
  ♣ Q 10 8 3    S         ♣ J 9 7 6
              ♠ K 9 6 5 2
              ♡ K 8 4 3 2
              ◇ 8 4
              ♣ A
```

West	North	East	South
Xu	*Chagas*	*Zhuang*	*Branco*
—	—	Pass	1♠
Pass	2◇	Pass	2♡
Pass	3♡	Pass	4♣
Pass	4◇	Pass	4♡
Pass	6♡	All Pass	

North's Two Diamond response was game forcing.

West led the eight of clubs.

Declarer won in hand with the ace and crossed to the ace of diamonds. He cashed dummy's king of clubs to discard a diamond and ruffed a diamond. A spade ruff was followed by a diamond ruff as East discarded, so declarer ruffed another spade and played a diamond. East ruffed this one with the ten of hearts. Branco overruffed and ruffed a spade, felling the ace. Now he cashed the ace of hearts and played the master diamond, thus losing only to the jack of hearts.

Declarer had combined the setting up of the diamond suit by utilizing the power of his trumps. The hand would not be out of place in the next section.

Cross-ruffing

This is a way of making tricks by using your trumps separately. It happens quite often, especially when declarer is trying to scramble as many tricks as possible in a poor contract. It is usually a good idea to take your winners in the side suits before embarking on the crossruff – otherwise a defender may be able to discard from a side-suit and subsequently ruff one of your winners.

Love All
Dealer North

```
                    ♠ J 6 4 2
                    ♡ A K 10 5
                    ◇ A 9 8 6 5
                    ♣ —

  ♠ 10                               ♠ K 9 8 3
  ♡ Q 8 6          N                 ♡ J 9 7 4
  ◇ K J 10 7 3 2  W   E              ◇ Q
  ♣ A 9 2          S                 ♣ Q 8 6 4

                    ♠ A Q 7 5
                    ♡ 3 2
                    ◇ 4
                    ♣ K J 10 7 5 3
```

West	North	East	South
Wang X	*Rosenberg*	*Fu*	*Mahmood*
	1◇	Pass	1♠
Pass	3♠	Pass	4♣
Pass	4♠	All Pass	

Zia won the opening lead of the six of hearts and cashed the ace of diamonds, noting the appearance of East's queen. He ruffed a diamond, East discarding a club, ruffed a club, and cashed the ace of hearts. He ruffed a heart, ruffed a club and then ruffed a heart with the ace of spades. He ruffed a club with the jack of spades and then played a diamond, ensuring that the queen of spades would be his game-going trick whenever East held the king.

Notice how declarer was careful to ruff with high trumps towards the end to ensure that he could not be overruffed.

Counting the hand

In the introduction to this section I said that no special skill was required to count a bridge hand – but it does require a conscious effort. Let's look at an example from the 1999 World Junior Championships in Nymburk, Czech Republic, the largest International Junior Bridge event in history, with almost 400 participants from 30 countries.

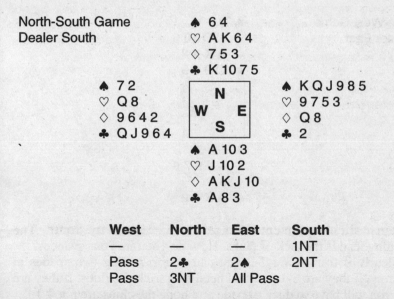

North-South Game
Dealer South

```
              ♠ 6 4
              ♡ A K 6 4
              ◇ 7 5 3
              ♣ K 10 7 5
♠ 7 2                          ♠ K Q J 9 8 5
♡ Q 8            N             ♡ 9 7 5 3
◇ 9 6 4 2     W     E          ◇ Q 8
♣ Q J 9 6 4      S             ♣ 2
              ♠ A 10 3
              ♡ J 10 2
              ◇ A K J 10
              ♣ A 8 3
```

West	North	East	South
—	—	—	1NT
Pass	2♣	2♠	2NT
Pass	3NT	All Pass	

Declarer ducked the first round of spades but, expecting East to have a six-card suit for his overcall, won the second trick with the ace of spades. Declarer now tried the jack of hearts and was delighted when West played the queen. He won with the ace of hearts and took the diamond finesse. When it held he cashed the king of diamonds and saw a second red queen appear. His next move was to cash the ten and king of hearts. When West discarded a club on the third round declarer could be almost certain that East's distribution was 6-4-2-1.

He came back to hand with the ace of clubs, East following with the two. He now took his remaining winners in the diamond suit before playing another club.

West did his best to put declarer to the test by following with the nine but declarer made no mistake, inserting the ten of clubs to score a valuable overtrick.

If West had split his honours declarer would have ducked, knowing that the enforced club return into dummy's tenace would give him the last two tricks.

This is more complicated. It comes from an International tournament in Madeira in 1998.

East-West Game	♠ 8
Dealer East	♡ K Q 10 5
	◇ A K 4 2
	♣ Q 9 8 5

```
        N
    W       E
        S
```

♠ 6 5 3
♡ A J 9 7 6
◇ J
♣ A K 6 2

Against silent opponents you reach Six Hearts by South. The opening lead is the jack of clubs. How do you rate your chances?

Clearly if trumps are 2-2 you can claim, ruffing two spades in dummy. If they are 3-1 you will need four tricks in clubs. If they are 4-0 you will have to duck a spade and hope the clubs are not 4-1.

To keep the club situation fluid you should win in hand, draw trumps – of course, they prove to be 3-1 – and give up a spade. You plan to win the return and cash the top diamonds. One spade can be ruffed in dummy and one diamond in hand.

Your idea is to try to get a picture of the distribution and ascertain who has the club length. While you are doing this East produces the three of clubs, a singleton trump, the ten, seven and six of diamonds, and the ten and two of spades.

Rien ne va plus!

This was the full deal:

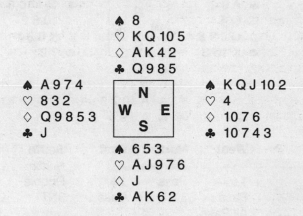

```
                    ♠ 8
                    ♡ K Q 10 5
                    ◇ A K 4 2
                    ♣ Q 9 8 5
   ♠ A 9 7 4                      ♠ K Q J 10 2
   ♡ 8 3 2          N             ♡ 4
   ◇ Q 9 8 5 3    W   E           ◇ 10 7 6
   ♣ J              S             ♣ 10 7 4 3
                    ♠ 6 5 3
                    ♡ A J 9 7 6
                    ◇ J
                    ♣ A K 6 2
```

If East has a doubleton club nothing matters so the danger holdings are zero, one or four. With a shortage he must have at least six spades and might have bid at some point. So you should play East for the club length.

Did you get it right?

You can draw many inferences from the bidding, both as to the length of suits and the number of points held by an opponent. This is especially true when a player opens the bidding and ends up defending.

This deal comes from a festival in Portugal in 1998.

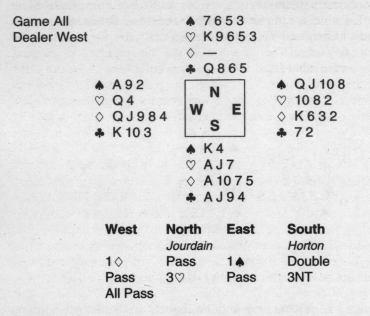

Game All
Dealer West

```
              ♠ 7653
              ♡ K9653
              ◇ —
              ♣ Q865

♠ A92              N              ♠ QJ108
♡ Q4                              ♡ 1082
◇ QJ984      W         E          ◇ K632
♣ K103             S              ♣ 72

              ♠ K4
              ♡ AJ7
              ◇ A1075
              ♣ AJ94
```

West	North	East	South
	Jourdain		*Horton*
1◇	Pass	1♠	Double
Pass	3♡	Pass	3NT
All Pass			

Patrick Jourdain judged his hand well, first showing some values with his jump to Three Hearts and then passing Three No-Trumps.

West led the queen of diamonds and declarer had to duck.

If West had realized South could hold only a doubleton spade he would have seen the advantage of switching to ace and another spade. Seeing no danger, he continued with the four of diamonds.

Declarer took East's king with the ace and crossed to dummy with the king of hearts to play a club to the jack and king. West cleared the diamonds and declarer crossed to dummy by overtaking the nine of clubs with the queen. The club suit would provide another entry to dummy so it was possible to play East for the queen of hearts. However, West had opened the bidding and so far turned up with the queen and jack of diamonds and the king of clubs. He surely held the ace of spades but needed another high card. Not a strong indication but enough to persuade declarer to play a heart to the ace and, on the appearance of the queen, to claim the rest of the tricks.

Deception

One of declarer's weapons is the gentle art of deception. After all he can see his side's combined assets, while the defenders have a harder task. Look at it like this: when a defender plays a card, he has to keep in mind the information that he is giving to partner. Declarer, on the other hand, owes no such obligation to the dummy!

There are many situations in which the play of the right card can lead a defender astray. Before we look at some examples from play, let's check out a few standard situations that come up on a regular basis.

```
                     ♠ 8 7 4
  ♠ 3 led        ┌──────────┐     ♠ J played
                 └──────────┘
                     ♠ K Q 6
```

If you win with the queen it will be clear to West that you must have the king as well. If you take the trick with the higher honour West will not be sure who has the queen.

```
                     ♠ 8 7 4
  ♠ 3 led        ┌──────────┐     ♠ J played
                 └──────────┘
                     ♠ A K 6
```

This simple little situation contains a number of possibilities. If you decide to duck the first round of the suit – as you might well do if playing in no-trumps – then you should win the second round with the ace, leaving East in the dark as to who has the king.

If you decide to win the first trick, then the king is a better card to play than the ace because no self-respecting declarer would use his only stopper on the first round of the suit unless he had to.

The correct use of the spot cards is every bit as important. It can be really easy to divert a defender from the right path.

```
                     ♡ Q 8 3
 ♡ A K J 9 7     ┌──────────┐     ♡ 10 5 4
                 └──────────┘
                     ♡ 6 2
```

If West, having bid hearts, now leads a top honour against a trump contract, you should follow from your hand with the six. If West notices the two is missing he may place his partner with a doubleton and continue the suit.

This is the reverse situation:

$$\heartsuit \ Q\,10\,6\,4$$

$$\heartsuit \ A\,K\,J\,8\,5 \qquad\qquad\qquad \heartsuit \ 3$$

$$\heartsuit \ 9\,7\,2$$

This time, when West leads the suit he has bid, you can see that East's three must be a singleton. If you play one of your intermediates, the only card West will know his partner can have is the two and he will continue the suit. You should play the two, hoping West will place his partner with three cards in the suit.

The easy way to remember these positions is to play as if you were defending. Play a high card if you want to tempt the defender into continuing the suit, but play a low one if you are trying to persuade him to switch.

There are many plays designed to persuade an opponent to do what you want. This is a well-known stratagem:

$$\diamondsuit \ 7\,4$$

$$\diamondsuit \ 6 \text{ led} \qquad\qquad\qquad \diamondsuit \ J \text{ played}$$

$$\diamondsuit \ A\,Q\,5$$

In no-trumps if you have one suit wide open and know you may have to lose a trick to West – say a finesse has to be taken into his hand – then you may elect to win with the ace! If West does gain the lead he will surely place his partner with the queen and underlead his king.

Our next example is a variation on the same theme.

$$\diamondsuit \ J\,10\,4$$

$$\diamondsuit \ K\,9\,7\,5\,3 \qquad\qquad\qquad \diamondsuit \ 6\,2$$

$$\diamondsuit \ A\,Q\,8$$

If West leads this suit you can try to encourage West to continue it if he regains the lead by playing the jack from dummy and the queen from hand – but this is unlikely to work if your opponents are using any sensible method of signalling!

It is not often that a brilliant play is made on VuGraph, but in the 1998 Junior European Championships in Vienna the capacity crowd saw a beautiful deceptive move by Grzejdziak in the match between Norway and Poland.

```
Game All              ♠ K 10 7 4
Dealer West           ♡ A K Q 8
                      ◇ 7 4 3
                      ♣ 9 5
       ♠ Q 9 8 6        ┌─────┐      ♠ J 2
       ♡ J 4 3          │  N  │      ♡ 10 7
       ◇ J 10 6       W │     │ E    ◇ Q 8 5
       ♣ A Q 4          │  S  │      ♣ K J 8 6 3 2
                        └─────┘
                      ♠ A 5 3
                      ♡ 9 6 5 2
                      ◇ A K 9 2
                      ♣ 10 7
```

West	North	East	South
Pass	1♣	Pass	1♡
Pass	2♡	Pass	4♡
All Pass			

West was on lead, and chose the eight of spades.

It is impossible, I think, for anyone to find a legitimate winning line of play, but Grzejdziak found an excellent deceptive play that made it difficult for West to find the killing defence. The first trick went spade eight, four, two, three! Cashing the ace of clubs could have been a disaster on a different layout, so West continued with the six of spades. South took East's jack with the ace, played three rounds of hearts and later finessed in spades and threw a club loser on the fourth spade. A club ruff made a total of ten tricks thanks to a very imaginative deception.

Here is a variation on an old theme that has caught out many a defender. It was played in the 1996 Junior European Championships in Cardiff.

Love All
Dealer East

```
                          ♠ K
                          ♡ 9 8 7
                          ◇ K 6 4 2
                          ♣ A Q 8 4 2
    ♠ Q J 9 8 6 4        ┌─────────┐        ♠ 7 5
    ♡ K 6                │    N    │        ♡ A J 10 4 3 2
    ◇ A 10               │ W     E │        ◇ J 9 5
    ♣ 10 7 6             │    S    │        ♣ 5 3
                         └─────────┘
                          ♠ A 10 3 2
                          ♡ Q 5
                          ◇ Q 8 7 3
                          ♣ K J 9
```

West	North	East	South
	Brink		Brink
—	—	Pass	1◇
2♠	3♠	Pass	3NT
All Pass			

A lot of players would have opened with a Weak Two-bid on the East hand.

Against Three No-Trumps, West led the queen of spades, taken by dummy's king.

With only seven tricks on top declarer needed to find two more and avoid what would almost certainly be a fatal switch to hearts.

Niel Brink found a neat way to discourage a heart switch. At trick two he played a heart to his queen!

West won with the king and naturally gave no thought to returning the suit. His actual choice of a small spade gave declarer one of the extra tricks he needed and all he had to do now was steal a trick in the diamond suit.

If East held the ace of diamonds he would be odds-on to follow it with a torrent of hearts so Niel played a small diamond towards the king. When that held he quickly ran for home.

Here is another ploy of a type that works over and over again. It comes from the 1997 Venice Cup played in Tunisia.

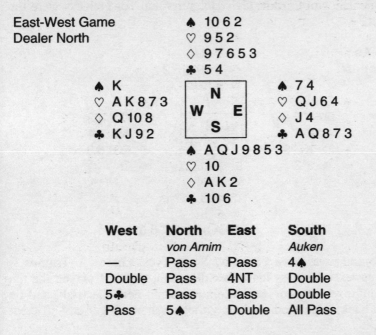

East-West Game
Dealer North

♠ 10 6 2
♡ 9 5 2
◇ 9 7 6 5 3
♣ 5 4

♠ K
♡ A K 8 7 3
◇ Q 10 8
♣ K J 9 2

N
W   E
S

♠ 7 4
♡ Q J 6 4
◇ J 4
♣ A Q 8 7 3

♠ A Q J 9 8 5 3
♡ 10
◇ A K 2
♣ 10 6

West	North	East	South
	von Arnim		*Auken*
—	Pass	Pass	4♠
Double	Pass	4NT	Double
5♣	Pass	Pass	Double
Pass	5♠	Double	All Pass

North faced a tough decision when her partner doubled Five Clubs and she took out insurance.

West started with her top hearts so Sabine Auken ruffed the second round and cashed the ace of spades. When the king appeared she continued smoothly with the two of diamonds! West won with the jack and, completely taken in, returned the suit! Now, after drawing the last trump and unblocking the diamonds, Sabine was able to reach dummy with the ten of spades and dispose of her losing clubs on the diamonds.

My final example pitted four of the finest players in the world against each other. Jeff Meckstroth was the man who stole a contract. The Norwegians Geir Helgemo and Tor Helness were the victims.

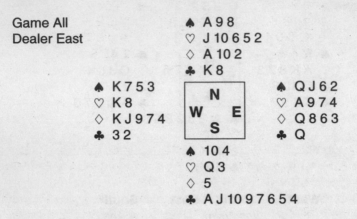

Game All
Dealer East

♠ A 9 8
♡ J 10 6 5 2
◇ A 10 2
♣ K 8

♠ K 7 5 3
♡ K 8
◇ K J 9 7 4
♣ 3 2

♠ Q J 6 2
♡ A 9 7 4
◇ Q 8 6 3
♣ Q

♠ 10 4
♡ Q 3
◇ 5
♣ A J 10 9 7 6 5 4

The contract was Five Clubs by South (yes, Three No-Trumps is much easier!). Helness led a low diamond, and Jeff played the ten from dummy! Of course, Helgemo's queen held the trick, and he played back a diamond. Suddenly there was no longer any efficient defence!

Meckstroth discarded a heart on the ace of diamonds and led a heart to his queen. Helness won this and fired back a spade – but it was too late. Meckstroth rose with the ace and played the jack of hearts. East had to put up the ace, which Meckstroth ruffed in hand. He cashed the ace of clubs, crossed to the king of clubs, and the ten of hearts took care of his spade loser.

More on finessing

The finesse is one of the easiest ways to try to make an extra trick. However, there are variations on a theme. The presence of a trump suit makes it possible for you to take a ruffing finesse as in this example from the 1999 Generali European Bridge Championships in Malta.

Love All
Dealer East

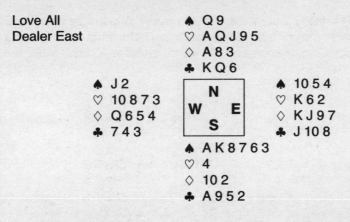

```
                      ♠ Q9
                      ♡ AQJ95
                      ◇ A83
                      ♣ KQ6
    ♠ J2                              ♠ 1054
    ♡ 10873          N                ♡ K62
    ◇ Q654       W       E            ◇ KJ97
    ♣ 743            S                ♣ J108
                      ♠ AK8763
                      ♡ 4
                      ◇ 102
                      ♣ A952
```

It was not a problem to reach the excellent contract of Six Spades, but West threw down the gauntlet by finding the only lead to trouble declarer: the four of diamonds.

After drawing trumps in three rounds, declarer had to find a way of getting rid of his losing diamond as he could hardly count on the clubs being divided 3-3. A simple finesse in hearts would allow East to win with the king and cash a diamond. However, declarer had a second string to his bow. He crossed to the ace of hearts and played the queen of hearts, taking a ruffing finesse. His plan was to discard the ten of diamonds if East did not cover with the king. West was welcome to win the trick as declarer would then be able to park his potentially losing club on the jack of hearts. When East proved to have the key card, declarer had no difficulty making all thirteen tricks. He ruffed the king of hearts and could now arrange for two more discards in the suit by crossing to dummy with a top club and ruffing a small heart, establishing the J-9 of hearts.

Another recent discovery is to use a manoeuvre described by the Brazilian wizard Gabriel Chagas, the "intra finesse".

Patrick Jourdain is one of those people who can be found at every major championship. He is usually a member of the team that prepares the daily bulletins but every now and then he makes an appearance at the table. This board was played in the 1998 World Championships in Lille.

East-West Game
Dealer South

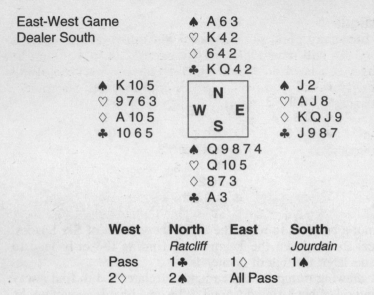

```
                    ♠ A 6 3
                    ♡ K 4 2
                    ◇ 6 4 2
                    ♣ K Q 4 2
    ♠ K 10 5              N          ♠ J 2
    ♡ 9 7 6 3                        ♡ A J 8
    ◇ A 10 5        W       E        ◇ K Q J 9
    ♣ 10 6 5             S           ♣ J 9 8 7
                    ♠ Q 9 8 7 4
                    ♡ Q 10 5
                    ◇ 8 7 3
                    ♣ A 3
```

West	North	East	South
	Ratcliff		*Jourdain*
Pass	1♣	1◇	1♠
2◇	2♠	All Pass	

West opened the defence by underleading his diamond ace. East won the trick with the jack and returned the nine of diamonds to his partner's ace. Thinking that East had overcalled on a five-card suit and worried that declarer might be about to discard a loser on the third round of clubs, West switched to the nine of hearts. East took the ace and cashed the king of diamonds before returning the eight of hearts. Declarer was now faced with the problem of how to avoid the loss of two trump tricks.

He won the heart with dummy's king and ran the six of spades. West took the trick with the ten and exited with a heart. Reasoning that, having overcalled on a four-card suit, East was more likely to be 2-3-4-4, declarer advanced the queen of spades from hand. This collected the trump suit for no further loser and eight tricks were made.

In the other room North came to rest in One No-Trump, a contract that failed by one trick when declarer tackled the spade suit by playing low to the queen. Thus the "Welsh Chagas" earned 4 IMPs for his team.

Notice that if East makes the strange-looking play of the jack of spades on the first round of the suit, declarer may go wrong, playing him for J-10 doubleton. This is not as difficult as it looks when you know your only hope of further tricks lies in the trump suit.

Technique

There are many good plays that do not fall into any specific category but will nevertheless repay careful study. I'll start by showing you a hand on which declarer failed to combine all his chances. It was played in the 1999 Forbo International in The Netherlands.

Love All
Dealer South

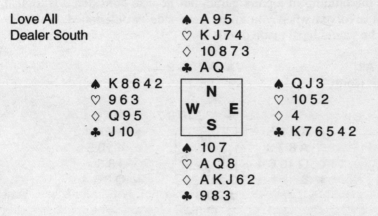

♠ A 9 5
♡ K J 7 4
◇ 10 8 7 3
♣ A Q

♠ K 8 6 4 2
♡ 9 6 3
◇ Q 9 5
♣ J 10

♠ Q J 3
♡ 10 5 2
◇ 4
♣ K 7 6 5 4 2

♠ 10 7
♡ A Q 8
◇ A K J 6 2
♣ 9 8 3

I played in Three No-Trumps from the South hand. In the other room, North was the declarer and emerged with eleven tricks when East led a low club.

I faced the more testing spade lead and ducked the first two rounds of the suit. When I won the third round with the ace, I discarded the seemingly useless three of clubs from my hand. It was clear that West held the spade length so I cashed the ace and king of diamonds, hoping the queen might appear. I was prepared to concede a trick to East but when West turned up with the guarded queen it was time to try the club finesse. When that lost I had to admit defeat.

Can you see the small extra chance that declarer missed? I was the first to spot it.

As three diamond tricks will be enough for game declarer can afford to throw a diamond on the third round of spades. Now you play off the top diamonds as before. When West proves to have three diamonds to the queen you turn once again to the club suit. The finesse still loses but, because the jack and ten of clubs are doubleton, you score a second trick in the suit with your nine of clubs.

According to the analysts, this represents only a 0.15% chance. I am still annoyed I didn't follow this line but at least it provided me with a good story. As I remarked, Sherlock Holmes would have called it "The 0.15% Solution".

The late Terence Reese wrote frequently that, if possible, one had to enter the bidding in a pairs game, but he also considered it foolish to get involved when you know your side is outgunned. I wonder what he would have made of this:

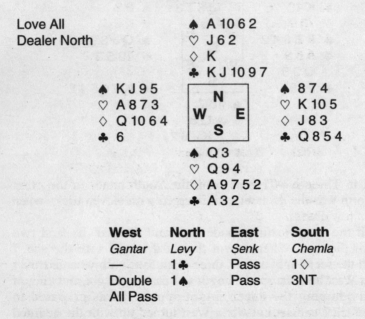

Love All
Dealer North

North
♠ A 10 6 2
♡ J 6 2
◊ K
♣ K J 10 9 7

West
♠ K J 9 5
♡ A 8 7 3
◊ Q 10 6 4
♣ 6

East
♠ 8 7 4
♡ K 10 5
◊ J 8 3
♣ Q 8 5 4

South
♠ Q 3
♡ Q 9 4
◊ A 9 7 5 2
♣ A 3 2

West	North	East	South
Gantar	*Levy*	*Senk*	*Chemla*
—	1♣	Pass	1◊
Double	1♠	Pass	3NT
All Pass			

West led the three of hearts to the two, ten and queen.

With West's double firmly in mind, Chemla crossed to the king of diamonds and ran the jack of clubs. He followed that with the ten of clubs and, when it held, he claimed nine tricks and a good score.

Chemla might have played the same way without the double, but how wise was West to get involved facing a partner who could not bid over One Club?

Apolinary Kowalski of Poland was the declarer who found this brilliancy that eluded some of the world's finest players. It occurred in the 1997 Bermuda Bowl match between Poland and the host country, Tunisia:

Game All
Dealer East

```
                    ♠ A Q J 5 3
                    ♡ A 8 3
                    ◇ A J 5 4 2
                    ♣ —
  ♠ K 10 7 6        ┌─────────┐        ♠ 8 2
  ♡ 10 9            │    N    │        ♡ K 7 4
  ◇ 9 7             │ W     E │        ◇ Q 10 8 6
  ♣ A K 8 4 2       │    S    │        ♣ Q 10 9 7
                    └─────────┘
                    ♠ 9 4
                    ♡ Q J 6 5 2
                    ◇ K 3
                    ♣ J 6 5 3
```

West	North	East	South
	Romanski		*Kowalski*
—	—	Pass	Pass
1♣	1♠	Pass	1NT
Pass	3◇	Pass	3♡
Pass	4♡	Double	All Pass

Kowalski was in Four Hearts doubled from the South seat. The play proceeded card for card, for the first six tricks, exactly as it did on VuGraph between USA1 and France, and in the match between Denmark and Venezuela. West led a high club ruffed in dummy. Declarer came to hand with the king of diamonds, and finessed in spades. Next came the ace of diamonds and a diamond, ruffed low and overruffed by West.

It has been suggested that, at this point, West should lead a club, but in practice all three Wests led a trump won by the ace in dummy, leaving this end-position with the lead in the North hand:

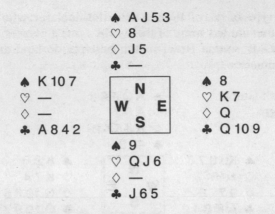

Declarer has made five tricks so far. When Zia was declarer, he ruffed a diamond low, ruffed a club, and played the winning diamond, but Perron, East, discarded his spade, and the game failed. When Vernon was declarer for Venezuela, he ruffed the diamond low, took another spade finesse and led a winner off the table. Now Koch-Palmund as East could have defeated the game by ruffing high and leading a trump. Declarer would be stuck in the South hand and have to concede two clubs at the end. But, East made the mistake of ruffing low, and now declarer succeeded by overruffing, ruffing a club, and making his last trump en passant.

Kowalski found the solution in the diagrammed ending. He ruffed the diamond high, keeping his precious six of trumps! Then he repeated the spade finesse and led a winning diamond off the dummy. He needed only three more tricks. If East does not ruff high and lead a trump, declarer easily makes his three remaining trumps, ruffing in hand, ruffing a club in dummy, and finishing with a coup *en passant*, leading a card from dummy thereby guaranteeing a trick for his remaining trump.

The Tunisian East did very well, correctly ruffing with his king of trumps and leading his seven of trumps. But now Kowalski's great foresight became relevant. He was able to play the six of trumps from his own hand and win the trick in dummy with the eight! The ace of spades in dummy and his remaining trump made ten tricks.

The next type of play happens so often that it has been given a special name that has become part of the sport's terminology.

The declarer won a prize for the best-played hand in the World Bridge Federation's World-Wide Epson contest in 1993.

North-South Game   ♠ A J 7 4
Dealer North   ♡ A 3
                 ◇ A K Q J 9
                 ♣ 10 2

♠ 10 2   ♠ K 9 8 5
♡ K 9 4 2   N   ♡ 8 7 5
◇ 10 7 6 2   W   E   ◇ 8 4
♣ Q 8 6   S   ♣ J 9 5 3

                 ♠ Q 6 3
                 ♡ Q J 10 6
                 ◇ 5 3
                 ♣ A K 7 4

West	North	East	South
	Rosenberg		*Zia*
—	1◇	Pass	1♡
Pass	2♠	Pass	2NT
Pass	3NT	Pass	5NT
Pass	6NT	All Pass	

West led a small heart.

The booklet that the players receive after the event noted that twelve tricks could be made on a neutral lead by starting spades with a low card from the dummy – but that would not be a natural way to play.

When the heart finesse won Zia realized that after cashing some diamond winners – either three or four – a low spade would catch East in a Morton's Fork Coup. If East rises with the king of spades, declarer will have three tricks in the suit, and if he ducks then declarer can abandon spades and develop an extra trick in hearts.

The coup derives its name from Henry VII's chancellor – if you spent a lot you could afford to give money to the king and if you didn't spend then you had money to spare for the king. Either way you were caught in the net.

Here is another example from the 1998 IOC Grand Prix staged in Lausanne.

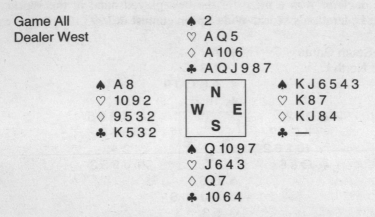

Game All
Dealer West

```
              ♠ 2
              ♡ A Q 5
              ◊ A 10 6
              ♣ A Q J 9 8 7
♠ A 8                      ♠ K J 6 5 4 3
♡ 10 9 2         N         ♡ K 8 7
◊ 9 5 3 2      W   E       ◊ K J 8 4
♣ K 5 3 2        S         ♣ —
              ♠ Q 10 9 7
              ♡ J 6 4 3
              ◊ Q 7
              ♣ 10 6 4
```

South was in Three No-Trumps after East had mentioned his spades.

The opening lead of the ace of spades collected a discouraging three from East, so West switched to a diamond. That was taken by East's king and he returned the suit. Declarer won with the queen and ran the ten of clubs. When it held, the finesse was repeated. Declarer now played dummy's queen of hearts, presenting East with a choice of evils. If he won with the king he would provide declarer with an entry to his hand to repeat the club finesse, but if he ducked then declarer could simply give up a club.

Safety play

When the declarer makes a safety play he is prepared to lose one trick in order to guarantee not losing a second trick whatever the layout. I like to think of it as paying a small insurance premium.

You can usually work out the correct way to play a suit combination at the table, but most players quickly learn to recognize some of the standard situations. Here are a few examples:

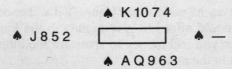

```
                    ♠ K 10 7 4
♠ J 8 5 2      [            ]      ♠ —
                    ♠ A Q 9 6 3
```

It would be a mistake to start with the king of spades on this layout.
You should start with one of the top honours from the South hand.
If it is West who shows out you can still avoid a loser in the suit.

♡ Q 6 4 3

♡ —   [   ]   ♡ K J 8

♡ A 10 9 7 5 2

Imagine this is your trump suit and you can afford to lose a trick.
The correct play is a small card away from the ace. If you cash the
ace you will be fine if West has all the missing hearts but not when
they are with East.

◇ K 9 7 4

◇ Q 10 8 2   [   ]   ◇ 3

◇ A J 6 5

This is one of my favourites. If you cannot afford a loser in this suit
your best chance is to finesse the jack of diamonds. However, if you
can afford one then you should start by cashing the ace! You follow
with a low card and all you have to do is cover West's card. Say he
plays the eight and you beat it with the nine. If East can win the
trick your king will take care of the missing card.

Now for a couple of combinations that I have seen misplayed.

♣ A Q 9 8 5 3

♣ K 10 5   [   ]   ♣ —

♣ J 7 6 2

The correct line is to lead the jack from your hand, catering for the
above layout. If you play a small club to the queen you will lose a
trick to West's K-10.

♠ A K J 10 6 4

♠ Q 9 8 2   ♠ 5

♠ 7 3

I have seen many players start with a top spade and end up losing a trick to West's queen. The correct technique is to finesse on the first round – only wrong if East has the singleton queen.

◇ Q 10 9 8 5

◇ K 7 6 2   ◇ J 3

◇ A 4

This is perhaps not so much a safety play as an example of good technique. If you need four tricks the correct line is to cash the ace and follow it with the four intending to play the queen if West plays a small card. At first glance it may seem to be a guess whether to play the queen or the ten. However, if the ten loses to king doubleton you will still lose a trick to West's jack, while if the queen drops East's jack doubleton you have succeeded in restricting your losers to one.

Patrick Jourdain, playing in a Camrose match between Wales and England some years ago, made front-page news by handling this chestnut correctly in a slam:

♡ A 10 8 7 5 3

♡ 9   ♡ Q J 6 2

♡ K 4

This was the trump suit. The correct safety play is to lead the ten and let it run. When this successfully pinned the singleton nine with West (Graham Kirby), the VuGraph audience was most impressed.

My next example has stuck in my mind because I saw a very good player mishandle the combination when it was his trump suit in a grand slam.

♣ A K 7 6 4

♣ Q 8 5 3   [   ]   ♣ —

♣ J 10 9 2

The point is that you get a nasty shock if you do what the declarer did, which was to play the jack and go up with king when West played low.

Here is one final example:

♡ K J 8 4

♡ 10 9 7 6   [   ]   ♡ Q 3

♡ A 5 2

If you need four tricks then you will have to finesse and hope West has the queen and the suit is 3-3. If three tricks will be enough, then you should play low to the king and then back to the ace intending to lead towards the jack if the queen has not appeared.

Ducking play

It is never easy to resist the temptation to win a trick when you can beat the defender's card. However, there are many occasions when ducking is the only way to succeed.

Here is a simple example based on a hand described to me by one of the world's best analysts, Martin Hoffman.

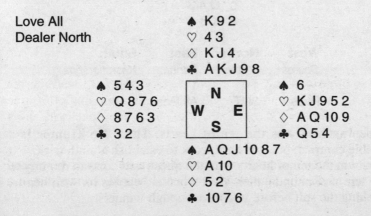

Love All
Dealer North

♠ K 9 2
♡ 4 3
◇ K J 4
♣ A K J 9 8

♠ 5 4 3   ♠ 6
♡ Q 8 7 6   ♡ K J 9 5 2
◇ 8 7 6 3   ◇ A Q 10 9
♣ 3 2   ♣ Q 5 4

♠ A Q J 10 8 7
♡ A 10
◇ 5 2
♣ 10 7 6

West	North	East	South
—	1♣	1♡	1♠
2♡	2♠	Pass	4♠
All Pass			

West led the six of hearts and declarer took East's king with the ace. He drew trumps and ran the ten of clubs. East won with the queen and played a heart to West's queen. The inevitable diamond switch spelt the defeat of the contract.

Can you see declarer's mistake?

All he has to do is duck the first heart. Now East has no way to get West in for the killing diamond lead, and declarer can develop the club suit at his leisure.

This deal from the 1998 European Junior Championships in Vienna demonstrates a more sophisticated form of hold-up.

North-South Game ♠ A K 5 2
Dealer North ♡ 8
  ◇ 10 9 7 6
  ♣ A Q J 7

♠ Q J 9 4   ♠ 8 7
♡ 10 9 2   ♡ K J 5 4 3
◇ K   ◇ A J 8 5 2
♣ 9 6 5 3 2   ♣ 10

  ♠ 10 6 3
  ♡ A Q 7 6
  ◇ Q 4 3
  ♣ K 8 4

West	North	East	South
Soares	*Mathisen*	*Fanha*	*Kristofferson*
—	1◇	1♡	2NT
Pass	3NT	All Pass	

The opening lead was the ten of hearts. Three No Trumps is a reasonable contract, but it is hard work to establish a ninth trick.

If you win the ten of hearts with the queen and cross to dummy to run the ten of diamonds, then West wins and carries on with hearts, establishing the suit before you have enough winners.

Say you win the second heart. This is no good as West will still
be able to play a heart when he wins with the king of diamonds.

Roderigo Soares found the star play of ducking two rounds of
hearts! Winning the third round, he crossed in clubs to run the ten
of diamonds. West won, but had no heart left, and now declarer
could establish his ninth trick in comfort.

Tackling trumps

The correct management of the trump suit is of the utmost
importance. We have seen some examples of the techniques
available.

In the 1996 Junior European Championships in Cardiff, the
games room contained a pinball machine called "The Theatre of
Magic" on which the balls vanished and then magically re-appeared
all over the place. On this deal, the declarer may have been
practising on the machine, as he indulged in a little magic of his
own.

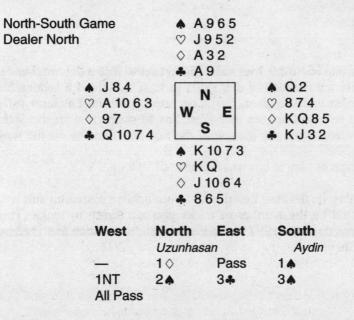

North-South Game
Dealer North

```
                    ♠ A 9 6 5
                    ♡ J 9 5 2
                    ◇ A 3 2
                    ♣ A 9
  ♠ J 8 4                          ♠ Q 2
  ♡ A 10 6 3          N            ♡ 8 7 4
  ◇ 9 7          W        E        ◇ K Q 8 5
  ♣ Q 10 7 4          S            ♣ K J 3 2
                    ♠ K 10 7 3
                    ♡ K Q
                    ◇ J 10 6 4
                    ♣ 8 6 5
```

West	North	East	South
	Uzunhasan		Aydin
—	1◇	Pass	1♠
1NT	2♠	3♣	3♠
All Pass			

West's bid promised hearts and clubs, at least 4-4. He led the four
of clubs and Ercan Aydin won with dummy's ace. Declarer then led
the two of hearts to his king. West took the trick with the ace and

returned the nine of diamonds ducked to East's queen. The club
return went to West's ten and he played a second diamond, declarer
winning with the ace in dummy.

Declarer led a heart to his queen, ruffed a club, cashed the jack of
hearts pitching a diamond and led dummy's last heart, ruffing in
hand while East pitched a diamond.

This was the ending:

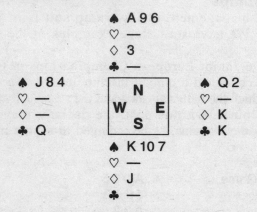

```
              ♠ A 9 6
              ♡ —
              ◇ 3
              ♣ —
♠ J 8 4                      ♠ Q 2
♡ —          ┌─────────┐     ♡ —
◇ —          │    N    │     ◇ K
♣ Q          │  W   E  │     ♣ K
             │    S    │
             └─────────┘
              ♠ K 10 7
              ♡ —
              ◇ J
              ♣ —
```

Declarer had lost three tricks and looked set to lose a diamond and a
trump. He led the jack of diamonds to East and all of a sudden his
trump loser had vanished. Say East returns a club. Declarer ruffs
with the seven of spades and West has to overruff with the jack.
Now declarer wins the trick with the ace and finesses on the way
back.

This type of play is known as the Devil's Coup.

It will often be the case that the way you tackle a particular suit will
be affected by the number of tricks you are trying to make. This
hand came up at the 1997 Malta Festival and was much analyzed by
Robert Sheehan.

Game All
Dealer North

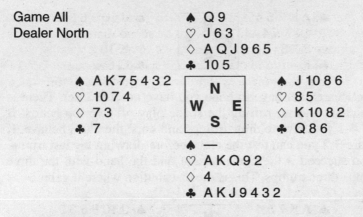

♠ Q 9
♡ J 6 3
◇ A Q J 9 6 5
♣ 10 5

♠ A K 7 5 4 3 2
♡ 10 7 4
◇ 7 3
♣ 7

♠ J 10 8 6
♡ 8 5
◇ K 10 8 2
♣ Q 8 6

♠ —
♡ A K Q 9 2
◇ 4
♣ A K J 9 4 3 2

This type of hand poses many questions.

For instance, should North open the bidding? Perhaps the ideal start would be a weak Two Diamonds, but that might not be available.

If the auction starts 1◇ – Pass – 2♣, how many spades should West bid?

Probably the majority vote for action on the West hand would be Three Spades. It is generally a good idea to crowd the auction, but this can assist declarer in the play.

Assuming East-West don't sacrifice in spades, how should South tackle the play in Six or Seven Hearts?

The correct play in Six is not the same as in Seven!

The technique in Six Hearts is to ruff the spade lead and play the ace of hearts. If all follow you are laydown if the clubs are no worse than 3-1. The trap is to continue to draw trumps. That will put you out of control if you have to lose a club trick and trumps are 4-1.

You should play off the ace of clubs and, if the queen doesn't fall play the king of clubs before drawing any more trumps. If someone ruffs the second club you are in control to ruff your third club with the jack of hearts and return to hand with a trump to draw the remainder and cash your winners.

This is the distribution of the East-West cards you are guarding against:

In Seven Hearts you have to hope you have no club loser. There is an extra chance. After ruffing the spade play off two top hearts. If they are 4-1 you have to draw trumps and hope the clubs behave. If trumps are 3-2 you can test the clubs before drawing the last trump. Then you succeed if the clubs are 3-1 and the hand with the three clubs holds three trumps. This is the distribution where it gains.

It looks risky to play on clubs before drawing all the trumps, but if the clubs behave it is no cost. If they don't you have extra chances.

Although I have already said that no special knowledge of the subject is required, there is no doubt that my final topic can give rise to some of the most interesting situations at the table, and the concept will allow many a contract that looks doomed to be made.

Squeeze play

I don't believe it is necessary for a player to have a special understanding of this aspect of the game. If you get hooked on the subjet there are plenty of books to help you on your way.

In its simplest form, an opponent is forced to throw away winning or potentially winning cards. The late Terence Reese wrote that it could not be "picked up" but had to be learned. I don't think that is necessarily correct, but it does help if you understand the mechanics of a squeeze.

The main point is that the combined holdings in the declarer's hand and dummy may be too much for one opponent, as between them those two hands contain twice as many cards as a single one. The combined holding may sometimes be too much for both opponents.

This simple ending illustrates the point:

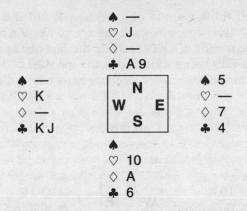

As you can see, West has to look after both hearts and clubs.

When South plays the ace of diamonds West has no safe discard. As a chess player would say, he is in "Zugzwang".

This hand was played at the 1999 World Junior Camp in Nymburk, Czech Republic.

	♠ J 8 6 3	
East-West Game	♡ A K 8 6	
Dealer South	◇ 10	
	♣ A K 10 8	

♠ A K 9		♠ 2
♡ 10 4	N	♡ Q J 5 3 2
◇ Q J 8	W E	◇ K 7 5 3
♣ Q 9 7 6 3	S	♣ J 4 2

	♠ Q 10 7 8 4	
	♡ 9 7	
	◇ A 9 8 4 2	
	♣ 5	

West	North	East	South
—	—	—	2♠
Pass	4◇	Pass	4♠
All Pass			

When West led the ten of hearts, declarer played on cross-ruff lines and emerged with eleven tricks.

It looks as if three rounds of spades will put the contract in jeopardy but declarer can win, cash the ace of diamonds, and ruff a diamond. Three rounds of clubs, ruffing the last one and a diamond exit will lead to East being squeezed in the red suits.

This will be the position when declarer exits with a diamond.

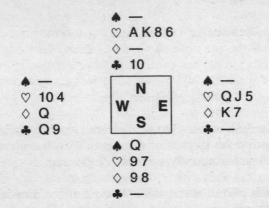

If West exits with a heart declarer wins in the dummy and plays the ten of clubs intending to ruff it. If East discards the king of diamonds then declarer's nine will score. If he parts with a heart then declarer will score three tricks in that suit.

This tragedy occurred in the 1998 IOC Grand Prix, played in the Olympic Museum in Lausanne.

North-South game
Dealer West

```
              ♠ K J 10 9
              ♡ A K Q 10 8
              ◇ 3
              ♣ K Q 7
  ♠ A 7 6 5        N        ♠ 4 2
  ♡ 7 3                     ♡ J 6 4 2
  ◇ 7          W     E      ◇ K J 10 9 8 5
  ♣ 10 9 8 6 5 4    S       ♣ 2
              ♠ Q 8 3
              ♡ 9 5
              ◇ A Q 6 4 2
              ♣ A J 3
```

West	North	East	South
Perron	*Failla*	*Chemla*	*Attanasio*
Pass	1♣	3◇	Double
Pass	3♡	Pass	4NT
Pass	5♡	Pass	6NT
All Pass			

North's One Club opening promised 17 or more points.

West cashed the ace of spades and continued the suit.

Declarer has ten top tricks and needs to find two more. The king of diamonds is clearly in the East hand so a finesse in that suit will bring declarer's total up to eleven. The twelfth trick will probably have to come from the heart suit.

The natural line of play for declarer is to cash the winners in the black suits before doing anything else.

This will help him to form a picture of the unseen hands.

When East discards on the second round of clubs and the third round of spades West is known to have started with ten black cards and cannot therefore have four hearts to the jack. Declarer can afford to test the suit by cashing the ace, king and queen. If the jack does not fall then only East can have it and he will have been squeezed when the black suits were cashed.

A finesse in diamonds will see declarer making the last three tricks in that suit.

East could see what was going to happen and he discarded four diamonds. Declarer now took the winning diamond finesse and cashed the ace. Losing concentration, he had miscounted the suit and did not realize he could cash another trick in the suit. He now played on hearts and had to concede a trick to East's jack.

The Hackett twins have a deserved reputation for aggressive bidding. Take a look at this deal from the 1998/99 British Premier League.

North-South Game
Dealer North

```
                    ♠ K 10 9 5
                    ♡ 2
                    ◇ A 9 7 5
                    ♣ A K 8 4
♠ Q J 8 6 4 2    ┌─────────┐    ♠ A 7 3
♡ K              │    N    │    ♡ 9 5 4
◇ Q J 6          │ W     E │    ◇ 10 2
♣ Q 7 3          │    S    │    ♣ 10 9 6 5 2
                 └─────────┘
                    ♠ —
                    ♡ A Q J 10 8 7 6 3
                    ◇ K 8 4 3
                    ♣ J
```

West	North	East	South
Thomas	*Jason*	*Goodman*	*Justin*
—	1♣	Pass	1♡
3♠	Pass	4♠	6♡
Pass	Pass	6♠	Pass
Pass	Double	All Pass	

At –1400 this "save" didn't have the appearance of being a bargain.
A preliminary analysis suggested that unless declarer had dropped
the king of trumps offside, Six Hearts would have failed.

However, if West leads the queen of spades, declarer can get
home. If he places the diamond length with West, the lead is
covered by both dummy and East, and declarer ruffs. He crosses to
dummy with the king of clubs and discards a diamond on the ace.
He then takes the losing heart finesse. West wins but will
subsequently find himself squeezed in spades and diamonds when
declarer runs the trumps. If declarer decides it is more likely that
East has the diamond length, he plays low on the first spade and
then it is East who is squeezed.

This hand comes from the 1997 Generali European Championships.

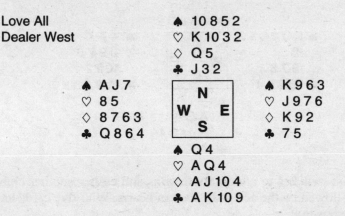

Love All
Dealer West

```
                    ♠ 10 8 5 2
                    ♡ K 10 3 2
                    ◇ Q 5
                    ♣ J 3 2
    ♠ A J 7           N         ♠ K 9 6 3
    ♡ 8 5                       ♡ J 9 7 6
    ◇ 8 7 6 3       W     E     ◇ K 9 2
    ♣ Q 8 6 4         S         ♣ 7 5
                    ♠ Q 4
                    ♡ A Q 4
                    ◇ A J 10 4
                    ♣ A K 10 9
```

At most of the tables Three No-Trumps was played from the South hand. Declarers who received a diamond lead were in no difficulty, being able to set up three club tricks to go with a similar number in both red suits.

For example, Russia's Helena Maitova simply played the nine of clubs from hand. It held, of course.

It was rather different when her compatriot, Andrew Choudnev, was playing against Portugal. He selected as his opening lead the jack of spades! Frightened that West held J-x, declarer ducked and it was now a simple matter for the defenders to take three more tricks in the suit. East, Gromov, exited with a club and declarer went one down. +50 went well with the +430 recorded at the other table.

Considering the hand for inclusion in this book, it struck me that it was not quite so simple. Between them, South and West have to find some discards. Say declarer parts with a couple of clubs and West throws a heart. That leaves the following:

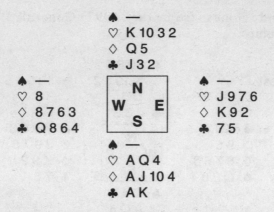

When East switches to a club South wins and cashes another club. That is followed by the ace and queen of hearts. With five cards left this is the position:

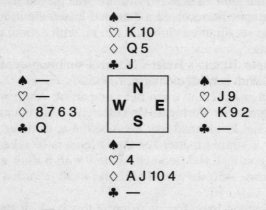

When declarer plays a heart to dummy's king West is not well placed. If he parts with a diamond then declarer will take four tricks in the suit via the finesse.

The previous examples have illustrated the situation where one defender is in trouble. Sometimes both can feel the pressure.

Love All
Dealer South

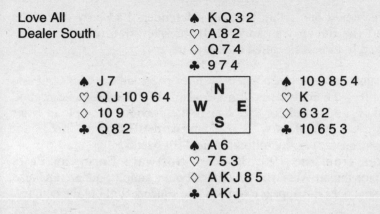

When South opened Two No-Trumps, North looked for a major-suit fit before settling in Six No-Trumps. West led the queen of hearts and declarer could see that there were eleven tricks on top with the obvious chance of a twelfth coming via the club finesse. When you are only one trick short of the number required for your contract a squeeze may be one possible answer. Here it costs nothing for declarer to duck the opening lead. East won with the king of hearts and switched to the ten of spades. Declarer won and set about cashing his winners. With everyone down to five cards this was the position:

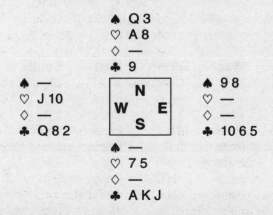

When declarer cashed dummy's ace of hearts East could not afford to part with a spade and so had to throw a club, South and West following suit. When the queen of spades was cashed West could not discard the master heart and he too had to release a club. Now declarer could be certain that both defenders had only two clubs left, so the queen was sure to drop. Each defender had been squeezed in turn, a so-called double squeeze.

Most squeezes take place when declarer needs all the tricks but one and, unless the contract is a grand slam, it will usually be a good idea to give up a trick, or tricks, as in the previous example in order to leave the defenders with no spare cards. However, this is not always necessary as the following deal illustrates.

Taken from the 1999 Prokom Software European Pairs Championship in Warsaw it illustrates both a simple squeeze and also a play that does not appear too often, the squeeze without the count.

East-West Game
Dealer East

	♠ K 9 6
	♡ A 9 8 5 4
	◇ K Q 9 4
	♣ A

West		East
♠ Q J 10 7	**N**	♠ 8 5 4 3 2
♡ K 10 2	**W E**	♡ Q 7
◇ J 3	**S**	◇ 8
♣ Q 9 8 6		♣ 10 7 5 4 2

	♠ A
	♡ J 6 3
	◇ A 10 7 6 5 2
	♣ K J 3

West	North	East	South
	Chodorowski		*Chodorowska*
—	—	Pass	1◇
Pass	1♡	Pass	2◇
Pass	2♠	Pass	2NT
Pass	3◇	Pass	3♡
Pass	4♣	Pass	4♠
Pass	4NT	Pass	5♡
Pass	6NT	All Pass	

Six Diamonds is the simple slam, a club ruff providing the twelfth trick. However, Jan Chodorowski was looking for one more top and the form of scoring persuaded him to try for the higher-scoring denomination.

West led the queen of spades and Irena Chodorowska won in hand, crossed to a diamond and played a low heart from dummy. East produced the seven and that was allowed to hold the trick. It was not easy for East to break up the impending squeeze by playing back the queen of hearts and, when he continued with a spade, the hand was quickly over. Declarer won in dummy, cashed the ace of clubs, and reeled off the diamonds. The last one was too much for West and he returned his cards to the board.

An alternative line is for declarer to cash the ace of clubs at trick two and then run all the diamonds. Assuming you can read the ending that will always work if the opening lead is from Q-J-10 of spades and West also has the queen of clubs. You will be able to cross to dummy with the ace of hearts and endplay West by playing king and another spade.

A close relative of the squeeze without the count is the stepping-stone.

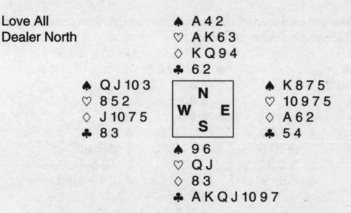

Love All
Dealer North

                    ♠ A 4 2
                    ♡ A K 6 3
                    ◇ K Q 9 4
                    ♣ 6 2

♠ Q J 10 3   ♠ K 8 7 5
♡ 8 5 2   N   ♡ 10 9 7 5
◇ J 10 7 5   W   E   ◇ A 6 2
♣ 8 3   S   ♣ 5 4

                    ♠ 9 6
                    ♡ Q J
                    ◇ 8 3
                    ♣ A K Q J 10 9 7

Of course, Six Clubs is an easy contract, but at one table the North-South pair lost their way and ended up in Six No-Trumps.

After an opening spade lead, declarer wins with the ace, and cashes all his club winners, reducing everyone to five cards.

This is the position with East still to play:

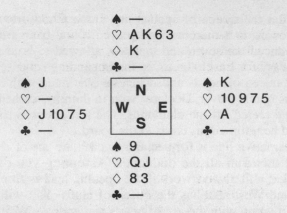

If East discards a heart or a diamond dummy will always make four tricks. The best he can do is throw a spade. But now declarer cashes the queen and jack of hearts and plays a diamond. East must win and give dummy the last two tricks.

This is another example of the squeeze in action. It comes from the 1996 EC Championships in Ostend.

Game All
Dealer North

♠ Q J 10 6 5
♡ 8 5
♢ 9 8 7
♣ 9 6 4

♠ 9 8 3 2
♡ Q 10 6
♢ A 6 3 2
♣ K 8

♠ A
♡ J 9 4 2
♢ 10 5 4
♣ J 10 7 3 2

♠ K 7 4
♡ A K 7 3
♢ K Q J
♣ A Q 5

West	North	East	South
	Handley		*Landy*
—	Pass	Pass	2NT
Pass	3♡	Pass	3♠
Pass	3NT	Pass	4♠
All Pass			

West led a trump to East's ace and East switched to a diamond. West won with the ace and played a second trump to declarer's king. Sandra Landy drew the remaining trumps, discarding a club from her hand to reach the following position:

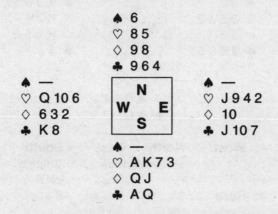

```
                    ♠ 6
                    ♡ 8 5
                    ◇ 9 8
                    ♣ 9 6 4
    ♠ —                           ♠ —
    ♡ Q 10 6        N             ♡ J 9 4 2
    ◇ 6 3 2      W     E          ◇ 10
    ♣ K 8           S             ♣ J 10 7
                    ♠ —
                    ♡ A K 7 3
                    ◇ Q J
                    ♣ A Q
```

There was no rush for declarer to take the club finesse as she could always get back to dummy by ruffing a heart. She simply cashed the queen and jack of diamonds. If East discards a heart on the second of these then declarer can establish a tenth trick by playing three rounds of hearts, so East had to release another club.

Sandra was sure that East had started with five clubs and four hearts and simply played the ace and queen of clubs establishing dummy's nine as the all-important tenth trick.

A small deception in the bidding led North astray on this deal from the 1999 Prokom Software European Pairs Championship in Warsaw and gave declarer the chance to execute a rare type of squeeze.

North-South Game
Dealer East

♠ Q 10 7 6 4 2
♡ A 10 3
◇ 10 4
♣ K 10

♠ 9 3
♡ 8 5 4 2
◇ J 6
♣ J 8 6 5 2

```
      N
   W     E
      S
```

♠ K J 8 5
♡ K 7 6
◇ K 8 5 3
♣ 4 3

♠ A
♡ Q J 9
◇ A Q 9 7 2
♣ A Q 9 7

West	North	East	South
	Saelendsminde		*Tislevoll*
—	—	Pass	2NT
Pass	3♡	Pass	3♠
Pass	3NT	All Pass	

The attractions of opening an off-centre Two No-Trumps are not entirely clear, but it was quite a popular action. North did well not to insist on a spade contract and West led a small club. That was a good start for declarer, who won with dummy's ten and ran the ten of diamonds to West's jack. He won the club continuation with the king and played a diamond to the nine. He then cashed the ace of diamonds and exited in that suit. If East had been certain of his partner's distribution he would have switched to a spade. However, it was hard to credit declarer with a singleton spade after the opening bid and he fatally preferred the other major.

Declarer won in hand with the queen and started to cash his minor-suit winners. This was the four-card ending:

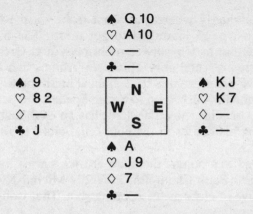

```
              ♠ Q 10
              ♡ A 10
              ◇ —
              ♣ —
  ♠ 9                        ♠ K J
  ♡ 8 2       ┌─────────┐    ♡ K 7
  ◇ —         │    N    │    ◇ —
  ♣ J         │  W   E  │    ♣ —
              │    S    │
              └─────────┘
              ♠ A
              ♡ J 9
              ◇ 7
              ♣ —
```

The ten of hearts was discarded on the winning seven of diamonds, leaving East with no good discard. This type of ending is known as a criss-cross squeeze.

My next example illustrates the fact that you may sometimes have to decide if the squeeze you have been playing for has operated.

Unless you have been living in a monastery or a convent for the last couple of years, you will be aware that bridge is inexorably moving towards inclusion in the Winter Olympics. One of the sports already there is ice-skating. That sport has a unique method of scoring, awarding points for technical merit and artistic impression.

One could easily award points in those categories on a number of bridge hands. Take for example this deal from the 1999 Generali European Open Teams Championship in Malta.

```
Game All          ♠ A J 8 6
Dealer North      ♡ A
                  ◇ A K Q 7 5
                  ♣ 7 6 3
  ♠ 10 5                        ♠ 9 7 4
  ♡ K 6 5 3     ┌─────────┐     ♡ J 9 8 7 4
  ◇ 10 9 6 3    │    N    │     ◇ 8 2
  ♣ K 5 2       │  W   E  │     ♣ Q J 9
                │    S    │
                └─────────┘
                  ♠ K Q 3 2
                  ♡ Q 10 2
                  ◇ J 4
                  ♣ A 10 8 4
```

Six Spades is clearly where you want to be on the North-South cards and most pairs managed to get there. The most notable exception was the match between Germany and Great Britain in which the teams reached only Three No-Trumps and Four Spades respectively. Not many marks for technical merit there.

A number of pairs pushed on to Seven Spades.

On a trump or a heart lead declarer has an easy route to thirteen tricks by using his entries in diamonds and clubs to ruff his losing hearts.

The one lead that dooms the slam at trick one is a club, so full marks to World Pairs Champion Poland's Michal Kwiecien who selected the five of clubs as his opening shot. That would be hard to beat for technical merit.

The only alternative remaining is a diamond. Two declarers, Frank Multon of France and Sweden's Tommy Gullberg, were faced by that opening salvo from West.

Multon won in hand, crossed to the ace of hearts and came back to hand with a trump. He now played the queen of hearts and ran it. A practical approach to a nasty problem that paid a huge dividend. Still, it would be difficult to give it much of an award for technical merit or artistic impression.

It is not immediately obvious that declarer has any legitimate line for the contract but Gullberg realized he could do it if either opponent held at least four clubs and the king of hearts.

If clubs are 3-3 then the heart honours have to be divided, with the king on the left and the jack to the right. In this case a double ruffing squeeze with a smother play in hearts (eventually pinning the jack) is the answer! Well, that is not encountered every day and would surely score a maximum for artistic impression.

This is the type of ending declarer must envisage:

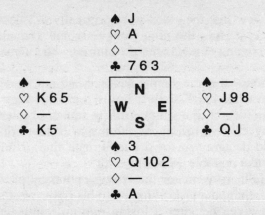

Both defenders have been forced to keep three hearts to prevent the ruffing/pinning variations. Now a club to the ace, a heart back to dummy and a club ruff scores +2210 and probably collects some prize for both player and writer as well as the Michelangelo award for artistic impression.

Gullberg won the first trick with the jack of diamonds and drew trumps.

On the third round of trumps, West discarded a club, a play that had significant ramifications later on. Declarer then played off his diamond winners finding they were 4-2, with East discarding hearts as West followed suit. On the last diamond, East gave the matter a lot of thought and eventually discarded a third heart. Meanwhile declarer has to pitch his small clubs.

This was the position and declarer had to decide how to proceed.

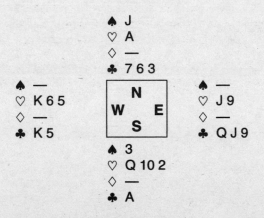

Taking the view that the clubs were originally 3-3 declarer cashed the heart ace, getting the nine from East and a small card from West. After coming to hand with the club ace "the moment of truth" had arrived.

Declarer knew that the simple squeeze had not worked but what happened at trick four? If East holds the heart king, then West subjected his partner to a simple ruffing squeeze by letting go of a club. Playing the ten, ruffing in dummy, will now bring down the king. Should declarer go for the legitimate line or rely on "table presence" and a possible defensive error?

Finally, Gullberg went for the wrong option by playing the ten, painfully watching the jack flying by to his right. West's "innocent" discard had given declarer a losing option. South will probably never get closer to a "maximum" for both technical merit and artistic impression.

Having told you how to make contracts I'm now going to show you how to break them!

TIME TO DEFEND

To be a good defender you need to be able to do many things: communicate with your partner by means of a signalling method; listen to the bidding and use the information to help you with the opening lead; and try to ascertain the distribution of declarer's hand and the number of points it contains.

It sounds difficult but it's really not complicated – all it takes is the ability to count up to thirteen and a lot of concentration.

I'll start by looking at the area where the defenders can put declarer under pressure right from the start.

Opening leads
A player who always made the best opening lead would undoubtedly win every prize the game has to offer.

Millions of contracts are won and lost on the opening lead every year. If you keep your ears open you will rapidly become known as one of those defenders who hardly ever seems to make declarer a present of the contract at trick one.

Keeping in mind that good defending is often all about the giving and receiving of information, a lot of thought has been put into how the opening lead can be best used to obtain it.

In these modern times, the general view is that if you are leading from a suit headed by the A-K then you lead the ace if you want partner either to encourage or discourage; if you lead the king you are asking your partner to tell you how many cards you have in the suit led. It is possible to extend this agreement down to suits headed by the K-Q, the queen asking partner to give an attitude signal.

The British expert Tony Forrester made it very clear that the opening lead is one of the most dangerous moments for the defence. Although he would be the first person to make an attacking lead when the bidding called for it, his golden rule was: "Don't lead away from a king if you have any decent alternative". Following this rule has saved me a lot of tricks over the years and my files are not overflowing with deals where a contract that made would have been defeated if I had underled a king.

Generally speaking, experts don't like leading trumps, and the combination of that and Tony's principle placed two-time World Champion Sally Brock in an interesting situation when she found herself looking at this hand:

♠ 6
♡ K 8 7 2
♢ K J 6 3
♣ K 9 5 4

Her opponents were a mine of information, bidding 1♠ – 4♠, and she had to find a lead. Given the restraints – don't lead away from a king and think twice before leading a trump – she appeared to have an insoluble problem.

If, like Sally, you led a diamond then go to the top of the class for this was the full deal:

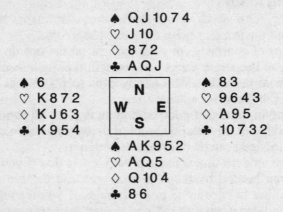

```
                    ♠ Q J 10 7 4
                    ♡ J 10
                    ◇ 8 7 2
                    ♣ A Q J
    ♠ 6                                ♠ 8 3
    ♡ K 8 7 2          N              ♡ 9 6 4 3
    ◇ K J 6 3      W       E          ◇ A 9 5
    ♣ K 9 5 4          S              ♣ 10 7 3 2
                    ♠ A K 9 5 2
                    ♡ A Q 5
                    ◇ Q 10 4
                    ♣ 8 6
```

Of course, she didn't simply close her eyes and hope for the best! She reasoned that if her partner held the queen of diamonds then leading that suit might set up two more tricks while a similar holding in either hearts or clubs would establish only one trick.

This deal from the 1999 Cap Gemini tournament in The Hague defeated many of the world's best players.

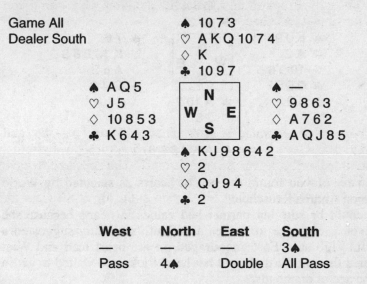

Game All
Dealer South

North
♠ 10 7 3
♡ A K Q 10 7 4
♢ K
♣ 10 9 7

West
♠ A Q 5
♡ J 5
♢ 10 8 5 3
♣ K 6 4 3

East
♠ —
♡ 9 8 6 3
♢ A 7 6 2
♣ A Q J 8 5

South
♠ K J 9 8 6 4 2
♡ 2
♢ Q J 9 4
♣ 2

West	North	East	South
—	—	—	3♠
Pass	4♠	Double	All Pass

Only one of the seven players who faced this lead problem selected a club. The others chose the jack of hearts for –790.

You know the raise to Four Spades is not based on wonderful trumps, so dummy probably has a good suit. That hardly figures to be clubs. If you are not sure, then the ace of spades will buy you time to check out the dummy and decide on your switch.

You can try the next hand as a problem.

♠ K J 9 8 4
♡ A 2
♢ 10 9 8 5
♣ 9 5

West	North	East	South
Rauscheid		*Nehmert*	
—	—	Pass	1♣
1♠	Double	1NT	Double
2♢	Pass	2♠	3NT
All Pass			

Dealer East
North-South Game

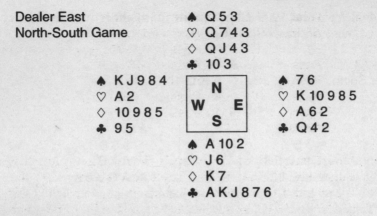

How many of you found the ace of hearts as selected by World Champion Andrea Rauscheid?

She could be sure her partner had values in hearts because she had given preference to spades and South's bidding suggested a powerful club suit. East encouraged on the heart lead and West continued the suit. East cleared her heart tricks and waited to get in with the ace of diamonds.

Pony Nehmert returned the compliment to her partner on this deal from the 1999 Generali European Women's Team Championship played in Malta.

Game All
Dealer North

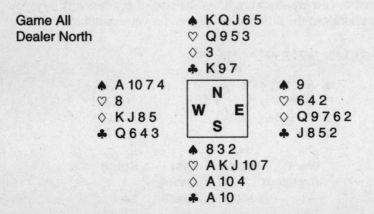

West	North	East	South
Nehmert	*Kara*	*Rauscheid*	*Aykut*
—	Pass	Pass	1NT
Pass	2♣	Pass	2♡
Pass	3♠	Pass	4♣
Pass	4◇	Pass	4NT
Pass	5◇	Pass	6♡
All Pass			

Pony Nehmert, another of Germany's World Championship winning team, heard North deny any key cards in response to the Four No-Trump bid. It was therefore just about a certainty that the king of spades would be in the North hand. She also knew her partner could not have much in the way of high cards. She led the ace of spades and, when her partner played the nine, she continued with a second spade defeating the slam.

In the other room West led a club and declarer had no problem in arriving at twelve tricks, ruffing two diamonds in the dummy and losing only to the ace of spades.

I have already mentioned that you need a good reason to lead away from a king. You need a very good reason to lead away from an ace, and even that is probably not enough. Look at this hand from the 1997 Bermuda Bowl in Tunisia.

East-West Game
Dealer South

```
                      ♠ 8 6 5
                      ♡ A 10 8 5
                      ◇ J 8 5
                      ♣ A K 2
  ♠ A J 10 9 4                      ♠ Q 7 2
  ♡ Q 9 6 4        N                ♡ K 7 3 2
  ◇ 7 3         W     E             ◇ Q 10 9
  ♣ J 5           S                 ♣ 9 8 7
                      ♠ K 3
                      ♡ J
                      ◇ A K 6 4 2
                      ♣ Q 10 6 4 3
```

Closed Room

West	North	East	South
Li	Soloway	Wang	Deutsch
—	—	—	1◇
1♠	Double	2♠	3♣
Pass	3♠	Pass	4♣
Pass	4◇	Pass	5◇
All Pass			

South had an awkward decision to make at his third turn. He had a spade stopper, but there were certainly layouts where Five of a Minor would be better than Three No-Trump, so he elected to bid out his shape.

It looked as if he was destined to go one down, but West led the ten of spades and, after winning with the king and cashing the ace and king of diamonds, declarer claimed his contract.

Open Room

West	North	East	South
Mahmood	Wang X	Rosenberg	Fu
—	—	—	1◇
1♠	Double	2♠	3♣
Pass	3♠	Pass	3NT
All Pass			

After a similar start to the bidding, South preferred the nine-trick game. He would have made it at most tables, as West led a spade, but Zia was not prepared to give a trick on the lead and he selected the four of hearts.

There was nothing declarer could do. He had eight tricks and no more. +50 and 10 IMPs for USA 1.

Some leads are simply brilliant. Take a look at this deal from the final of the 1997 European Mixed Teams Championship played in Monaco.

East-West Game
Dealer West

```
                    ♠ 10 8 6 3
                    ♡ K 4 2
                    ◇ K Q 9 2
                    ♣ A 8
   ♠ 9 2                              ♠ —
   ♡ 10 8 7 5          N              ♡ A Q J 9
   ◇ 10 8 4        W       E          ◇ A 7 6 3
   ♣ J 9 5 4           S              ♣ K Q 10 6 3
                    ♠ A K Q J 7 5 4
                    ♡ 6 3
                    ◇ J 5
                    ♣ 7 2
```

West	North	East	South
Nippgen	*Bessis*	*Auken*	*Bessis*
Pass	1◇	2♣	4♠
Pass	Pass	Double	All Pass

Georg Nippgen knew his partner's double was orientated for take-out but where could he go? It was unrealistic to expect Five Clubs to make so he decided to defend.

He found the brilliant lead of a heart – surely his partner had values there. Sabine Auken took the king with the ace and switched to the king of clubs to ensure one down.

West	North	East	South
Chemla	*von Arnim*	*Saul*	*Reps*
Pass	1NT	2♠	4♠
Pass	Pass	Double	All Pass

The "mini" 10-12 no-trump made no difference, as Two Spades had promised a club suit. West led the five of clubs and all declarer has to do is cover with the eight – do you remember the advice on ducking in the section on declarer play?

The point is that East cannot get West in to play a heart. At the table, Klaus Reps won with the ace of clubs and, when Saul came in with the ace of diamonds, she underled her club honours, putting West on play to make the killing switch to a heart.

Let me give you another problem to solve. It comes from the 1999 Cap Gemini tournament played in The Hague. Let me set the scene.

It's been a tough day. So far you have played 50 boards against some of the finest players in the world. This is your hand on number 51, and you are sitting West:

    ♠ 9 7 6
    ♡ K 7 6
    ◇ 10 8 6
    ♣ 8 7 4 3

It seems unlikely that you will have any significant contribution to make, but experience has frequently taught you otherwise. This turns out to be no exception!

West	North	East	South
—	—	—	1♣
Pass	1♡	2◇	Pass
Pass	Double	Redble	3♠
Pass	4♠	Double	All Pass

What are you going to lead? Get it right and you will be a star, go wrong and you will be just another extra.

I hope you selected the eight of clubs for this was the full deal:

Game All
Dealer North

            ♠ A 5 3 2
            ♡ Q 10 9 8
            ◇ 9 4
            ♣ K J 5

    ♠ 9 7 6   ♠ Q 10
    ♡ K 7 6   N   ♡ A J 5 4 2
    ◇ 10 8 6   W   E   ◇ A Q J 7 5 2
    ♣ 8 7 4 3   S   ♣ —

            ♠ K J 8 4
            ♡ 3
            ◇ K 3
            ♣ A Q 10 9 6 2

Your partner will ruff and routinely underlead the ace of hearts!

Don't worry if this proved to be too difficult to find – it defeated everyone faced by it at the table.

"Fourth best of your longest and strongest" is perhaps the best-known maxim in the game. It certainly worked well on this deal from the Brighton Summer Festival in 1997.

Game All
Dealer South

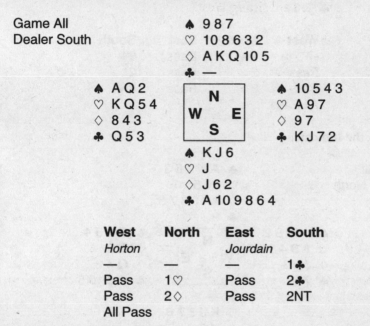

```
                    ♠ 9 8 7
                    ♡ 10 8 6 3 2
                    ◇ A K Q 10 5
                    ♣ —
   ♠ A Q 2                          ♠ 10 5 4 3
   ♡ K Q 5 4          N             ♡ A 9 7
   ◇ 8 4 3         W     E          ◇ 9 7
   ♣ Q 5 3            S             ♣ K J 7 2
                    ♠ K J 6
                    ♡ J
                    ◇ J 6 2
                    ♣ A 10 9 8 6 4
```

West	North	East	South
Horton		*Jourdain*	
—	—	—	1♣
Pass	1♡	Pass	2♣
Pass	2◇	Pass	2NT
All Pass			

West kicked off with the four of hearts.

Patrick Jourdain won with the ace of hearts and switched to the three of spades. Declarer put in the jack, which lost to the queen, and West continued with the five of hearts. Declarer might have reasoned that West must be strong in hearts to have selected that suit for the opening lead but, not unreasonably, he put in the eight of hearts which lost to the nine.

The four of spades from East now posed South an awkward question and playing the king was the wrong answer.

Two No-Trumps made – but by the defenders not the declarer!

The question of which particular card to lead from a suit is one that has posed a problem for bridge players through the ages. What would you lead from the West hand shown below?

♠ J 10 9 2
♡ A 9 4 3
◇ J 9 3
♣ 7 6

West	North	East	South
—	1♠	Pass	2♣
Pass	2◇	Pass	2♡
Pass	3◇	Pass	3NT
All Pass			

Here is the full deal:

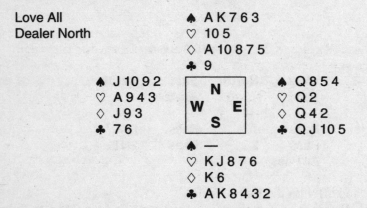

Love All
Dealer North

            ♠ A K 7 6 3
            ♡ 10 5
            ◇ A 10 8 7 5
            ♣ 9

♠ J 10 9 2   N   ♠ Q 8 5 4
♡ A 9 4 3   W   E   ♡ Q 2
◇ J 9 3   S   ◇ Q 4 2
♣ 7 6   ♣ Q J 10 5

            ♠ —
            ♡ K J 8 7 6
            ◇ K 6
            ♣ A K 8 4 3 2

A spade was the choice of the experts I asked and they all made the point that you might as well lead the two as the jack. After all, you are playing partner for a reasonable holding.

Declarer elected to play on clubs rather than hearts and the contract was defeated.

The message from this deal and the one that follows is simply this: "When the bidding seems to call for a particular suit to be led, don't be afraid to depart from conventional wisdom."

Geir Helgemo is indisputably one of the top players in the world, and he quite frequently produces IMPs out of thin air. His opening lead on this board, from Norway's match against Italy in the 1997 Bermuda Bowl in Tunisia, contributed greatly to Norway's impressive 22-8 win.

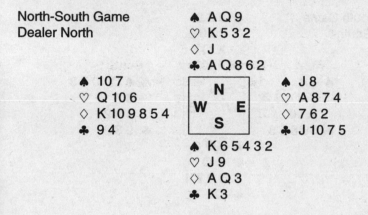

North-South Game
Dealer North

♠ A Q 9
♡ K 5 3 2
◇ J
♣ A Q 8 6 2

♠ 10 7
♡ Q 10 6
◇ K 10 9 8 5 4
♣ 9 4

♠ J 8
♡ A 8 7 4
◇ 7 6 2
♣ J 10 7 5

♠ K 6 5 4 3 2
♡ J 9
◇ A Q 3
♣ K 3

The Italians Versace & Lauria produced the following auction to end in the good contract of Six Spades:

North	South
1♣	1♠
2♡	2NT
3♡	3♠
4♣	4◇
4♡	4NT
5♠	6♠
Pass	

If I interpreted the Italian auction correctly, Two Hearts was artificial and a series of cuebids followed by RKCB led to the slam. Which card would you put on the table at trick one?

Geir Helgemo found the only lead to give Lorenzo Lauria a problem – the ten of hearts!

Lauria pondered for a considerable amount of time, and he finally concluded that Geir was clever enough to underlead the ace and so called for dummy's king. Tor Helness took his ace and quickly fired back a low heart to beat the slam; 17 IMPs to Norway.

The next deal comes from the 1997 Venice Cup and demonstrates the skill of the World and European Ladies Pairs Champions, Sabine Auken & Daniela von Arnim. It also illustrates the point that the bidding will sometimes serve as a beacon for the defender on lead.

North-South Game
Dealer South

	♠ 8 5 2	
	♡ 10 9 5	
	◇ K Q 6 5	
	♣ A K 7	

♠ J 4		♠ A Q 10 7 3
♡ K J 4 3 2	N	♡ 8 7
◇ A 10	W E	◇ 8 3 2
♣ 10 8 6 5	S	♣ 9 3 2

	♠ K 9 6	
	♡ A Q 6	
	◇ J 9 7 4	
	♣ Q J 4	

Open Room

West	North	East	South
	Gladiator		Vogt
—	—	—	1NT
Pass	3NT	All Pass	

Vogt & Gladiator play the weak no-trump and their simple auction gave the Italian West little information. She led a heart. Declarer won cheaply, knocked out the diamond ace, and later led towards the spade king for her ninth trick.

Closed Room

West	North	East	South
von Arnim		Auken	
—	—	—	1◇
1♡	Double	1♠	Pass
2♣	Double	Pass	2NT
Pass	3NT	All Pass	

At the other table, the strong no-trump was part of the North-South system, and a much more informative auction followed.

Daniela von Arnim therefore led the jack of spades and Sabine Auken carefully overtook it with the queen. Declarer was forced to duck this, or the defence could run the spades when they were in with the diamond ace. When the spade queen held, Auken, with no entry to her spades, switched smartly to a heart. Declarer played low and the jack won. Now von Arnim went back to spades. Auken won with the ace to play a second heart, establishing West's suit. When von Arnim won her ace of diamonds, she completed a devastating defence by cashing the rest of the hearts to put declarer three light.

Here is a final spectacular example from the 1999 World Junior Bridge Camp held in the Czech Republic.

```
Love All            ♠ A Q 6 3
Dealer East         ♡ K Q 10 5
                    ◇ Q 10 7 5
                    ♣ 6
  ♠ 7 4               ┌─────────┐        ♠ K J 10
  ♡ A 9 7 4 2         │    N    │        ♡ J 6 3
  ◇ K 8 4           W │ W     E │ E      ◇ J 9 6 2
  ♣ K 10 5            │    S    │        ♣ 8 4 2
                     └─────────┘
                    ♠ 9 8 5 2
                    ♡ 8
                    ◇ A 3
                    ♣ A Q J 9 7 3
```

West	North	East	South
—	—	Pass	1♣
Pass	1♡	Pass	1♠
Pass	2◇	Pass	3♣
Pass	3♠	Pass	3NT
All Pass			

West, Greece's Dimitri Ballas, found the devastating lead of the king of diamonds! That removed the entry to the club suit and left declarer with no way of making the contract.

Forcing declarer

If the defenders can successfully attack declarer's trump holding they may be able to gain control of the hand.

In 1997 the World Bridge Federation introduced a new form of contest, the World Transnational Teams Championship. This deal from the first event in Tunisia illustrates an important principle – when you have length in the trump suit, consider the possibility of a forcing defence.

```
East-West Game          ♠ 8 4
Dealer South            ♡ A K 2
                        ◇ 6 3
                        ♣ A K J 6 5 2
     ♠ K 9 5                              ♠ 10 7 3
     ♡ Q 8 6 5        ┌───────┐          ♡ 10
     ◇ J 9 8 7 2      │   N   │          ◇ A Q 10 5 4
     ♣ 9            W │       │ E        ♣ Q 7 4 3
                      │   S   │
                      └───────┘
                        ♠ A Q J 6 2
                        ♡ J 9 7 4 3
                        ◇ K
                        ♣ 10 8
```

Closed Room

West	North	East	South
Møller		*Schaffer*	
—	—	—	1♠
Pass	2♣	Pass	2♡
Pass	3◇	Double	3♡
Pass	4♡	All Pass	

Guided by the lead-directing double, Kirsten Steen Møller's opening salvo was the two of diamonds. Lauye Schaffer took his ace and returned the four of diamonds, ruffed by declarer, who played a heart to the ace and took a losing spade finesse. Now Kirsten found the killing defence of a third diamond, offering a ruff and discard!

This ensured that she would make two heart tricks and declarer soon conceded one down.

Open Room

West	North	East	South
	J Auken		*S Auken*
—	—	—	1♠
Pass	2♣	2♦	2♡
4♦	Double	Pass	4♡
All Pass			

Here West started with his singleton club, which gave Sabine Auken a
chance. She won with the king and took a losing spade finesse. West
switched to a diamond, taken by his partner, ruffed the club return and
exited with a diamond. Sabine ruffed and played a heart to the king.
When East's ten dropped, she returned to hand with the jack of spades
and considered the position. She knew East had four clubs, one heart
and at least five diamonds. He had followed to two spades, playing the
three and the seven. Weighing the evidence, she advanced the jack of
hearts, running it when West played low. +420 and 10 IMPs.

The defenders can also force dummy to ruff as in this deal from the
1997 Generali European Championships.

Game All
Dealer West

```
                    ♠ A 8 6 2
                    ♡ A Q
                    ◇ K Q 9 4 3
                    ♣ J 10
   ♠ 7                                ♠ Q J 10 9 5
   ♡ J 8 6 5         N               ♡ 10 3
   ◇ 8 6 5       W       E           ◇ J 7 2
   ♣ A K 7 5 3       S               ♣ Q 8 6
                    ♠ K 4 3
                    ♡ K 9 7 4 2
                    ◇ A 10
                    ♣ 9 4 2
```

West	North	East	South
Holowski	*Basalyga*	*Gotard*	*Sotniku*
Pass	1◇	Pass	1♡
Pass	2♠	Pass	3♣
Double	Pass	Pass	3♡
Pass	4♡	All Pass	

Andreas Holowski led the ace of clubs, his partner playing an upside-down count signal with the eight.

It seemed East would hold little in the way of high cards so the trump suit would have to provide the two extra tricks needed by the defence. He continued with the king of clubs and a third round of the suit, forcing dummy to ruff. When his partner turned up with the vital ten of hearts, West's vision was rewarded.

Deception

It is not only the declarer who can be deceptive as you will see from the following examples.

This is a situation that is worth knowing. It comes from the 1970 Spingold Teams.

```
Game All                    ♠ K J 10 8
Dealer North                ♡ K Q 4
                            ◇ A Q J 10
                            ♣ K 2
        ♠ 7 2             ┌─────────┐        ♠ A Q 6
        ♡ J 10 3 2        │    N    │        ♡ 9 8 7
        ◇ 9 7 6           │ W     E │        ◇ 8 4
        ♣ A J 10 7        │    S    │        ♣ Q 9 5 4 3
                          └─────────┘
                            ♠ 9 5 4 3
                            ♡ A 6 5
                            ◇ K 5 3 2
                            ♣ 8 6
```

West	North	East	South
—	1◇	Pass	1♠
Pass	4♠	All Pass	

West leads the jack of hearts. Declarer wins in hand to play a small spade to the jack. If East wins with the queen, declarer will use his remaining entry to hand, the king of diamonds, to lead towards the king of clubs. However, if East wins with the ace of spades, declarer will undoubtedly prefer to repeat the spade finesse. East will win and lock declarer in dummy with a heart. In due course, two club tricks will be lost and the contract will fail.

Here is a more recent example from the 1999 Generali European Bridge Championships. Guido Ferraro is well known as one of the best VuGraph commentators, usually spotting the winning line of play at a glance and frequently predicting a sparkling piece of play well in advance of its appearance on the table.

At these championships the boot was on the other foot, so to speak, as he was a member of the high-flying Italian team, thereby giving his fellow commentators a chance to see if he could practise what he preaches.

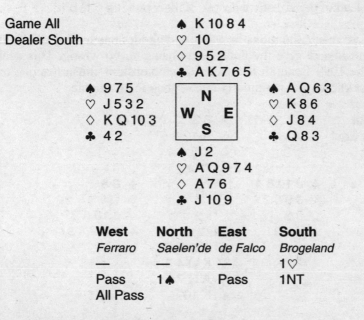

Game All
Dealer South

```
              ♠ K 10 8 4
              ♡ 10
              ◇ 9 5 2
              ♣ A K 7 6 5
♠ 9 7 5                        ♠ A Q 6 3
♡ J 5 3 2          N           ♡ K 8 6
◇ K Q 10 3     W       E       ◇ J 8 4
♣ 4 2              S           ♣ Q 8 3
              ♠ J 2
              ♡ A Q 9 7 4
              ◇ A 7 6
              ♣ J 10 9
```

West	North	East	South
Ferraro	*Saelen'de*	*de Falco*	*Brogeland*
—	—	—	1♡
Pass	1♠	Pass	1NT
All Pass			

Opening lead: queen of diamonds
Result: down one, Italy +50

When this result from the Closed Room appeared on the screen it caused some surprise. How can declarer possibly lose seven tricks?

An examination of the play record revealed the following. The opening lead was ducked, as was a second diamond that went to the jack. Declarer won the third diamond and ran the jack of clubs to East's queen. The eight of hearts was returned and when the queen held the contract was safe.

Looking for some extra tricks, declarer now ran the jack of spades. Ferraro, East, won with the *ace* and played the king of hearts. Winning in hand with the ace declarer played a second spade to the ten, taking the "marked" finesse. But East won and put his partner in with a heart to cash the thirteenth diamond, the seventh defensive trick. Do you blame declarer for being taken in? Notice that unblocking the eight of hearts would have produced another trick for the defence if West had held the seven.

In the other room declarer made nine tricks in Two No-Trumps on the lead of the six of spades, so Italy picked up 6 IMPs.

There are many situations in which a defender has to play the right card in order to give the declarer a chance to go wrong. This deal from the 1999 Generali European Championships illustrates one of the best known and potentially one of the most valuable.

Love All
Dealer East

```
                      ♠ 6 3
                      ♡ A 10 8 5
                      ◇ K 8 6 4
                      ♣ A Q 5
  ♠ J 10 8 4                            ♠ 9 5 2
  ♡ J 9 6 2        N                    ♡ 7
  ◇ 9 3         W     E                 ◇ J 10 5 2
  ♣ J 6 2          S                    ♣ 9 8 7 4 3
                      ♠ A K Q 7
                      ♡ K Q 4 3
                      ◇ A Q 7
                      ♣ K 10
```

West	North	East	South
Smith	*Gothe*	*Davies*	*Swanstrom*
—	—	Pass	2NT
Pass	3◇	Pass	3♡
Pass	3NT	Pass	4♣
Pass	4◇	Pass	4NT
Pass	5♡	Pass	7♡
All Pass			

North's Three Diamonds was a variation of the Stayman convention and her next bid of Three No-Trumps was a slam try agreeing

hearts as trumps. At the other table Great Britain had stopped in Six
No-Trumps so it looked as if Sweden would make a major gain.

West led the jack of spades and declarer won in hand and played
the king of hearts. West followed with the nine and East with the
seven. That gave declarer an option and she decided to play a low
trump. When West followed with the two of hearts declarer
realized that it was possible for West to hold J-9-6-2 but what if
she had 9-2 or even 9-6-2? When she put up the ace the grand slam
had to go down.

There are four points to consider. If West does not play the nine
then declarer cannot go wrong as she can only cope with four
trumps in the West hand. An expert West is three times more
likely to hold J-9-x-x and drop the nine than to hold the singleton
nine.

Notice East's card was the seven of hearts. If West has a singleton
then that is from J-7-6-2. The defender can only make this play
when the ten is in dummy. Why? Imagine what a disaster it would
be if your partner was looking at the singleton ten!

Here is another example of a defender outwitting declarer. It comes
from the 1996 Olympiad in Rhodes.

```
Game All              ♠ K 7 5
Dealer South          ♡ Q 9 3
                      ◇ J 9 4 2
                      ♣ J 4 2

    ♠ A                   N           ♠ J 10 9 8 3 2
    ♡ K J 8 7 6 5 4 2               ♡ —
    ◇ 10 3          W       E        ◇ 6
    ♣ 6 5                S           ♣ K Q 10 8 7 3

                      ♠ Q 6 4
                      ♡ A 10
                      ◇ A K Q 8 7 5
                      ♣ A 9
```

West	North	East	South
Buratti	*Robbins*	*Lanzarotti*	*Goldfein*
—	—	—	1◇
3♡	Pass	Pass	3NT
All Pass			

Buratti led the six of clubs on which his partner played the queen (yes, the queen).

Goldfein can hardly be blamed for misreading the position. He won with the ace and played a spade. Buratti won with the ace perforce and, for want of anything better to do, returned a club. When East produced the card he could not have, the ten of clubs, the contract was two down.

If East had played the ten of clubs at trick one declarer could hardly go wrong since it never costs to duck in case the suit happens to be 2-6.

Here is a fantastic piece of play from the 1999 Prokom Software European Pairs Championship played in Warsaw. This was perhaps the hand of the tournament. Bridge journalist Marc Smith was the man to get the story.

East-West Game		♠ K 8 6	
Dealer West		♡ J 3 2	
		◇ 10 9 8	
		♣ Q 8 7 3	

♠ A J		♠ 10 9 7 4 3 2
♡ Q 10 7 6	N	♡ 9 8 5
◇ J 5 3	W E	◇ K 7 6
♣ 9 5 4 2	S	♣ 10

	♠ Q 5	
	♡ A K 4	
	◇ A Q 4 2	
	♣ A K J 6	

Three No-Trumps was the universal contract. This was a typical auction:

West	North	East	South
Glowacki	*Svoboda*	*Szymborski*	*Kurka*
Pass	Pass	Pass	2♣
Pass	2◇	Pass	2NT
Pass	3NT	All Pass	

Glowacki made a bad start when he selected a heart. Declarer went up with the jack and ran the ten of diamonds to West's jack. It was now clear to Glowacki that at best his partner had the king of diamonds. Declarer must have the rest of the points. Realizing that desperate measures were called for he switched to the jack of spades!

Put yourself in South's position.

Taking a second diamond finesse now appears to put the contract at risk as West may win and play a second spade through dummy's king – hardly the result you were looking for having been gifted a trick by the opening lead. Seeing the possibility of an endplay, declarer won the trick with the queen of spades and cashed his winners in clubs and hearts before exiting with the ace and another diamond. East had to win and, as hoped, declarer had to lead a spade.

It was a bemused declarer who saw West produce the ace of spades and the thirteenth heart, thereby holding the contract to nine tricks. North-South were +400 but East-West had scored the matchpoints.

Now for one of the most amazing plays that has ever been seen. It comes from the Macallan International Pairs Championship played in London.

Game All
Dealer North

		♠ A K 8		
		♡ 7 2		
		◇ K Q 6		
		♣ Q 7 6 5 3		

♠ 6 4 3 2		**N**		♠ 9 7 5
♡ 9 8 6	**W**		**E**	♡ K Q J 5 4
◇ A 10 7 5		**S**		◇ J 3 2
♣ J 9				♣ K 4

		♠ Q J 10		
		♡ A 10 3		
		◇ 9 8 4		
		♣ A 10 8 2		

West	North	East	South
Goldman	*Replinger*	*Soloway*	*Mari*
—	1♣	1♡	2NT
Pass	3NT	All Pass	

West led the six of hearts and Christian Mari took the third round. His plan was to prevent East getting in to cash his heart winners.

He played a spade to dummy and led the queen of clubs. East covered with the king so Mari played the ace on which Goldman dropped the jack!

Placing East with an original club holding of K-9-4 Mari went back to the dummy with a spade and took the "marked" finesse, playing a club to his eight. Goldman won with the nine and played a spade. Now declarer had only eight tricks and when he played a diamond West won with the ace and cashed his remaining spade, the setting trick.

If West had played the nine on the first round of clubs declarer would have simply continued the suit, hoping West had both the jack of clubs and the ace of diamonds.

Goldman was so excited when his play worked that on winning with the nine of clubs he almost forgot to play a spade!

Suit-preference signals

Suit-preference signals are an important weapon in the defenders' armoury. The intelligent use of high and low cards can help the defence to defeat contract after contract. To an expert almost every card played has some meaning.

This is one of my favourite deals on the subject. It comes from the 1991 Bermuda Bowl in Yokohama.

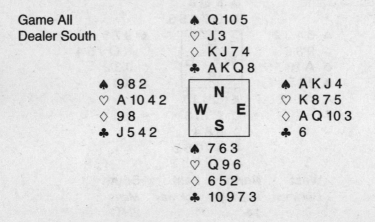

```
Game All            ♠ Q 10 5
Dealer South        ♡ J 3
                    ◇ K J 7 4
                    ♣ A K Q 8

        ♠ 9 8 2          N          ♠ A K J 4
        ♡ A 10 4 2                  ♡ K 8 7 5
        ◇ 9 8       W         E     ◇ A Q 10 3
        ♣ J 5 4 2        S          ♣ 6

                    ♠ 7 6 3
                    ♡ Q 9 6
                    ◇ 6 5 2
                    ♣ 10 9 7 3
```

West	North	East	South
Robson	*Meckstroth*	*Forrester*	*Rodwell*
—	—	—	Pass
Pass	1NT	Double	2♣
Double	All Pass		

Robson led the nine of diamonds and Tony Forrester took dummy's jack with the queen. He knew the lead must be either a singleton or a doubleton but before he gave his partner a ruff he carefully cashed the king of spades to make it clear he wanted a spade continuation. On this trick Robson played the two.

Forrester now cashed the ace of diamonds and followed it with the three, ruffed by West, who returned the nine of spades.

Forrester knew his partner had started with three spades and by playing back his highest spade at this point he was clearly showing something good in hearts. After cashing a third spade winner Forrester played a low heart to his partner's ace. He won the heart return and played his remaining diamond enabling East to score a further trick with the jack of clubs. That added up to a penalty of 1,100 points!

The principle is neatly illustrated by this deal from the 1998 Junior European Championships in Vienna.

North-South Game
Dealer North

```
                    ♠ J 9 3
                    ♡ A Q J 4
                    ◇ A K Q
                    ♣ K Q J
    ♠ A 7 4                         ♠ K Q 8 5 2
    ♡ 10 5         N                ♡ 9 8 6
    ◇ J 10 9 5 4   W   E            ◇ —
    ♣ A 10 4           S            ♣ 9 8 7 6 2
                    ♠ 10 6
                    ♡ K 7 3 2
                    ◇ 8 7 6 3 2
                    ♣ 5 3
```

West	North	East	South
Vreeswijk	*Kapala*	*Drijver*	*Buras*
—	2◇	Pass	2♡
Pass	2NT	Pass	3♣
Pass	3♡	Pass	4♡
Pass	Pass	Double	All Pass

There was nothing wrong with North-South's bidding but they were about to be punished by East's bold double.

West could tell from his hand that his partner must be hoping to ruff something so he led the jack of diamonds. Bas Drijver ruffed and, interpreting the jack of diamonds as an indication that West had something in the spades, boldly returned the eight of spades. His confidence was rewarded when his partner produced the ace. East ruffed the next diamond and cashed the king of spades.

Now came one of those lapses in concentration that I keep warning you about.

East was feeling pretty pleased with the success of his speculative double and hadn't noticed the diamond his partner had played on the previous trick. It was the four, and a club switch would have enabled his partner to give him a third ruff. East tried the queen of spades so declarer escaped for two down.

A defender should always think a problem through rather than blindly follow a signal.

Look at this deal from the 1997 Generali European Women's Team Championship.

Love All
Dealer North

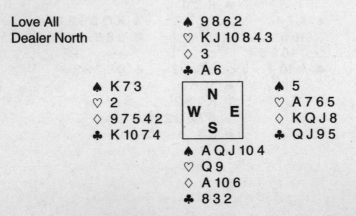

```
                    ♠ 9 8 6 2
                    ♡ K J 10 8 4 3
                    ◇ 3
                    ♣ A 6
      ♠ K 7 3                         ♠ 5
      ♡ 2              N              ♡ A 7 6 5
      ◇ 9 7 5 4 2    W   E           ◇ K Q J 8
      ♣ K 10 7 4       S             ♣ Q J 9 5
                    ♠ A Q J 10 4
                    ♡ Q 9
                    ◇ A 10 6
                    ♣ 8 3 2
```

West	North	East	South
Vriend	*Auken*	*v d Pas*	*von Arnim*
—	1♡	Pass	1♠
Pass	2♠	Pass	4♠
All Pass			

For an aggressive player like Sabine Auken, the North hand constitutes an automatic opening bid.

West led the four of clubs taken by dummy's ace. The spade finesse lost and West continued with the seven of clubs taken by East with the jack. The moment of truth had arrived. East thought the contract might depend on the heart guess, so she played the king of diamonds. Now declarer could draw trumps and concede a heart.

West	North	East	South
Rauscheid	*Pasman*	*Schreck'r*	*Simon*
—	Pass	1♢	1♠
3♢	4♢	Pass	4♠
All Pass			

Here North preferred to pass, hoping to be able to describe her hand later. A perfectly playable approach, but I recall the old adage, "Twice armed is she who's cause is just but three times armed is she who gets her blow in first!" Still the contract was the same.

West led her singleton heart and East won with the ace and returned the seven of hearts for West to ruff. West switched to a diamond and declarer was out of danger, being able to knock out the king of spades.

From East's point of view, her partner did not have to have the king of spades. If she had the ace of diamonds an underlead was vital.

But West could already see three tricks for her side. The ace of diamonds was unlikely to run away, but if a club trick needed to be established it was vital to switch to that suit immediately.

The lesson is not to rely entirely on signals – think the situation through.

A matter of entries

The defenders have to be wide awake, not only to preserve communications between themselves, but also to execute the types of play that can cause declarer a problem. You have already seen some of the spectacular plays that can be made.

This deal was played in the 1999 Prokom Software European Pairs Championship in Warsaw.

Followers of the Eurovision song contest will certainly remember the occasion when the Norwegian entry failed to score a point. An encounter between Germany and Norway saw an unfortunate pair from the Scandinavian country in a similar situation.

East-West Game
Dealer West

```
                        ♠ A 4 3 2
                        ♡ Q 4 3
                        ◇ 4 3
                        ♣ A J 10 4
        ♠ K 6                          ♠ Q 8 7
        ♡ A 6 5          N             ♡ J 2
        ◇ K Q 9 6 5    W   E           ◇ J 8 7
        ♣ 9 3 2          S             ♣ K Q 7 6 5
                        ♠ J 10 9 5
                        ♡ K 10 9 8 7
                        ◇ A 10 2
                        ♣ 8
```

West	North	East	South
Kondoch		*Kornek*	
1◇	Pass	1NT	2♡
Pass	4♡	Double	All Pass

An insurance company would not underwrite East's double but his partner justified his decision. Hartmut Kondoch led the king of diamonds and declarer ducked. The German pair was using the "obvious switch" method of signalling championed by Matthew & Pamela Granovetter. East had played the eight of diamonds and, interpreting that correctly, Kondoch smartly switched to the king of spades!

It created an entry to his partner's hand and, in the fullness of time, East came in with the queen of spades and gave his partner a spade ruff.

That was an entry-creating play and its close relative is the entry destroying play as demonstrated by the following deal from the 1999 Prokom Software European Pairs Championship.

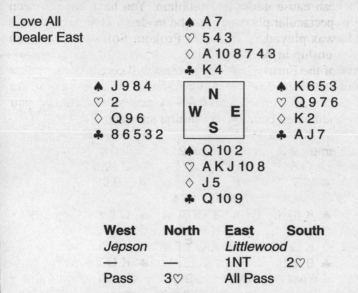

Love All
Dealer East

```
                    ♠ A 7
                    ♡ 5 4 3
                    ◇ A 10 8 7 4 3
                    ♣ K 4
  ♠ J 9 8 4                          ♠ K 6 5 3
  ♡ 2              N                 ♡ Q 9 7 6
  ◇ Q 9 6       W     E              ◇ K 2
  ♣ 8 6 5 3 2      S                 ♣ A J 7
                    ♠ Q 10 2
                    ♡ A K J 10 8
                    ◇ J 5
                    ♣ Q 10 9
```

West	North	East	South
Jepson		*Littlewood*	
—	—	1NT	2♡
Pass	3♡	All Pass	

The British pair sitting East-West had to work hard on this deal to secure an average, as the majority of the field played the North-South cards in game and usually went one down.

West led the six of diamonds against Three Hearts and declarer played low in dummy, allowing East to win with the king. Declarer should have unblocked the jack to make sure he could win a subsequent diamond in the dummy but, when he failed to do so, East was able to return the suit, forcing declarer to win in hand.

Declarer now played the ace, king and jack of hearts, putting East on play with the queen. Appreciating the danger posed by the diamond suit Peter Littlewood switched to the king of spades! The removal of the only certain entry to dummy left the fate of the contract dependent on declarer's view in the club suit.

The defenders were rewarded when, after winning with the ace of spades, declarer led the ace of diamonds from dummy, ruffed and overruffed. He now ran the ten of clubs. East won with the jack and switched to a spade. When the finesse of the ten lost to West's jack, the ace of clubs was the setting trick.

Avoiding the endplay

One of declarer's weapons is the threat to force a defender to make a damaging lead. It will sometimes be necessary for a defender to get rid of a high card in order to avoid the danger.

This illustrative deal comes from the 1998 IOC Grand Prix played in Lausanne.

```
East-West Game              ♠ 10 6
Dealer South                ♡ A K 9 7
                            ◇ A 6 4
                            ♣ K 9 3 2
    ♠ K 9 7 5 4 2    ┌─────────────┐    ♠ A J 8 3
    ♡ Q 4 3          │      N      │    ♡ J 5 2
    ◇ Q 8            │  W       E  │    ◇ J 10 5 2
    ♣ J 5            │      S      │    ♣ 10 6
                     └─────────────┘
                            ♠ Q
                            ♡ 10 8 6
                            ◇ K 9 7 3
                            ♣ A Q 8 7 4
```

West	North	East	South
Branco	*Hu*	*Chagas*	*Wang*
—	—	—	1♣
1♠	Double	2♠	Pass
Pass	3♠	Pass	4♣
Pass	5♣	All Pass	

Four Hearts is obviously a good contract on the North-South cards but difficult to reach. North might have tried Four Hearts over Four Clubs.

Apart from the small chance that the queen-jack of hearts are doubleton, Five Clubs appears to have little hope. There is only one real chance.

West leads a spade. East wins and plays a second spade ruffed by declarer, who then leads a heart to the king, a club to the queen, and a second heart to the ace. He now cashes a second trump and the top diamonds. If West is still in possession of the queen of hearts declarer can now exit with a heart, forcing West to win and concede a ruff and discard.

Did the brilliant Brazilian star Marcelo Branco allow himself to be endplayed? Well, even Homer is supposed to have nodded off once!

Pretending to have a doubleton

As you know, the general rule is to play high-low with a doubleton and low from an odd number. It can sometimes pay dividends to try to persuade the declarer that you are about to ruff.

Look at this deal from the match between USA1 and China in the 1997 Bermuda Bowl played in Tunisia.

```
North-South Game          ♠ 10 6 5 3
Dealer North              ♡ A K Q J 2
                          ◇ Q
                          ♣ K 5 4

     ♠ Q J              ┌──────────┐         ♠ A 2
     ♡ 9 7 6            │    N     │         ♡ 10 5 3
     ◇ K 9 8 6 4        │  W   E   │         ◇ 10 7 5
     ♣ 10 8 3           │    S     │         ♣ A Q 9 7 2
                        └──────────┘
                          ♠ K 9 8 7 4
                          ♡ 8 4
                          ◇ A J 3 2
                          ♣ J 6
```

The bidding was identical at both tables:

West	North	East	South
Li	Soloway	Wang	Deutsch
Mahmood	Wang X	Rosenberg	Fu
—	1♡	Pass	1♠
Pass	3♠	Pass	4♠
All Pass			

Li led the three of clubs and in no time at all Wang had cashed the queen and ace and played a third round. He went up with the ace of spades on the first round of the suit and played another club to promote his partner's jack of spades. Fantastic!

Seymon Deutsch joked later that once West had dropped the queen of spades under the ace he would have finessed on the next round! Of course, he knew East would not have played the ace from A-J-2.

Zia led ... the eight of clubs! Rosenberg took the queen and cashed the ace, Zia playing the three. Of course, he followed to the next round but just as in the other room the contract was now defeated by the promotion.

Underleading

When a defender wants to reach his partner's hand, he may have to resort to something dramatic.

When Mario Dix took out his cards on this deal from the third session of the Cara IMP Pairs in the 1998 World Championships in Lille he was looking forward to a delicate auction.

```
East-West Game        ♠ A 8 7 3
Dealer North          ♡ J 10 9 3
                      ◇ A Q J 4
                      ♣ 3
        ♠ 10 2                        ♠ J 5
        ♡ 7 6 4 2        N            ♡ A K Q 8 5
        ◇ 9 8 6 2    W       E        ◇ —
        ♣ 10 7 2        S            ♣ A K Q J 6 5
                      ♠ K Q 9 6 4
                      ♡ —
                      ◇ K 10 7 5 3
                      ♣ 9 8 4
```

West	North	East	South
Parnis-England		*Dix*	
—	1◇	6♣!	6◇
Pass	Pass	6♡!	6♠!!
Pass	Pass	Double	All Pass

As you can see things turned out rather differently!

Once North opened the bidding Mario decided to dispense with science. South was not going to risk Six Clubs being cold when his side clearly had a cheap save in diamonds. However, the man from Malta was not finished yet. He used the second string to his bow and tried for a different slam. North must have been itching to get his hands on Six Hearts but South was not going to let East have any fun and he tried for a different save.

After East had doubled, the spotlight went across the table to Margaret Parnis-England. She had a shrewd idea what was going on and she fished out the two of diamonds. Mario ruffed and, realizing that it takes something special to make the headlines, he returned the five of clubs! A surprised Margaret won with the ten and gave him another ruff.

The Zonal final of the J M Weston Mixed Pairs Championship in the World Championships played in Lille witnessed this hot defence from one of the leading Egyptian pairs.

East-West Game
Dealer South

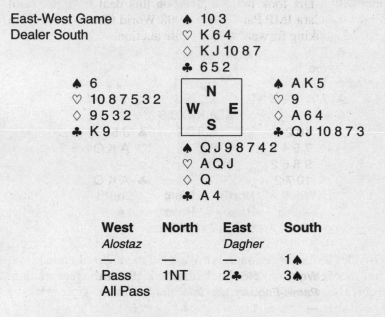

♠ 10 3
♡ K 6 4
◇ K J 10 8 7
♣ 6 5 2

♠ 6
♡ 10 8 7 5 3 2
◇ 9 5 3 2
♣ K 9

N
W   E
S

♠ A K 5
♡ 9
◇ A 6 4
♣ Q J 10 8 7 3

♠ Q J 9 8 7 4 2
♡ A Q J
◇ Q
♣ A 4

West	North	East	South
Alostaz		*Dagher*	
—	—	—	1♠
Pass	1NT	2♣	3♠
All Pass			

West started with the king of clubs and declarer, perhaps unwisely, elected to win at once with the ace. He played a trump to the ten and East won and switched to his singleton heart. Declarer won in hand and played the queen of spades. East won and had a delicate decision to make: who had the nine of clubs?

Reflecting on his partner's discard of the two of diamonds and the fact that at many tables the contract might well be Four Spades, Hani Dagher bravely underled his club honours. Moments later he was a happy man as his partner won and gave him a heart ruff.

This deal comes from the 1998 Brighton Summer Festival.

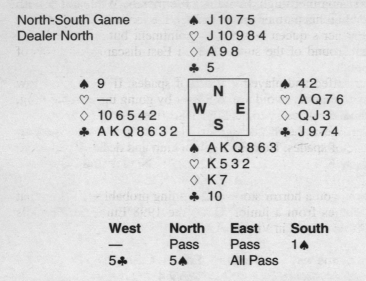

North-South Game
Dealer North

♠ J 10 7 5
♡ J 10 9 8 4
◇ A 9 8
♣ 5

♠ 9
♡ —
◇ 10 6 5 4 2
♣ A K Q 8 6 3 2

♠ 4 2
♡ A Q 7 6
◇ Q J 3
♣ J 9 7 4

♠ A K Q 8 6 3
♡ K 5 3 2
◇ K 7
♣ 10

West	North	East	South
—	Pass	Pass	1♠
5♣	5♠	All Pass	

Five Spades looks safe enough but West led the eight of clubs!

After recovering from the shock of winning with the jack of clubs East quickly switched to the ace and another heart, giving West a ruff.

Discarding

A player may be able to transmit important information even when he is not following suit. Consider the following deal:

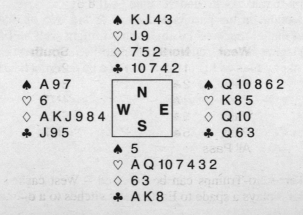

♠ K J 4 3
♡ J 9
◇ 7 5 2
♣ 10 7 4 2

♠ A 9 7
♡ 6
◇ A K J 9 8 4
♣ J 9 5

♠ Q 10 8 6 2
♡ K 8 5
◇ Q 10
♣ Q 6 3

♠ 5
♡ A Q 10 7 4 3 2
◇ 6 3
♣ A K 8

South was in Four Hearts.

Hoping his partner might be short in diamonds, West started with the king. When his partner followed with the ten he carried on with the ace. Partner's queen was a disappointment but West persisted with a third round of the suit on which East discarded the two of spades.

Declarer ruffed and played the five of spades. If West plays low declarer will not only avoid a spade loser by going up with the king, he will also have an entry to take the heart finesse.

However, West placed his partner with five spades and went up with the ace of spades. He exited with a club and declarer had to go down.

Let me show you a horror story. The bidding probably tells you that the hand comes from a junior event, the 1998 European Schools Championship played in Vienna.

East-West Game
Dealer North

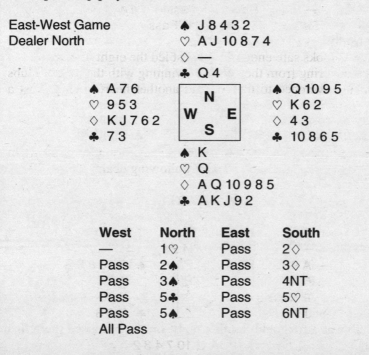

♠ J 8 4 3 2
♡ A J 10 8 7 4
◇ —
♣ Q 4

♠ A 7 6
♡ 9 5 3
◇ K J 7 6 2
♣ 7 3

♠ Q 10 9 5
♡ K 6 2
◇ 4 3
♣ 10 8 6 5

♠ K
♡ Q
◇ A Q 10 9 8 5
♣ A K J 9 2

West	North	East	South
—	1♡	Pass	2◇
Pass	2♠	Pass	3◇
Pass	3♠	Pass	4NT
Pass	5♣	Pass	5♡
Pass	5♠	Pass	6NT
All Pass			

Even Three No-Trumps can be defeated – West cashes the ace of spades and plays a spade to East, who switches to a diamond.

At the table West led the three of hearts and declarer had to play low from dummy. It would be asking too much for East to play low, which would have ensured that the contract goes several down, but when he took the king and failed to find the spade switch, his side were in trouble. On his diamond return, declarer went up with the ace, crossed to the queen of clubs and ran the hearts, discarding the five, eight, nine and queen of diamonds and the king of spades before rattling off his winning clubs. In the two-card ending West had to discard either the ace of spades or the king of diamonds. He got it wrong.

Sensible discarding by East should really leave West with no problem – unless of course he fails to pay attention!

Cashing out

There is nothing more frustrating for the defenders than failing to beat a contract that can be defeated by force. This hand comes from Britain's premier competition, the Gold Cup.

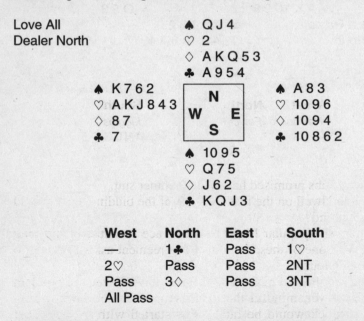

Love All
Dealer North

                    ♠ Q J 4
                    ♡ 2
                    ◇ A K Q 5 3
                    ♣ A 9 5 4

    ♠ K 7 6 2   ♠ A 8 3
    ♡ A K J 8 4 3   N   ♡ 10 9 6
    ◇ 8 7   W   E   ◇ 10 9 4
    ♣ 7   S   ♣ 10 8 6 2

                    ♠ 10 9 5
                    ♡ Q 7 5
                    ◇ J 6 2
                    ♣ K Q J 3

West	North	East	South
—	1♣	Pass	1♡
2♡	Pass	Pass	2NT
Pass	3◇	Pass	3NT
All Pass			

One Club was strong and South's reply simply promised more than 8 points.

West led the king of hearts and had to try to find a way of giving his partner the lead.

He tried the seven of clubs.

The way to approach this type of problem is to consider where declarer's tricks are coming from. Assuming he has five diamond tricks, two tricks in spades and the ace of clubs still only gives a total of eight. That should be enough for West to find the devastating switch to a spade.

Here is another example from Britain's Premier League.

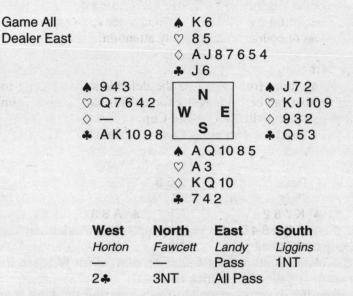

Game All
Dealer East

	♠ K 6		
	♡ 8 5		
	◇ A J 8 7 6 5 4		
	♣ J 6		
♠ 9 4 3			♠ J 7 2
♡ Q 7 6 4 2	N		♡ K J 10 9
◇ —	W E		◇ 9 3 2
♣ A K 10 9 8	S		♣ Q 5 3
	♠ A Q 10 8 5		
	♡ A 3		
	◇ K Q 10		
	♣ 7 4 2		

West	North	East	South
Horton	*Fawcett*	*Landy*	*Liggins*
—	—	Pass	1NT
2♣	3NT	All Pass	

West's Two Clubs promised hearts and another suit.

Rather than dwell on the inadequacies of the bidding, how should East-West defend?

Remember the popular leading style is ace for attitude and king for count with one of these honours by agreement asking partner to unblock an honour.

Here the king would have done that and have solved the problem at once. However, mindful that if either declarer or dummy held J-x-x an unblock would be fatal, West started with the ace, East playing the five. With no certainty that that his partner's card was encouraging, West pressed on with the king catering for a doubleton queen with declarer or partner. When East inexplicably retained the queen of clubs it was all over.

A final thought: suppose South had started with J-x-x-x of clubs and East with Q-x? Then you have to lead a low club at trick one.

Game All
Dealer East

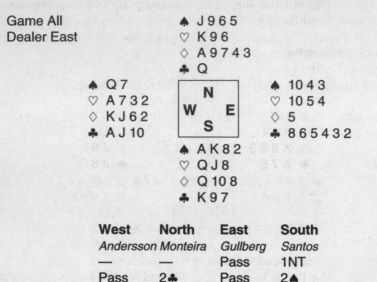

```
                    ♠ J 9 6 5
                    ♡ K 9 6
                    ◇ A 9 7 4 3
                    ♣ Q
      ♠ Q 7                          ♠ 10 4 3
      ♡ A 7 3 2         N            ♡ 10 5 4
      ◇ K J 6 2      W     E         ◇ 5
      ♣ A J 10          S            ♣ 8 6 5 4 3 2
                    ♠ A K 8 2
                    ♡ Q J 8
                    ◇ Q 10 8
                    ♣ K 9 7
```

West	North	East	South
Andersson	*Monteira*	*Gullberg*	*Santos*
—	—	Pass	1NT
Pass	2♣	Pass	2♠
Pass	4♠	All Pass	

To make things easier – for his partnership – Lars Andersson kept silent during the bidding.

Who can blame South for the following play, when West put the seven of spades on the table at trick one?

Small from the dummy, spade ten from East and the king from declarer. It seemed to poor South that West might have led away from a small doubleton in the trump suit, so why not start to establish the diamond suit?

The diamond queen was covered by West's king and, when dummy had taken the diamond ace, Santos played a spade to his eight – and the roof came down.

West could now take his spade queen and defeat the contract by taking one trick in each side-suit – and finish the show by giving his partner a diamond ruff!

At the other table, V Diegues as West also found the spade lead against the same contract. But, unluckily, his choice was the highest card from two.

Ducking

It is not only declarer who is allowed to withhold a high card. Look at this example from the 1996 European Schools Championship played in Cardiff.

East-West Game
Dealer South

```
                    ♠ 5 2
                    ♡ A J 6 2
                    ◇ A Q 10 7
                    ♣ 6 4 3
        ♠ 10 9 4                   ♠ 8 3
        ♡ 8 5 4        N           ♡ Q 10 9 7 3
        ◇ K 9 5 3   W     E        ◇ J 6 2
        ♣ A 7 5        S           ♣ J 8 2
                    ♠ A K Q J 7 6
                    ♡ K
                    ◇ 8 4
                    ♣ K Q 10 9
```

West led a trump against South's Six Spades.

The simple line is to draw trumps, unblock the king of hearts and play the king of clubs. If the jack is not singleton, you will cross to dummy with the ace of diamonds, get rid of your losing diamond on the ace of hearts, and take the club finesse.

South started along those lines but, after unblocking the king of hearts, he tried a diamond finesse. When that worked, declarer played a club to the king smoothly ducked by West. Declarer went back to dummy and played another club. When East played low declarer tried the queen. The arrival on the scene of the ace of clubs meant one down.

If West had taken the ace of clubs at the first opportunity declarer could not have gone wrong.

Trump promotion

This hand illustrates a classic trump promotion:

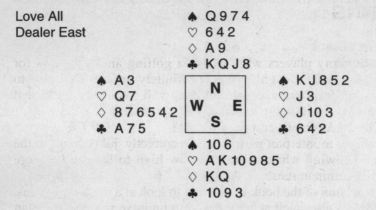

Love All
Dealer East

```
                    ♠ Q 9 7 4
                    ♡ 6 4 2
                    ◇ A 9
                    ♣ K Q J 8
    ♠ A 3                          ♠ K J 8 5 2
    ♡ Q 7          N               ♡ J 3
    ◇ 8 7 6 5 4 2  W    E          ◇ J 10 3
    ♣ A 7 5           S            ♣ 6 4 2
                    ♠ 10 6
                    ♡ A K 10 9 8 5
                    ◇ K Q
                    ♣ 10 9 3
```

If South is the declarer in Four Hearts West can lead the ace of spades and a second spade. A third round of the suit promotes the queen of hearts into the setting trick.

Time to move on to the final section.

BIDDING

There are many players who, to use a golfing analogy, "Bid for show and play for dough!" That is definitely not the best way to treat the subject. Good, accurate bidding will frequently mean that you don't have to struggle to make your contract.

So what makes a player a good bidder?

The ability to interpret partner's bids correctly, judgement, in the sense of knowing when, what and how high to bid, and a large amount of common sense.

In this section of the book I am going to look at a number of ideas. Most of them are aimed at helping you to improve your bidding, but one or two are designed to make like awkward for your opponents.

There is far more to good bidding than simply counting up your points. You have to know what your hand is worth in real terms. Take a look at this deal from the match between Brazil and Poland in the 1997 Bermuda Bowl in Tunisia.

```
Love All                    ♠ 8 4
Dealer North                ♡ K 8 3 2
                            ◇ Q J 6 3
                            ♣ Q 6 3
        ♠ Q 10 9 5      ┌─────────┐      ♠ 7 6 2
        ♡ 10 5          │    N    │      ♡ A 9
        ◇ 4 2          W│         │E      ◇ K 10 8
        ♣ J 10 9 7 5    │    S    │      ♣ A K 8 4 2
                        └─────────┘
                            ♠ A K J 3
                            ♡ Q J 7 6 4
                            ◇ A 9 7 5
                            ♣ —
```

West	North	East	South
Kowalski	Branco	Romanski	Cintra
—	Pass	1NT	2◇
Pass	2♡	All Pass	

Cintra showed hearts and another suit with his bid of Two Diamonds. He did not judge the hand well when he passed North's Two Hearts as he would have almost certainly have had a play for game if North had an otherwise worthless hand that contained as little as K-x-x-x in hearts.

Judgement comes with experience but it can be reinforced by the application of a number of ideas.

What do you think the following hand is worth?

♠ A 10 8 3
♡ A J 10 7 4
◇ 8 6 3
♣ 5

You are playing in an International Team event and your partner opens One Club and raises your response of One Heart to Two Hearts.

Should you bid on over Two Hearts?

A lot of players would argue that with only 9 points a pass is indicated but your hand is worth much more than that. As soon as your five-card suit has been supported you can be almost certain that your fifth heart will be a winner. To make it easy to evaluate your hand, think of the extra trick as a king. With 40 high card points in the pack each "extra" king is worth almost exactly one trick.

With 9 points and one "extra" king you have a total of 12 points. Enough to bid game, especially when playing teams. It's not laydown but the cards were well placed and it made in comfort at the other table.

Your partner's hand looks like this:

♠ Q 5
♡ K Q 5
◇ K 7
♣ A 8 7 6 4 2

In real life the player with this hand rebid Two Clubs and that became the final contract. Even though you only have three card heart support your club suit is moth-eaten and as a general rule you should try and show good support for a suit bid by your partner as soon as possible.

As far as I am aware, this idea of adding on an "extra king" was first proposed by Tony Sowter. It makes a lot of sense, as does the principle of supporting partner, preferably at the earliest opportunity.

The Lawman

Although bridge appears to have been around for a long time, set against most other sports its life span has been rather short. So, just as the cyclist is always on the lookout for a better bicycle the bridge player is constantly searching for ways in which to improve the accuracy of his bidding.

In recent years the idea first proposed by Jean René Vernes and brilliantly re-introduced by Larry Cohen has been sweeping the world.

His "Law of Total Tricks" is that on most bridge deals, the total number of tricks will be approximately equal to the total number of trumps.

If you assume that on any given hand each side will try and play in its best trump fit it becomes possible to calculate the number of tricks each side can take. That number is usually very close to or exactly equals the total number of trumps on that particular deal. This example will show you how that works:

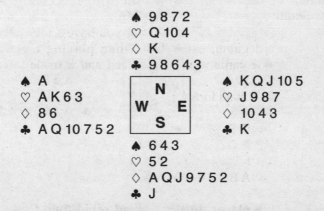

North-South have an eight-card fit in diamonds and East-West have an eight-card fit in hearts. That means there are 16 total trumps.

North-South can make seven tricks if diamonds are trumps, East-West ten playing in hearts. That gives us 17 total tricks.

The time to use this law is when both sides are competing for the contract. It does not override other considerations such as those situations where you know your side has enough points to bid a game or slam.

- If you have an eight-card fit you should be prepared to bid to the two level.
- With a nine-card fit be prepared to bid to the three level.
- With a ten-card fit bid be prepared to bid to the four level.

When Larry wrote his Bols Bridge Tip about the law he coined the phrase: "Eight never, Nine ever".

The idea was that it would remind you not to compete at the three level if your side has only eight trumps. On the other hand, with nine trumps you should always compete to the three level.

Pre-empting

Of course, it's easier to judge the value of your hand when you are given plenty of time and space. While many modern players favour a style of very weak pre-empts, the old fashioned variety are still capable of doing plenty of damage.

```
Game All              ♠ Q 7 5 2
Dealer South          ♡ A 8 7 6
                      ◇ 10 5 2
                      ♣ Q 3
      ♠ K 8 4 3       ┌─────────┐      ♠ 9 6
      ♡ Q J 4 2       │    N    │      ♡ K 5 3
      ◇ 9 8 4         │ W     E │      ◇ J
      ♣ 10 8          │    S    │      ♣ A J 9 7 5 4 2
                      └─────────┘
                      ♠ A J 10
                      ♡ 10 9
                      ◇ A K Q 7 6 3
                      ♣ K 6
```

West	North	East	South
Pass	Pass	3♣	4◇
Pass	5◇	All Pass	

In Five Diamonds declarer was faced by a club lead to the ace and a club return. He won and cashed the ace of diamonds. Seeing the jack he crossed to the ten of diamonds and played a spade to the jack and king.

Now West could switch to a heart, removing the entry to dummy before declarer could untangle the spades.

Declarer did not make the best of things, especially in the bidding. With a club stopper and an excellent source of tricks he should have preferred Three No-Trumps. In the play the jack or ten of spades might have followed the ace of diamonds. West can win but cannot remove both entries to the dummy.

Players who open very light run the risk of setting partner a problem rather than the opponents! Suppose you partner opens Three Clubs. If your partner's pre-empt can be based on a suit as poor as say Q-9-7-5-4-3 then it makes it very difficult for you to bid constructively. Contrast that approach with this deal:

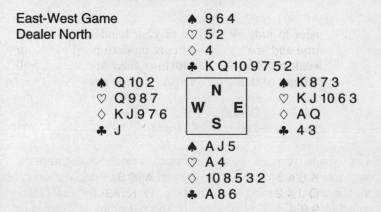

East-West Game
Dealer North

```
              ♠ 9 6 4
              ♡ 5 2
              ◇ 4
              ♣ K Q 10 9 7 5 2
♠ Q 10 2          N          ♠ K 8 7 3
♡ Q 9 8 7      W     E       ♡ K J 10 6 3
◇ K J 9 7 6       S          ◇ A Q
♣ J                          ♣ 4 3
              ♠ A J 5
              ♡ A 4
              ◇ 10 8 5 3 2
              ♣ A 8 6
```

When North opened Three Clubs, South, knowing his partner's style, had an easy conversion to Three No-Trumps.

The deal was played in a match and the other North player was unable to open Three Clubs because his suit was too strong! He had to pass and East opened One Heart, raised to Four Hearts by West. Although that contract might have been defeated by a diamond ruff it wasn't and a double game swing was recorded.

Interfere over strong clubs!

There are many pairs who use a system where all strong hands are
opened One Club. Experience has taught me that left to their own
devices they will nearly always bid fluently to the best contract.
However, you can frequently put a spanner in the works by
intervening. Take a look at this deal from the 1995 Dunhill Cup
played in Bonn.

East-West Game
Dealer South

```
                ♠ A 6 2
                ♡ K Q 9 5
                ◇ Q 5
                ♣ 10 8 7 4
  ♠ 8 3              N        ♠ J 9 5
  ♡ 4                         ♡ J 10 8 7 3
  ◇ 9 7 6 4    W       E      ◇ 10 3
  ♣ A K J 9 5 3    S          ♣ Q 6 2
                ♠ K Q 10 7 4
                ♡ A 6 2
                ◇ A K J 8 2
                ♣ —
```

West	North	East	South
Winter	Nilsland	Horton	Fallenius
—	—	—	1♣
1♠	Double	2♣	2♠
3♣	4♠	All Pass	

West's One Spade overcall showed either the majors or the minors.

I never cease to be amazed at how even modest intervention can
sometimes disrupt a strong club auction. Here South was clearly
worth another bid, Five Clubs being the obvious way to start.
Assuming North then bids Five Hearts, a slam is sure to be reached.
Sweden had missed the boat, but at the other table it was "full speed
ahead" and the English pair Gus Calderwood and Dick Shek had no
trouble bidding a grand slam.

There are many excellent defences to Strong Club systems. This
is my favourite:

TRAP

This defence is an amalgam of four others, Transfers, Robinson, Amsbury and Panama, hence its name.

This is how it works:

Bid	Meaning
Double	Hearts
1◇	Spades
1♡	Spades and clubs, or hearts and diamonds
1♠	Spades and hearts, or diamonds and clubs
1NT	Spades and diamonds, or hearts and clubs
2♣	Diamonds, or hearts and spades
2◇	Hearts, or spades and clubs
2♡	Spades, or clubs and diamonds
2♠	Clubs, or diamonds and hearts
2NT	Hearts and clubs
3♣	Diamonds and spades

One advantage of this system is that there are several ways of describing the same hand. That can be an important consideration depending on the vulnerability. For example take a look at this hand:

```
♠ K Q 9 4 2
♡ 6
◇ 6 5
♣ 9 7 4 3 2
```

After a One Club opening bid you can choose between One Diamond (showing spades), One Heart (two suits of the same colour) or Two Diamonds (Hearts or the black suits).

If the vulnerability is in your favour it is almost mandatory to bid over a strong club. Tony Forrester did not hesitate to enter the bidding with this hand:

```
♠ 10 8 4 2
♡ 10 7 5 3
◇ 7 4 2
♣ J 9
```

Responding to these bids is a simple exercise in common sense.

> ♠ Q J 8 6 4
> ♡ 5
> ◇ Q J 6 3
> ♣ 7 5 2

After 1♣ – 1♡ – Pass, your partner has promised clubs and spades or diamonds and hearts. You can choose between Two Spades or Three Diamonds depending on how pre-emptive you want to be and the vulnerability.

> ♠ —
> ♡ K J 10 6 4
> ◇ 7 3
> ♣ J 10 9 7 4 2

After 1♣ – 1♠ – Pass, you can jump all the way to Four Hearts! If your partner has the majors it may be a make and if he has the minors Five Clubs should be a good save.

> ♠ 10 5 3 2
> ♡ A 6
> ◇ Q 7 4 3 2
> ♣ 7 4

After 1♣ – 2♡ – Pass, you have excellent support for spades but you can afford to bid Three Diamonds, as that is obviously what you prefer when partner has the minors.

Fit jumps
These have become popular since the idea was explained in *Partnership Bidding in Bridge* by Andrew Robson and Oliver Segal. This illustrative deal from the Junior European Championships in Vienna in 1998 will show you the idea.

Game All
Dealer South

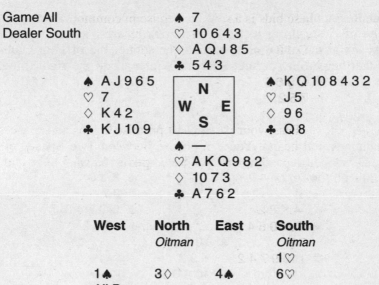

♠ 7		
♡ 10 6 4 3		
◊ A Q J 8 5		
♣ 5 4 3		

♠ A J 9 6 5   ♠ K Q 10 8 4 3 2
♡ 7   ♡ J 5
◊ K 4 2   ◊ 9 6
♣ K J 10 9   ♣ Q 8

♠ —
♡ A K Q 9 8 2
◊ 10 7 3
♣ A 7 6 2

West	North	East	South
	Oitman		*Oitman*
			1♡
1♠	3◊	4♠	6♡
All Pass			

When West overcalled North's jump to Three Diamonds showed a
reasonable suit and promised a fit for hearts.

This style allows a partnership to realize very quickly the degree
of fit they have on a deal and can help them to judge high-level
situations. When your side has a double fit there are likely to be
plenty of tricks available for both sides because the opponents will
have a double fit as well.

Defensive bidding

Thinking players are always on the lookout for bids that will help
partner to judge what to do. Take a look at this example from a
match between England and Belgium.

You are at favourable vulnerability. After two passes West opens
One Spade and your partner makes a weak jump overcall of Three
Hearts. East bids Three Spades and you, South, are looking at:

♠ 10 5
♡ K 9 2
◊ 10 9 6 5
♣ K Q 9 3

What do you bid?

The obvious thing to do is bid Four Hearts, which is what happened at the other table. I made the subtler bid of Four Clubs and that helped my partner Richard Winter to do the right thing. This was the full deal:

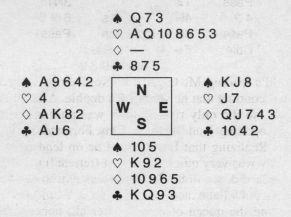

```
                    ♠ Q 7 3
                    ♡ A Q 10 8 6 5 3
                    ◇ —
                    ♣ 8 7 5
   ♠ A 9 6 4 2              N        ♠ K J 8
   ♡ 4                               ♡ J 7
   ◇ A K 8 2        W         E      ◇ Q J 7 4 3
   ♣ A J 6              S            ♣ 10 4 2
                    ♠ 10 5
                    ♡ K 9 2
                    ◇ 10 9 6 5
                    ♣ K Q 9 3
```

At the other table West was allowed to play in Four Spades but Richard, knowing he was facing values in clubs, went on to Five Hearts. East-West could not be sure they could make Five Spades so they were left with doubling and collecting +300 against the +650 scored at the other table.

Here is a more recent example from the Cap Gemini played in The Hague in 1999.

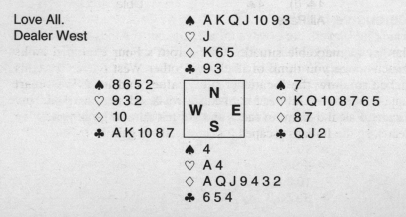

```
Love All.            ♠ A K Q J 10 9 3
Dealer West          ♡ J
                     ◇ K 6 5
                     ♣ 9 3
   ♠ 8 6 5 2              N        ♠ 7
   ♡ 9 3 2                         ♡ K Q 10 8 7 6 5
   ◇ 10             W         E    ◇ 8 7
   ♣ A K 10 8 7          S         ♣ Q J 2
                     ♠ 4
                     ♡ A 4
                     ◇ A Q J 9 4 3 2
                     ♣ 6 5 4
```

This deal caused huge swings all around the room because East almost always found himself on lead against a slam as in this case:

West	North	East	South
Chemla	*Forrester*	*Levy*	*Zia*
Pass	1♠	3♡	3NT
4♡	4NT	Pass	6♢
Pass	6NT	Pass	Pass
Dble	7♠	All Pass	

To the world's leading Mr Cigar, Six No-Trumps looked so much like the final contract that he ventured a double. After all, he was on lead himself, so the only risk he took was pulling out the wrong card for his opening lead. Against Tony Forrester, you had better think twice. Realizing that Levy would be on lead against a spade contract, Tony was very quick to convert (retreat?) to Seven Spades. When Chemla did not double this, it was extremely difficult for Levy to work out what exactly was going on. Would you blame him for not leading the queen of clubs? After all, nobody led clubs at any table. On the actual heart lead, Tony had thirteen tricks, and he could enter +1,510 as his score.

However, this is how Buratti & Lanzarotti wrong footed Helgemo & Helness:

West	North	East	South
Lanzarotti	*Helness*	*Buratti*	*Helgemo*
Pass	1♠	3♡	3NT
4♣ (!)	4♠	5♡	Dble
All Pass			

This is a remarkable situation. Lanzarotti's Four Club bid looks obvious once you think of it. Yet, no other West player took his chance to show the location of his values and imply his heart support. With the club lead marked, North-South no longer had any chance to steal a slam. In fact, they did not dare to go beyond Five Hearts, so the Italians escaped for only −100 to gain 11 IMPs.

Doubles

A double is a very flexible bid when it is simply used to carry the message to partner that you have some values.

Some doubles have been assigned a special meaning.

SUPPORT DOUBLES

Eric Rodwell is a professional player and writer who lives in Clearwater Florida. He won the Bermuda Bowl in 1981 and 1995, the World Open Pairs in 1986 and the Olympiad in 1988. His partnership with Jeff Meckstroth is one of the most famous in the world. An outstanding theoretician, Eric was responsible for the invention of the now popular convention, the support double.

The idea is that the opening bidder can distinguish between hands with three or four card support for partner's suit. This is a typical example:

West	North	East	South
1◇	Pass	1♡	1♠
Double			

If you raise to Two Hearts partner may not be sure that you have four card support. However, playing support doubles your bid promises four hearts. With only three you tell partner by doubling.

This is a similar situation:

West	North	East	South
1◇	Pass	1♠	Double
Redouble			

Your redouble promises three-card support for spades. Bidding Two Spades would show four.

These hands would qualify for a support double:

West	North	East	South		
1◇	Pass	1♡	2♣	♠ 7 5	
Double				♡ Q J 6	
				◇ A K J 7 3	
				♣ K 8 6	

You are showing nothing special with your double, simply the possession of three hearts.

West	North	East	South	♠ 10 7 5
1◇	Pass	1♡	2♣	♡ A J 6
Double				◇ A K Q J 7 3
				♣ 8

You are probably tempted to rebid your excellent diamonds but if you do you will be denying three hearts.

LIGHTNER DOUBLES

Over a period of time Theodore A Lightner observed that many slam contracts could be defeated if the defender on lead did something out of the ordinary. Searching for an answer he realized that in the vast majority of cases it was hardly likely that one would want to want to double a slam for penalties. Sensible players who bid to a slam in the expectation of making their contract were hardly going to present you with the opportunity to collect a sizeable penalty. The combination of these two thoughts led him to arrive at a solution.

His idea has survived the test of time as this example illustrates. It was played in the 1999 final of the Vanderbilt Knockout Teams Championship.

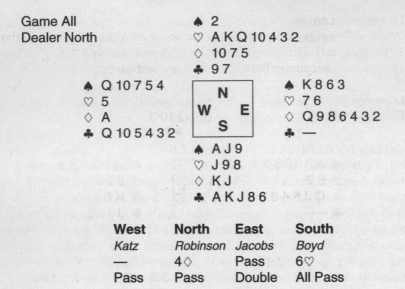

Game All	♠ 2
Dealer North	♡ A K Q 10 4 3 2
	◇ 10 7 5
	♣ 9 7

♠ Q 10 7 5 4		♠ K 8 6 3
♡ 5	**N**	♡ 7 6
◇ A	**W E**	◇ Q 9 8 6 4 3 2
♣ Q 10 5 4 3 2	**S**	♣ —

	♠ A J 9
	♡ J 9 8
	◇ K J
	♣ A K J 8 6

West	North	East	South
Katz	*Robinson*	*Jacobs*	*Boyd*
—	4◇	Pass	6♡
Pass	Pass	Double	All Pass

There are a lot of clubs in a golf bag. The secret is using the right one at the right time. Most experts come to the table armed with lots of conventions. It is terribly tempting to use them as often as possible but even the slightest deviation can frequently lead to disaster.

North's opening bid of Four Diamonds theoretically promised a solid heart suit and eight tricks so he was off-centre on two counts.

East could not be sure his side would take two tricks but by doubling Six Hearts he was suggesting to his partner that an unusual lead might get his side off to a good start.

It was clear to West that his partner would be able to ruff the first round of clubs but looking for a big penalty he cashed the ace of diamonds before switching to the two of clubs. East ruffed and was not hard pressed to return a diamond for his partner to ruff. A further club allowed East to secure a second ruff and that meant a penalty of 800 points.

When one of your opponents makes a Lightner double you should always consider retreating to no-trumps. If South had done that here he would have saved a lot of points.

Before I leave the topic of doubles I want to look at one more situation.

DAFT DOUBLES

What will surely be remembered as the most dramatic deal of the 1997 Generali European Team Championships took place in the Open series encounter between Germany and Sweden.

```
Love All              ♠ —
Dealer North          ♡ A K Q 10 3
                      ◇ A 10 9 7
                      ♣ K Q 7 6
   ♠ A K 10 6 3 2          ┌─────┐          ♠ Q 9 8
   ♡ 6 2                   │  N  │          ♡ J 7 5
   ◇ Q J 6 4 3          W  │     │  E       ◇ K 8 5 2
   ♣ —                     │  S  │          ♣ J 10 8
                           └─────┘
                      ♠ J 7 5 4
                      ♡ 9 8 4
                      ◇ —
                      ♣ A 9 5 4 3 2
```

Closed Room

West	North	East	South
Holowski	Nilsland	Gotard	Fallenius
—	1♡	Pass	2♡
4♠	Pass	Pass	Double
All Pass			

In theory North-South can take the first six tricks against Four Spades doubled, but only if the opening lead is a double dummy diamond. In practice it was even worse, as the defenders failed to find even one diamond ruff, so declarer was able to claim ten tricks. +590 to Germany

In the replay Four Spades also became a possible contract, but this time South would have been declarer! This was the remarkable sequence produced at the table:

Open Room

West	North	East	South
Friedin	*Rath*	*Eriksson*	*Tomski*
	1♡	Pass	1♠
2♠	4♠!	Pass	Pass!!
Double!!!	4NT	Pass	5♣
Pass	6♣	Pass	7♣!
All Pass			

West's Two Spades was natural, so North thought it would be clear that he was making a cuebid when he leapt to Four Spades. South didn't see it in that light, but West came to the rescue with a double that will surely cause him to have many sleepless nights.

His double was for penalties but North promptly took it out!

West could scarcely believe it when his opponents bid on to the cold Seven Clubs for +1,440 and 19 IMPs.

In desperation he called for the Tournament Director.

All they could offer him was sympathy and a wry smile!

I hope you see the point. West knew his opponents were in a silly contract. He also knew that North could not possibly have intended his bid of Four Spades to be natural so it was more than likely his opponents had a better, making contract available. He should have been content to pass and collect what would normally have been an excellent result. He will know better next time.

Conventional assistance

I imagine everyone would find the game much harder if they were not allowed to play any conventions. The best ones are undoubtedly an aid to judgement. I recently asked a number of top class players a simple question: 'If you were limited to just five conventions, which would they be?'

By a significant majority these are the five that topped the list:

- Take out Doubles
- Negative Doubles
- Transfers
- Stayman
- Splinters

We have already considered the first four. So here is an outline of
Splinter bids followed by a brief look at some of my favourite
conventions. They all make bidding easier.

SPLINTER BIDS

Dorothy Hayden Truscott is credited with the invention of this
convention. Apart from winning four World Championship titles
she has collected a vast number of national titles. In 1965 she was a
member of the American team that finished second in the Bermuda
Bowl and in 1996 she was third in the World Open Pairs
Championship, unique achievements for a woman.

This convention is undoubtedly one of the most popular in the
world today. Its inherent simplicity and the frequency with which it
can be applied easily explain that.

A splinter bid is a double jump, usually by responder but it can
also be an option for the opening bidder. It shows a shortage in the
suit bid (a singleton or void), four-card support for partner's suit
and at least the values for game. These are typical examples:

North	South	
1♠	?	♠ K Q 7 3
		♡ A K 4
		◇ Q 8 5 3 2
		♣ 6

South bids Four Clubs.

North	South	
1♡	?	♠ A Q 8 4
		♡ K 10 7 5
		◇ 8
		♣ A J 7 3

This time South shows his hand with a bid of Four Diamonds.

North	South	
1♠	?	♠ A Q 7 3
		♡ 7
		◇ K J 8 2
		♣ K Q J 7

This time South bids Four Hearts. This cannot be to play as South
would respond Two Hearts and then bid Four Hearts.

North	South	
1♠	2♣	♠ K Q J 7 3
?		♡ A J 7 4
		◇ —
		♣ A Q 8 4

You give partner the good news about you support for clubs with a jump to Four Diamonds. Notice that good as your hand is it would be wrong to resort to Blackwood. A one-ace response of Five Diamonds would leave you in the dark as it could be in diamonds or spades.

Such is the popularity of splinters that players are constantly looking for ways to increase their use. The mini-splinter has been gaining in popularity. This is an example:

North	South	
1◇	?	♠ A K Q 4
		♡ 9
		◇ Q 8 5 3 2
		♣ K 7 4

Using mini-splinters the correct response is Three Hearts.

RUBINSOHL

This is one of my personal favourites that has proved its worth at the table again and again. The name is a strange amalgam of the surnames of the three people who have contributed to the development of the idea.

Jeff Rubens represented the USA in the 1973 Bermuda Bowl and has won several national titles. His book, *The Secrets of Winning Bridge,* is one of the essential texts for the aspiring player. He is the editor of the renowned periodical, *The Bridge World.*

Ira Rubin was a member of the American Bermuda Bowl winning team in 1976 and was one of the outstanding players of his generation, winning numerous national titles. Like many great players he has a reputation for being difficult to play with – his nickname is "The Beast"!

Bruce Neill, a well-known Australian player, suggested that the idea could be extended in an article in *The Bridge World* in May 1983.

The most important area in which this convention has gained favour is when the opponents intervene over your partner's opening bid of One No-Trump.

The basic idea involves the use of a series of transfer bids. The original idea was that you either had a weakish hand that simply wanted to compete or a hand with at least invitational values. I have found it more useful to reserve the bid for the latter hand-type. These are the possible bids:

West	North	East	South	
1NT	2♠	?	2NT	clubs
			3♣	diamonds
			3♦	hearts
			3♡	four hearts
			3♠	the values for 3NT but without a heart suit or a spade stopper
			3NT	A spade stopper and the values for game

Here are some typical examples:

West	North	East	South	♠ 7 4
1NT	2♠	?		♡ J 6
				♦ K 7 3
				♣ K Q 8 7 4 2

By bidding Two No-Trumps you show your club suit. If partner simply bids Three Clubs you intend to pass but the knowledge that you have a fair suit may enable him to bid Three No-Trumps.

West	North	East	South	♠ Q 7 3
1NT	2♡	?		♡ A Q 9 6
				♦ Q 7 4
				♣ K 7 3

Sorry, this is a trick question! Obviously you have more than enough to make a penalty double of Two Hearts.

West	North	East	South	♠ K 6
1NT	2♠	?		♡ A J 10 5
				◇ K 6 3
				♣ J 10 7 3

Here you bid Three Hearts to show your four-card suit. Partner will raise with a fit for hearts, bid Three No-Trumps with a spade stopper or, lacking both, use a bid of Three Spades to ask you for one.

West	North	East	South	♠ 7 4
1NT	2♠	?		♡ Q 6
				◇ K Q 9 7 6 3
				♣ K 8 4

Here you have a choice of actions; either Three Spades to show the values for game without four hearts or a spade stopper or Three Clubs intending to follow up with Three Spades. The second route might allow you to reach Five Diamonds rather than Three No-Trumps.

If the overcall is made at a lower level then the responder will have room to make some natural bids as well. For example, if the overcall is Two Clubs then responder can bid any of the three remaining suits naturally at the two level, in each case simply showing a desire to compete.

This system can be used even when the overcall of One No-Trump is conventional.

This method can also be used when the opening bid is natural and the opponents use a weak jump overcall. The meaning attached to responder's bids is exactly as before:

West	North	East		
1◇	2♠	?	2NT	clubs
			3♣	diamonds
			3◇	hearts
			3♡	four hearts
			3♠	the values for 3NT but without a heart suit or a spade stopper
			3NT	To play

Let's look at a few examples:

West	North	East	South	♠ 7 4
1♢	2♠	?		♡ J 6
				♢ K 7 3
				♣ K Q 8 7 4 2

By bidding Two No-Trumps you show your club suit. If partner simply bids Three Clubs you intend to pass but the knowledge that you have a fair suit may enable him to bid Three No-Trumps.

West	North	East	South	♠ 7 4
1♢	2♠	?		♡ A Q 8 7 4
				♢ K 7 3
				♣ K J 6

You have a good hand but no spade stop. You bid Three Diamonds to show at least five hearts intending to follow it with Three Spades.

West	North	East	South	♠ K 7 3
1♢	2♠	?		♡ A J 8 7
				♢ K 7
				♣ K J 6 4

This time you only have a four-card heart suit but you also have a spade stop. The correct bid is Three Hearts to be followed by Three No-Trumps.

Before we leave this topic, it's a good idea to take a look at the actions of the opening bidder after partner has used this conventional aid. I'll assume the bidding has started like this:

West	North	East	South
1♢	2♠	2NT	Pass
?			

♠ 7 2
♡ K J 5
♢ A K 9 7 3
♣ Q 8 4

You have a good fit for clubs but for the moment all you can do is comply with partner's request and bid Three Clubs.

♠ 9 3
♡ A 6
◇ A K Q 9 2
♣ K J 7 3

With a fantastic fit for clubs the right action is to jump to Four Clubs. You already have visions of a slam providing partner has first or second round spade control.

♠ K 9 7
♡ Q J 10 5
◇ A K 10 8 4
♣ 6

You have to bid Three Clubs and hope for the best.

KOKISH

Eric Kokish is undoubtedly one of the most famous players and writers of the twentieth century. He is recognized as a leading authority on every aspect of bidding all over the world. He has coached many national teams to international success and somehow still finds to play in the odd tournament. He was a member of the Canadian team that won the silver medals in the 1996 Bermuda Bowl.

One of his many contributions to theory is the Kokish relay.

One of the great weaknesses of all natural systems is the bidding of very strong hands. Eric's idea is designed to facilitate the bidding of very strong balanced hands.

When the bidding starts:

North	South
2♣	2◇
2♡	

The bid of Two Hearts is used to describe one of two possible hand types; either natural with hearts or a strong balanced hand that is too strong for an immediate rebid of Two No-Trumps. The idea is to enable the responder to use stayman and transfers at the three level if opener has the balanced hand type.

North	South
2♣	2♦
2♡	2♠

Responder must reply with Two Spades, a relay bid simply waiting for partner to clarify his hand type.

CAPPELLETTI

There are many defences to an opening bid of One No-Trump. This recent idea that has been gaining converts was developed in the USA.

The bids are easy to remember:

Bid	*Meaning*
2♠	Spades and a minor
2♡	Hearts and a minor
2♦	Spades and hearts
2♣	Any one-suited hand
Double	Penalties

A double by a passed hand promises a four-card major and a minor. Your partner bids Two Hearts if he wants to play in the major and Two Clubs if he wants to play in the minor.

When you have both majors 4-4 is OK if you are aggressive, otherwise you need 4-5 or even 5-5. You may have to wait a long time for that last option.

Here is a typical hand for the each of the four main options:

♠ A Q J 7 4   ♠ 8
♡ 9 3   ♡ A K J 8 4
◇ 8   ◇ K Q 9 6 3
♣ K J 10 7 5   ♣ 7 3

Bid Two Spades   Bid Two Hearts

♠ A J 10 8 4   ♠ 8 3
♡ K Q J 5   ♡ K 7 4
◇ 7 4 2   ◇ A K J 10 8 6
♣ 6   ♣ 9 5

Bid Two Diamonds   Bid Two Clubs

In reply to the Two Club bid the responder is allowed to pass with a
reasonable six-card club suit. The "normal" response is Two
Diamonds but it is allowed to introduce a good five-card or better
major, or bid Two No-Trumps with a balanced 11+ points. One
wrinkle worth thinking about is to use the sequence:

West	North	East	South
1NT	2♣	Pass	2◇
Pass	2NT		

to show clubs and four or more diamonds.

If the overcall is Two Diamonds then the simple style is for
responder to use limit bids in support of the appropriate major.

After an overcall of Two of a major the responder can use a bid of
Two No-Trumps to locate the promised minor suit. If that is
followed by a return to Three of partner's major, it is invitational
and stronger than a direct raise.

No convention comes with a written guarantee but used wisely the
ones I have described will hopefully lead you to better results.
Good luck!

PART THREE

The World of Bridge

BRIDGE BOOKS YOU SHOULD READ

If you asked 20 players to name the "best" bridge book they had ever read, you would probably get 15 different answers. However, if you asked those same 20 players to name their "Top 10" there would be a reasonable degree of consensus. "Best" is a very subjective term, but there is little doubt that most players would benefit from reading a selection from the books listed below.

The books are divided into four categories: Classics, Books for Beginners, Books for Advancing Players, and Books for Experienced Players. Within each category, I have tried to select a range of Bidding, Declarer Play and Defensive works. Those books in the "Classic" section should all be part of any serious player's library.

Classic books
GENERAL
Five Weeks to Winning Bridge by Alfred Sheinwold (*Novice*)
Countless players have learned to play from this book. With over a million copies sold, it is the most successful bridge book of all time.
Bid Better, Play Better by Dorothy Hayden (*Novice-Intermediate*)
Reading and rereading this classic cannot help but improve your game
Matchpoints by Kit Woolsey (*Experienced+*)
The best book ever written about expert-level matchpoints strategy.

BIDDING
Commonsense Bidding by Bill Root (*Novice-Intermediate*)
A complete guide to modern bidding concepts.
To Bid or Not to Bid by Larry Cohen (*Intermediate+*)
The best-selling book of the 1990s. This book will change the way you evaluate your hand in competitive auctions, and significantly improve your decision making.
Bridge Conventions Complete by Amalya Kearse (*Intermediate+*)
The definitive reference work on conventions.
The Complete Book of Hand Evaluation (*Intermediate+*)
Good advice on everything from basic counting to expert-level inferences.

The Complete Book of Overcalls by Mike Lawrence
(*Intermediate+*)
The definitive work on the subject.

DECLARER PLAY
Watson's Play of the Hand by Louis H. Watson (*Novice-Intermediate*)
Rather dated, but still one of the most complete works on the subject. It is fairly slow going, but what you learn will be invaluable.
How to Read Your Opponents Cards by Mike Lawrence
(*Intermediate+*)
ABTA Book of the Year, and rightly so! This classic offers great insights into how the experts read the subtle clues at the table.
Card Play Technique by Victor Mollo & Nico Gardener
(*Intermediate+*)
Your game is bound to be improved by reading this classic.
Reese on Play by Terence Reese (*Experienced+*)
Reese cuts to the heart of the matter. Worth reading many times.
The Expert Game by Terence Reese (*Experienced+*)
One of the all-time greats.
Play These Hands With Me by Terence Reese (*Intermediate+*)
Excellent hands presented in an unusual format. This book is one you can read time and time again.
Bridge Squeezes Complete by Clyde Love (*Experienced+*)
Not light reading, by any means, but the definitive work on squeeze play.
The Dictionary of Suit Combinations by Jean-Marc Roudinescu
(*Experienced+*)
The definitive reference work on handling suit combinations.
Adventures in Card Play by Hugh Kelsey and Géza Ottlik
(*Experienced+*)
Perhaps the most complex card play book ever written. You will either love it or hate it. This book introduced many of the more obscure squeeze position for the first time.

DEFENCE
Killing Defence at Bridge by Hugh Kelsey (*Experienced+*)
If you can solve most of these problems the first time through, you are probably a World champion already.

Opening Leads by Robert Ewen (*Intermediate+*)
The classic book on trick one strategy.

ENTERTAINMENT
Why You Lose at Bridge by S J Simon (*Intermediate+*)
Voted the #1 book of all time in the December 1994, *ACBL Bulletin* survey.
Right Through the Pack by Roger Darvas and Norman de V. Hart (*Intermediate+*)
A brilliant fantasy featuring ingenious hands and humour as each card in the deck tells its own tale. Each of the 52 stories offers shrewd advice for players of all levels. Voted one of the top three books of all time in the ACBL survey.
Bridge Humor by Eddie Kantar (*Intermediate+*)
One of the funniest bridge books ever written.
The Best of Kantar by Eddie Kantar (*Intermediate+*)
Be prepared to laugh.
Bridge in the Menagerie by Victor Mollo (*Intermediate+*)
The first of a classic series. It is impossible not to love Mollo's characters.
Miracles of Card Play and other "Abbot" books by David Bird & Terence Reese (*Intermediate+*)
Another classic series; the characters rival those of Mollo and Simon.
Bridge with the Blue Team by Pietro Forquet (*Experienced+*)
A collection of wonderful hands.
The Bridge Bum by Alan Sontag (*Intermediate+*)
An entertaining look at the life of a professional bridge player

Books for beginners
GENERAL BOOKS
Bridge for Dummies by Eddie Kantar
A detailed introduction to the basics of bidding and play. Winner of the 1996 ABTA "Bridge Book of the Year" award.
Win at Bridge in 30 Days by David Bird
A daily lesson on bidding and card play.
Bridge for Bright Beginners by Terence Reese
A succinct summary of bidding plus the fundamentals of both play and defence.
Bridge Basics by Ron Klinger
A ten-lesson course on all aspects of duplicate bridge.

Teach Me to Play – A First Book of Bridge by Jude Goodwin &
Don Ellison
Perfect for teaching young children, as it has plenty of cartoons and
quizzes
Bridge for Beginners by Zia Mahmood & Audrey Grant
A compilation of three earlier books, and now a single volume
covering the three major aspects of the game.
Bridge for Beginners by Nico Gardener & Victor Mollo
A complete course for the novice player.
Beginning Bridge by Alan & Maureen Hiron
A suitable text for beginners of all ages.

BIDDING
Teach Yourself Basic Bidding by Dorothy & Alan Truscott
An effective outline of Standard American methods.
Basic Acol by Ben Cohen & Rhoda Barrow
All you need to know to be able to sit down and play Acol.
Really Easy Bidding (published by the English Bridge Union)
Another Acol-based book. Laid out ideally for novices.

DECLARER PLAY
Introduction to Declarer's Play by Eddie Kantar
A popular book featuring easy-to-understand "how-to"s on all the
basics.

DEFENSIVE PLAY
Introduction to Defender's Play by Eddie Kantar
Similar to the above, but this time about defence.

Books for advancing players
GENERAL BOOKS
Winning Contract Bridge Complete by Edgar Kaplan
Two books in one – a basic course and an advanced course.
The Complete Book of Bridge by Terence Reese & Albert Dormer
A broad outline of all aspects of the game. Plenty of tips to be
picked up here.
The Mistakes You Make at Bridge by Terence Reese &
Roger Trézel
An illuminating insight into costly, common and forgivable errors
in all aspects of the game.

BIDDING

Points, Schmoints! by Marty Bergen
How to evaluate a bridge hand. You'll certainly bid more after reading this book.

25 Conventions You Should Know by Barbara Seagram &
Marc Smith
You will leave each chapter convinced that you understand the convention just discussed. Starts with the simplest conventions and progresses to the more advanced ones. 1999 ABTA Book of the Year.

Modern Bridge Conventions by Bill Root & Richard Pavlicek
A broad look at just about any convention you might wish to add to your arsenal

Judgement in Bridge by Mike Lawrence
Improve your judgement.

Hand Evaluation in Bridge by Brian Senior
A good overview of how to judge your playing strength and choose the best bid for your hand and the auction so far.

Pre-empts from A-Z by Ron Andersen and Sabine Zenkel
The definitive work on pre-emptive bidding.

Raising Partner by Brian Senior
How to choose the most descriptive bid with a good hand, and the most effective one when you do not.

Precision Bidding in Acol & Acol in Competition by Eric Crowhurst
If Acol is your preferred system, then these two books should be read over and over again.

Washington Standard by Steve Robinson
If you play Standard American methods, then this book will add a great deal to your understanding of how bidding works.

DECLARER PLAY

Countdown to Winning Bridge by Tim Bourke & Marc Smith
If you can count to thirteen, you can improve your game by reading this book.

The Basic Elements of Play and Defence by G C H Fox
A solid grounding in card play techniques.

Play of the Hand Complete by Eddie Kantar
A definitive work on declarer play

Guide to Better Card Play by Ron Klinger
An easy to read book with plenty of tips. An ABTA "Book of the Year" winner.

DEFENCE
Kantar for the Defense Volumes 1 & 2.
A total of 200 challenging problems, with clear explanations of the solutions.
Opening Leads by Mike Lawrence
Blind leads are for deaf players... adjust your hearing aid with one of the world's best writers
Step by Step Signalling by Mark Horton
Make sure you are on the same wavelength as your partner.
Kantar Teaches Advanced Bridge Defense by Eddie Kantar
It is impossible not to pick up some useful tips from this book. An ABTA Book of the Year winner.

Books for experienced players
GENERAL
The Complete Book of BOLS Tips edited by Sally Brock
It would be impossible not to gain from some of the tips presented by the world's top players.
The Secrets of Winning Bridge by Jeff Rubens
Detailed discussion of many topics only touched upon in other books.
For Experts Only edited by Matthew Granovetter
A collection of excellent articles.
Matchpoint Bridge by Hugh Kelsey
An insight into expert-level matchpoint strategy
Hoffman on Pairs Play by Martin Hoffman
Another work concentrating on the matchpoint game.
Expert Tuition for Tournament Players by Raymond & Sally Brock
Sit in on the authors' post-mortem discussion of a match.

BIDDING
Partnership Bidding by Andrew Robson & Oliver Segal
The ultimate book on modern competitive bidding theory.
The Modern Losing Trick Count by Ron Klinger
An alternative to point counting...
Better Bridge with Bergen Volumes 1 & 2 by Marty Bergen
A thorough discussion of how to approach competitive and uncontested auctions – best read with your regular partner.
Precision and Super Precision Bidding by Giorgio Belladonna & Benito Garozzo
The definitive book of the Precision system.

Powerhouse Hands by Albert Dormer
Somewhat dated now, but this book still contains plenty of sound advice on the subject of slam bidding.
Aces Scientific by Bobby Goldman
This book about the methods developed by the famous Dallas Aces team contains much that is still just as relevant today.

DECLARER PLAY
Step by Step: Deceptive Declarer Play by Barry Rigal
How to make life difficult for your opponents.
Advanced Play at Bridge by Hugh Kelsey
Not an easy read, but well worth the effort.
Secrets of Expert Card Play by David Bird & Tony Forrester
An insight into expert thinking as declarer.
Simple Squeezes by Hugh Kelsey
An introduction to basic squeeze play.
Positive Declarer's Play by Terence Reese & Julian Pottage
A series of quiz hands to test your card-play.
Bridge: Tricks of the Trade by Terence Reese & David Bird
An insight into many aspects of expert thinking.

DEFENCE
Dynamic Defense by Mike Lawrence
An outline of how expert defenders think, with plenty of tips for less experienced players too.
Secrets of Expert Defence by David Bird & Tony Forrester
An insight into expert defensive methods.
Step-by-Step: Deception in Defence by Barry Rigal
How to make life difficult for declarer.
Partnership Defense in Bridge by Kit Woolsey
This book will help to improve your individual judgement in defence, but for maximum benefit both members of the partnership should read and discuss it.
Positive Defence by Terence Reese & Julian Pottage
A series of quiz hands to test your defensive thinking.

PERSONAL BRIDGE SOFTWARE

Thanks to Jim Loy for allowing me to use the results of his research

There are many ways to use your computer for bridge activities. We have become accustomed to getting results almost as soon as play has finished, irrespective of the size of the event, and for many years that was the primary role of computers in the world of bridge. No longer! Now there are many more personal bridge uses to which computers can be put. One kind of bridge software (such as *Bridge Base III* or *Borel*) allows you to do things such as generate practice hands or test the validity of your bidding decision making. Then there is the type of software that allows you to play bridge online against other live users.

In this section, I look at some of the software packages available in two other categories. First, bridge-playing programs that provide two opponents against whom you can compete. What's more, these programs also provide you with a partner. Some of the programs referred to here also allow network/modem play too. Right at the end of this section, I will also review briefly some of instructional software packages on the market.

For more information on these programs and many more, visit Jim Loy's Bridge Software web site at www.mcn.net/~jimloy/.

Only a very small number of the packages mentioned in this section are available from High Street stores. The vast majority are sold through specialist outlets, a brief list of which can be found at the very end of this section.

Bridge-playing software

We all want programs that play to a level similar to our own, or a little better. Although bridge-playing programs are still some way behind their chess-playing counterparts, they are definitely getting better. At the 1998 World Bridge Championships in Lille, France, a program finished in the top third of a field containing 34 of the world's leading players competing in a contest to solve 'fiendishly difficult' problems. This result was so surprising that it was even reported on the front page of the *Daily Telegraph* (UK).

With more than 50 octillion possible deals in bridge before a single card is played, the programmers face an awesome task but they are getting there, and bridge players the world over now use software to help them sharpen their skills in every aspect of the game. The programs themselves now compete annually in the World Bridge Computer Championships.

It is my opinion that the programs awarded "5 Stars" below bid to a standard similar to the average club player, while their play and defence is a little worse than that.

SKILL RANKINGS

The Skill Rankings of each program were determined by short matches and by the programs' performances in bidding quizzes. Here is a very rough ranking of the bidding and play skill of the top programs. The packages are given stars (from 0-5 with 5 being the best) based on their performance in the various tests.

Rank	Program	bidding (out of 15)	play (out of 15)	total
5 Stars *****				
1	GIB	9	7+	16+
2	Bridge Baron 9	9	7	16
2	Q-plus Bridge	9	7	16
4	Micro Bridge 8	8	7	15
4	Meadowlark Bridge	9+	6–	15
4	Bridge Buff 6.0	9	6(peeks)	15
4	Saitek Pro Bridge 510	9+	6–	15
8	Endless Bridge 4.1	9	6–(peeks)	15–
9	Blue Chip Bridge	9+	5	14+
4 Stars ****				
10	Bridge Baron Lite	9	4	13
10	Bicycle Bridge	9	4	13
10	Oxford Bridge	9	4	13
13	Bridge Master Class (Omar)	7	4	11
13	Bridge Deluxe II (Omar)	7	4	11
13	Bridge Mate 3	5	6	11
16	Let's Play Bridge 98.6	6	4	10
17	MVP Bridge Deluxe/Windows	6	3	9
17	GOTO Bridge	6	3	9
17	Grand Slam Bridge II	6	3(peeks)	9

Rank	Program	bidding (out of 15)	play (out of 15)	total
3 Stars *				
20	Bridge Master (Capstone)	6	3-	9-
21	Finesse Bridge 2.2	5	3	8
21	Winning Bridge	5	3	8
21	Bridge for the Dummy	5	3	8
21	Easy Bridge	5	3	8
21	Smart Bridge	5	3	8
2 Stars **				
26	Play 'n Learn Bridge	4	3	7
26	Perfect Partner	4	3	7
26	Hoyle Bridge...	3	4	7
29	Bridge Olympiad	3	4–(peeks)	7-
30	Eddie Kantar's Br. Companion	3	3	6
30	Bridge 8.0	3(peeks)	3(peeks)	6

The following packages play very poorly and receive either a "1 Star" or "No Stars" ranking: Saitek Pro Bridge 310, Randy's Bridge, Classic 5 Games, Bridge Pal, Bridge for Windows, Bridge Partner Alice, TRBridge, Expert Cardgames Classics

PROGRAM FEATURES

The standard to which the programs play may not be that important to you, but perhaps you expect it to have certain features. All the top-ranking programs offer outstanding graphics and lots of features. In this section, the various packages are awarded stars from 1-5 (5 being the best) based on the following criteria:

- User friendliness;
- Number of conventions available;
- Bugs;
- Extra features such as: Are takebacks allowed? Can you input your own hands? Can you choose which compass position you occupy? etc.

In the table below, packages which perform particularly well or badly in a specific area are annotated by: ! = Great feature, + = Good feature, – = Bad feature

5 STARS ***
GIB – Ginsberg's Intelligent Bridge Player
Just Write, Inc, 29585 Fox Hollow Rd, Eugene OR 97405
Web site: www.gibware.com
Win. CD – $79.95 + s/h (133 MHz Pentium)
+ 46 conventions
! Systems = Standard American, Acol, Two-over-One forcing,
   Kaplan/Sheinwold
! Skill levels = many
+ Closed room
! Deal types = many
! Several lead & signal options

This program, popularly referred to as GIB, is the reigning World
Champion and is based on the program that generated all the
excitement at Lille in 1998. Unlike other programs it uses
techniques from artificial intelligence and its outstanding card-
playing ability is based on an extremely fast double dummy solver.
It uses the method known as *partition searching* to deal the
opponents' cards at random over and over again until it arrives at a
solution based on the bidding and play up to that point. It uses
similar methods to arrive at a choice of bid
    Like all the programs on offer it comes with a wide range of
features including a number of pre-packaged hands. These allow
you to compare your results with those achieved by some of the
world's top players. For example, you can try all the deals played in
the final of the 1997 Bermuda Bowl.
    GIB needs a CPU running at 133MHz or faster and at least 32
Mbytes of memory. Windows 95/98/NT or Linux. You need a
display resolution of 800x600 pixels.
**Summary: Easily the best card-playing program currently
available.**

 Bridge Baron 9
Great Game Products Inc., 8804 Chalon Drive, Bethesda, MD 20817
Tel: 1-800-GAMES-4-U
Email: brbaron@erols.com Web site: www.bridgebaron.com
DOS/Windows/Mac(ver 7.6) – $59.95 + $7 s/h
The DOS version is nice looking, but not as fancy
10 conventions

Systems = Five-card Majors, Two-over-One forcing and Acol
+   Skill levels = 7
!   Deal types = really tremendous variety
+   Duplicate matches
!   Explains the bids in numerous ways, including interactive flow
    charts
!   Tutorial – Blackwood Bridge Challenges
!   You can compete in weekly worldwide tournaments
+   Defensive signals
!   Network/modem
–   They sometimes take forever to answer email on complaints

The 1997 World Champion remains one of the most popular
programs. It offers a choice of Acol, Standard American or Two-
over-One bidding systems. It includes 24 challenge hands designed
by Easley Blackwood, the man responsible for inventing one of the
best-known conventions in bridge. It has one of the best deal
generators and produces really interesting hands. It offers hints
during both the bidding and the play and can be asked to defend
double dummy. You can set up a network and by getting online you
can compete in weekly worldwide tournaments.

   Unlike almost all the other programs it is available in both PC
and MAC versions.

   You need Windows 3.1 or higher on at least a 386 with 4MB of
Ram free on your hard disk.
Summary: An excellent all-round program.

Q-plus Bridge (v5)
Q-plus Software, Belfortstrasse 10, D-81667 Munich, Germany
Email: 100675.1114@compuserve.com Web site: www.q-plus.com
Windows CD- $60
USA & Canada: ACBL & Baron Barclay & Writewoman
Other countries, see the Q-plus www page, above
!   Systems: Acol (basic & advanced), Standard American (basic &
    advanced), Kaplan-Sheinwold, Precision (simple & advanced),
    Schenken
!   120+ conventions
+   Skill levels = many
+   Explains bids (alerts artificial bids and all doubles and shows
    point-count ranges)

! Deal types = tremendous variety
! Several lead & signal options
Note: There is a version (P-plus) for the Psion Series 5.

Developed in Germany by Johannes Leber, this became one of the
most popular programs following its debut in the 1994 World
Computer Championships in Albuquerque. One of the most varied of
the programs currently available, it can play no less than five different
systems: Acol, Precision Club, Standard American, Kaplan-Sheinwold
and Schenken's "Big Club". Its wide range of features include the
ability for you to specify the type of hand you would like to have
including the number of high-card points and the length of the suits.
    Requires Windows 3.1 on a 386.
**Summary: Entertaining and easy to use. Ideal for players at
every level.**

Micro Bridge 8
Tomio Uchida, 2-1-7 Mizonuma, Asaka-shi, Saitama-ken 351,
Japan
Email: mcbridge@tky.threewebnet.or.jp
Web site: www.threeweb.ad.jp/~mcbridge
USA & Canada: ACBL
Windows CD – $70 (cash or MO) includes s/h (no personal checks)
+   52+ conventions. Define your own conventions
+   Systems = Acol, Four-card Majors, Five-card Majors, Two-over-
    One Game Force, Japan Standard, Club series, or define your
    own systems
!   Deal types = Tremendous variety
!   Skill levels = 10 (some very very slow on most machines)
+   Pairs & team matches
+   Defensive signals
!   Download free demo
!   Network/modem
Note: Micro Bridge 7 (a DOS program) is still available?

This popular program has performed consistently well in the World
Championships. It offers a wide choice of systems including Acol,
four-card majors, five-card majors, Two-over-One Game Force, and
Japan Standard. If you don't like any of those you can define your
own system! It also offers you the chance to play on a network. One

of its best features is the huge amount of data that has been stored from major events allowing you to play in both Pair and Teams tournaments in the comfort of your own home. Unlike many of its competitors it comes on a CD.

Summary: Excellent features for Pair and Teams play.

Meadowlark Bridge v1.3

Meadowlark Software, 2718 N. Broadway #283, Fargo, ND 58102
Email: meadowlark@rrnet.com Web site: rrnet.com/meadowlark
Windows – $59.95 + $5 s/h
+ 50+ conventions
! Systems = Five-card Majors, Two-over-One forcing,
   Kaplan/Sheinwold, SAYC, Simple
! Skill levels = 3 bidding, 3 play (various bird personalities)
! Tournaments with numerous computer teams
+ Deal types = great variety
– You must play South
+ Defensive signals
! A demo version can be downloaded from Meadowlark's www
   page. Allows you three 24-hand tournaments before repeating
   the hands
! Print hands shows all alerts and artificial bids, as well as a list of
   all conventions that both partnerships use

***** Bridge Buff 6.0

BridgeWare, PO Box 65077, 358 Danforth Ave, Toronto, Ontario
M4K 3Z2 Canada
Tel: 1-800-WEAK-1NT
Email: bbuff@user.bridgebuff.com Web site: www.bridgebuff.com
$99.95 + $5 s/h – Windows or MSDOS $49.95 upgrade if you
registered an earlier version
+ 30 conventions (+ several non-optional conventions)
Systems = Five-card Majors, Two-over-One forcing, Kaplan-
Sheinwold
! Create your own systems and conventions
– Peeks at the other hands during play
! Skill levels = 2
! Kibitzer explains bids, Post Mortem estimates how various
   contracts would do
+ Defensive signals

Visual Deal ($99.95 or $49.95 if you have Bridge Buff) – really tremendous variety of deal types and more

Saitek Pro Bridge 510
Saitek Ltd, 12/F, 414 Kwun Tong Rd, Kwun Tong, Hong Kong
Baron Barclay, 3600 Chamberlain Lane, Suite 230, Louisville, KY 40241
Tel: 1-800-274-2221
Email: bbarclay@iglou.com
Web site: www.iglou.com/baronbarclay/
$349 – stand-alone laptop computer, liquid crystal display
16 conventions
Systems: Five-card Majors, Four-card Majors, Acol, French Five-card Majors, Precision
Most of the good features of other programs
!   Pro Bridge 310 ($149) can be used as plug-in terminal
Cannot print hand
Note: The model 310 has very few features, by itself.

Endless Bridge 4.1
455 Alfreton Rd, Nottingham, NG7 5LX, UK
$147.50 – MSDOS
9 conventions
Systems = Acol, 5-Card Majors
!   Deal types = tremendous variety
Defensive signals = first trick only (attitude or high from doubleton)
–   Copy protection = Original diskette must be in drive
Has extensive manual, instead of help messages
+   Closed room
–   A few minor bugs
–   Cannot take back bid
–   Peeks at the other hands during play
Note: This is the English version of Eindeloos Bridge, from Bridgesoft, in Holland.

Blue Chip Bridge 3.0.1
Blue Chip Bridge Ltd, P O Box 167, Waltham Cross, EN7 5GB UK
Web site: www.bluechipbridge.co.uk (free upgrade?)
£65.00 (Free p&p in UK, elsewhere at £2.50) – Windows
13 conventions

System = Acol + five-card majors
!   You can define your own bidding conventions and systems with difficulty
!   Deal types = tremendous variety
+   Defensive signals
+   Bidding and card-play tutorials
Note: peeking at card-play is default setting, called "best play"

In the United Kingdom, Acol and the "weak no-trump" are the universal bidding methods employed by players at home or in clubs and tournaments, and Blue Chip is way ahead of its competitors when it comes to this phase of the game. In the current world-ranking list it ties for first place with two other programs.

Its bidding strength is derived from a vast editable bidding database containing hundreds of thousands of sequences. Possessing all the standard technical options, it includes a number of unique features including a "Bidding Tutor" that offers tips and advice during the auction. It recently played in and won a club duplicate, making it the first program to win a tournament against human players!

The inventors, Ian Trackman & Mike Whittaker, are quietly confident about its chances in the next World Championships in January 2000 in Bermuda.

You need a Pentium with Windows 95 or better and at least 16 Mbytes of memory.
Summary: The number one program for Acol players.

4 STARS**
Bridge Baron Lite
Great Game Products Inc., 8804 Chalon Drive, Bethesda, MD 20817
Tel: 1-800-GAMES-4-U
Email: brbaron@erols.com Web site: www.bridgebaron.com
Windows – $20 + $5 s/h ($45 + $5 s/h upgrade to Bridge Baron)
7 conventions
Systems = Five-card Majors
Skill levels = 2
Deal types = some
+   Duplicate matches
!   Explains the bids in numerous ways, including interactive flow charts
!   You can compete in weekly worldwide tournaments

Defensive signals
Note: This is a cheaper version of Bridge Baron, fewer options, only 10,000 deals

Bicycle Bridge
Expert Software, 800 Douglas Rd., Coral Gables, FL 33134
About $10 – Windows 3.1 and 95 on one CD
System = Standard American
- 7 conventions
- Cannot print deal

Oxford Bridge v4.58
Thinking Games, Cedar Lodge, The Crescent, Pattishall, Northants NN12 8NA England
email: ob@thinkgam.demon.co.uk www.thinkgam.demon.co.uk
Windows £59.95 or DOS £49.95
DOS version uses text mode (boxes & suit symbols)
+ Systems: Standard American, Acol, European Five-card Majors
   25+ conventions
! Skill levels = many
! You can define your own bidding conventions and systems
! Explains bids in numerous ways
+ Count signals (only?)
+ Closed room
! Very detailed manual (substitutes for help messages)
Copy protection – must uninstall before reinstalling

Bridge Master Class with Omar Sharif
Oxford Softworks, Stonefield House, 198 The Hill, Burford, Oxford, OX18 4HX, UK
Web site: www.demon.co.uk/oxford-soft/bridge.html
£40 + s/h – MSDOS CD
About 25 conventions
Systems: Acol & Standard American (Five-card Majors)
+ Defensive signals
Very fancy looking
+ Deal types = many
! Can install on to a very small hard disk
- Both partnerships must use the same conventions
! CD has good lectures by Omar Sharif ! Network/modem

Bridge Deluxe II with Omar Sharif
Interplay Productions, 17922 Fitch Ave, Irvine, CA 92714
Email: orderdesk@interplay.com
Web site: www.interplay.com (has patches for older programs)
$29.95 – MSDOS CD (Mac and Windows versions planned) Mac
version is Bridge Deluxe with Omar Sharif, from MacPlay
25 conventions
Systems: Acol & Standard American (Five-card Majors)
+   Defensive signals (rare?)
Very fancy looking
+   Deal types = many combinations
!   Can install onto a very small hard disk
−   Both partnerships must use the same conventions
!   CD has good lectures by Omar Sharif
!   Network/modem

This brand new program was released in the summer of 1999. Its
number one feature is a fully interactive video tutorial with Omar
Sharif acting as your personal tutor. It also offers an Internet play
option – most programs don't. Designed to resemble the human
style of play, the program never peeks at the hidden hands.
   It offers Acol, five-card majors and Standard American, and you
can also design and save your own bidding configurations.
   Requires Windows 95, CD-ROM.
**Summary: A fine introduction to computer bridge at an
attractive price.**

Bridge Mate 3
Bridge Mate, 6374 Chinook Dr, Clinton, WA 98236
Email: bobr@whidbey.com
Windows – $69.95 (upgrade $34.95)
!   237+ conventions, much more than any other
!   Systems = Standard American, Two-over-One forcing, Goren,
    Kaplan/Sheinwold, Precision
−   Peeks at the cards, after opening lead
!   Deal types = Really tremendous variety
+   Skill levels = 9
+   Closed Room
!   Lots of lead & signal options
!   Explains the bids in numerous ways, including alerting

Let's Play Bridge – 98.6

Terry Inc, PO Box 21289, Carson City, NV 89721
Email: lpb@letsplaybridge.com
Web site: www.letsplaybridge.com (plenty of info)
Windows – Shareware – $39.95 to register to unlock features
System: Five-card Majors (Weak no-trump, artificial strong raises)
10 conventions (several non-optional conventions)
download free demo from www page, only deals 9 hands
Deal types = 4 types
! All upgrades are free
+ Suit preference signals
! Network/modem
– No card-play hints, no takeback, no play review, can't print deal
   (cards disappear when you go to menu)

MVP Bridge Deluxe for Windows v3.2 (and v.3.03 for DOS)

MVP Software, P.O. Box 888281, Grand Rapids, MI 49588
Tel: 1-800-968-9684
Email: 74777.1116@compuserve.com
Web site: www.mvpsoft.com
$39.95 – Windows ($20 upgrade for registered users) $29.95 –
DOS (same skills, looks different) free – MVP Bridge (shareware,
use for limited time)
13 conventions
Systems: Four-card Majors (Goren) & Five-card Majors (Standard
American)
+ Closed room
+ Deal types = several
– Cannot take back bids, no play review, cannot print deal
+ Tutorial hands
! Network/modem

GOTO Bridge v1.52

GOTO Informatique, Chateau de la Bonnerie, 111 rue de Croix,
59510 HEM, France
Email: bridge@goto.fr Web site: www.goto.fr/us
Windows – Shareware (download from www site) – register $9.95
Conventions: several, none optional
Systems: Five-card Majors (French standard), Weak Twos, Standard
American, Acol

! Deal types = tremendous variety
+ Nice looking bidding box
− Cannot see deal at end of play, cannot take back bids
Note: Weak 1NT response often gets to game if opener rebids

**** Grand Slam Bridge II
Electronic Arts, P O Box 7578, San Mateo, CA 94403-7578
about $15 − MSDOS or Windows CD
8 conventions
Systems: Five-card Majors & Four-card Majors
− Peeks at the hands during play
! Deal types = tremendous variety
− Cannot print deal
− Bug = will bid Jacoby transfers over 2NT, but won't recognize it
  when partner bids it

3 STARS***
*** Bridge Master
There is a bridge tutoring program of the same name
Capstone, 7200 N.W. 19th Street, Ste. 500, Miami, FL 33126
About $10 − MSDOS or Windows (There is also a Mac version)
4 conventions
Systems = Standard American − Five-card Majors
Network/modem?
DOS version crashes on Windows computers

Finesse Bridge 2.2
Wild Card Software, P.O. Box 208, Hockessin, DE 19707-9954
Tel: 1-800-334-2722
Email: mark@wildcards.com Web site: www.wildcards.com
Free during test period − Windows
− 0 conventions
Systems: Standard American − Four- or Five-card Majors (strong
Two-bids)
Signals high/low with a doubleton
− A few bidding quirks (mainly with strong 2-bids & Two-over-
  One response can be very weak)
− Cannot print deal
! Network/modem (new version 2)
+ Free Internet play during testing period

*** Winning Bridge (Older version called WinBridge)
Pik A Program, 13 Saint Marks Place, New York, NY 10003
Europe: Gerald Wilson, WinBridge orders, 36, Ferndale Rd, Church
Crookham, FLEET, Hampshire, GU13 0LN, UK
Email: 100046.670@compuserve.com
Windows – Shareware – register $29.95 + $4 s/h
Systems: Acol 5 conventions
– Can't takeback bids, no play review, can't print deal
Registered version has more features

Bridge for the Dummy 1.2
Butler Software Development, P O Box 451786, Los Angeles, CA
90045
Email: sales@b4td.com Web site: www.b4td.com
Shareware ($35 to register)
0 conventions
Systems: Five- or Four-card Majors
– Cannot print deal
+ Tutorial
Play review, must step through each card played

Easy Bridge
Steven Han
Email: shan@nyx.net
Web site: www.thegrid.net/shan/EasyBridge.htm
Free – Win95/NT/98
23 conventions
Systems: Five- or Four-card Majors
+ Explains bids and card play
Many deal types

**** SmartBridge 2.1
Francesco Barcio, Viale Abruzzo 154, 66013 Chieti (CH), Italy
ZDNet
Web site: www6.zdnet.com/cgi-bin/texis/swlib/hotfiles/info.html?
fcode=000NQQ
Shareware (reg = $25) – Windows
Systems: Five-card Majors, Canapé
9 conventions
+ English and Italian
– Cannot take back bid

2 STARS**
Play 'n Learn Bridge 1.0
Digital Frontier, Box 561, Brookline, MA 02146
Email: info@yourpace.com Web site: www.yourpace.com/bridge
$39.95 – Windows CD
System = Standard American (strong Two-bids)
- 0 conventions
+ Contains tutorial
Note: 3 modes – beginner = computer bids and plays, intermediate = user bids and plays, advanced = you cannot get hints or take back bids or plays

**** Perfect Partner
Positronic Software Inc, 164 Braemar Dr, Unit 106, Dartmouth, Nova Scotia, Canada, B2T 2T3
Tel: 1-800-565-4005
Email: mailto: david.positronic@ns.sympatico.ca
Web site: www3.ns.sympatico.ca/david.positronic/HOME.HTM
About $40 – Windows or Mac
! Will, in time, learn your bidding system, if close to Standard American
20 conventions – Bids and plays and loads slowly
Systems: Five-card Majors, Two-over-One forcing
- The bidding systems that come with the program, bid very poorly (half the time). They are apparently meant to be a foundation upon which you can build your own system.
- You must play South
+ Closed room
+ Skill levels = several
+ Defensive signals
+ Modem/network
- Only deal hands similar to those used to develop the bidding system
! Tutorials

*** Hoyle Bridge (Windows CD) about $12
*** Hoyle Classic Card Games (diskette) $40.95?
*** Hoyle Classic Games (Windows CD) $34.95
Sierra On-Line, Coarsegold, CA 93614
Price – see above

+   Nice looking (Hoyle Classic Card Games lower resolution)
+   Hoyle Classic Card Games = Crazy 8s, Old Maid, Hearts, Gin
    Rummy, Cribbage, Klondike, Bridge, Euchre + Hoyle Classic
    Games = Draw Poker, Bridge, Cribbage, Gin Rummy, Hearts,
    Solitaire, Old Maid, Crazy 8s, Backgammon, Checkers
0 conventions
System: Five-card Majors (limit raises)
−   No hints, no takeback, can't see deal at end, no play review,
    can't hand-enter, can't print deal

*** Bridge Olympiad
QQP (Quantum Quality Products), 495 Highway 202, Flemington,
NJ 08822
About $10 – MSDOS CD
Systems: Standard American, Natural, or Precision (crude)
+   Nice looking
0 conventions
−   No play review after last trick, no hand-entered deals, can't save
    hand, can't print hand
Many psychic bids from some partners or opponents (the program
calls this "cheating")
−   Peeks at the hands during play
−   Copy protection – You must look up a word in the manual
Note: Some people enjoy this program a lot

*** Eddie Kantar's Bridge Companion
Lifeware, 63 Orange St., St. Augustine, FL 32084-3584
Email: lsg@lifeware.com Web site: www.lifeware.com
About $12 – Windows CD
Systems – Goren & Five-card Majors
9 conventions
Systems: Four- & Five-card Majors
!   Several card-play tutorials
-   Won't let you pass out a hand
-   Bugs in the bidding

*** Bridge 8.0 (v6.0122)
Artworx, Penfield, NY 14526
Email: artworx@frontiernet.net Web site: www.artworx.com
$54.95 + $4 s/h – MSDOS or Mac

1 convention
System: Standard American (sort of) – Five-card Majors
– Peeks at your cards during play and bidding
! Download upgrade (v6.0122) from www page (press V at main menu to find out your version number).

DEFINITIONS OF TERMS USED IN THIS SECTION
Peeking = Some programs actually look at your cards, when making their decisions.
Closed room (and similar options) = The program rebids and replays the hand, so you can compare your auction and cardplay.
Deal types = You can specify what kinds of hands you want dealt, for practice (slam hands, Flannery hands, pre-empt hands...).

Instructional bridge software
Bridgemaster
Bridge Base Inc £49.99
The program presents a series of instructional deals that are certain to improve the user's declarer-play. Unlike human players the program always defends perfectly so if you make a mistake you will be defeated. A "bridge movie" accompanies each deal, explaining the correct line of play and the reasoning behind it. The problems are set at different skill levels so it can be used by players of all levels of ability, from beginners to World Champions. When you have completed all the deals – it will take you a long time – you can purchase additional sets of deals.
Requires Windows 3.1 with 1MB free hard disk space.
Summary: A terrific teaching tool and addictive fun.

Counting at Bridge
Bridge Base Inc £39.95
Using the same style of on screen presentation as *Bridgemaster*, Mike Lawrence, three times a World Champion and recognized as one of the leading writers of his generation, talks you through a series of problems. The majority relate to declarer play and the essential technique of learning to count your opponents' cards and points. At every stage you are faced by a question "How many

spades does West have?" or "How are the missing hearts divided?" After you have answered, rightly or wrongly, Mike shows you how the correct answer can be reached.

As in all the teaching programs you cannot put in your own hands but must play the ones that have been preloaded. At the end of a deal a "Post Mortem" summarizes all the key points you need to remember.

Requires Windows 3.1 on a 386.

Summary: An outstanding interactive tuition program.

Private Bridge Lessons I & II
Bridge Base Inc £39.95

The sequels to *Counting at Bridge* unravel the mysteries surrounding a variety of card play techniques. The first includes Endplays, Safety Plays and Simple Squeezes. The second describes, amongst others, the Crossruff, Dummy Reversals and Loser-on-Loser plays.

Requires Windows 3.1 on a 386.

Summary: Packed with advice for players of all abilities.

Defense
Bridge Base Inc £39.99

The latest program from the creators of *Counting at Bridge* and *Private Bridge Lessons* has over one hundred hands showing you exactly how good defenders take their tricks and why.

Requires Windows 3.1 or Windows 95/98, 3MB hard disk space.

Summary: A brilliant survey of defensive play.

The Master Solvers Club
Bridge Base Inc £34.99

Another program from the creators of *Counting at Bridge*, *The Master Solvers' Club* contains all the Master Solvers' Club problems that appeared in *The Bridge World* magazine (USA) in 1994, 1995 and 1996. (*Extra years 1989–1993 avaialble at £14.95 per year.*) A panel of experts help you to solve hundreds of difficult bidding and opening lead problems.

Requires Windows 3.1

Summary: A bidding masterclass.

Learn Bridge
CD £39.99
Interactive tutorial for beginners and improvers. Practise bidding, defence and card play, with an unlimited hand generator. Multimedia features include video animation and commentary. Uses five-card majors bidding system.
Requires CD drive, Windows 3.1, Windows 95, Windows 98, 8 MB of Ram, Sound card
Summary: An excellent introduction

Bobby Wolff's Bridge Mentor (ABTA Award 1999)
Bridge Trix £39.95
This is the latest product to come to the market. It is the first in a series of teaching programs designed to help you systematically to master the elements of card-play. This one deals with the most important techniques in no-trump play. It demonstrates a wide range of practical techniques which frequently arise. Uniquely, it uses video clips where ten times World Champion Bobby Wolff explains how you should arrive at the correct line of play. That feature reminds me of the old advertisement about having a bank manager in your cupboard – a World Bridge Champion is much more useful!

The problems can be tackled in several ways: they can be taken randomly, or in order, or grouped by topic. There are plenty of options that allow users to progress at their own pace.

The second in the series is expected to appear late in 1999.
Summary: Suitable for players at every level.

Where to get your bridge software

The London Bridge Centre, 369 Euston Road, London NW1 3AR
Tel: 0171-388 2404 Fax: 0171-388 2407
Email: bridgeshop@easynet.co.uk
Web site: www.bridgemagazine.co.uk
Bridge Plus Magazine, Box 384, Reading, Berks RG1 5YP, England
Tel: 0118-935 1052 Fax: 0118-935 1052
Email: bridgeplus@patrol.i-way.co.uk
Mr Bridge, Ryden Grange, Bisley, Surrey GU21 2TH, England
Tel: 01483 489961 Fax: 01483 797302
Email: bridge@mrbridge.demon.co.uk
Bridge Suppliers Scotland, Hope Street, Glasgow G2 6AB, Scotland
Tel: 0141 248 2887

English Bridge Union, Broadfields, Bicester Road, Aylesbury,
Bucks HP19 3BG, England
Tel: 01296 394414
Blue Chip Bridge Ltd
Tel: 01992 636074
Email: mike@bluechipbridge.co.uk
Oxford Softworks
Tel: 01993 823 463
Master Point Press, 22 Lower Village Gate, Toronto, Ontario,
M5P 3L7, Canada
Tel: (1)-416-932 9766 Fax: (1)-416-932 2816
Email: masterpointpress@home.com
ACBL, 2990 Airways Boulevard, Memphis TN 38116, USA
Tel: (1)-901-332 5586
Email: 74431.3434@compuserve.com
Baron Bridge Supplies, 3600 Chamberlain Lane, Suite 230,
Louisville, KY 40241, USA
Tel: (1)-502-426 0410 Fax: (1)-502-426 2044
E-mail: bbarclay@iglou.com
C & T Bridge Supplies, 3838 Catalina Street, Los Alamitos, CA
90720, USA
Tel: (1)-310-598 7010

ONLINE COMPUTER BRIDGE

Even if you have not yet played online bridge, you will no doubt have realized that it is one of the fastest-growing forms of the sport today. The attractions of playing online are numerous. Perhaps you do not have time to play a complete four-hour session, but would like to play for half an hour before you go to work or while waiting for dinner to cook. Perhaps your local club doesn't allow you to smoke at the table, and that bothers you. Maybe you are on-call, and must therefore hang around the house in case you are urgently needed at work. Maybe your car has broken down, so getting to the club tonight is difficult, or perhaps the weather is just too awful to go out. Whatever the reason, online bridge means you can play your favourite sport without leaving the comfort of your armchair.

The growth of online bridge is also a godsend for many serious partnerships who do not live in the same town, state or even country. Now they can practise together regularly without having to travel miles to do so.

We are not yet at the stage where online bridge has replaced face to face (FTF) games, but it is not inconceivable that it one day will.

So, what's it all about?

In this section, we offer a brief description of many of the online bridge clubs, as well as details of how to find them. You may wonder at the description of these online sites as "clubs", but to those who play regularly that is exactly what they are. They are "places" where you can "go" to play, to kibitz, to attend lessons or supervised practice sessions, or just to meet friends and chat.

These sites can be divided into two distinct groups – free sites, most of which offer bridge as well as many other games, and subscription sites.

Pay sites
OKBRIDGE
OKBridge is the biggest and the best of all the commercial online bridge clubs. It was also the first. Not enough can be said about this great live bridge game, invented and presented by Matthew Clegg.

Players are able to play pairs, IMP pairs, team games or rubber bridge, and they can also enter tournaments and knock-out team events – everything you might want from a regular bridge club! Of all the online sites, this one is probably the most formal, and by that I mean that it has the most in common with a conventional club or tournament.

OKBridge also offers by far the best service in terms of graphics, ease of use, and any other criteria you can think of. The software allows communication between players and their opponents, and one-way communication between players and the gallery (the kibitzers). It is common practice to self-alert conventional bids, and to provide the opponents (and the spectators) with explanations of your own bids, none of which can be seen by your partner. You can also store convention cards for regular partners, or use one of the standard OKB versions. Either Standard American Yellow Card or OKBridge Two over One are the most common systems played here.

OKBridge is an excellent place to meet new bridge-playing friends and chat with players from around the world. There are also plenty of opportunities to kibitz some of the world's greatest players. You will also find plenty of teachers and professional players available if you are looking for formal instruction. No matter your level, you will find a game to suit your tastes at OKBridge.

OKBridge currently boasts in excess of 15,000 subscribers. The catch is that it is also the most expensive of all the online clubs — the current cost of a regular membership is $99/year, and you must double that for a "Tournament membership", which allows you to participate in the daily matchpointed or IMP-pairs competitions.

The OKBridge software is easy to download and very user-friendly. When you log in the OKBridge server, you will see a list of tables currently in play (and you can click on any of them to see not only who is playing, but also who is watching). You will also see a list of players who are in "the lobby". Whenever a table needs a fourth or a pair, a request can be sent to the lobby. Such messages will usually indicate the level of player preferred, the type of scoring, and any other information. For example, such a message might read, "Intermediate player needed for friendly IMP game for a half hour". If you don't see a game you like, you can always start (or serve) your own table.

OKBridge requires players to adhere to certain standards of etiquette too, just as you would expect from a FTF club (and this is one reason that players are willing to pay to play there rather than using one of the free services). For example, it is customary to ask if it is all right to take a vacant seat, rather than rushing to sit down. Vacant seats are often filled on a first-come basis, and someone else may have arrived before you. The "server" at a table also has the facilities for disconnecting anyone who is rude or unco-operative.

The number of tables in play at any one time varies according to the time of day. The busiest time, and thus the time when there is the biggest choice of tables to join or partners to play with, is 18.00–03.00 Eastern time. At these times it is normal to find upwards of 200 tables in play and over 1000 players online. At quieter times, you might find as few as 10 tables going and a handful of players hanging out or looking for a game.

In addition to the regular club activities, subscribers to OKBridge also receive via email a free monthly magazine called *The OKBridge Spectator*. This magazine includes news of current and future OKBridge events as well as regular columns by writers such as Mike Lawrence, Matt Granovetter, Marc Smith and Frank Stewart.

OKBridge is not cheap, but it is well worth the money, particularly when you compare it with the cost of playing in a local club game.

To join OKBridge or to set up a free trial membership, visit their web site at www.okbridge.com or email info@okbridge.com.

BRIDGE PLAYER LIVE

This is a popular UK-based online bridge club with facilities for kibitizing and chatting as well as playing. The graphics are good here also, but the number of players online, and thus the choice of tables to join, is less than at OKBridge. An advantage (or disadvantage) of BPL is that the "standard" system here in Acol, rather than Standard American.

Software is easy to download and run. Current subscription rates for BPL are $83/year for unlimited play. Free trial memberships are available.

For more information, visit the BPL web site at www.bridgeplayerlive.com.

WIREPLAY

This is another UK site. This one is owned by BT (British Telecom) and designated as "a direct-dial gaming service".

If you are used to BPL or OKBridge, then you will be disappointed with the graphics here. There are usually only 2-3 tables in play at any one time, although it is very club-like in that you will tend to meet up with the same players regularly.

In addition to playing together on Wireplay, many of the players who frequent this particular club are also on an email-based chat group through which they exchange stories, hands and problems.

For more information, visit the Wireplay web site at www.wireplay.com/uk/mindgames/

Free sites

THE MICROSOFT INTERNET GAMING ZONE

Known simply as "The Zone", this is a popular site featuring all kinds of games. It is not uncommon for more than 10,000 people to be visiting the site at any one time, hundreds of whom will be playing bridge. What's more, it is absolutely free, but you must have Windows 95/98/NT to operate the software – hardly surprising since the site is maintained and financed by Microsoft.

The bridge software has recently been vastly improved by Canadian computer whiz kid and Bermuda Bowl silver medallist, Fred Gitelman.

The software is easy to download and use. The graphics are also excellent. You will be required to choose an online "handle" and a pictorial icon. The listing of the tables in play are depicted by the players' icons seated around a table. If there is an open chair, you may sit down and play.

One excellent feature of this site is that, unlike most other online clubs, you do not have to wait until you have four players in order to play. A bridge-playing "robot" will make up the table until another live player shows up to replace it. Of course, the robot's bidding and play are generally hopeless, but their presence does at least allow you to begin play immediately if you wish to do so. When another human arrives, the robot is automatically ejected from the game and replaced by the live player. This does have a downside of course, since you may replace a robot halfway through a hand, having not heard the bidding or seen the previous tricks.

The atmosphere at "The Zone" is friendly and informal. Players come and go, often without announcement. You can choose to play matchpoints, IMPs or rubber bridge, and the various choices are then subdivided according to standard.

In addition to the playing facilities, this site also offers regular lectures by guest experts.

"The Zone" is a lot of fun, and certainly worth checking out, particularly since it is free.

For more information, visit the web site at www.zone.com.

GO NETWORK

This is another free site, and features numerous classic games including bridge. You will have to register to enter the site, but once there you can play bridge or any other game on offer.

Go Network also has robot players (like "The Zone") to fill in when the table is not full.

This site is aimed at the novice player. Besides the actual game facilities, novices will find plenty of information such as what is called a "Bidding Primer" – a simple set of rules for basic bidding.

For more information, visit the Go Network web site at www.go.com/Center/Games/Play/Classic_games.

WINBRIDGE

This is a relatively new site, and clearly a lot of effort went into designing it. The graphics are great and the software has plenty of features.

Perhaps it just hasn't caught on yet, but at the time of writing there do not seem to be many players using this site . However, the software is easy to download and it's a free site, so the chances are that it will become popular as more players discover it.

For more information visit the web site at www.winbridge.com.

YAHOO JAVA BRIDGE

The Yahoo Games site includes bridge. Everyone with Internet access has probably used the Yahoo search engines at some point. For many of our web-searching needs, Yahoo does everything we need it to do, but their Games site is another matter.

The Yahoo Games site is free. That's the good news. However, the registration process is tediously lengthy, particularly if you happen to live in a country that is not called the USA. Having fought your way through the registration, it's time to download the software. All I can say is, "I hope you don't have anything else to do today."

Then there is that word "Java". For most PC-based uses, the Java interface is clunky and time-consuming, with lots of annoying screen refreshes. If you do something the Java applet does not like, they can be unforgiving. Even if you manage to avoid crashing so often that you decide to take up needlework and throw the PC away, the other players at the table may not be so lucky. As you will quickly discover when you get into the world of online bridge, it is exceedingly frustrating when players crash during a hand. I have not yet managed to play a complete hand at the Yahoo Games site, and I doubt I ever will.

If you still want to investigate the site for yourself, point your browser to play.yahoo.com/games/login?game=Bridge

PLAY SITE
This is another Java-based site, and a brand new one at the time of writing. This is the site's advertising blurb:

> "100% Java, latency-tolerant, multiplayer board and card games that incorporate chat, messaging, tournaments and player ratings. The PlaySite team is currently developing new and original multiplayer games to add to PlaySite, which has been recognized as the premier Java gaming site on the World Wide Web."

It is hard to believe that with the Java base this site can compete with places such as OKBridge and "The Zone".

For information, visit the web site at www.playsite.com.

FLOATER
Software is available for Mac, Unix and Windows users.

This is another free site, although not as yet a particularly popular one, although not for want of effort on the part of its creators, Geoff Pike and Jim Foster at the University of California at Berkeley.

The software is easy to download, install and play.

For more information, check the web site at cs.berkeley.edu/~pike/floater/

PASSPORT2

A new look site from Legacy Software. The Passport2 network has bridge, backgammon, and chess all fully up and running as well as the first multiplayer educational game for kids (Spell-O-Rama). Players must be using Windows 95 or better.

For information, check out the web site at: www.passport2.com

New sites

The following sites are either brand new at the time of writing, or scheduled to open soon. I include their details, and a web page address so that you can check them out if you feel so inclined, although I can offer no recommendations, and any comments below are those made by the site's advertising blurb.

CYBER CITY INTERNATIONAL BRIDGE

www.netfun.com./cybercity/
Must install the full Cyber-City software. Windows only.

THE JAVA MULTIGAME MACHINE

paul.rutgers.edu/~xuelin/ypc/bridge.html

SONY ONLINE ENTERTAINMENT CLASSIC GAMES

www.station.sony.com/classics/
Sony Online Entertainment expands – new "Classic Games" Area.

ONLINE BRIDGE RESOURCES

I have looked elsewhere at online sites where you can play bridge, but that is only one aspect of what the Internet has to offer bridge players. Details of bridge magazines, software, and organizations can also be found in other sections.

Here, are some pointers to other online bridge resources. This is not intended as a definitive list, far from it, but as a starting point. The World Wide Web offers an incredible variety of bridge sites including online bridge schools, bookshops, bridge travel organizers, and bidding forums as well as an enormous library of bridge articles, stories, etc. Some of these sites are players' personal pages. Here are the addresses of some of the best sites I have found, as well as some sites containing a wide range of bridge links...

Bridge link sites
Great Bridge Links: www.cbf.ca/GBL/
The ultimate bridge links site.
The ACBL Bridge Links Site: www.acbl.org/links.stm
A comprehensive list of links to bridge sites around the world. Everything is sorted geographically which would be a help for those looking for information about bridge in a certain part of the world.
The Internet Bridge Archive: rgb.anu.edu.au/Bridge
At this comprehensive (and impressive!) web site, Markus Buchhorn (Australia) provides archives of "anything and everything electronically available that is related to the card game (nay, sport!) of bridge that I can find". All the questions you ever have regarding bridge could very well be answered with a visit to the IBA...
Bridge Arkade: home.sol.no/~torskogl/enindex.htm
A Norwegian site with plenty of links.
Bridge Odyssey: rrnet.com/~rludwig/odyssey.html
Courtesy of Rodney A Ludwig, this bridge links list is extremely well laid out, comprehensive and informative.

Tournament sites
The World Bridge Federation: www.bridge.gr
Probably the most important of the sites currently available on the
Internet. It includes details of all forthcoming major events
worldwide. During major championships you can log on for up-to-
the-minute online reporting or to download the daily bulletins.

Bridge Plaza: www.bridgeplaza.com
Perhaps the best of all the bridge sites on the Internet, this is where
you can watch all the world's major events *live*, on VuGraph. You
can also watch the recorded VuGraph from these same events for
the past three of four years. Plus, there are photographs, results, and
much more. Be sure to add this site to you "Favourites" list.

Commercial online bridge schools
Bridge Forum International: www.bridge-forum.com
A fully-fledged online bridge school run by Harold Schogger of the
UK and Ellen Pomer from Canada, both experienced teachers with
many years experience. Expert tuition, lectures and supervised
practice sessions are provided by Mike Lawrence of the US, Ron
Klinger from Australia, Marc Smith of the UK, and Leo Glaser
from Canada.

In addition to pages containing monthly articles for novices,
intermediate and advanced players, the BFI site also features a
monthly "Bid with the Experts" competition, with prizes donated
by Master Point Press and a panel of world-class players to discuss
the hands.

The Bridge Today University: www.bridgetoday.com
BTU offers lessons "direct by email", with an emphasis on learning
how to think. Resident professors are Pamela and Matthew
Granovetter, Larry Cohen and Marshall Miles.

Learn Bridge Online: www.learn-bridge-online.com
Play bridge for free, pay for lessons, or pay to watch lessons. Larry
Cohen, Rhoda Walsh, Karen McCallum and Mark Lair are your
instructors at LBO. Free software is available to download
(Windows 95, 98, or NT only though). Nice graphics.

Onedown's Bridge School: www.escape.ca/~onedown/teac4.htm
This new school run by Richard Ternouth from Canada is a
gathering of teachers from North America and Europe.

Free on-line learning resources
The Fifth Chair Foundation: www.fifthchair.org
FCF is an international non-profit organization dedicated to
fostering bridge education on the Internet and attracting new
players to the game.

Learn to Play Bridge: www.acbl.org/notices/ltpb.stm
This program was written by Fred Gitelman, one of the top bridge
software authors, and is being given away free by the American
Contract Bridge League. You can download the program on to your
computer, and take the lessons at your own pace, offline. You don't
need any prior card-playing experience to take these lessons. After
you finish all the lessons, you'll be ready for one of the most
exciting, challenging hobbies – playing bridge. ACBL is providing
this $60 program to you free in order to promote bridge. The
program requires Windows 95, 98, 2000, or NT. Your monitor must
be set to at least 800x600.

Warren's Free Bridge Lessons Workshop: www.jps.net
Warren Hawley offers free party-bridge lessons online. You can
read the lesson notes and email questions. Challenges beginners,
intermediates and seniors to raise the level of their play, the easy
way.

North Shore Bridge: northshorebridge.com
Download a "Free Web Book" from this site in Laie, Hawaii. The
book contains duplicate bidding instruction for advancing players in
a free downloadable form. It is based on popular modern American
bidding methods using Losing Trick Count for hand evaluation. You
will also find book reviews, articles, and some advanced transfer
bidding theory at this site.

Welcome to Competitive Bridge: worldwidefolks.com
At this site you can try out Bob McConnell's "Competitive Bridge"
series. This is a six-part series for beginning duplicate and
tournament bridge players. All the little details about hand records

and travellers and kibitzers, sessions and sections, etc. There is also a full treatment of Two Over One methods for players new to duplicate. Free.

How to Score
Shirley Silverman shows beginning players how to keep score at various forms of the game. The links to each form of scoring are:
Matchpoints: www.iglou.com/baronbarclay/matchpt.htm
Duplicate: www.iglou.com/baronbarclay/duplscor.htm
Rubber Bridge: www.iglou.com/baronbarclay/rubbscor.htm
Chicago: www.iglou.com/baronbarclay/chicago.htm

Bridge for the Dummy: www.b4td.com
Tom Butler's site includes a wonderful "About Bridge" collection of pages, with extensive writing on all aspects of the game at a social level including Scoring, Definitions, General Approach, Offensive and Defensive bidding, and more.

**Introduction to the Game of Bridge:
www.pagat.com/boston/bridge.html**
Here you will find a comprehensive site with lots of information on how to play including Scoring, Common Terms, Types of Play, etc. While you're here, enjoy the huge collection of card games pages, card sites, and more – loads of Internet resource for card lovers of all kinds!

Online bridge libraries
Karen's Bridge Library: www.prairienet.org/bridge
Divided into sections for beginners, intermediate and advanced. This is a great collection of class handouts and reference sheets. Lots of quick tips, conventions, strategies and more. You'll learn it all here!

**The Bridge World Magazine's Introduction to Bridge:
www.bridgeworld.com/begin.html**
This site features great articles by well-known bridge writers.

The American Contract Bridge League Library: www.acbl.org
The ACBL site features an extensive online library

Richard Pavlicek's Home Page: www.gate.net/~pavlicek/rpbr.htm
This site contains a large collection of articles for players of all
levels, as well as quizzes, systems information, etc.

Online bridge columns
Ron Klinger columns: www.ron-klinger.com.au/columns.htm
Mr Klinger produces three weekly newspaper columns. Many can
be found at this site. Updated twice a month.
Alan Truscott columns: www.nytimes.com/diversions
Alan Truscott's newspaper columns on Mondays, Thursdays and
Sundays are posted here. There are also Internet-only columns on
Tuesdays and Fridays, and on Wednesdays during newsworthy
events.

Bobby Wolff columns: www.bridgetrix.com/aces_on_bridge.htm
The "Aces on Bridge" daily column appears at this web site.

The Laws of Bridge
Inside the Laws: www.blakjak.demon.co.uk/lws_menu.htm
The Laws of Bridge in all its forms. David Stevenson's Bridge
Page is home of the ultimate online discussion of bridge law
around the world, with articles on the Laws, discussions of
interpretations, and links to online Law books, as well as other
information. There is also a page here detailing the ACBL Alert
Procedure.

Bridge Proprieties: www.txdirect.net/users/biigal/d16bprop.htm
An outline of the game's Proprieties hosted by the ACBL's Unit 16
web site

Bidding forums
Bridge Forum International: www.bridge-forum.com
Conducted by British international Marc Smith, the expert panel
includes the likes of Paul Soloway, Eddie Kantar, Eric Kokish,
David Bird, Karen McCallum, Marshall Miles, and many more.
Prizes awarded monthly to the competition winners.

District 8 Solvers' Forum: www.priarienet.org/bridge
For those of you who like bidding quizzes, our District 8 "Solvers
Forum" column is now available on the Web. It's written every

other month in the style of *The Bridge World*'s Master Solver Club – six bidding problems answered and analysed by a panel of our local Midwest "experts".

Dutch Solvers Club: www.bridge.nl/ladder.htm
The Dutch Bridge Magazine *Bridge* has made a special edition of the Dutch Solvers Club on Internet. Answer the problems and send them to The Netherlands!
The International Bidders' Club: www.bridgespace.com
Try out each month's problems and compare your answers with those of the experts.

Bidding pages
All the Conventions You Could Want (for now): home.sprynet.com/sprynet/marlowc/allcon~1.htm
There are more than 270 conventions described and explained on this site. Chris Marlow is trying to obtain as many new conventions and sample hands as possible to make it "the most complete bridge convention guide on the net." Good luck Chris on a huge challenge!

The Internet Bridge Archives – Conventions area: rgb.anu.edu.au/Bridge/Bidding/Conventions

The Internet Bridge Archives – Systems area: rgb.anu.edu.au/Bridge/Bidding/Systems

The Bidding Systems Page: www.geocities.com/Vienna/1193/BridgeNsysIndex.html
Vlatko Primorac's web site contains links to every bidding system description that he can find on the net.

Standard English System: http://www.ebu.co.uk/ses.htm
The English Bridge Union's pages outline the Standard English System.

Acol Based Bidding Systems: www.cavendish.demon.co.uk/bridge
Chris Ryall's Acol site.

Standard American Yellow Card: www.annam.co.uk/sayc.htm
This is one of the many sites on the web where an outline of the most commonly played Internet system can be found.

Bridge World Standard: www.bridgeworld.com/bws.html

Commercial products
The Bridge Shopping Mall: http://www.cbf.ca/BridgeMall/

Bridge book suppliers
The London Bridge Centre: www.bridgemagazine.co.uk
Europe's biggest online bridge bookshop.

Master Point Press: www.pathcom.com/~raylee/homepage.html
North America's bridge publisher.

Jannersten Forlag AB: www.jannersten.se/
Sweden's major site for books and bridge supplies.

The Bridge Shop: www.bridgeshop.com.au/
Australia's premier place for books and bridge supplies.

BridgeRus: www.bridgerus.com/
A postage-free site for buying bridge books.

The Bridge Bookstore at Amazon:
www.prairienet.org/bridge/books.htm
A terrific place to browse through bridge books

The Mr Bridge Bookshop:
www.mrbridge.demon.co.uk/booksh.htm
A UK-based site that sells books and many other bridge-related items

The Bridge World Bookshelf:
www.bridgeworld.com/bookshelf.html
Books available from America's oldest bridge magazine.

Baron/Barclay Bridge Supplies: www.iglou.com/baronbarclay/
The world's biggest supplier of bridge books.

Vince Oddy Bridge Supplies: www.interlog.com/~voddy/
For the latest books, software and supplies.

Bridge travel and vacations

The Academy Bridge School: www.your1source.com/bridge/
A seven-day, six-night bridge vacation with Eddie Kantar in Calgary, Alberta. (Tip: Take the optional tour to Banff and Lake Louise, awesome countryside.)

Mercian Bridge: www.merciantravel.co.uk/
A UK-based company offering a wide range of speciality bridge playing holidays are available to some of the world's most exotic and interesting destinations.

Finesse Bridge Breaks: www.finessebridge.com/
The premier bridge vacation company.

Ron Klinger Bridge Holidays: www.ron-klinger.com.au/hol.htm
Bridge vacations "Down Under".

Bridge Pro Travel: http://web.wt.net/bridgepro/
Catering to players travelling to all of the major tournaments.

Professional players' associations

Professional Bridge Services: www.in.net/pro/
You want to hire a professional partner? This is a good place to start. Choose a name and read his/her resumé.

JUNIOR BRIDGE

Junior, in bridge terms, means under 25, although not so long ago, the age limit for juniors was, remarkably, 35. Many countries stage tournaments for junior players, with Zonal and World Championships, both pairs and teams, held biennially. Some countries also have events specifically for even younger players and, in 1997, the first Under-20 European Championship was held.

The first World Junior Teams Championship was held in 1987. The 1999 championships were played in Fort Lauderdale, Florida.

World Junior Teams
(for the ORTIZ PATINO TROPHY)

1987 PLAYED IN AMSTERDAM, NETHERLANDS:

1st **The Netherlands:**
Berry Westra, Enri Leufkens, Wubbo de Boer, Marcel Nooyen
2nd France:
Christian Desrousseaux, Alexis Damamme, Frank Multon, Bénédicte Cronier, Jean-Christophe Quantin

1989 PLAYED IN NOTTINGHAM, ENGLAND

1st **Great Britain:**
John Pottage, Andrew Robson, Derek Patterson
John Hobson, Stuart Tredinnick, Gerald Tredinnick
2nd Argentina:
Alejandro Bianchedi, Leonardo Rizzo, Claudio Varela
Marcelo Cloppet, Juan Martin Quitegui, Alexix Pejacsevich

1991 PLAYED IN ANN ARBOR, MICHIGAN, USA

1st **United States:**
John Diamond, Jeff Ferro, Debbie Zuckerberg
Martha Benson, Brian Platnick, Wayne Stuart
2nd Canada:
Fred Gitelman, Geoff Hampson, Mark Caplan
Bronia Gmach, Michael Roberts, Eric Sutherland

1993 PLAYED IN ARHUS, DENMARK
1st   Germany:
Klaus Reps, Roland Rohowsky
Markus Joest, Guido Hopfenheit
2nd   Norway:
Geir Helgemo, Lasse Aaseng, Svein-Gunnar Karlberg
Jorgen Molberg, Espen Kvam, Knut-Ove Thomassen

1995 PLAYED IN BALI, INDONESIA
1st   Great Britain:
Jason Hackett, Justin Hackett, Tow Townsend,
Jeff Allerton, Phil Souter, Danny Davies
2nd   New Zealand:
Del'Monte, Bach, Ker, Kearney, Smith, Ackerley

1997 PLAYED IN HAMILTON, ONTARIO, CANADA
1st   Denmark:
Morten Lund Madsen, Lars Lund Madsen, Freddi Brøndum
Jacob Røn, Mik Kristensen, Mikkel Bensby Nohr
2nd   Norway:
Boye Brogeland, Øyvind Saur, Bjørn-Morten Mathiesen
Christer Kristoffersen, Espen Erichsen, Thomas Charlsen

1999 PLAYED IN FORT LAUDERDALE, FLORIDA, USA
1st   Italy:
Bernardo Biondo, Riccardo Intonti, Mario d'Avossa,
Andrea Mallardi, Furio diBello, Stelio di Bello
2nd   USA:
Eric Greco, Chris Willenken, Tom Carmichael,
Joel Wooldridge, David Wiegand, Chris Carmichael

In 1991, the European Bridge League introduced an international pairs tournament for Juniors to precede the biennial Junior Camp (see below). When the WBF took over the running of the Junior Camps in 1995, they also took over the competition, and thus the World Pairs Championship was born. The medal winners are listed here:

World Junior Pairs medallists

1991 HELD IN FIESCH, SWITZERLAND
1st   Seidel & Wodniansky (Austria)
2nd   Korus & Tomski (Germany)
3rd   Bruun & Iversen (Denmark)

1993 HELD IN OBERREIFENBERG, GERMANY
1st   Dall & Thomsen (Denmark)
2nd   Puczynski & Puczynski (Poland)
3rd   Skoglund & Torhaug (Norway)

1995 HELD IN GHENT, BELGIUM
1st   Brogeland & Helgemo (Norway)
2nd   Erichsen & Charlsen (Norway)
3rd   Kristensen & M Madsen (Denmark)

1997 HELD IN FORLI, ITALY
1st   Solebrand & Wademark (Sweden)
2nd   Drøgemuller & Reim (Germany)
3rd   Brogeland & Hantviet (Norway)

1999 HELD IN FORLI, ITALY
1st   Saurer & Gloyer (Austria)
2nd   Stromberg & Nystrom (Sweden)
3rd   Biondo & Mazzadi (Italy)

Europe has led the way in encouraging Junior Bridge. The European Junior Championships have been held biennially since 1968.

European Junior Teams Championships

1968	Sweden	1984	France
1970	Denmark	1986	The Netherlands
1972	Poland	1988	France
1974	Sweden	1990	Norway
1976	Austria	1992	Italy
1978	Great Britain	1994	Great Britain
1980	Norway	1996	Norway
1982	Poland	1998	Italy

In addition to competitive events for juniors, the European Bridge League instituted a biennial Junior Camp in 1973. In 1995, the World Bridge Federation took over responsibility for the Junior Camp.

In 1989, as part of their general effort to encourage the development of Junior Bridge worldwide, the WBF instituted The Youth Awards. The intention of these awards is to reward those Junior Camp participants who display outstanding aptitude, diligence and international spirit.

In introducing the Youth Awards, WBF President at the time, Denis Howard of Australia, said: "The top players are not the WBF's only concern. Development of all young players is a priority in our plan, and in this respect we acknowledge the tremendous growth of Junior Bridge in Europe. It is therefore fitting for the WBF to institute a new award which, unlike almost all other distinctions in the world of bridge, honours aptitude, diligence and friendly behaviour, rather than performance at the bridge table."

Current WBF President, José Damiani, who was then President of the European Bridge League, added: "Among the many distinctions provided for those who shine in competition, these awards are special. They are not made for bidding, or play or defence, but for the spirit in which young people participate at Junior Camps. The Camps are not for the privileged, but for the common mortals: young people with many common interests, doubts and ambitions. When they arrive, they have bridge as a common hobby; when they leave they know much more about other people's mentality and feel comfortable in an international environment. To be able to distinguish yourself in such a forum is most commendable."

Below are the winners of the WBF Youth Awards since their inception in 1989.

WBF Youth Award Winners
1989 YOUTH AWARDS
announced at the 8th European Junior Camp in Mragovo, Poland:

Wim Hendriks (The Netherlands)
Andrew J Merrison (Great Britain)
Witold Tomaszek (Poland)
Sergej Zernov (USSR)

1991 YOUTH AWARDS
announced at the 9th European Junior Camp in Fiesch, Switzerland:

Lennart Heip (Belgium)
Julia Korus (Germany)
Stephan Magnusson (Switzerland)
Peter Pade (Denmark)

1993 YOUTH AWARDS
announced at the 10th European Junior Camp in Obereiffenberg, Germany.

Panos Papadopoulos (Greece)
Marco Pengov (France)
Brian Powell (Great Britain)
Ruth Sorrell (Israel)

1995 YOUTH AWARDS
announced at the 1st World Junior Camp in Ghent, Belgium

Andrei Mihailescu (Switzerland)
Henrik Røn (Denmark)
Tony Seto (USA)
Shelley Unger (Austria)

1997 YOUTH AWARDS
announced at the 2nd World Junior Camp in Santa Sofia, Italy

Mette Drøgemüller (Denmark)
Daniel Stanghelle (Norway)
Schelte Wijma (The Netherlands)
Daniel Zagorin (USA)

1999 YOUTH AWARDS
announced at the 3nd World Junior Camp in Nymburk, Czech Republic

Josh Heller (Canada)
Monika Miroslaw (Germany)
Kathrine Stensrud (Norway)
Thomas Schønfeldt (Denmark)

BRIDGE MAGAZINES OF THE WORLD

Magazines in English
ACBL Bulletin
– the official publication of the American Contract Bridge League

Address:	American Contract Bridge League
	1990 Airways Boulevard
	Memphis TN 38116-3847
Phone:	(1)-901-332 5586
Editor:	Brent Manley
Regular features:	Reports of ACBL and major international events
	Information on upcoming ACBL events
	Masterpoint information
	New Players' Section
	Intermediate Players' Section (articles by Kantar, Bergen, etc)
	"Master Pointers" (articles by Lawrence, Kantar, Kokish, etc)
	"Partnership Bridge with the Granovetters"
Issues per year:	12
Subscription:	US$18 to non-members
	US$10 to ACBL members paid with annual subscriptions

Australian Bridge

Address:	P O Box 429, Willoughby, NSW 2068, Australia
Telephone:	(61)-2-9967 0444
Email:	ab@grandslam.com.au
Publisher/Editor:	Stephen Lester
Regular features:	"Twenty Years Ago"
	"State Reports" – a round-up of recent Australian tournaments
	"Bidding Forum"
	"Test Your Opening Leads"
	"Problems for Average Players"
	"Bidding Challenge"

Issues per year:	6 (increasing to 12 in 1999)
Subscription:	AU$37.50 within Australia
	AU$48.50 to New Zealand
	AU$60.50 to the USA
	AU$62.50 to Europe

Bridge Canada
— the official publication of the Canadian Bridge Federation

Address:	20284 121 Ave, Maple Ridge BC
	V2X 9S4, Canada
Telephone:	(1)-604-465 2933
Fax:	(1)-604-465 2979
Email:	jude@cbf.ca
Web site:	www.cbf.ca
Editor:	Jude Goodwin-Hanson
Regular features:	Articles by Canadian bridge authors
	Articles about Canadian bridge players
	Reports of local, national and international competitions
	News from the Canadian Bridge Federation Board to members
Issues per year:	3
Subscription:	Distributed free to CBF members

BRIDGE Magazine

Address:	The London Chess Centre, 369 Euston Road
	London NW1 3AR, England
Telephone:	(44)-0171-388 2404
Email:	chesscentre@easynet.co.uk
Web site:	www.bridgemagazine.co.uk
Editor:	Mark Horton
Deputy Editor:	Sally Brock
Regular features:	Sandra Landy's Diary
	"Partnership Profile"
	"Marks & Comments"
	Tournament reports from Britain and around the world
	"Modern Bidding Theory"
	David Bird's Abbot stories
	Barry Rigal's "Letter from America"

Issues per year: 12
Subscription: £ 29.95 within the UK
               £ 38.95 to Europe and Rest of World
               US$60 to the USA

The first ever magazine, founded in 1926.

Bridge Plus
Address: P O Box 384, Reading, Berks RG1 5YP,
               England
Telephone: (44)-118-935 1052
Email: bridgeplus@patrol.i-way.co.uk
Editor: Elena Jeronimidis
Regular features: "Meet the Stars"
               "The Batsford Acol Bidding Quiz"
               "Cyberbridge"
               Ron Klinger's "Play a Hand with the Expert"
               Dave Huggett's "Improver's Page"
               Freddie North's "It Happened That Way"
               "Director, Please!"
               Derek Rimington's "Bridge with an Expert"
Issues per year: 12
Subscription: £28.00 within the UK
               £32.50 to Europe
               £43.00 to Rest of the World

Bridge Today
Address: Griffin Enterprises, 3329 Spindletop Dr NW
               Kennesaw, GA 30144-7336
Fax: (1)-440-446 9537
Email: Matt@Bridgetoday.com
Web site: Bridgetoday.com
Editors: Matthew & Pamela Granovetter
Regular features: Everything dedicated to the tournament player
               Contributors include: Larry Cohen, Eddie
               Kantar, Michael Rosenberg and Al Roth
Issues per year: 6
Subscription rates: US$29 within the US
               US$34 within Canada
               US$41 outside North America

The Bridge World

Address:	717 White Plains Road, Suite 106
	Scarsdale NY 10583-6713, USA
Telephone:	(1)-914-725 6712
Fax:	(1)-914-725 6713
Email:	mail@bridgeworld.com
Web site:	www.bridgeworld.com
Editor:	Jeff Rubens
Regular features:	Reports on major events, usually from a player closely involved
	"Test Your Play"
	"Fifty Years Ago"
	Book and software reviews
	"Challenge of the Champs"
	"Master Solvers Club"
	"Improve Your Bidding"
	"Improve Your Play"
	"Improve Your Defense"
Issues per year:	12
Subscription:	US$52 within the U.S
	US$62 elsewhere
	Discounts on subscriptions of more than one year

The oldest bridge magazine in the USA, founded in 1929 by Ely Culbertson.

English Bridge

— the official publication of the English Bridge Union

Address:	Wynford, Awliscombe, Honiton
	Devon EX14 0NT, England
Telephone:	(44)-1404-43259
Email:	100731.2141@compuserve.com
Editor:	Ken Rowe
Regular features:	Sandra Landy's "Bridge for All"
	"Conventions You Need to Know"
	"The Origins of the Game"
	"Develop Your Bidding Judgement"
	"Beat the Experts" – a bidding challenge with David Bird

"Competitions Round-Up" – results of recent
English events
Information of upcoming events
"County News"

Issues per year: 6
Subscription: Distributed free to English Bridge Union members

The IBPA Bulletin
– the official publication of the International Bridge Press Association
Address: 8 Felin Wen, Rhiwbina, Cardiff,
Wales CF4 6NW
Telephone: (44)-1222-628839
Fax: (44)-1222-615234
Email: PatrickJourdain@compuserve.com
Editor: Patrick Jourdain
Regular features: Reports of all major tournaments
Interesting hands from around the world
"Column Service" by Barry Rigal
Results and highlights from World and Zonal
Championships
Issues per year: 12+
Subscription: Distributed free to IBPA members

Irish Bridge Journal
Address: Arcadia Road, Athlone
Eire
Telephone: (44)-902-72390/74430
Fax: (44)-902-74665
Editor: Úna Walsh
Regular features: Play Quiz
CBAI and IBU Notes
Bidding quiz
Reports on Irish events
Issues per year: 6
Subscription: £8

The Kibitzer and the Kibitzer Online
— the official publication of the Chicago Contract Bridge
Association

Address:	5765 N. Lincoln Ave.
	Suite 17
	Chicago IL 60659
	USA
Telephone:	(1)-773-271 0133
Fax:	(1)-773-271 3012
Email:	stansubeck@prodigy.net
Editor:	Suzi Subeck
Regular features:	Articles on the most recent bridge events within the Chicago area
	Details of special club games and Unit and District events
	Results of local tournaments
	A "Novice Niche" for new players
Issues per year:	10
Subscription:	Free to ACBL members living in the Chicago (Unit 123) area

The OKBridge Spectator
– the official publication of OKBridge

Email:	editor@okbridge.com
Editor:	Roberto Scaramuzzi
Regular features:	Letters to the Editor
	"On the Horizon" by Matt Clegg
	"Hand o' the Month" by Frank Stewart
	"Test Your Bidding" by Eddie Kantar
	"Modern Bidding Theory" by Marc Smith
	"Bridge Makes Fools of Us All" by Matthew Granovetter
	"Tuna's Netiquette" by Tony "Tuna" Reus
	"This Month's Angelfish" by Tony "Tuna" Reus
	"Technical Tips" by Leslie Beaver
	Calendar of Events
Subscription:	Distributed free via email to OKBridge subscribers

Magazines in other languages

...IN DANISH
Dansk Bridge
Asminderødgade 53, DK - 3480 Fredensborg, Denmark
Tel: (45)-4847 5213 Fax: (45)-4847 6213 Email: dansk@bridge.dk
Editor: Ib Lundby
Issues per year: 10 (not June or August)
Subscription: DKR 200 within Denmark; DKR 230 to other Nordic
countries; DKR 270 to the rest of the world

...IN DUTCH
IMP Magazine
Prinsegracht 28 A, 2512 GA The Hague, The Netherlands
Tel: (31)-70-360 5902 Fax: (31)-70-364 0841;
Email: jvcleeff@xs4all.nl Web site: www.imp-bridge.nl/
Editor: Jan Van Cleeff
Issues per year: 8
Subscription: Df 69

NBB
André Boekhorst Centrum, Willem Dreeslaan 55, 3515 GB Utrecht,
The Netherlands
Tel: (31) 30 275 99 99 Fax: (31) 30 279 99 00
Email: NBB@bridge.nl Web site: www.bridge.nl
Issues per year: 11
Subscription: Df11.50 per issue

...IN FRENCH
Le Bridgeur
28 rue de Richelieu, 75001 Paris, France
Tel: (33) 1 42 96 25 50 Fax: (33) 1 40 20 92 34
Email: bridgeur@compuserve.com Web site: www.lebridgeur.fr
Editor: Jean-Paul Meyer
Issues per year: 12
Subscription: 47Ff per issue

...IN GERMAN
Bridge Magazin
DBV-Geschäftsstelle, Postfach 2453, 32014 Herford, Germany
Tel: (49) 52 21 8 36 63 Fax: (49) 52 21 5 40 94

Email: sback@t-online.de
Editor: Stefan Back
Issues per year: 12
Subscription: 84Dm (Germany); 126Dm (overseas)

...IN ITALIAN
Bridge d'Italia
Via C Menotti, 11-Scala C, 20129, Milan, Italy
Tel: (39)-2-700004 83 Fax: (39)-2-700013 98
Email: fedbridge@galactica.it Web site: www.federbridge.it
Editor: Riccardo Vandoni

...IN NORWEGIAN
Bridge i Norge (Bridge in Norway)
Dag Hammarskjølds vei 2, 5144 Fyllingsdalen, Norway
Tel: (47)-55-169400 Fax: (47)-55-169401
Email: bridge@online.no
Editor: Boye Brogeland
Issues per year: 6
Subscription: NKr 350 within Norway; NKr 370/£30 Scandinavia;
NKr 400/£33 Europe; NKr 430/£35 outside Europe

...IN POLISH
Brydz
Jagiellonia SA, 31-072 Kraków, ul Wielopole 1, Poland
Tel: (48)-12-619 9226 Fax: (48)-12-619 9225
Email: brydz@jagiellonia.krakow.pl
Editors: Marian Szulc, Jan Chodorowski, Szawomir Zawizlak
Subscription rate: PLN 110; US$ 30 for overseas

...IN SWEDISH
Bridgetidningen
Storgatan 7, SE-243 30 Höör, Sweden
Tel: (46)-413-22448 Fax: (46)-413-23140
Email: ml@bridgetidningen.com
Web site: www.bridgetidningen.com
Editor: Magnus Lindkvist
Issues per year: 10
Subscription: 290 SEK in Sweden; more elsewhere

PART FOUR

Essential Bridge

Information

HISTORY OF THE WORLD CHAMPIONSHIPS

In this section of the book we outline the history of the various World Championship events. You will find here the names of the medallists in the various events. (Only the Open and Women's events are included in this section – for details of Junior Championships, see the section on Junior Bridge.)

The oldest World Championship sponsored by the WBF is the Bermuda Bowl. When held for the first time in Bermuda in 1950, it was a three-way match between teams representing Great Britain, the United States and Europe. The Americans were comfortable winners:

1950
1st Bermuda Bowl in Bermuda
USA beat Great Britain by 3,660 total points, and Sweden/Iceland by 4,720 points.

1st   USA:
J R Crawford, C H Goren, G Rapee, H Schenken, S M Stayman, S Silodor

2nd   Great Britain:
M Harrison-Gray, L W Dodds, N Gardener, K W Konstam, J Tarlo, L Tarlo

3rd   Sweden-Iceland:
Dr E Werner, G Gudmundsson, R Kock, N-O Lilliehook, E Thorfinsson, J Wohlin

The competition then developed into a regular challenge match between the USA and a team representing Europe. The Americans dominated in the early days.

1951
2nd Bermuda Bowl in Naples, Italy
USA defeated Italy by 116 IMPs.

1st   USA:
       J R Crawford, B J Becker, G Rapee, H Schenken,
       S M Stayman
2nd   Italy:
       P Baroni, P Forquet, M Franco, A Ricci, G Siniscalco

1953
3rd Bermuda Bowl in New York City, NY, USA
USA defeated Sweden by 8,260 total points

1st   USA:
       J R Crawford, B J Becker, G Rapee, H Schenken,
       S M Stayman, T A Lightner
2nd   Sweden:
       Dr E Werner, R Kock, N-O Lilliehook, J Wohlin,
       G Anuldh, R Larsen

1954
After three consecutive European defeats, France came close to
unseating a new-look American team:

4th Bermuda Bowl in Monte Carlo, Monaco
USA defeated France by 49 IMPs

1st   USA:
       C W Bishop, M Q Ellenby, D A Oakie, L L Mathe,
       W A Rosen, D Steen
2nd   France:
       J Amouraben, R Bacherich, P Ghestem, J Besse,
       P Kornblum, K Schneider

1955
Twelve months later, the America domination came to an end. Great
Britain became the first European team to win a World Bridge
Championship and, although no one knew it at the time, it was to be
15 years before an American team again won the Bermuda Bowl.

5th Bermuda Bowl in New York City, NY, USA
Great Britain defeated USA by 5,420 total points.

1st   Great Britain:
        L W Dodds, K W Konstam, J T Reese, B Schapiro,
        J Pavlides, A Meredith
2nd   USA:
        M Field, C H Goren, L Hazen, R F Kahn, C J Solomon,
        S M Stayman

1956

The following year, it was the turn of the French, whose team
included two players who had been on the losing side two years
previously:

6th Bermuda Bowl in Paris, France
France defeated USA by 56 IMPs.

1st   France:
        R Bacherich, P Ghestem, P Jaïs, R Latter,
        R Trézel, B Romanet
2nd   USA:
        M Field, C H Goren, L Hazen, R F Kahn,
        C J Solomon, S M Stayman

1957

What followed was an era of total dominance that is unlikely ever to
be repeated. The Italian Blue Team began their run of consecutive
victories on American soil. The Italian team in those early days
included two players who are now recognized as two of the greatest
ever to play the game – Pietro Forquet and Giorgio Belladonna. The
other notable occurrence was the American selection of Helen Sobel,
the first woman player to compete in the event.

7th Bermuda Bowl in New York City, NY, USA
Italy defeated USA by 10,150 total points.

1st   Italy:
        W Avarelli, G Belladonna, P Forquet, M D'Alelio,
        E Chiaradia, G Siniscalco

2nd USA:
C H Goren, H Sobel, B Koytchou, P A Leventritt,
H A Ogust, W E Seamon

1958
The eighth Bermuda Bowl saw the expansion of the event to include the champions of the South American zone for the first time, although it would not be until 1965 that their representatives would win even a single match in the event.

8th Bermuda Bowl in Como, Italy
Italy defeated USA by 37 IMPs and Argentina by 72 IMPs.

1st Italy:
W Avarelli, G Belladonna, P Forquet, M d'Alelio,
E Chiaradia, G Siniscalco
2nd USA:
B J Becker, J R Crawford, G Rapee, S Silodor,
A I Roth, T Stone
3rd Argentina:
A Castro, C Cabanne, R Calvente, M Lerner, A Blousson

1959
9th Bermuda Bowl in New York City, NY, USA
Italy defeated USA by 50 IMPs and Argentina by 40 IMPs.

1st Italy:
W Avarelli, G Belladonna, P Forquet, M D'Alelio,
E Chiaradia, G Siniscalco
2nd USA:
H J Fishbein, S Fry Jr, L Hazen, S H Lazard,
I Stakgold, L B Harmon
3rd Argentina:
A Castro, R Calvente, A Berisso, C Dibar, E Rocchi, A Jaques

1960
There was no Bermuda Bowl in 1960, as the WBF introduced two new competitions, the World Team Olympiad and the Women's World Team Olympiad, open to teams from any member country. The French, fielding a team including four members of their

victorious 1956 Bermuda Bowl squad, won the Open event, while the United Arab Republics surprised the prominent bridge-playing nations by winning the Women's event.

1st World Team Olympiad in Turin, Italy

1st   France:
        R Bacherich, P Ghestem, P Jaïs, R Trézel,
        C Delmouly, G Bourchtoff
2nd   Great Britain:
        J T Reese, B Schapiro, A Rose, N Gardener,
        M J Flint, R Swimer
3rd   USA:
        J R Crawford, S Silodor, B J Becker, N Kay,
        G Rapee, T Stone

1st Women's World Team Olympiad in Turin, Italy

1st   United Arab Republics:
        H Camara, A Choucry, S Fathy, L Gordon,
        J Morcos, S Naugib
2nd   France:
        Mrs Chanfray, Miss Morenas, Mrs Gray,
        Miss Rouviere, Mrs Pouldjian, Mrs Alexandre
3rd   Denmark:
        A Faber, O Dam, R Fraenckel, L Schaltz, G Skotte

1961

For the tenth Bermuda Bowl, the event was expanded to four teams – the defending champions, the reigning Olympiad champions, North America, and South America. It was also the first time the event was staged outside of either North America or Europe. There was also a significant addition to the Italian team – Benito Garozzo – who was destined to join Forquet and Belladonna as legends of the game.

10th Bermuda Bowl in Buenos Aires, Argentina

Italy defeated N America by 120 IMPs, France by 110, and Argentina by 140.
N America defeated France by 26 IMPs and Argentina by 127.
France defeated Argentina by 52 IMPs.

1st   Italy:
       W Avarelli, G Belladonna, P Forquet,
       M D'Alelio, E Chiaradia, B Garozzo
2nd   North America:
       J Gerber, P Hodge, N Kay, P A Leventritt,
       S Silodor, H Schenken
3rd   France:
       R Bacherich, P Ghestem, R Trézel, J LeDentu,
       C Deruy

1962

Persisting with the four-team format, the eleventh Bermuda Bowl was contested by the defending champions and teams representing the three WBF zones, North America, South America and Europe. 1962 also saw the introduction of three new World Championship events — the World Mixed Teams, the World Open Pairs and the World Women's Pairs.

11th Bermuda Bowl in New York City, NY, USA

Italy defeated N America by 26 IMPs, Great Britain by 79, and Argentina by 112.
N.America defeated Great Britain by 13 IMPs and Argentina by 158.
Great Britain defeated Argentina by 7 IMPs.

1st   Italy:
       W Avarelli, G Belladonna, P Forquet,
       M D'Alelio, E Chiaradia, B Garozzo
2nd   North America:
       C Coon, M Key, G R Nail, L L Mathe,
       E R Murray, R Von der Porten
3rd   Great Britain:
       N Gardener, K W Konstam, R A Priday, C Rodrigue,
       A F Truscott, A Rose

By winning the 1st World Open Pairs, Pierre Jaïs & Roger Trézel became the first players to complete the Triple Crown – Bermuda Bowl, Olympiad and World Pairs.

Meanwhile, British stalwarts Rixi Markus & Fritzi Gordon won both the Women's Pairs and the Mixed Teams.

1st World Open Pairs in Cannes, France
1st   France: Pierre Jaïs & Roger Trézel
2nd   Great Britain: Terence Reese & Boris Schapiro
3rd   France: René Bacherich & Pierre Ghestem

1st World Women's Pairs in Cannes, France
1st   Great Britain: Rixi Markus & Fritzi Gordon
2nd   France: Fanny Pariente & Marianne Serf
3rd   USA: Dorothy Hayden & Helen Portugal

1st World Mixed Teams in Cannes, France
1st   Great Britain:
       Mrs R Markus, Mrs F Gordon, N Gardener, B Schapiro
2nd   The Netherlands:
       Mme Westerfield, Mme Hoogenkamp,
       H Filarski, A Kornlijnsliper

1963
12th Bermuda Bowl in St Vincent, Aosta, Italy
Italy defeated N.America by 19 IMPs, France by 185, and
Argentina by 90.
N.America defeated France by 89 IMPs and Argentina by 235.
France defeated Argentina by 134 IMPs.

1st   Italy:
       G Belladonna, P Forquet, M d'Alelio, E Chiaradia,
       B Garozzo, C Pabis Ticci
2nd   North America:
       G R Nail, J Jacoby, H Schenken, P A Leventritt,
       A G Robinson, R F Jordan
3rd   France:
       R Bacherich, P Ghestem, G Desrousseaux, Dr G Theron,
       J Stetten, L Tintner

1964
Unlike 1960, each country (or National Contract Bridge
Organization – NCBO) was allowed to enter only one team in the
World Team Olympiad (and one in the Women's event). With six
consecutive Bermuda Bowl triumphs behind them, the Italians
emphasized their superiority by winning the first of three successive

Olympiad titles. Meanwhile, the British ladies collected their first World team title, winning every match except the last (when the title was already assured). For Rixi Markus & Fritzi Gordon, this victory gave them an unprecedented triple – the Olympiad, the World Women's Pairs and the World Mixed Teams.

The Open event consisted of a 29-team Round Robin from which the leading four teams qualified for a knockout stage. The Women's event, with only 15 teams, was contested over a Round Robin only.

2nd World Team Olympiad in New York City, NY, USA
Italy defeated Great Britain by 6 IMPs in one semi-final.
USA defeated Canada by 16 IMPs in the other.
Italy defeated USA by 46 IMPs in the final.
Great Britain won the playoff for third place by 11 IMPs.

1st	Italy: G Belladonna, P Forquet, M d'Alelio, E Chiaradia, B Garozzo, C Pabis Ticci
2nd	USA: R D Hamman, D P Krauss, S M Stayman, V Mitchell, A G Robinson, R F Jordan
3rd	Great Britain: M Harrison-Gray, M J Flint, K W Konstam, J Tarlo, J T Reese, B Schapiro

2nd Women's World Team Olympiad in New York City, NY, USA
1st	Great Britain: R Markus, F Gordon, A L Fleming, J Juan, M Moss, D Shanahan
2nd	USA: A Gordon, M Kaplan, A Kempner, H Portugal, S Rebner, J Stone
3rd	France: S Baldon, A Chanfray, Mme De Gailhard, J Velut, M Serf, G Morenas

1965
The thirteenth Bermuda Bowl will always be remembered for the cheating allegations levelled against the British pairing of Reese & Schapiro. Although the WBF inquiry did not reach any conclusion

at the time, and the BBL investigation subsequently found in favour
of the players due to lack of evidence, the British captain at the time
forfeited all his team's matches. One upshot of these concessions
was that the South American champions won their first Bermuda
Bowl match (in their sixth appearance in the event). The other
significant occurrence was the presence of Dorothy Hayden in the
American team, the second and, to date, the last woman to represent
North America in the Bermuda Bowl.

13th Bermuda Bowl in Buenos Aires, Argentina
Italy defeated N America by 74 IMPs, Great Britain by 121, and
Argentina by 88.
N America defeated Great Britain by forfeit and Argentina by 109
IMPs.
Argentina defeated Great Britain by forfeit.

1st   Italy:
       W Avarelli, G Belladonna, P Forquet, M d'Alelio,
       C Pabis Ticci, B Garozzo
2nd   North America:
       B J Becker, Mrs D Hayden, I Erdos, K Petterson,
       H Schenken, P A Leventritt
3rd   Argentina:
       E Rocchi, L Attaguile, M Santamarina, A Berisso,
       M Lerner, C Cabanne

1966
The fourteenth Bermuda Bowl in 1966 saw a number of firsts as the
event was expanded to include a fifth team. There were debuts for
Venezuela and The Netherlands as the champions of their respective
zones, and for Thailand as the first ever representatives of the new
WBF Asian zone. There were also the first Bermuda Bowl victories
at the table for a South American champion, but the Asian team
would have to wait at least one more year for their first win. There
was to be no change at the top though, with the Italians collecting
their eighth consecutive Bermuda Bowl victory.

14th Bermuda Bowl in St Vincent, Aosta, Italy
Italy beat N America by 57 IMPs, Venezuela by 159, the Dutch by
128, and Thailand by 343.

N America defeated Venezuela by 138 IMPs, the Dutch by 234, and Thailand by 125.
Venezuela defeated The Netherlands by 84 IMPs and Thailand by 36.
The Netherlands defeated Thailand by 63 IMPs.

1st	Italy:
	W Avarelli, G Belladonna, P Forquet, M D'Alelio, C Pabis Ticci, B Garozzo
2nd	North America:
	P Feldesman, R D Hamman, L L Mathe, I S Rubin, E R Murray, S R Kehela
3rd	Venezuela:
	R Benaim, D Berah, R Rossignol, M Onorati, F Vernon, R Straziota

1966
The second World Open Pairs was held in The Netherlands, and Kreijns/Slavenburg collected the host country's first ever World bridge title. The event also saw America's Dorothy Hayden collecting a bronze medal, a remarkable feat when considering that the World Open Pairs has now been held a total of ten times (through 1998), and no other woman player has finished in the top 15 places. Meanwhile, in the women's event, a British pair collected the gold medals for the second time in as many attempts.

2nd World Open Pairs in Amsterdam, The Netherlands
1st   The Netherlands: Hans Kreijns & Cornelius Slavenburg
2nd   USA: Jim Jacoby & Dr John Fisher
3rd   USA: B Jay Becker & Mrs Dorothy Hayden

2nd World Women's Pairs in Amsterdam, The Netherlands
1st   Great Britain: Jane Juan & Joan Durran
2nd   USA: Nancy Gruver & Sue Sachs
3rd   USA: Mary-Jane Farell & Peggy Solomon

1st World Mixed Pairs in Amsterdam, The Netherlands
1st   USA: Mary-Jane Farell & Ivan Erdos
2nd   Great Britain: Joan Durran & Maurice Weissburger

1967

The format of the Bermuda Bowl was altered in 1967. Instead of the five competing teams playing a complete Round Robin of long matches, the teams played three Round Robins of 20-board matches, with the results of each short match converted to victory points. In this, their second appearance in the competition, Thailand won their first Bermuda Bowl matches (the first by any Asian team) and also avoided the wooden spoon. Having finished third in 1966, winding up at the bottom of the heap at their second attempt was a disappointment for Venezuela.

The two teams with the most VPs after the three Round Robins qualified to play a 128-board head-to-head match for the Bermuda Bowl title. Needless to say, though, the Italians would have won their ninth straight title irrespective of the format, and they beat the North American team comfortably in the first Bermuda Bowl Final.

15th Bermuda Bowl in Miami Beach, Florida, USA
Italy defeated North America by 111 IMPs in the final.

1st　　Italy:
　　　　W Avarelli, G Belladonna, P Forquet, M d'Alelio,
　　　　C Pabis Ticci, B Garozzo
2nd　　North America:
　　　　E Kaplan, N Kay, S R Kehela, E R Murray,
　　　　W S Root, A I Roth
3rd　　France:
　　　　J-M Boulenger, J Pariente, J-M Roudinescu, L Tintner,
　　　　J Stetten, H Szwarc

1968

The Italians retained the Harold S Vanderbilt Trophy by winning their second consecutive World Team Olympiad. In the Women's Olympiad, the British did not defend their title and the Swedish team won the first ever World bridge championship for their country. As in 1964, the Open event was decided with a knockout stage, whereas the women played a Round Robin only.

3rd World Team Olympiad in Deauville, France
Italy defeated Canada by 51 IMPs in one semi-final.
USA defeated The Netherlands by 32 IMPs in the other.

Italy defeated USA by 53 IMPs in the final.
Canada won the playoff for third place by 15 IMPs.

1st	Italy:
	G Belladonna, P Forquet, M d'Alelio, E Chiaradia, B Garozzo, C Pabis Ticci
2nd	USA:
	E Kaplan, N Kay, W S Root, A I Roth, A G Robinson, R F Jordan
3rd	Canada:
	C B Elliott, W J Crissey, E R Murray, S R Kehela, G Charney, P E Sheardown

3rd Women's World Team Olympiad in Deauville, France

1st	Sweden:
	B Blom, K Eriksson, E Martensson, R Segander, G Sllborn, B Werner
2nd	South Africa:
	T Beron, G Goslar, P Mansell, E Sender, R Jacobson, A Schneider
3rd	USA:
	H Baron, R Walsh, S Sachs, N Gruver, E-J Hawes, D Hayden,

1969

For the first time in the event's history, the fate of the sixteenth Bermuda Bowl was not decided by a match involving an American team. The Italians won the Round Robin qualifier with 185 VPs, Taiwan were second with 166, and the Americans a distant third on 141. This Bermuda Bowl also marked the end of an era, with the Italians announcing their retirement at its conclusion. Their win gave them ten consecutive Bermuda Bowl titles. Two victories in the World Team Olympiad meant twelve World Championships for the Azurri in 13 years – a remarkable record indeed.

16th Bermuda Bowl in Rio de Janeiro, Brazil.

Italy defeated Taiwan by 247 IMPs in the final.

1st   Italy:
        W Avarelli, G Belladonna, P Forquet, M d'Alelio,
        C Pabis Ticci, B Garozzo
2nd   Taiwan:
        F Huang, P Huang, C S Shen, K W Shen,
        K Suchartkul, M F Tai
3rd   North America:
        R D Hamman, E B Kantar, W Eisenberg, R Goldman,
        S H Lazard, G Rapee

1970

The North American team recaptured the Bermuda Bowl in 1970, to
end a European dominance of the event that had lasted since 1955. For
the second year running, Taiwan reached the final, but they were again
easily beaten. The team that represented Italy was a pale shadow of
the great Blue Team, and they duly finished in last place. No member
of this team ever represented Italy again. The Americans, meanwhile,
were represented for the first time by the Dallas Aces team.

17th Bermuda Bowl in Stockholm, Sweden
North America defeated Taiwan by 141 IMPs in the final

1st   North America:
        R D Hamman, R S Wolff, W Eisenberg, R Goldman,
        J Jacoby, M S Lawrence
2nd   Taiwan:
        P Huang, M F Tai, C Cheng, E Hsiao, H Lin
3rd   Norway:
        E Hoie, T Jensen, K Koppans. L A Strom,
        B Larsen, W Varnas

That same year, Austria won its first ever World Bridge
Championship, in the Open Pairs. Meanwhile, the Italians reminded
the bridge world that they were still around by collecting the silver
and bronze medals. In the World Women's Pairs, Mary-Jane Farell
switched partners and improved two places on her bronze medal of
four years previous, while Great Britain's gold medallists from
1960 returned to collect silver this time.

The World Mixed Pairs was a triumph for a man who had been
an outstanding auction bridge player, and had contested the first

ever international bridge match 40 years previously. At the age of 74, Waldemar von Zedwitz's win established him as the oldest World Champion – a record unlikely to be broken for some time to come.

3rd World Open Pairs in Stockholm, Sweden
1st   Austria: Fritz Babsch & Peter Manhardt
2nd   Italy: Benito Garozzo & Federico Mayer
3rd   Italy: William Saulino & Italo Zanasi

3rd World Women's Pairs in Stockholm, Sweden
1st   USA: Mary-Jane Farell & Marilyn Johnson
2nd   Great Britain: Rixi Markus & Fritzi Gordon
3rd   Sweden: Britt Blom & Gunborg Silborn

2nd World Mixed Pairs in Stockholm, Sweden
1st   USA: Barbara Brier & Waldemar von Zedwitz
2nd   Great Britain/Switzerland: Rixi Markus & George Catzeflis
3rd   Israel: Riva Sinfer & Michael Hochzeit

1971
The eighteenth Bermuda Bowl was the first World Bridge Championship held on the Asian continent. It was also the first time that two American teams competed in the event – the Aces played as the defending champions, while the team designated as "North America" were there as that NCBO's champions, and established new lows by finishing in last place. Asia was represented by host country, Taiwan, and Australia made their debut as the Pacific zonal champions. The Australian team included Jim and Norma Borin – the only married couple ever to play in the Bermuda Bowl.

This was also the first time since 1956 that a Bermuda Bowl had been contested without an Italian team present.

18th Bermuda Bowl in Taipei, Taiwan
The Aces defeated France by 62 IMPs in the final.
Australia defeated Taiwan by 40 IMPs in the 3rd-place playoff.
Brazil defeated North America by 16 IMPs in the playoff for 5th place.

1st   The Aces:
R D Hamman, R S Wolff, W Eisenberg, R Goldman,
J Jacoby, M S Lawrence

2nd   France:
J-M Boulenger, J-M Roudinescu, H Szwarc, J-L Stoppa,
R Trézel, P Jaïs

3rd   Australia:
J Borin, Mrs N Borin, D Howard, R J Cummings,
T P Seres, R A Smilde

1972

The Italian Blue Team came out of retirement to defend their
Olympiad crown, and they dominated the field en route to the final
against the reigning World Champions Dallas Aces (with Paul
Soloway replacing Billy Eisenberg) who were representing the
USA. The Italians won the final comfortably and, not to be outdone,
their ladies team also won the Women's event, while South Africa
and the USA repeated their silver and bronze medal performances
of four years earlier.

4th World Team Olympiad in Miami Beach, Florida, USA

Italy defeated France by 90 IMPs in one semi-final.
USA defeated Canada by 118 IMPs in the other.
Italy defeated U.S.A. by 65 IMPs in the final.
Canada won the playoff for third place by 73 IMPs.

1st   Italy:
G Belladonna, P Forquet, M D'Alelio, E Chiaradia,
B Garozzo, C Pabis Ticci

2nd   USA:
R D Hamman, R S Wolff, P Soloway, R Goldman,
J Jacoby, M S Lawrence

3rd   Canada:
B Gowdry, W J Crissey, E R Murray, S R Kehela,
G Charney, D R Phillips

4th Women's World Team Olympiad in Miami Beach, Florida, USA

1st   Italy:
M Bianchi, R Jabes, M A Robaudo, L C Romanelli,
A Valenti, M V Venturini

2nd   South Africa:
        T Beron, J Disler, G Goslar, P Mansell,
        R Jacobson, A Schneider
3rd   USA:
        E-J Hawes, D Hayden-Truscott, M-J Farell, M Johnson,
        P Solomon, J Mitchell

1973

For the nineteenth Bermuda Bowl, the Italians fielded a Blue Team containing their three greatest stars. The Aces returned also, as defending champions, and in the Round Robin qualifying stage those two teams were totally dominant. The final Round Robin standings were: the Aces 177 and Italy 176, with Brazil a distant third on 148. The final though, was not such a close affair.

One notable situation was the presence of B Jay and Michael Becker in the North America team – the only father-son combination ever to play in the Bermuda Bowl.

19th Bermuda Bowl in Guaruja, Brazil

Italy defeated the Aces by 128 IMPs in the final.
1st   Italy:
        G Belladonna, B Bianchi, P Forquet, B Garozzo,
        V Pittala, G Garabello
2nd   The Aces:
        R D Hamman, R S Wolff, M E Blumenthal, R Goldman,
        J Jacoby, M S Lawrence
3rd   Brazil:
        P P Assumpcao, G P Chagas, M Branco, P Branco,
        C Fonseca, G Cintra

1974

Having lost the title in Brazil the previous year, the Americans were entitled to field only one team in the twentieth Bermuda Bowl. That team was the Aces, but the reincarnated Blue Team, with the addition of two new members, beat them in one of the closest finals for some time. There was one new face this year, with New Zealand making their Bermuda Bowl debut as champions of the Pacific zone.

1974 also saw the introduction of another new competition – the Venice Cup, a women's event that would in time mirror the Bermuda Bowl. For this first Venice Cup though (and the second two years later) the format would be a challenge match between the champion women's teams from Europe and North America. The Italians fielded five of the team that had won the Women's World Team Olympiad two years earlier, but the Americans beat them in a close match.

20th Bermuda Bowl in Venice, Italy

Italy defeated North America by 29 IMPs in the final.
Brazil won the playoff for third place by 1 IMP.

1st   Italy:
        G Belladonna, B Bianchi, P Forquet, B Garozzo,
        S De Falco, A Franco
2nd   North America:
        R D Hamman, R S Wolff, M E Blumenthal, R Goldman,
        E R Murray, S R Kehela
3rd   Brazil:
        P P Assumpcao, G P Chagas, M Branco, P Branco,
        C Fonseca, G Cintra

1st Venice Cup in Venice, Italy

USA defeated Italy by 35 IMPs.

1st   USA:
        B Cohn, B-A Kennedy, E-J Hawes, D Hayden-Truscott,
        M Passell, C Sanders
2nd   Italy:
        M Bianchi, R Jabes, M A Robaudo, L Canessa,
        A Valenti, M V Venturini

In the World Open Pairs, America's Hamman-Wolff added a second World title to their two Bermuda Bowl wins, while Italy's Italo Zanasi collected a bronze medal for the second time in the event.

In the Women's Pairs, Rixi Markus & Fritzi Gordon won the event for the second time – two wins and one second-place finish in four attempts is a remarkable record. South Africans Gerda Goslar & Rita Jacobson added to their collection of silver medals, having twice finished second in the Olympiad.

4th World Open Pairs in Las Palmas, Canary Islands
1st   USA: Bob Hamman & Bobby Wolff
2nd   Italy: Adriano Abate & Leandro Burgay
3rd   Italy: Federico de Paula & Italo Zanasi

4th World Women's Pairs in Las Palmas, Canary Islands
1st   Great Britain: Rixi Markus & Fritzi Gordon
2nd   South Africa: Gerda Goslar & Rita Jacobson
3rd   USA: Emma-Jean Hawes & Dorothy Hayden-Truscott

3rd World Mixed Pairs in Las Palmas, Canary Islands
1st   Swizerland: Loula Gordon & Tony Trad
2nd   USA: Jacqui Mitchell & Jimmy Cayne

2nd World Mixed Teams in Las Palmas, Canary Islands
1st   USA:
      Mrs J Morse, Mrs P Lipsitz, R H Lipsitz,
      S W Robinson, S J Parker
2nd   USA:
      Mrs J L Stayman, Mrs J Mitchell, V Mitchell,
      J Cayne, M Granovetter

1975

To commemorate the 25th anniversary of the event, the 1975 Bermuda Bowl was held in Bermuda. However, controversy in the form of a cheating scandal once again plagued the event. For the first time, screens were used, so that players could not see their partner, but the space beneath the table was left open. Two Italian players, Zucchelli and Facchini, were accused of transmitting information by tapping their feet under the table, and they have since become infamous as the "Italian Foot Soldiers". Although exactly what information they were transmitting was never determined, the WBF reprimanded the pair but unaccountably permitted not only the Italian team, but also the offending pair, to continue playing. American npc Alfred Sheinwold threatened to withdraw his team if Zucchelli-Facchini played, but the Italians avoided further confrontation by playing four-handed throughout the latter stages of the event. The final was one of the most exciting of all time. The Americans held a substantial lead (more than 70 IMPs) late in the final, but a dramatic Italian recovery saw the Blue

Team retain their title for the 13th (and what was to be the last) time.

Of the great Italian players, Belladonna was the only one who had played in all of the Italian wins – 13 Bermuda Bowls and three Olympiads. Forquet was present for all but the final victory in 1975. Garozzo had joined the team in 1961, so he had missed the first three victories and thus finished with a record of ten Bermuda Bowls and three Olympiads.

21st Bermuda Bowl in Bermuda
Italy defeated Indonesia by 146 IMPs in one semi-final.
North America defeated France by 12 IMPs in the other.
Italy defeated North America by 26 IMPs in the final.

1st   Italy:
       G Belladonna, B Garozzo, A Franco, V Pittala,
       S Zucchelli, G Facchini
2nd   North America:
       R D Hamman, R S Wolff, P Soloway, E B Kantar,
       J C Swanson Jr, W Eisenberg
3rd   France:
       J-M Boulenger, H Szwarc, M Lebel, C Mari,
       E Vial, F Leenhardt

1976
1976 was a busy year, as both the World Team Olympiads and the Bermuda Bowl/Venice Cup were staged in the same year. There were two NCBOs sending teams to the Bermuda Bowl for the first time – Israel as European champions, and Hong Kong as the Asian representatives. For the first time too, the great Italian Blue Team were beaten – and twice too! They reached the final of the Bermuda Bowl but lost to the Aces. This was indeed the end of an era – the Italians have come close to winning the Bermuda Bowl since 1975, but have not yet done so (although they have qualified for the 2000 Bermuda Bowl in Bermuda having won the 1999 European Championships for the third time in succession).

22nd Bermuda Bowl in Monte Carlo, Monaco
North America defeated Italy by 34 IMPs in the final.

1st   North America:
      P Soloway, W Eisenberg, I S Rubin, H L Ross,
      E Paulsen, F Hamilton
2nd   Italy:
      G Belladonna, B Garozzo, P Forquet, A Franco,
      V Pittala, A Vivaldi
3rd   Israel:
      J Frydrich, M Hochzeit, S Lev, Y Levit, P Romik, E Shaufel

2nd Venice Cup in Monte Carlo, Monaco
USA defeated Great Britain by 184 IMPs.

1st   USA:
      B-A Kennedy, E-J Hawes, D Hayden-Truscott,
      C Sanders, J Mitchell, G Moss
2nd   Great Britain:
      C Esterson, N P Gardener, S Landy, R Oldroyd,
      R Markus, F Gordon

In the Olympiad, the Italians lost their crown to the Brazilians, whose victory meant a first World bridge title to representatives of the South American zone.

In the Women's events, the Italians retained their Olympiad crown, while the Americans repeated their Venice Cup success of two years earlier by beating the British European Champions.

There were no playoffs in either event – just a complete Round Robin with the results of each match converted to victory points.

5th World Team Olympiad in Monte Carlo, Monaco
1st   Brazil:
      P P Assumpcao, G P Chagas, S Barbosa, M Branco,
      G Cintra, C Fonseca
2nd   Italy:
      G Belladonna, P Forquet, B Garozzo, A Franco,
      C Mosca, S Sbarigia

5th Women's World Team Olympiad in Monte Carlo, Monaco
1st   Italy:
      M Bianchi, R Jabes, M A Robaudo, A Valenti,
      L Capodanno, M B d'Andrea

2nd   Great Britain:
        C Esterson, N P Gardener, S Landy, R Oldroyd,
        R Markus, F Gordon
3rd   USA:
        B-A Kennedy, E-J Hawes, D Hayden-Truscott,
        C Sanders, J Mitchell, G Moss

1977

As had happened before when the Americans were holders, there were two North American Teams in the 23rd Bermuda Bowl – designated as "Defending Champions" and "North America". (Curiously, the North American team included two players – Soloway and Eisenberg – who had been members of the Defending Champions team when they won the event the previous year.) On previous occasions, the format of the event was a Round Robin qualifying stage with two semi-finals and a final, and a built-in requirement that if two teams from the same zone reached the knockout stage then they had to meet in the semi-finals. In 1977, the format was a Round Robin qualifying stage with the top two teams to meet in the final. The Round Robin was won convincingly by the Defending Champions, with North America well clear of third-placed Sweden. The result of this was the unsatisfactory situation of having the World Championship final contested by two American teams.

23rd Bermuda Bowl in Manila, Philippines
North America defeated the Defending Champions by 30 IMPs in the final

1st   North America:
        P Soloway, R D Hamman, R S Wolff, J C Swanson,
        E B Kantar, W Eisenberg
2nd   Defending Champions:
        I S Rubin, H L Ross, E Paulsen, F Hamilton,
        M Passell, R von der Porten
3rd   Sweden:
        A Brunzell, S-O Flodqvist, H Göthe, J Lindqvist,
        A Morath, P-O Sundelin

1978

The Venice Cup was staged in 1978, and accredited with full World Championship status. Instead of just two teams, there were five challengers this time around, the champion women's team from each of the WBF zones. That seemed to make little difference to the American team, who won comfortably and retained their 100% record in the event.

3rd Venice Cup in New Orleans, Louisiana, USA
USA defeated Italy by 89 IMPs in the final.

1st   USA:
       E-J Hawes, D Hayden-Truscott, J Mitchell, G Moss,
       M-J Farell, M Johnson
2nd   Italy:
       M Bianchi, A Valenti, L Capodanno, M B D'Andrea,
       E Gut, A M Morini
3rd   Argentina:
       M T B de Diaz, M E Iacapraro, A C de Martinez de Hoz,
       M Martienzo, M G de Schenone, C Monsegur

The WBF also introduced an additional World teams championship in 1978, the World Knockout Teams for the Rosenblum Cup, thus completing the cycle that is currently operational today. Henceforth, the Bermuda Bowl and Venice Cup would be staged in the odd-numbered years. The two Olympiads would be held every four years, and in the fourth year of each cycle the World Knockout Teams would be held in tandem with the three World Pairs events. Unlike the other major teams championships, the Rosenblum Cup is an open event in that NCBOs can enter as many teams as they wish. Thus, for many players, who cannot, for some reason or other, get into their national team, the Rosenblum Cup represents their only chance to play in a World teams championship. The women's equivalent of the World Knockout Teams, the McConnell Cup, would be introduced in 1994.

The first winners of the new event were Poland, giving that NCBO (and any Eastern European country) its first World title.

1st World Knockout Teams in New Orleans, Louisiana, USA
Poland defeated Brazil by 84 IMPs in the final.

1st   Poland:
       M Frenkel, A Macieszszak, J Polec, A Wikosj
2nd   Brazil:
       P P Assumpcao, G P Chagas, M Branco,
       G Cintra, S Barbosa, Taunay

In the Open Pairs, the Brazilians went one better, giving Marcelo
Branco & Gabino Cintra a second World title to go with their
victory in the Olympiad two years earlier. Meanwhile, the second
place finish by Eric Kokish & Peter Nagy brought Canada closer
than they had yet been to a World title.

In the Women's Pairs, Carol Sanders & Betty-Ann Kennedy just
failed to add a second title to their double Venice Cup wins. Sanders
also collected a bronze medal in the Mixed Pairs, where the
Americans swept the board.

5th World Open Pairs in New Orleans, Louisiana, USA
1st   Brazil: Marcelo Branco & Gabino Cintra
2nd   Canada: Eric Kokish & Peter Nagy
3rd   USA: John Mohan & Roger Bates

5th World Women's Pairs in New Orleans, Louisiana, USA
1st   USA: Judi Radin & Kathie Wei
2nd   USA: Betty-Ann Kennedy & Carol Sanders
3rd   France: Claude Blouquit & Elizabeth Delor

4th World Mixed Pairs in New Orleans, Louisiana, USA
1st   USA: Kerri Shuman & Barry Crane
2nd   USA: Heitie Noland & Jim Jacoby
3rd   USA: Carol Sanders & Lou Bluhm

1979
The North American and Italian teams met in the final of the
Bermuda Bowl yet again in 1979, with the Americans emerging
victorious in the closest final in the event's history. For the first
time, there was a team representing the WBF's newest zone —
Central American and the Caribbean (CAC).

24th Bermuda Bowl in Rio de Janeiro, Brazil
North America defeated Italy by 5 IMPs in the final.

1st   North America:
       M K Brachman, W Eisenberg, R Goldman, P Soloway,
       E B Kantar, M Passell
2nd   Italy:
       G Belladonna, B Garozzo, V Pittala, L Lauria,
       S de Falco, A Franco
3rd   Australia:
       J Borin, N Borin, R J Cummings, T P Seres,
       R A Richman, A Reiner

1980

The French, who had won the first World Team Olympiad in 1960, won their first World title in 20 years, beating the USA team in a close final. The format in the Open divided the teams into two pools, with four teams from each advancing to the second stage. At that point the eight qualifiers were again divided into two for a second Round Robin, with the winning team from each group advancing to the final.

The Women's Olympiad was played as a complete Round Robin, and for the first time in six attempts the USA team emerged victorious. However, this was not a first World title for any of the American women, as they were reigning Venice Cup holders. This win completed the Women's Triple Crown for Johnson and Farell – the Olympiad, the Venice Cup and the World Women's Pairs – the first women to achieve that distinction. Indeed, Farell had now achieved a unique quartet of victories, having also won the World Mixed Pairs. The victory also elevated Dorothy Truscott (previously Hayden) to the number one spot in the WBF world women's rankings, taking over from Britain's Rixi Markus, who had held that position for the previous ten years. Farell also overtook Markus to move into second place behind Truscott. The Italian team, containing four players who had been on the winning team at the last two Women's Olympiads, collected silver medals this time around.

6th World Team Olympiad in Valkenburg, The Netherlands
France defeated USA by 20 IMPs in the final.

1st   France:
       P Chemla, C Mari, M Lebel, M Perron, H Szwarc, P Soulet

2nd   USA:
       P Soloway, I S Rubin, R D Hamman, R S Wolff,
       M Passell, F Hamilton

6th Women's World Team Olympiad in Valkenburg, The Netherlands

1st   USA:
       E-J Hawes, D Truscott, J Mitchell, G Moss,
       M-J Farell, M Johnson
2nd   Italy:
       M Bianchi, A Valenti, L Capodanno, M B D'Andrea,
       E Gut, A M Morini

1981

Thanks to India's performance at the 1980 Olympiad, the WBF's Middle East zone had earned a place at the 1981 Bermuda Bowl. That place was taken by Pakistan who, led by the hitherto unknown Zia Mahmood, proceeded to surprise everyone by reaching the final. Besides Pakistan, current World Knockout Team champions Poland also made their Bermuda Bowl debut as European Champions. The American team contained few familiar faces, and Bobby Levin's victory at the age of 24 made him the youngest ever World Bridge Champion. This was also the Bermuda Bowl debut for a pair who have since dominated the event, and the American bridge scene since then – Jeff Meckstroth & Eric Rodwell.

    Meanwhile, in the women's event, Great Britain broke the USA's stranglehold on the trophy by defeating the reigning Venice Cup and Olympiad champions in a close final.

25th Bermuda Bowl in Port Chester, New York, USA

USA defeated Poland by 59 IMPs in one semi-final.
Pakistan defeated Argentina by 60 IMPs in the other.
USA defeated Pakistan by 89 IMPs in the final.

1st   USA:
       R J Levin, R D Arnold, A E Reinhold, J Solodar,
       J J Meckstroth, E V Rodwell
2nd   Pakistan:
       N Abedi, N Ahmed, J-e-A Fazli, M Ata-Ullah,
       Z Mahmood, M Salim

3rd   Poland:
         A Jezioro, J Klukowski, M Kudla, K Martens,
         A Milde, T Przybora

4th Venice Cup in Port Chester, New York, USA
Great Britain defeated USA by 39 IMPs in the final.

1st   Great Britain:
         N P Gardener, P Davies, S J Sowter, S Landy,
         M Dennison, D Williams
2nd   USA:
         N Gruver, E Kemp, B-A Kennedy, J Radin,
         C Sanders, K Wei
3rd   Brazil:
         A Mandelot, S F de Mello, M E Murtinho,
         S Powidzer, A Saade, M L Silva

1982

Having not won a World title for 20 years, the French picked up their second in two years. On a personal level, Michel Lebel and Philippe Soulet added the World Knockout Teams to their Olympiad title won two years earlier.

2nd World Knockout Teams in Biarritz, France
France defeated USA by 15 IMPs in the final.

1st   France:
         M Lebel, P Soulet, D Pilon, A Feigenbaum
2nd   USA:
         C U Martel, L Stansby, H L Ross, P A Pender,
         E A Manfield, C R Woolsey

Americans Chip Martel and Lew Stansby arrived on the international scene with a flourish, collecting silver medals in the World Knockout Teams and then winning the World Open Pairs. Holland's Anton Maas & Max Rebattu collected silver – the best performance by any Dutch competitors in World championship events since Kreijns/Slavenburg won the 2nd World Pairs in 1966.

In the Women's Pairs, Carol Sanders & Betty-Ann Kennedy improved by one place on their 1978 performance to move up from silver to gold, and add the World Pairs title to their two Venice Cup crowns. Second place also went to an American pair, and was the first international success for Lynn Deas, who would rise to the forefront of World women's bridge over the next decade. In third, were Britain's Sally Horton (previously Sowter) & Sandra Landy, reigning Venice Cup holders.

In the Mixed Pairs, Dianna Gordon & George Mittelman produced a first ever World Championship title for Canada.

6th World Open Pairs in Biarritz, France
1st   USA: Chip Martel & Lew Stansby
2nd   The Netherlands: Anton Maas & Max Rebattu
3rd   Brazil: Gabriel Chagas & Roberto de Mello

6th World Women's Pairs in Biarritz, France
1st   USA: Betty-Ann Kennedy & Carol Sanders
2nd   USA: Lynn Deas & Beth Palmer
3rd   Great Britain: Sally Horton & Sandra Landy

5th World Mixed Pairs in Biarritz, France
1st   Canada: Dianna Gordon & George Mittelman
2nd   USA: Peggy Sutherlin & John Sutherlin
3rd   France: M & Mme Viennois

1983
There was no Venice Cup in 1983, and the Bermuda Bowl was held in Scandinavia for the second time. It proved notable for two reasons. The first was the final Bermuda Bowl appearance of Italy's legendary Giorgio Belladonna and Benito Garozzo. The second was one of the most exciting contests ever. Spectators had become accustomed to the Americans building a substantial lead and then seeing the Italians overhaul them, but this time it was the Italians who faltered at the final hurdle. Having said that, as the competition approached the end of the qualifying stages, few people expected the Italians to be staying on for the knockout matches as anything more than spectators. The format of the event pre-qualified the first-ranked teams from North America (USA 1) and Europe (France) to the semi-final stage. The remaining eight teams, including a second American team and a second European team (Italy), had to battle through a Round Robin qualifying stage.

That the Italians emerged from an incredibly close finish to the Round Robin, then survived a tense battle with the French in the semi-finals, with sufficient energy and composure to take the final right down to the wire says a great deal about their status as true champions.

26th Bermuda Bowl in Stockholm, Sweden
USA 1 defeated USA 2 by 102 IMPs in one semi-final.
Italy defeated France by just 1 IMP in the other.
USA 1 defeated Italy by 5 IMPs in the final.

1st	USA 1:
	R D Hamman, R S Wolff, M M Becker, R D Rubin, P M Weichsel, A Sontag
2nd	Italy:
	G Belladonna, B Garozzo, S De Falco, A Franco, L Lauria, C Mosca
3rd	France:
	P Cronier, M Corn, M Lebel, H Mouiel, H Szwarc, P Soulet

1984
The 7th World Team Olympiad was a showcase for European bridge. In the Open, all four semi-finalists came from that single WBF zone. Poland won its second World team title in six years, although none of the 1984 winners had previously won at this level.

Three of the four semi-finalists in the Women's event were also European teams, but here it was the Americans who emerged as triumphant, retaining the Olympiad title won in The Netherlands four years earlier. Two members of that team survived (Moss & Mitchell), while the other four successful players in Seattle had each won the World Women's Pairs.

Having also won the Venice Cup, Carol Sanders and Betty-Ann Kennedy join Mary-Jane Farell and Marilyn Johnson as the only players to have completed the Women's Triple Crown – the Olympiad, the Venice Cup and the World Women's Pairs.

For the first time ever (and, hopefully, the last, as the rules have since been changed) the team winning the final of a World Championship event did not win the title. The USA team had beaten the British by 45 IMPs in their Round Robin qualifying match, and the rules in force stated that when (if) they met later in the knockout stage then half of that advantage was carried forward. Therefore, although the British team defeated the Americans 102-87 in the 64-board final, this only reduced the Americans' carried forward lead by 15, so the Americans won the title by 7 IMPs.

7th World Team Olympiad in Seattle, Washington, USA

Poland defeated Austria by 4 IMPS in one semi-final.
France defeated Denmark by 15 IMPS in the other.
Poland defeated France by 80 IMPs in the final.

1st   Poland:
       P Gawrys, H Wolny, T Przybora, P Tuszynski,
       J Romanski, K Martens
2nd   France:
       P Chemla, M Perron, H Szwarc, H Mouiel,
       F Covo, F Paladino
3rd= Denmark:
       S Werdelin, J Auken, S Schou, J Hulgaard,
       P Schaltz, K-A Boesgaard
       Austria:
       W Meinl, H Berger, J Fucik, F Terraneo, A Milavec, F Kubak

7th Women's World Team Olympiad in Seattle, Washington, USA

USA defeated France by 31 IMPS in one semi-final.
Great Britain defeated The Netherlands by 132 IMPs in the other.
USA defeated Great Britain by 7 IMPs (including the carry-forward) in the final.

1st   USA:
       G Moss, J Mitchell, K Wei, C Sanders,
       B-A Kennedy, J Radin
2nd   Great Britain:
       N P Gardener, P Davies, S J Horton, S Landy,
       S Scarborough, G Scott-Jones
3rd= The Netherlands:
       P Kaas, B Vriend, L van der Brom, M van Mechelen,
       E Schippers, M van der Pas
       France:
       N Cohen, H Zuccarelli, C Blouquit, E Delor,
       F Pariente, A C de l'Epine

1985

The format of the 27th Bermuda Bowl followed that used in 1983, with USA and Austria, the European champions, exempted through to the semi-finals, while everyone else played a Round Robin with the top two to join the seeded teams in the knockout stage. The teams contesting the Round Robin were Canada and Israel (the second teams from North America and Europe respectively), Brazil as the hosts, and one team from each of the other four WBF zones.

For Hamman/Wolff this was their second consecutive victory, and their fifth in all. For Hamman it was his ninth final, and for Wolff his eighth. They had also won the World Pairs. Hugh Ross was also a previous Bermuda Bowl winner, while Martel/Stansby were current World Open Pairs champions.

Although the Americans were very impressive in their demolition of Austria in the final, they were fortunate to survive the semi-final clash with Brazil, a match they won on the very last board in somewhat bizarre fashion. Look for Brazil, who have done little capitalize on their Olympiad title in 1976, to make a major impact on the World bridge scene before too much longer.

In the Venice Cup, Great Britain retained the title won four years earlier, hammering USA 1 in the final. In a remarkable display of stamina, Britain's Sandra Landy & Sally Horton (formerly Sowter) played a remarkable 656 boards in the event, more than any other pair in either the Venice Cup or Bermuda Bowl. The format was similar to that used in the Bermuda Bowl, with USA 1 and European Champions France seeded to the semi-finals.

27th Bermuda Bowl in Sao Paulo, Brazil

USA defeated Brazil by 3 IMPs in one semi-final.
Austria defeated Israel by 88 IMPs in the other.
USA defeated Austria by 75 IMPs in the final.
Israel won the playoff for third place by 32 IMPs.

1st   USA:
       R D Hamman, R S Wolff, C U Martel, L Stansby,
       P A Pender, H L Ross
2nd   Austria:
       H Berger, J Fucik, K Feichtinger, W Meinl,
       K Rohan, F Terraneo

3rd   Israel:
        D Birman, J Frydrich, M Hochzeit, S Lev,
        S Zeligman, E Shaufel

5th Venice Cup in Sao Paulo, Brazil
USA 1 defeated Chinese Taipei by 96 IMPs in one semi-final.
Great Britain defeated France by 35 IMPs in the other.
Great Britain defeated USA 1 by 110 IMPs in the final.
France won the playoff for third place by 39 IMPs.

1st   Great Britain:
        N P Gardener, P Davies, S J Horton, S Landy,
        M Brunner, G Scott-Jones
2nd   USA 1:
        B-A Kennedy, J Radin, C Sanders, K Wei,
        G Greenberg, J Mitchell
3rd   France:
        V Bessis, D Gaviard, G Chevalley, F Pigeaud, S Willard, C Saul

1986
The winning American team in the World Knockout Teams included
two players (Woolsey & Manfield) who had lost in the final four years
earlier. Zia Mahmood's Pakistan squad again reached a World
Championship final.

3rd World Knockout Teams in Miami Beach, Florida, USA
USA defeated Pakistan by 150 IMPs in the final.

1st   USA:
        S W Robinson, P A Boyd, R H Lipsitz, N Silverman,
        E A Manfield, C R Woolsey
2nd   Pakistan:
        Z Mahmood, J-e-A Fazli, N Ahmed, N Abedi
3rd   Sweden:
        B Fallenius, M Lindkvist, M Nilsland, A Wirgren

Jeff Meckstroth & Eric Rodwell won the World Open Pairs by a
huge margin, adding to their Bermuda Bowl triumph of five years
earlier and establishing themselves among the world's top pairs.

Austria's Berger/Meinl collected their second silver medals in two years, while Australia's Burgess/Marston climbed into third place to collect their country's first World Championship medals.

In the Women's Pairs, the American's took gold, Denmark the silver, and Landy/Horton of Great Britain their second consecutive bronze medals in this event. With this victory, Jacqui Mitchell joined Mary-Jane Farell, Marilyn Johnson, Betty-Ann Kennedy and Carol Sanders as only the fifth player ever to have completed the Women's Triple Crown – the Olympiad, the Venice Cup and the World Women's Pairs.

For the second time in five attempts, the Americans swept the medals in the Mixed Pairs, with first and third places going to married couples. Kerri Shuman, who had won gold eight years ago playing with Barry Crane, had to settle for silver with Bob Hamman this time around.

7th World Open Pairs in Miami Beach, Florida, USA
1st   USA: Jeff Meckstroth & Eric Rodwell
2nd   Austria: Wolfgang Meinl & Heinrich Berger
3rd   Australia: Paul Marston & Stephen Burgess

7th World Women's Pairs in Miami Beach, Florida, USA
1st   USA: Jacqui Mitchell & Amalya Kearse
2nd   Denmark: Charlotte Palmund & Bettina Kalkerup
3rd   Great Britain: Sally Horton & Sandra Landy

6th World Mixed Pairs in Miami Beach, Florida, USA
1st   USA: Pam Wittes & John Wittes
2nd   USA: Kerri Shuman & Bob Hamman
3rd   USA: Rozanne Pollack & Bill Pollack

1987
The Americans defended their Bermuda Bowl crown, with only one change (Mike Lawrence replacing Peter Pender) from the team that had won two years earlier. This time Great Britain were the losing finalists. Again, the USA team and Sweden, as European champions, were seeded to the semi-final stage. This victory tied the USA with Italy, now each with 13 wins.

In the Venice Cup, it was the two American teams and the two European teams who survived to the knockout stage. USA 2 upset their senior team, while France overcame Italy to reach the final, where they lost to the Americans. There were still only two names – USA and Great Britain – on the Venice Cup after six contests.

With this victory, Kathie Wei and Judi Radin join that elite group (now up to seven in number, all Americans) who had completed the Women's Triple Crown – the Olympiad, the Venice Cup and the World Women's Pairs.

28th Bermuda Bowl in Ocho Rios, Jamaica
USA defeated Chinese Taipei by 131 IMPs in one semi-final.
Great Britain defeated Sweden by 47 IMPs in the other.
USA defeated Great Britain by 64 IMPs in the final.

1st   USA:
       R D Hamman, R S Wolff, C U Martel, L Stansby,
       M S Lawrence, H L Ross
2nd   Great Britain:
       A R Forrester, G T Kirby, J Armstrong, R S Brock,
       M J Flint, R M Sheehan
3rd   Sweden:
       B Fallenius, M Lindkvist, T Gullberg, H Göthe,
       P-O Sundelin, S-O Flodqvist

6th Venice Cup in Ocho Rios, Jamaica
USA 2 defeated USA 1 by 26 IMPs in one semi-final.
France defeated Italy by 49 IMPs in the other.
USA 2 defeated France by 32 IMPs in the final.

1st   USA 2:
       J Radin, K Wei, L Deas, B Palmer, J Chambers, C Bjerkan
2nd   France:
       V Bessis, D Gaviard, G Chevalley, S Willard,
       H Bordenave, B Cronier
3rd   Italy:
       L Capodanno, M d'Andrea, C Gianardi, M Bianchi,
       A Valenti, G Olivieri

1988
In 1988, at the eighth attempt, the USA finally broke their duck in the World Team Olympiad. For four of the American team, Bob

Hamman, Bobby Wolff, Jeff Meckstroth and Eric Rodwell, this was the third leg of their Triple Crown – the Olympiad, the Bermuda Bowl and the World Open Pairs. This feat had previously achieved only by Roger Trézel and Pierre Jaïs of France, more than 25 years earlier, when they won the first World Pairs in 1962. For Hamman this was his fourth Olympiad final, and for Wolff his third. Curiously, Austrians Heinrich Berger and Wolfgang Meinl completed a Triple Crown also, but with silver medals, having finished second in the 1986 World Pairs, the 1985 Bermuda Bowl, and now the 1988 Olympiad.

The Women's event was won by Denmark – that country's first World bridge title. It was their third silver medal in this event for Great Britain's Sandra Landy and Nicola Smith (formerly Gardener).

8th World Team Olympiad in Venice, Italy
1st   USA:
       R D Hamman, R S Wolff, J J Meckstroth, E V Rodwell,
       S Deutsch, J Jacoby
2nd   Austria:
       H Berger, J Fucik, W Meinl, A Kadlec, F Terraneo, F Kubac

8th Women's World Team Olympiad in Venice, Italy
1st   Denmark:
       K Moeller, D Shaltz, B Kalkerup, C Palmund,
       T Dahl, J Norris
2nd   Great Britain:
       N P Smith, P Davies, S Landy, E McGowan,
       S Penfold, M Brunner

1989

The 29th Bermuda Bowl, staged for the first time in Australia, saw a momentous first – a victory for a team from outside both North America and Europe. The Brazilians, who had been on the fringes for so long, finally reached the final and defeated the American team in convincing fashion. For Marcelo Branco too, this was the final leg of the Triple Crown, and he became the seventh player in history to achieve the feat of winning the Bermuda Bowl, the Olympiad and the World Open Pairs.

This loss ended an American run of seven consecutive Bermuda Bowl victories going back to 1976.

The two teams seeded to the semi-finals were USA and Poland. Brazil, and the hosts Australia, finished atop the qualifying Round Robin to join them in the knockout stage.

In the Venice Cup, USA retained the trophy with a team including two members (Deas & Palmer) from the one that had won two years earlier. The Dutch were the beaten finalists. One of the beaten semi-finalists was Germany, which is as close as any team from that country had previously come to a World title.

29th Bermuda Bowl in Perth, Australia
USA defeated Australia by 60 IMPs in one semi-final.
Brazil defeated Poland by 42 IMPs in the other.
Brazil defeated USA by 104 IMPs in the final.

1st   Brazil:
      G P Chagas, M Branco, P Branco, R Mello, C Camacho, R Janz
2nd   USA:
      H L Ross, P A Pender, C U Martel, L Stansby,
      M S Lawrence, C R Woolsey
3rd   Poland:
      A Zmudzinski, C Balicki, K Moszczynski, J Klukowski,
      K Martens, M Szymanowski

7th Venice Cup in Perth, Australia
USA defeated Canada by 47 IMPs in one semi-final.
The Netherlands defeated Germany by 21 IMPs in the other.
USA defeated The Netherlands by 34 IMPs in the final.

1st   USA:
      B Palmer, L Deas, K Shuman, K T McCallum,
      K Bethe, M Gwodzdzinsky
2nd   The Netherlands:
      E Bakker, I Gielkens, C Arnolds, B Vriend,
      M van der Pas, E Schippers
3rd   Canada:
      D Gordon, S Reus, M Paul, F Cimon, K Thorpe, G Silverman

1990
Germany broke their World title duck sooner than expected, and from an unforeseen direction, by defeating an American team in the

final of the 1990 World Knockout Teams. Not that their win was free of controversy – in the semi-final, they overcame a strong Canadian team by 3 IMPs, thanks to a scoring error in the final set! They were then 30 IMPs down with one set remaining in the final, and gained 43 IMPs in the last set to win by 13.

4th World Knockout Teams in Geneva, Switzerland
Germany defeated Canada by 3 IMPs in one semi-final.
USA (Moss) defeated USA (Rapee) by 42 IMPs in the other.
Germany defeated USA (Moss) by 13 IMPs in the final.

1st   Germany:
        B Ludwig, J Bitschene, G Nippgen, R Rohowsky
2nd   USA:
        M Moss, C Coon, D Casen, M E Seamon

Hot from their victory in the 1989 Bermuda Bowl, Brazilians Marcelo Branco & Gabriel Chagas added the World Open Pairs crown to their growing collection of titles. For Branco, this was his second victory in the event, having won in 1978 playing with Gabino Cintra, and he is the only player to have won this event twice. The win also completed the Triple Crown for Chagas, and he became the eighth player in history to have won the Bermuda Bowl, the Olympiad and the World Open Pairs.

The Women's Pairs was also won by a pair who had been on a winning team in Perth a year earlier – America's Karen McCallum & Kerri Shuman. This win gave Shuman a Triple Crown of sorts – the Women's Pairs, the World Mixed Pairs and the Venice Cup. (This is not a unique achievement, as Mary-Jane Farell had previously won these three events too, as well as the Women's Team Olympiad.) Previous winners of the event (in 1978), Judi Radin and Kathie Wei, finished second.

The Americans also collected the gold in the Mixed Pairs, but their clean sweep of the event was spoiled this time around by Sweden's Göthe/Anderson, who won the silver medals.

At these World Championships, the WBF also introduced another new event – the World Seniors Pairs.

8th World Open Pairs in Geneva, Switzerland
1st   Brazil: Gabriel Chagas & Marcelo Branco
2nd   USA: Peter Nagy & Ralph Katz
3rd   Poland: Adam Zmudzinski & Cezary Balicki

8th World Women's Pairs in Geneva, Switzerland
1st   USA: Karen McCallum & Kerri Shuman
2nd   USA: Judi Radin & Kathie Wei
3rd   The Netherlands: Bep Vriend & Carla Arnolds

7th World Mixed Pairs in Geneva, Switzerland
1st   USA: Juanita Chambers & Peter Weichsel
2nd   Sweden: Eva-Liss Göthe & Lars Anderson
3rd   USA: Kathie Walvick & Walt Walvick

1st World Seniors Pairs in Geneva, Switzerland
1st   Great Britain: Albert Dormer & Alan Hiron

1991
The 30th Bermuda Bowl, held in Japan for the first time, was full of surprises. There was a new format for a start – for the first time, the winners would have to win three head-to-head matches, with eight teams proceeding to the knockout stage.

The upsets began early, with both American teams failing to reach the semi-final stage. One semi-final was a rematch from Perth two years earlier, but this time it was Poland who overcame Brazil, thus unseating the holders and ensuring that a new name would be inscribed on the famous trophy. The other semi-final featured two Nordic countries, and when Iceland edged past Sweden it was front-page news back in the small North Atlantic country where bridge is one of the primary national sports.

Sweden, Poland and Brazil had all won previous World bridge titles, and when Iceland emerged victorious another country was added to that list, and on their first appearance in the Bermuda Bowl at that.

The Venice Cup was more predictable, and after eight contests for that trophy there were still only two countries that had won – USA and Great Britain. The two American teams contested one semi-final, while in the other Austria saw off China. In the quarter-finals, two rising European powers (Germany and Austria) met in one of the most exciting matches in Venice Cup history. Austria established a huge lead by the halfway point, but the Germans came back strongly. Their recovery eventually fell just 10 IMPs short, but the bridge world was left with the feeling that it was only a matter of time for them. One other point of note was the presence of Jane and Kay Preddy in the British team – the first time a mother and daughter had played in the same team at this level.

30th Bermuda Bowl in Yokohama, Japan
In the quarter-finals:
Iceland beat USA-2 by 87 IMPs.
Poland beat Great Britain by 87 IMPs.
Sweden beat Argentina by 26 IMPs.
Brazil beat USA-1 by 8 IMPs.
Iceland defeated Sweden by 12 IMPs in one semi-final.
Poland defeated Brazil by 52 IMPs in the other.
Iceland defeated Poland by 39 IMPs in the final.
Sweden won the playoff for third place by 29 IMPs.

1st   Iceland:
       O Arnthorsson, G R Johannsson, J Baldursson, G P Arnarson,
       T Jonsson, A Jorgensen
2nd   Poland:
       A Zmudzinski, C Balicki, K Martens, M Szymanowski,
       P Gawrys, K Lasocki
3rd   Sweden:
       P-O Sundelin, T Gullberg, B Fallenius, M Nilsland,
       A Morath, S-A Bjerregard

8th Venice Cup in Yokohama, Japan
In the quarter-finals:
USA 2 beat Great Britain by 2 IMPs.
China beat Chinese Taipei by 32 IMPs.
Austria beat Germany by 10 IMPs.
USA 1 beat Japan by 134 IMPs.
USA 2 defeated USA 1 by 94 IMPs in one semi-final.
Austria defeated China by 88 IMPs in the other.
USA 2 defeated Austria by 102 IMPs in the final.

1st   USA 2:
       L Deas, S Cohen, S Osberg, S J Picus, N B Cahn, N L Passell

2nd   Austria:
      M Erhart, G Bamberger, D Fischer, T Weigkricht,
      B Widengren, R Spinn
3rd   USA 1:
      J Chambers, K Schulle, C Bjerkan, J J Meyers,
      P S Wittes, R Montin

1992

In 1992, the Olympiads followed the Bermuda Bowl and Venice Cup formats by qualifying eight teams to the knockout stage.

Great Britain reached its fifth Women's World Team Olympiad final in nine attempts, but for the fourth time (and the third consecutive occasion) they came away with the silver medals. This time it was the Austrian team, three of whom had lost in the final of the Venice Cup a year earlier, that claimed the World Championship title.

In the Open, the USA team matched the British women's achievement exactly by reaching their fifth final and losing for the fourth time. Meanwhile, the French reached their fourth final and equalled Italy's record of three victories in the event. The Danish team included a married couple – Peter and Dorthe Schaltz – and in reaching the quarter-finals they established the best ever performance by such a pair. The same Danish team also featured a pair of brothers – Lars and Knut Blakset – and this was the first time such a pair had reached the latter stages of an Olympiad.

In the Open, six European teams emerged from the Round Robin stage. The only non-European teams in the knockout stages were the USA and a surprise African representative, Egypt. In the Women's, Europe did even better by qualifying seven teams to the knockout rounds, the only exception being China.

9th World Team Olympiad in Salsomaggiore, Italy

In the quarter-finals:
USA beat Egypt by 71 IMPs.
The Netherlands beat Israel by 9 IMPs.
Sweden beat Poland by 75 IMPs.
France beat Denmark by 4 IMPs.
USA defeated Sweden by 71 IMPs in one semi-final.
France defeated The Netherlands by 37 IMPs in the other.
France defeated USA by 80 IMPs in the final.

1st   France:
       P Chemla, M Perron, A Levy, H Mouiel, M Auhaleu, P Adad
2nd   USA:
       R D Hamman, R S Wolff, J J Meckstroth, E V Rodwell,
       S Deutsch, M Rosenberg
3rd=   Sweden:
       B Fallenius, M Nilsland, A Morath, S-A Bjerregard,
       A Brunzell, J Nielsen
       The Netherlands:
       J van der Neut, M Nooijen, E Leufkens, B Westra,
       W de Boer, B Muller

9th Women's World Team Olympiad in Salsomaggiore, Italy

In the quarter-finals:
France beat China by 54 IMPs.
Austria beat Sweden by 51 IMPs.
Germany beat Denmark by 76 IMPs.
Great Britain beat The Netherlands by 120 IMPs.
Great Britain defeated Germany by 26 IMPs in one semi-final.
Austria defeated France by 14 IMPs in the other.
Austria defeated Great Britain by 48 IMPs in the final.

1st   Austria:
       M Erhart, B Lindinger, D Fischer, T Weigkricht,
       J Smederevac, H Gyimesi
2nd   Great Britain:
       E McGowan, S Penfold, S Landy, M Handley,
       N P Smith, P Davies
3rd=   Germany:
       S Zenkel, D von Arnim, W Vogt, B Nehmert,
       M Moegel, K Caesar
       France:
       C Lise, E Delor, S Willard, V Bessis, D Avon, A C de l'Epine

1993

The 31st Bermuda Bowl, held in Chile for the first time, threw up yet
more surprises in two exciting weeks of competition. For the second
time two teams who had never previously won the event reached the
final. Not that it seemed likely they would during two nail-biting
semi-finals in which Norway overcame former champions Brazil by

just 3 IMPs, while The Netherlands saw off USA-1 by the same margin. Indeed, the Dutch beat both American teams en route to the final.

In the Venice Cup, the USA won for the seventh time in nine attempts and, with Great Britain having won on the other two occasions, the trophy was still waiting for a third name to be engraved upon it after 20 years of competition. This time it was Germany who made it to their first final, only to be turned away by the powerful American squad.

31st Bermuda Bowl in Santiago, Chile

In the quarter-finals:
The Netherlands beat USA-1 by 28 IMPs.
Norway beat Poland by 141 IMPs.
USA 2 beat Denmark by 9 IMPs.
Brazil beat China by 178 IMPs.
The Netherlands defeated USA 2 by 3 IMPs in one semi-final.
Norway defeated Brazil by 3 IMPs in the other.
The Netherlands defeated Norway by 34 IMPs in the final.

1st	Netherlands:
	W DeBoer, B Muller, P Jansen, J Westerhof,
	E Leufkens, B Westra
2nd	Norway:
	G Groetheim, T Aa, A Rasumssen, J Sveindal,
	G Helgemo, T Helness
3rd=	USA 2:
	C Russell, S Lev, L N Cohen, D Berkowitz,
	M Bergen, E V Rodwell
	Brazil:
	G P Chagas, M Branco, P Branco, R Mello,
	C Camacho, O Barbosa

9th Venice Cup in Santiago, Chile

In the quarter-finals:
USA 2 beat Italy by 116 IMPs.
Sweden beat Canada by 15 IMPs.
Germany beat USA 1 by 129 IMPs.
Argentina beat Chinese Taipei by 74 IMPs.
USA 2 defeated Argentina by 55 IMPs in one semi-final.

Germany defeated Sweden by 20 IMPs in the other.
USA 2 defeated Germany by 64 IMPs in the final.

1st   USA 2
        K Schulle, J J Meyers, K Sanborn, K McCallum,
        S Osberg, S J Picus
2nd   Germany:
        S Zenkel, D von Arnim, W Vogt, B Nehmert,
        M Moegel, K Caesar
3rd=   Argentina:
        A Blum, M Tiscornia, M Matienzo, M Hernandez,
        C Suaya, G Rosenfeld
        Sweden:
        L Langstrom, C Midskog, P Flodqvist, M Ryman,
        B Odlund, L Astrom

1994

1994 saw the introduction of a Women's event to run concurrently
with the Rosenblum Cup – the McConnell Cup for the Women's
World Knockout Teams.

The American team's victory in the Rosenblum gave Lew
Stansby and Chip Martel a unique Triple Crown – they were the
first players to have won the Bermuda Bowl, the World Knockout
Teams and the World Pairs.

The Americans have dominated Women's bridge, and they
emphasized that by qualifying four teams for the semi-final stage of
the McConnell Cup. There was plenty of exciting bridge played,
with the final and one semi-final decided by single-figure margins.

Judi Radin's victory assured her of legendary status in World
Women's bridge, as she became the only player to have achieved a
unique quartet of victories – the Venice Cup, the Woman's Team
Olympiad, the World Women's Pairs, and now the Women's World
Knockout Teams.

5th World Knockout Teams in Albuquerque, New Mexico, USA
In the quarter-finals:
USA (Deutsch) beat USA(Rotman) by 30 IMPs.
Israel beat France by 3 IMPs.
Sweden beat USA (Binsky) by 20 IMPs.

Poland beat Italy by 13 IMPs.
USA defeated Israel by 91 IMPs in one semi-final.
Poland defeated Sweden by 21 IMPs in the other.
USA defeated Poland by 31 IMPs in the final.

1st	USA:
	S Deutsch, M Rosenberg, G Kasle, R W Bates,
	C U Martel, L Stansby
2nd	Poland:
	E Otvosi, M Borewixcz, C Balicki, A Zmudzinski,
	P Gawrys, K Lasocki
3rd=	Sweden:
	Auby, Brenning, Gullberg, Gustawsson
	Israel
	Levit, Cohen, Podgur, Kalish

1st Women's World Knockout Teams in Albuquerque, New Mexico, USA

In the quarter-finals:
USA (Woolsey) beat The Netherlands by 5 IMPs.
USA (Letizia) beat Israel by 31 IMPs.
USA (Alder) beat USA (Chambers) by 91 IMPs.
USA (Tornay) beat Great Britain by 75 IMPs.
USA (Letizia) defeated USA (Tornay) by 78 IMPs in one semi-final.
USA(Woolsey) defeated USA (Alder) by 8 IMPs in the other.
USA (Letizia) defeated USA (Woolsey) by 5 IMPs in the final.

1st	USA (Letizia):
	M Letizia, J Blanchard, J Radin, R Pollack, S Picus
2nd	USA (Woolsey):
	S Woolsey, D Cohen, K Allsion, J-A Casen,
	J Glasson, J-A Manfield
3rd=	USA (Tornay):
	C Tornay, J Cody, J-A Stansby, L Perlman,
	S Lapkoff, C Steiner
	USA (Alder):
	J Lilie, J Morse, T Deutsch, M Breed, J Mitchell, A Kearse

1994

After a number of near misses in the major teams events, a Polish pair struck gold in the World Open Pairs. For Holland's Anton Maas, the bronze medal was a step down from the silver he had won 12 years perviously. His wife, Bep Vriend, ensured the Dutch flag was flying high though, by winning the Women's Pairs with Carla Arnolds – an improvement of two places on their performance four years before. Like Maas, the bronze medallists in the women's event, Beth Palmer and Lynn Deas, had also collected silver in 1982.

The gold medals in the World Mixed Pairs went to a non-American pair for only the third time in eight attempts – Poland's Hocheker/Kowalski helping their country take two of the three pairs titles. Meanwhile Marcin Lesniewski, who won the Open Pairs, also collected a bronze in the Mixed to make it a great fortnight for Poland (who had also collected silver in the Open Teams). Bob Hamman finished second for the second time, partnering Germany's Sabine Zenkel on this occasion.

North America swept the medals at the World Seniors Pairs – USA collecting gold and silver, while the bronze went to Canada.

9th World Open Pairs in Albuquerque, New Mexico, USA
1st   Poland: Marcin Lesniewski & Marek Szymanowski
2nd   USA: Bob Hamman & Michael Rosenberg
3rd   The Netherlands: Anton Maas & Eric Kirchhoff

9th World Women's Pairs in Albuquerque, New Mexico, USA
1st   The Netherlands: Bep Vriend & Carla Arnold
2nd   France: Veronique Bessis & Catherine Saul
3rd   USA: Lynn Deas & Beth Palmer

8th World Mixed Pairs in Albuquerque, New Mexico, USA
1st   Poland: Danuta Hocheker & Apolinary Kowalski
2nd   Germany/USA: Sabine Zenkel & Bob Hamman
3rd   Poland: Eva Harasimowicz & Marcin Lesniewski

2nd World Seniors Pairs in Albuquerque, New Mexico, USA
1st   USA: Fred Hamilton & Hamish Bennett
2nd   USA: Simon Kantor & Murray Melton
3rd   Canada: Duncan Phillips & Bill Solomon

1995

In 1995, the World Championships moved to China for the first
time. There was good news and bad news for North American
teams. The Open team recovered the Bermuda Bowl for the first
time since 1987, and their opponents in the final were their northern
neighbours – Canada. For the Canadians, this was their country's
best ever result at this level. This win also gave the Americans their
14th Bermuda Bowl win – one more than Italy.

The bad news was that the Venice Cup at last, at the tenth attempt,
would have a third name engraved upon it. Germany overcame the
USA team in the final to win their country's second World title.

32nd Bermuda Bowl in Beijing, China

In the quarter-finals:
USA 2 beat Indonesia by 49 IMPs.
Canada beat South Africa by 85 IMPs.
France beat China by 3 IMPs.
Sweden beat The Netherlands by 45 IMPs.
USA 2 defeated France by 78 IMPs in one semi-final.
Canada defeated Sweden by 71 IMPs in the other.
USA 2 defeated Canada by 43 IMPs in the final.

1st   USA 2:
       R D Hamman, R S Wolff, J J Meckstroth, E V Rodwell,
       F T Nickell, R A Freeman
2nd   Canada:
       F A Gitelman, G Mittelman, E O Kokish, J Silver,
       B Baran, M Molson
3rd= Sweden:
       B Fallenius, M Nilsland, Bennett, A Wirgren,
       A Morath, S-A Bjerregard
       France:
       M Perron, P Chemla, M Lebel, P Cronier,
       R Reiplinger, P Soulet

10th Venice Cup in Beijing, China

In the quarter-finals:
Germany beat Japan by 36 IMPs.
China beat Venezuela by 200 IMPs.
France beat South Africa by 103 IMPs.

USA 1 beat USA 2 by 58 IMPs.
Germany defeated France by 93 IMPs in one semi-final.
USA 1 defeated China by 74 IMPs in the other.
Germany defeated USA 1 by 68 IMPs in the final.

1st   Germany:
      S Zenkel, D von Arnim, A Rauscheid, B Nehmert,
      M Moegel, K Caesar
2nd   USA 1:
      S J Picus, C Simon, K Munson, R Pollack,
      K T McCallum, K Sanborn
3rd= China:
      G Ling, Z Yaian, S Ming, Hongli, L P Wang, Y Liu
      France:
      C Lise, C Blouquit, C Saul, S Willard, V Bessis, B Cronier

1996

Victory in the 10th World Team Olympiad made France the most successful nation in the event. Since its inception in 1960, the French had recorded four victories – one more than the great Italian Blue Team achieved. The losing finalists were Indonesia, and although they had been one of the leading Asian teams, and thus regular participants at the Bermuda Bowl for many years, this was easily their most successful event to date. The bronze medals went to Denmark, a strong European bridge-playing nation, but one still seeking its first Open World bridge title. One curious note to this event was the appearance of Jason, Justin and Paul Hackett in the British team – the first time that three family members (in this case, father and twin brothers) had ever played in the same team.

In the Women's Olympiad, it was business as usual and another victory for the Americans. For Juanita Chambers, her victory in Rhodes gave her an unusual treble – she is the only player to have won the Venice Cup, the Women's Olympiad and the World Mixed Pairs. China were the losing finalists, which is the closest they have yet come to a World bridge title, and it can only be a matter of time before they break their duck. One notable achievement was the victory of America's former Russian Irina Levitina, who became the first person to have won a World title at both bridge and chess.

10th World Team Olympiad in Rhodes, Greece
1st   France:
       M Bompis, A Levy, C Mari, H Mouiel, F Multon, H Szwarc
2nd   Indonesia:
       K Lasut, E Manoppo, D Sacul, Karwur, Panelewan, Watulingus
3rd   Denmark:
       J Auken, L Blakset, D Kock-Palmund,
       Schaeffer, Christensen, L Andersen

10th Women's World Team Olympiad in Rhodes, Greece
1st   USA:
       J Blanchard, J Chambers, L Deas, G Greenberg,
       S Quinn, I Levitina
2nd   China:
       Gu, S Ming, Wang H, Wang W, Zhang Y, Zhang Yu
3rd   Canada:
       D Gordon, S Reus, B Kraft, F Cimon,
       R Habert, B J Saltsman

1997
For the first time, the World Championships were held in Africa. Tunisia was the host country. The WBF also introduced an additional event – the World Transnational Teams – that would run concurrently with the latter stages of the main events.

Arguably the two best teams in the world met head on in the final of the 33rd Bermuda Bowl. The Americans were the defending champions, while the French were current World champions having won the Olympiad the year before. Both teams had breezed through the earlier rounds, but something had to give. In the end, it was the Americans.

Remarkably, this was the first French victory in the event since 1956 – a gap of more than 40 years. For Bob Hamman, this was his 16th World Championship final, now just two short of the late, great Giorgio Belladonna's record (although Hamman's eight wins are well behind Belladonna's record of 16).

The Venice Cup saw the eighth American win in eleven attempts. The most exciting matches all involved North American teams – USA 2 edged past Canada by 2 IMPs and then fell 5 IMPs short in the semi-final against USA 1.

33rd Bermuda Bowl in Hammamet, Tunisia

In the quarter-finals:
USA 1 beat China by 50 IMPs.
USA 2 beat Chinese Taipei by 34 IMPs.
Norway beat Italy by 12 IMPs.
France beat Poland by 31 IMPs.
USA 2 defeated USA 1 by 131 IMPs in one semi-final.
France defeated Norway by 63 IMPs in the other.
France defeated USA 2 by 26 IMPs in the final.
Norway won the playoff for third place by 30 IMPs.

1st	France:
	M Perron, P Chemla, A Levy, C Mari, H Mouiel, F Multon
2nd	USA 2:
	R D Hamman, R S Wolff, J J Meckstroth, E V Rodwell, F T Nickell, R A Freeman
3rd	Norway:
	T Aa, G Groetheim, T Helness, G Helgemo, B Brogeland, E Saelensminde

11th Venice Cup in Hammamet, Tunisia

In the quarter-finals:
USA 2 beat Canada by 2 IMPs.
China beat Great Britain by 74 IMPs.
France beat The Netherlands by 120 IMPs.
USA 1 beat Italy by 24 IMPs.
China defeated France by 21 IMPs in one semi-final.
USA 1 defeated USA 2 by 5 IMPs in the other.
USA 1 defeated China by 65 IMPs in the final.
USA 2 won the playoff for third place by 48 IMPs.

1st	USA 1:
	T Sokolow, M Breed, L Berkowitz, M Letizia, J Meyers, R Montin
2nd	China:
	Gu Ling, Yalan Zhang, Sun Ming, Wenfei Wang, Yan Lu, Yu Zhang
3rd	USA 2:
	K Wei-Sender, L Deas, J Chambers, K Sanborn, B Palmer, I Levitina

1st World Transnational Teams in Hammamet, Tunisia
1st   Italy/Poland:
       S de Falco, L Buratti, M Lesniewski, K Martens, F Mariani
2nd   Poland:
       K Jassem, Gardynik, T Przybora, M Kwiecen, J Pszczola

1998

In the Rosenblum Cup, teams from seven different countries reached the quarter-final stage. Curiously, not one of those was from the host country – double-reigning World Champions, France. Sweden was the only nation with two survivors at that point. Every round had its close matches – the Brazilian squad who eventually collected the silver medals survived by just 1 IMP (having been 50 down at half-time) in the Round of 64. The Italians only made it through their semi-final against the Americans by 3 IMPs.

The final was always going to have a momentous outcome. Had the Brazilians won, then Garbiel Chagas and Marcelo Branco would have become the only players thus far to add the World Knockout Teams to the Triple Crown they already held. As it was, the Italians emerged victorious – remarkably, this was Italy's first World Team championship since 1975, a gap of 24 years.

Four years previously in the first McConnell Cup, the semi-finals had been competed by four American teams. This time around, four American teams made it to the quarter-finals, and two of those survived to the semis. However, both lost to former Venice Cup winners, and it was Austria against Germany in the final. The final was a one-sided affair, with the Austrians striking early and often.

6th World Knockout Teams in Lille, France
In the quarter-finals:
Italy beat The Netherlands by 51 IMPs.
USA(Bramley) beat Denmark by 67 IMPs.
Sweden (Lindkvist) beat Great Britain by 8 IMPs.
Brazil beat Sweden (Sundelin) by 26 IMPs.
Italy defeated USA by 3 IMPs in one semi-final.
Brazil defeated Sweden by 23 IMPs in the other.
Italy defeated Brazil by 79 IMPs in the final.

1st   Italy:
       A Versace, L Lauria, A Sementa, L Buratti, M Lanzarotti
2nd   Brazil:
       G P Chagas, M Branco, M Villas Boas, J P Campos
3rd=   Sweden (Lindkvist):
       M Lindkvist, P Fredin, B Fallenius, M Nilsland
       USA:
       B Bramley, S H Lazard, S Garner, H M Weinstein,
       W Pollack, D Casen

2nd Women's World Knockout Teams in Lille, France

In the quarter-finals:
USA (Wood) beat France by 12 IMPs.
Austria beat China by 19 IMPs.
USA (Truscott) beat USA (Allison) by 32 IMPs.
Germany beat USA(Solodar) by 90 IMPs.
Austria defeated USA(Truscott) by 23 IMPs in one semi-final.
Germany defeated USA(Wood) by 50 IMPs in the other.
Austria defeated Germany by 94 IMPs in the final.

1st   Austria:
       M Erhart, S Terraneo, T Weigkricht, D Fischer
2nd   Germany:
       S Auken, D von Arnim, K Farwig, B Stawowy
3rd=   USA (Wood):
       N Wood, C Tornay, T Michaels, E Lewis, M Kivel
       USA (Truscott):
       D Truscott, C Sanders, T Sokolow, J-A Sprung,
       S Quinn, J Meyers

Poland won the World Open Pairs for the second consecutive time.
America's Cohen/Berkowitz were unlucky, having led for the whole
five-session final except for after the final two boards. Sweden's
Lindkvist/Fredin collected their second bronze medals of the
tournament, having also tied for third in the Rosenblum Teams.

   In the Women's Pairs, America's Quinn/Meyers moved up to gold
having collected bronze in the teams. Bessis and d'Ovidio
(formerly Catherine Saul) collected the bronze medals, having
finished second four years earlier. Germany's Auken/von Arnim
collected silver, the same as in the teams. Sabine Auken also won

bronze in the Mixed Pairs, playing with husband Jens, to complete
an interesting two weeks of bridge. The Mixed Pairs title went to
Italy in the form of Antonio Vivaldi and Enza Rosano.

   The medal winners in the Seniors Pairs read like a *Who's Who* of
world bridge. Boris Schapiro's remarkable achievement in winning at
the age of 89 established a record unlikely to be beaten for some
time, if ever, and it is thought that he is the oldest ever winner of a
World Championship title in any sport. Meanwhile, collecting silver
was former Italian superstar Benito Garozzo, now representing the
USA.

9th World Open Pairs in Lille, France
1st   Poland: Michel Kwiecien & Jacek Pszczola
2nd   USA: Larry Cohen & David Berkowitz
3rd   Sweden: Magnus Lindkvist & Peter Fredin

10th World Women's Pairs in Lille, France
1st   USA: Jill Meyers & Shawn Quinn
2nd   Germany: Sabine Auken & Daniela von Arnim
3rd   France: Veronique Bessis & Catherine d'Ovidio

9th World Mixed Pairs in Lille, France
1st   Italy: Enza Rosano & Antonio Vivaldi
2nd   France: Claude Blouquit & Marc Bompis
3rd   Germany/Denmark: Sabine Auken & Jens Auken
1998: 3rd World Seniors Pairs in Lille, France
1st   Great Britain: Boris Schapiro & Irving Gordon
2nd   USA: Lea Dupont & Benito Garozzo
3rd   Germany: W Hoger & G Vavensleben

1999
There was no World Championship competition in 1999, as the
Bermuda Bowl and Venice Cup scheduled for that year will be held
in January 2000, in Bermuda, to commemorate the 50th
Anniversary of the first Bermuda Bowl. What appears above is
therefore a complete record of the first 50 years of World Bridge
Championships.

Leading players and countries in each event
THE BERMUDA BOWL
Total number of contests   33
Winners by country   USA (14)
                               Italy (13)
                               France (2)
                               GB, Iceland, Netherlands, Brazil (1)
Most consecutive wins   Italy (10)
                               USA (7)
                               USA (4)
Wins by individuals   Giorgio Belladonna (13)
                               Pietro Forquet (12)
                               Benito Garozzo, Massimo D'Alelio (10)
                               Walter Avarelli (9)
                               Bob Hamman, Bobby Wolff (7)
                               Eugenio Chiaradia (6)
                               Camillo Pabis Ticci,
                               Billy Eisenberg (5)
                               Guglielmo Siniscalco, George Rapee,
                               Howard Schenken, Sam Stayman,
                               Bobby Goldman, Paul Soloway, Mike
                               Lawrence (3)

THE VENICE CUP
Total number of contests   11
Winners by country   USA (8)
                               GB (2)
                               Germany (1)
Most consecutive wins   USA (4)
                               USA (3)
                               GB (2)
Wins by individuals   Dorothy Truscott (Hayden), Emma-
                               Jean Hawes, Lynn Deas (3)
                               Carol Sanders, Betty-Ann Kennedy,
                               Jacqui Mitchell, Gail Moss, Sandra
                               Landy, Nicola Smith (Gardener), Sally
                               Brock (Horton/Sowter), Pat Davies,
                               Beth Palmer, Sue Picus, Sharon
                               Osberg, Jill Meyers, Karen McCallum,
                               Kerri Sanborn (Shuman) (2)

WORLD OPEN TEAM OLYMPIAD

Total number of contests	10
Winners by country	France (4)
	Italy (3)
	Poland, USA, Brazil (1)
Most consecutive wins	Italy (3)
Wins by individuals	Walter Avarelli, Giorgio Belladonna, Benito Garozzo, Pietro Forquet, Camillo Pabis Ticci, Massimo d'Alelio (3)
	Paul Chemla, Michel Perron, Henri Szwarc, Hervé Mouiel, Christian Mari, Alain Levy (2)

WOMEN'S WORLD TEAMS OLYMPIAD

Total number of contests	10
Winners by country	USA (3)
	Italy (2)
	Sweden, GB, UAR, Denmark, Austria (1)
Most consecutive wins	Italy (2)
Wins by individuals	Gail Moss, Jacqui Mitchell, Anna Valenti, Marissa Bianchi, Rina Jabes (2)

TOTAL WORLD CHAMPIONSHIP WINS

Open		Women	
16	Giorgio Belladonna	5	Jacqui Mitchell
15	Pietro Forquet	4	Fritzi Gordon
13	Benito Garozzo		Rixi Markus
	Massimo D'Alelio		Judi Radin
12	Walter Avarelli		Kerri Sanborn (Shuman)
9	Bob Hamman		Carol Sanders
	Bobby Wolff		Betty-Anne Kennedy
8	Camillo Pabis Ticci		Lynn Deas
6	Eugenio Chiaradia		Mary-Jane Farrel
5	Billy Eisenberg		Dorothy Truscott
4	Marcelo Branco		Emma-Jean Hawes
	Jeff Meckstroth	3	Karen McCallum
	Eric Rodwell		Sue Picus

Chip Martel

Lew Stansby

3 Guglielmo Siniscalco

George Rapee

Howard Schenken

Sam Stayman

Bobby Goldman

Paul Soloway

Mike Lawrence

Paul Chemla

Michel Perron

Herve Mouiel

Christian Mari

Alain Levy

Jim Jacoby

Pierre Jaïs

Roger Trézel

Gabriel Chagas

Kathie Wei

Jill Meyers

Gail Moss

MAJOR NATIONAL EVENTS — THE WINNERS

The British Bridge League Gold Cup

The BBL Gold Cup was first presented in 1931. The list of winners contains most of the greatest names in British bridge. The format is a straight knockout played throughout the year. Teams enter from England, Scotland and Wales. In recent times, nine consecutive victories have been required in order to win (ignoring possible byes in an early round). The most successful individual is Boris Schapiro, who first won in 1945, and in 1998 was victorious for the 11th time.

1931-32: E E Mayer (Capt);
Col H M Beasley, H H Renshaw, P V Tabbush

1932-33: R Lederer (Capt);
C H Collingwood, H Newmark, W Rose

1933-34: R Lederer (Capt);
W Rose, C H Collingwood, N Kosky

1934-35: A Wolfers (Capt);
L Wolfers, E P C Cotter, E L Tottenham

1935-36: H Ingram (Capt);
S E Hughes, H Newmark, T Simmons

1936-37: M Harrison-Gray (Capt);
S J Simon, J C H Marx, I Macleod, C Harding

1937-38: N Mudie Bach (Capt);
L W Dodds, E P C Cotter, E L Tottenham, L Ritte

1938-39: R Lederer (Capt);
J Tarlo, L Tarlo, J Janes

1945-46: L Baron (Capt);
N Goldinger, H Leist, P Juan, B Schapiro, N Squire

1946-47: M Harrison-Gray (Capt);
B Schapiro, J C H Marx, S J Simon, E N Furse

1948: J T Reese (Capt);
B Schapiro, A Meredith, Dr H Leist, Dr S Lee, P Juan

1949:   G F Mathieson (Capt);
            M Harrison-Gray, K W Konstam, J Pavlides,
            L W Dodds, E Payne
1950:   J T Reese (Capt);
            B Schapiro, A Meredith, Dr H Leist,
            Dr S Lee, Mrs A L Fleming
1951:   L Tarlo (Capt);
            N Gardener, L Baron, A Rose
1952:   J T Reese (Capt);
            B Schapiro, A Meredith, Dr H Leist,
            Dr S Lee, S Booker
1953:   J T Reese (Capt);
            B Schapiro, A Meredith, Dr H Leist,
            Dr S Lee, S Booker
1954:   L Tarlo (Capt);
            H Franklin, N Gardener, A Rosc, N Squire
1955:   R Preston (Capt);
            R Swimer, J Nunes. B P Topley
1956:   J T Reese (Capt);
            B Schapiro, L W Dodds, K W Konstam,
            A Meredith, P Juan
1957:   Dr S Lee (Capt);
            Mrs F Gordon, S Booker, C Rodrigue, L Tarlo
1958:   N Gardener (Capt);
            A Rose, J Nunes, N Squire,
            A G Dormer, D C W Rimington
1959:   J Lazarus (Capt);
            S Blaser, F Farrington, B Franks, I Morris
1960:   L Tarlo (Capt);
            L W Dodds, H Franklin, K W Konstam,
            B Schapiro, J T Reese
1961:   Mrs R Markus (Capt);
            Mrs F Gordon, L W Dodds, H Lever MP,
            J Tarlo, M Wolach
1962:   M Harrison-Gray (Capt);
            J Sharples, R Sharples, Dr M Rockfelt,
            F North, J M Pugh
1963:   A G Dormer (Capt);
            A M Hiron, J Nunes. A Rose,
            K Barbour, H P F Swinnerton-Dyer

1964:   J T Reese (Capt);
           B Schapiro, K W Konstam, M J Flint,
           C Rodrigue, R A Priday

1965:   J T Reese (Capt);
           B Schapiro, M J Flint, K W Konstam,
           J D R Collings, J Cansino

1966:   M Harrison-Gray (Capt);
           A Rose, J Sharples, R Sharples

1967:   M Harrison-Gray (Capt);
           R A Priday, N Gardener, A Rose, J Sharples, R Sharples

1968:   M Harrison-Gray (Capt);
           R A Priday, N Gardener, A Rose,
           J Sharples, R Sharples

1969:   S Leckie (Capt);
           V Goldberg, W Coyle, V A Silverstone,
           T N Culbertson, H W Kelsey

1970:   R A Priday (Capt);
           N Gardener, J Sharples, R Sharples,
           J Amsbury, Dr M Rockfelt

1971:   K E Stanley (Capt);
           J C H Marx, J G Faulkner, D Romain,
           E W Crowhurst, A E Wardman

1972:   R M Sheehan (Capt);
           C P Dixon, R A Priday, Mrs A J Priday,
           M Esterson, D A Edwin

1973:   V A Silverstone (Capt);
           W Coyle, V Goldberg, Dr J A Matheson,
           S Leckie, B J Shenkin

1974:   R A Priday (Capt);
           C Rodrigue, L Tarlo, C P Dixon,
           D A Edwin, M I Esterson

1975:   K E Stanley (Capt);
           M E Dilks, Miss N P Gardener, I P Gordon,
           D J Greenwood, K Loveys

1976:   R A Priday (Capt);
           C Rodrigue, M Rosenberg, B J Shenkin,
           V Goldberg, P D Jourdain

1977:   B Posner (Capt);
           G N Breskal, J D R Collings, G Haase,
           J Nunes, D Smerdon

1978:   Dr A P Sowter (Capt);
              J Amsbury, M Nardin, S J Lodge, A Woo, T Cope
1979:   W Pencharz (Capt);
              R S Brock, J Sharples, R Sharples
1980:   W Mitchell (Capt);
              Dr J R Bennett, H W Kelsey, M J McMonagle,
              K Baxter, J E Paterson
1981:   I M Morrison (Capt);
              A H Bishop, Mrs S C Bruce, D S Liggat,
              J Patrick, M White
1982:   Dr G Haase (Capt);
              W Coyle, G Cuthbertson, V Goldberg, B J Shenkin
1983:   G N Breskal (Capt);
              A I Calderwood, A R Forrester,
              R S Brock, G O J Cooke
1984:   Mrs S Landy (Capt);
              Mrs S J Horton, R S Brock, Mrs N P Smith,
              Dr A P Sowter, S J Lodge
1985:   C P Dixon (Capt);
              V A Silverstone, M J Flint, I N Rose, R M Sheehan
1986:   R S Brock (Capt);
              A R Forrester, G T Kirby, J M Armstrong,
              Dr A P Sowter, S J Lodge
1987:   J K Morris (Capt);
              J W Hassett, R Churney, T Reveley,
              R Dempster, S Whittleton
1988:   R M Plackett (Capt);
              J Bacon, P J Crouch, A C L Dyson, J O Hobson
1989:   G T Kirby (Capt);
              J M Armstrong, R S Brock, A R Forrester,
              Mrs S J Horton, S J Lodge
1990:   A R Forrester (Capt);
              R S Brock, G T Kirby, J M Armstrong,
              Mrs S J Horton, S J Lodge
1991:   B Rigal (Capt);
              P Czerniewski, A. Calderwood, D. Shek,
              N P Smith, P Davies
1992:   A R Forrester (Capt);
              R S Brock, G T Kirby, J M Armstrong,
              R M Sheehan, W Coyle

1993:   G T Kirby (Capt);
           J M Armstrong, R M Sheehan, W Coyle,
           A R Forrester, B R Senior
1994:   D Patterson (Capt);
           G A Tredinnick, S P Tredinnick, P N Rosen,
           P G King, P Collins
1995:   D Patterson (Capt);
           G A Tredinnick, S P Tredinnick, P N Rosen,
           P G King, P Collins
1996:   A Dyson (Capt);
           G Liggins, P J Crouch, S J Lodge,
           J M Armstrong, G T Kirby
1997:   A Mould (Capt);
           G W Hyett, J Helme, P A Bowyer,
           J D R Collings, M A Jones
1998:   H Cohen (Capt);
           R M Sheehan, B Schapiro, I P Gordon,
           N Sandqvist, F Wrang

Crockford's Cup
The English Open Teams Championship for the Crockford's Cup
has been held since 1950. The format of the event is a nationwide
knockout competition until there are just eight teams remaining,
at which stage teams play in an all-play-all Round Robin Final.

1950:   Mrs A L Fleming, E B Parker, K W Konstam,
           G Mathieson, J T Reese, B Schapiro
1951:   J Pavlides, B Oliner, L W Dodds, E P C Cotter,
           S Merkin, E Rayne
1952:   L Ellison, J Tarlo, J Sharples, R Sharples
1953:   Dr P Browne, V Garard, I P Gibb, A Wolfeld
1954:   L Tarlo, H Franklin, N Gardener, A Rose,
           R Preston, R Swimer
1955:   J Pavlides, S Booker, L Bradley, L W Dodds, Dr S Lee
1956:   N Gardener, A Rose, R Preston, R Swimer, N Squire
1957:   N Gardener, A Rose, R Preston, R Swimer, N Squire
1958:   J Lazarus, B H Franks, S Blaser, I M Morris,
           W Wong, F Farrington
1959:   G Griffiths, P Richardson, E J Spurway, P F Spurway

1960:	L Tarlo, H Franklin, K W Konstam, Mrs R Markus, B Schapiro, M Wolach
1961:	S Blaser, I M Morris, F Farrington, J Meizis
1962:	S Booker, L Bradley, Dr S Lee, Mrs P Forbes, G F Mathieson
1963:	M Harrison-Gray, Dr M Rockfelt, H P F Swinnerton-Dyer, J Sharples, R Sharples, K R Barbour
1964:	M Harrison-Gray, J D R Collings, J Cansino, A M Hiron, Miss D Shanahan, H P F Swinnerton-Dyer
1965:	R Myers, D Myers, M Blank, M Lipworth, N F Choularton, B M Hargreaves
1966:	J D R Collings, J Cansino, A M Hiron, I N Rose, J Nunes, A B Milford
1967:	L Tarlo, C Rodrigue, F North, J Pugh
1968:	J T Reese, M J Flint, J Cansino, A Milford
1971:	C Dixon, R Sheehan, M Esterson, D Edwin
1972:	I Rose, J T Reese, J Cansino, M J Flint, G O J Cooke
1973:	J D Beattie, R E Seabrook, M J K Butler, D Jones
1976:	D C Rimington, R J Rowlands Miss N Gardener, Mrs S Landy, M E Dilks, R Butland
1979:	A M G Thompson, J Reardon, P Collins, C Bishop
1981:	R A Priday, Mrs J Priday, C Simpson, M Hoffman
1982:	R S Brock, G T Kirby, J M Armstrong, A R Forrester, B R Senior, S J Ray
1983:	B Posner, J Nunes, D Smerdon, J Sadler, A Waterlow, D C Oram
1985:	G T Kirby, J M Armstrong, A R Forrester, Mrs S J Horton, Dr A P Sowter, S J Lodge
1986:	R S Brock, J F Pottage, Mrs C Fishpool, S Fishpool, A I Calderwood, D Shek
1987:	G T Kirby, J M Armstrong, A R Forrester, Mrs S J Horton, Dr A P Sowter, S J Lodge
1989:	J Niblett, B J Callaghan, R A Cliffe, C Fishpool, P Jackson, D L Parry
1990:	A R Forrester, R J Fleet, S J Lodge, Mrs S J Horton
1991:	P Collins, M Lewis, G A Tredinnick, S P Tredinnick
1992:	S J Ray, Mrs G E Ray, D L Roberts, R J Winter, M H Horton, G M Foster

1993:	D Patterson, D O'Donovan, T Ward, P J Bailey, C C Thame
1994:	D J Jones, G J Watson, S J Green, M A Jones, M Allen
1995:	P D Hackett, J P Hackett, J T Hackett, A R Forrester, I Monahan
1996:	D Patterson, D O'Donovan, W Whittaker, P Law, P Collins
1997:	T G Townsend, L Steel, D S Mossop, P G King, D G W Price
1998:	W K Ford, I Swanson, A R Lunn, S O'Neill, W Hodgkiss, R A Clarke
1999:	T G Townsend, L Steel, D S Mossop, P G King, D G W Price, A R Forrester

British Spring Foursomes

A double-elimination teams knock-out, the Spring Foursomes, that has long been acknowledged as the strongest and most prestigious British tournament event. From its inception until 1991, the event was staged in two heats (North and South) and occasionally in three. Since 1992, the event has been staged with just a single field, and thus only one winner.

1979: North (Harrogate):
B J Shenkin, V A Silverstone, V Goldberg, I P Gordon
South (Eastbourne):
J Ortiz-Patino, J Besse, P Bernasconi, E Jacobi
1980: North (Harrogate):
J M Armstrong, G T Kirby, A R Forrester, R Smolski, R G Upton, J Salisbury
South (Eastbourne):
D F Huggett, E W Crowhurst, Miss N P Gardener, M R Pomfrey, K E Stanley, R D Bretherton
1981: North (Harrogate):
J M Armstrong, G T Kirby, A R Forrester, R Smolski, R G Upton, J Salisbury
South (Eastbourne):
D F Huggett, E W Crowhurst, Miss N P Gardener, M R Pomfrey, K E Stanley, R D Bretherton

1982:   North (Harrogate):
             G M Foster, R Smolski, Mrs S J Horton, M H Horton,
             N Stevens, W P Crook
             South (Brighton):
             I M Panto, M Wlodarczyk, I N Rose, J D R Collings

1983:   North (York):
             H Cohen, B Teltscher, D J Greenwood, I P Gordon,
             B Schapiro, L Tarlo
             South (Brighton):
             G Breskal, J D R Collings, A I Calderwood,
             A R Forrester, R S Brock

1984:   North (Leeds):
             D Shek, P Czerniewski, B J Rigal, M Clack
             South (Brighton):
             A J Mayo, M J Grounds, G Hiller, D E S Muller

1985:   North (Leeds):
             P Czerniewski, B J Rigal, M D Graham, P Franklin
             South (Brighton):
             D A L Burn, R O'Reilly, U M Durmus, K Loveys,
             R J Fleet, P Jackson

1986:   (Eastbourne):
             G N Breskal, A I Calderwood, D J Greenwood,
             S Fishpool

1987:   North (Leeds):
             J M Armstrong, G T Kirby, A R Forrester, R S Brock,
             Dr A P Sowter, S J Lodge
             South (Eastbourne):
             R J Rowlands, D Carlisle, N Selway, R Samson

1988:   North (Leeds):
             P J Hawkes, S Wood, M H Horton, R J Winter,
             I Reissman, R Pike
             South (Eastbourne):
             C J Elliott, Mrs S Landy, T E D Quibell, P W Poulter

1989:   North (Leeds):
             D J Banks, S Eginton, B L Ewart, W J Holland
             South (Eastbourne):
             P Czerniewski, B J Rigal, J F Pottage, R J Fleet

1990:   North (Leeds):
             D J Banks, S L Eginton, B L Ewart, W J Holland

South (Eastbourne):
P Czerniewski, B J Rigal, Mrs N P Smith, A J Mayo,
A I Calderwood, D Shek
West (Bath):
P D Jourdain, P Goodman, F S Kurbalija, A Thomas

1991: North (Leeds)
Mrs J Preddy, Mrs V Mitchell, C F J Outred, I Murdoch
South (Eastbourne):
S W Burton, Dr A D Clark, A M G Thompson,
J Y Pottage, L Young
West (Birmingham):
P Czerniewski, B J Rigal, A R Forrester, S J Lodge

1992: (Stratford)
Mrs N P Smith, Miss P Davies, A I Calderwood,
D Shek, J L Reardon, R J A Butland

1993: (Stratford)
S J Lodge, R J Fleet, G Liggins, A C L Dyson

1994: (Stratford)
S J Lodge, R J Fleet, G Liggins, A C L Dyson

1995: (Stratford)
G A Tredinnick, S P Tredinnick, P N Rosen, P G King

1996: (Stratford)
P D Hackett, A R Forrester, I Monachan, A M Robson,
A J Waterlow

1997: (Stratford)
I Monachan, N Selway, P Czerniewski, U M Durmus,
D G W Price

1998: (Stratford)
G A Tredinnick, S P Tredinnick, P N Rosen,
A McIntosh

1999: (Stratford)
D S Mossop, T G Townsend, J T Hackett, J P Hackett,
A R Forrester, G Helgemo

The Sunday Times/Macallan Invitational Pairs

1963: France: Pierre Jaïs & Roger Trézel
1964: England: Terence Reese & Boris Schapiro
1966: France: George Theron & Gerard Desrousseaux
1967: England: Claude Rodrigue & Louis Tarlo

1968:	France/Egypt: Claude Delmouly & Leon Yallouze
1969:	Switzerland/England: Jean Besse & John Collings
1970:	England: Nico Gardener & Tony Priday
1971:	Poland: Andrezej Wilkosz & Lukasz Lebioda
1972:	USA: Alan Sontag & Steve Altman
1974:	Italy: Gianfranco Faccini & Sergio Zucchelli
1975:	USA: Alan Sontag & Peter Weichsel
1976:	Scotland: Barnet Shenkin & Michael Rosenberg
1977:	France: Henri Szwarc & Jean-Michel Boulenger
1978:	Sweden: P-O Sundelin & Sven-Olov Flodqvist
1979:	Brazil: Gabriel Chagas & Pedro Paulo Assumpcao
1980:	Scotland: Barnet Shenkin & Victor Goldberg
1981:	Sweden: P-O Sundelin & Sven-Olov Flodqvist
1990:	England: Andrew Robson & Tony Forrester
1991:	France: Paul Chemla & Michel Perron
1992:	Brazil: Gabriel Chagas & Marcelo Branco
1993:	USA: Bobby Levin & Gaylor Kasle
1994:	Poland: Adam Zmudzinski & Cezary Balicki
1995:	USA: Jeff Meckstroth & Eric Rodwell
1996:	USA: Jeff Meckstroth & Eric Rodwell
1997:	Italy: Lorenzo Lauria & Alfredo Versace
1998:	Norway: Geir Helgemo & Tor Helness
1999:	Norway: Geir Helgemo & Tor Helness

The Cap Gemini World Top Invitational Pairs

1987:	Austria: Jan Fucik & Franz Terraneo
1988:	USA: Jeff Meckstroth & Eric Rodwell
1989:	Austria: Jan Fucik & Franz Terraneo
1990:	England: Andrew Robson & Tony Forrester
1991:	USA/Italy: Billy Eisenberg & Benito Garozzo
1992:	USA/Pakistan: Michael Rosenberg & Zia Mahmood
1993:	Brazil: Gabriel Chagas & Marcelo Branco
1994:	Norway: Geir Helgemo & Tor Helness
1995:	USA/Pakistan: Michael Rosenberg & Zia Mahmood
1996:	Norway: Geir Helgemo & Tor Helness
1997:	Brazil: Gabriel Chagas & Marcelo Branco
1998:	England/Pakistan: Tony Forrester & Zia Mahmood
1999:	USA: Larry Cohen & David Berkowitz

The Forbo Krommenie International Teams

1996: Germany:
Steve Haas, Michael Elinescu, Andrzej Holowski, Tomasz Gotard.

1997: Italy:
Alfredo Versace, Norberto Bocchi, Andrea Buratti, Massimo Lanzarotti

1998: Germany:
Michael Elinescu, Encho Wladow, Peter Splettstöser, Helmut Hausler

1999: Netherlands:
Schelte Wijma, Jaap Brulleman, Frans ten Brink, Hans de Vrind

The North American Board-a-Match Teams

Played annually at the Fall NABC, from 1929 until 1965 this event was contested for the Chicago Trophy. Since then, the prize has been the Reisinger Trophy, and it is by this name that the event is now commonly known. The Board-A-Match scoring accounts for the high number of ties for first or second. Originally a four-session event, there are now two qualifying sessions and two semi-final sessions, leading to a two-session ten-team all-play-all final.

The Chicago Trophy

1929: M M Cohen, L J Haddad, R W Halpin, N M Webster
1930: W K Barrett, W J Carpenter, E Culbertson, J Rau
1931: Mrs E Banfield, W S Liggett Jr, F Newman, G Unger
1932: B J Becker, S G Churchill, G Reith, W K von Zedtwitz
1933: C A Hall, A Steiner, P Steiner, R M Wildberg
1934: H S Dinkelspiel Jr, L Jaeger, B Rabinowitz, M Seiler
1935: F R Buck, J E Cain, L J Welch, E T Wood
1936: Mrs M Anderson, D G Farquharson,
Mrs J A Faulkner, P E Sheardown
1937: J R Crawford, C H Goren, C J Solomon, Mrs S Young
1938: J R Crawford, C H Goren, C J Solomon, Mrs S Young
1939: B J Becker, J R Crawford, C H Goren,
C J Solomon, Mrs S Young
1940: H Feinberg, J Glick, M J Glick, L Newman
1941: P A Leventritt, S Rossant, Mrs H Sobel, Mrs M Wagar
1942: B J Becker, C H Goren, S Silodor, J R Crawford

1943: B J Becker, C H Goren, S Silodor, Mrs H Sobel
1944: S Becker, Mrs P Golder, Mrs R Sherman, C J Solomon
1945: L Hazen, G Rapee, S M Stayman, W K von Zedtwitz
1946: A M Barnes, J R Crawford, A I Roth, Mrs E Seligman
1947: Mrs P Bacher, Mrs J Jaeger, Mrs K M Rhodes,
         Mrs S Young
1948: G Boeckh, C B Elliott, Mrs A Gordon, Mrs C Sidway
1949: L Hazen, L Hirsch, R Kahn, P A Leventritt, J Shore
1950: B J Becker, M F Field, C H Goren, S Silodor, Mrs H Sobel
1951: C Boland, C B Elliott, M M Miller, P E Sheardown
1952: H Harkavy, Mrs E Kemp, A I Roth, T Stone
1953: B J Becker, J R Crawford, G Rapee, S M Stayman
1954: B J Becker, J R Crawford, G Rapee, S Silodor
1955: B Fain, G Heath, P H Hodge, J Jacoby, O Jacoby
1956: B J Becker, J R Crawford, G Rapee, S Silodor
1957: C H Goren, H A Ogust, W S Root, H Schenken,
         Mrs H Sobel
1958: L B Harmon, R Hirschberg, E Kaplan,
         A Sheinwold, I Stakgold
1959: L L Mathe, D A Oakie, M Schleifer, E O Taylor
1960: O Adams, W Hann, S H Lazard, L L Mathe
1961: J R Crawford, N Kay, A I Roth, S Silodor, T Stone
1962: 1= P Allinger, H B Guiver, L L Mathe,
            R Von der Porten, E Paulsen, E O Taylor
            R D Hamman, E B Kantar, D P Krauss, M Miles,
            W Eisenberg
1963: C H Goren, P A Leventritt, H A Ogust, H Schenken
1964: J Gerber, P H Hodge, M Key, H Rockaway
1965: E B Kantar, M S Lawrence, M Miles, L Stansby
The Reisinger Trophy
1966: R F Jordan, E Kaplan, N Kay, A G Robinson
1967: R F Jordan, E Kaplan, N Kay, A G Robinson,
         W S Root, A I Roth
1968: K Larsen, E Paulsen, P A Pender, H L Ross,
         H Schenken
1969: P Feldsman, W P Grieve, I S Rubin, G Westheimer
1970: 1= W Eisenberg, R Goldman, R D Hamman, J Jacoby,
            M S Lawrence, R S Wolff
            G S Baze, A H Dionisi, W P Grieve, H S Lewis,
            P A Pender, G Rapee

1971:   W P Grieve, E Kaplan, N Kay, D P Krauss,
              L L Mathe, G Rapee

1972:   L Bluhm, S Goldberg, S J Parker, S W Robinson

1973:   L Cohen, Dr R H Katz, A E Reinhold, A Sontag,
              P M Weichsel

1974:   F Hamilton, E Paulsen, H Ross, I S Rubin

1975:   F Hamilton, E Paulsen, H L Ross, I S Rubin

1976:   M K Brachman, W Eisenberg, R Goldman,
              E B Kantar, M Passell, P Soloway

1977:   J Cayne, A Greenberg, J Jacoby, K Larsen,
              M S Lawrence

1978:   I G Corn Jr, F Hamilton, R D Hamman, I S Rubin,
              R S Wolff

1979:   1= R D Arnold, R J Levin, J J Meckstroth,
                 A E Reinhold, E V Rodwell
                 I G Corn Jr, F Hamilton, R D Hamman, I S Rubin,
                 R S Wolff

1980:   R E Andersen, M K Brachman, R Goldman,
              E B Kantar, M S Lawrence, P Soloway

1981:   C U Martel, P A Pender, H L Ross, L Stansby

1982:   W S Root, R Pavlicek, E Kaplan, N Kay

1983:   O Jacoby, E Kaplan, N Kay, W S Root, R Pavlicek

1984:   1= W S Root, R Pavlicek, E Kaplan, N Kay
                 F M Stewart, S M Weinstein, A Stauber, M Smolen
                 S M Stayman, R Reisig, G Tornay, S Bronstein
                 J Robison, J Wittes, R Grabel, S Touchtidis

1985:   C U Martel, P A Pender, H L Ross, L Stansby

1986:   S W Robinson, C U Martel, H L Ross, P A Boyd,
              P A Pender, L Stansby

1987:   Z Mahmood, J Shivdsani, W E Cohen, R Smith

1988:   J Cayne, R D Hamman, M Passell, M Lair,
              C F Burger, R S Wolff

1989:   Z Mahmood, M Rosenberg, S Lev, C Compton,
              M Molson

1990:   R Pavlicek, W S Root, E Kaplan, N Kay, B Glubok

1991:   C Russell, S Lev, L N Cohen, D Berkowitz,
              M A Bergen, B Fallenius

1992:   J Cayne, M Passell, M Lair, C F Burger,
              G P Chagas, M C Branco

1993:   F T Nickell, R A Freeman, R D Hamman,
              R S Wolff, J J Meckstroth, E V Rodwell
1994:   F T Nickell, R A Freeman, R D Hamman,
              R S Wolff, J J Meckstroth, E V Rodwell
1995:   F T Nickell, R A Freeman, R D Hamman,
              R S Wolff, J J Meckstroth, E V Rodwell
1996:   Z Mahmood, M Rosenberg, C U Martel, L Stansby
1997:   B Bramley, H M Weinstein, S Garner, S H Lazard
1998:   Mrs R Shugart, A M Robson, G Helgemo,
              A R Forrester

The Vanderbilt Knockout Teams

Held annually at the Spring NABC, the format has changed over the years, but this has been one North America's premier events since its inception. In 1928 it was scored by Board-a-Match, hence the tie. From 1929 until 1965 it was a double elimination knockout teams. From 1966 until 1969 qualifying rounds were followed by knockout, and since 1970 it has been a straight knockout competition.

1928:   1= R Richards, G M Scott, E A Wetzlar,
              W C Whitehead
              A Brown, Mrs S Lovell, Mrs C Taylor, N M Wester
1929:   M T Gottlieb, L Langdon, J P Mattheys, H B Raffel
1930:   E Culbertson, Mrs J Culbertson, T A Lightner,
              W K von Zedtwitz
1931:   D Burnstine, O Jacoby, W S Karn, P H Sims
1932:   W S Karn, P H Sims, H S Vanderbilt,
              W K von Zedtwitz
1933:   P Abramsohn, B Feuer, F A Rendon, S Rusinow
1934:   D Burnstine, R L Frey, M Gottlieb, O Jacoby,
              H Schenken
1935:   D Burnstine, M Gottlieb, O Jacoby, H Schenken,
              S Stearns
1936:   P Abramsohn, I Epstein, H J Fishbein, F D Kaplan
1937:   D Burnstine, O Jacoby, M D Maier, H Schenken,
              S Stearns
1938:   D Burnstine, O Jacoby, M D Maier, H Schenken,
              S Stearns
1939:   M Alexander, S Dornbusch, S Gintell, L Hazen,
              H B Raffel

1940:   E Hymes Jr, C S Lockridge, R A McPherran,
            H S Vanderbilt, W K von Zedtwitz

1941:   J R Crawford, M Fuchs, R A McPherran, S Stearns

1942:   L R Bachner, S Dornbusch, R L Frey, L Hazen,
            S M Stayman

1943:   H Fagin, H J Fishbein, F D Kaplan, A I Roth, T Stone

1944:   B J Becker, C H Goren, S Silodor, Mrs H Sobel

1945:   B J Becker, C H Goren, S Silodor, Mrs H Sobel

1946:   J R Crawford, O Jacoby, G Rapee, H Schenken,
            S M Stayman

1947:   D B Clarren, H Feinberg, H J Fishbein, L Hirsch,
            J E Low

1948:   R Appleyard, J T Feigus, W M Lichtenstein,
            H Sonnenblick, A Weiss

1949:   M Elis, H J Fishbein, L Hazen, L Hirsch,
            C S Lockridge

1950:   J R Crawford, G Rapee, H Schenken, S Silodor,
            S M Stayman

1951:   B J Becker, J R Crawford, G Rapee, S M Stayman

1952:   N Drucker, I Kass, S Mandell, M Moss, J Sloan

1953:   R Kahn, E Kaplan, P A Leventritt, W V Lipton,
            Mrs R Sherman

1954:   Dr K Apfel, F P Begley, N Drucker, S Mandell, M Moss

1955:   B J Becker, J R Crawford, G Rapee, H Schenken,
            S Silodor

1956:   B J Becker, J R Crawford, G Rapee, H Schenken,
            S Silodor

1957:   B J Becker, J R Crawford, G Rapee, H Schenken,
            S Silodor

1958:   H J Fishbein, S Fry Jr, L B Harmon, L Hazen,
            I Stakgold

1959:   B J Becker, J R Crawford, N Kay, G Rapee,
            S Silodor, T Stone

1960:   J R Crawford, N Kay, S Silodor, T Stone

1961:   C Coon, R F Jordan, E R Murray, A G Robinson

1962:   L Kolker, Mrs C Levitt, J Levitt, G Nash, G de Runtz

1963:   H Harkavy, Mrs E Kemp, A I Roth, C Russell,
            W Seamon, A Weiss

1964:   R D Hamman, E B Kantar, D P Krauss,
            P A Leventritt, L L Mathe, H Schenken

1965: P Feldesman, J Fisher, J Jacoby, O Jacoby,
I S Rubin, A Weiss

1966: P Feldesman, R D Hamman, S R Kehela,
L L Mathe, I S Rubin

1967: J Jacoby, M S Lawrence, L L Mathe, G R Nail,
R Von der Porten, L Stansby

1968: R F Jordan, E Kaplan, N Kay, A G Robinson,
W S Root, A I Roth

1969: G F Hallee, P Soloway, J C Swanson Jr, R Walsh

1970: E Kaplan, N Kay, S R Kehela, S H Lazard,
E R Murray, G Rapee

1971: W Eisenberg, R Goldman, R D Hamman, J Jacoby,
M S Lawrence, R S Wolff

1972: S B Altman, E Neiger, T M Smith, A Sontag,
J H Stuart, P M Weichsel

1973: M E Blumenthal, R Goldman, R D Hamman,
M S Lawrence, R S Wolff

1974: D M Crossley, R E Crossley, E O Kokish, J Silver

1975: R W Bates, L Cohen, Dr R H Katz, J Mohan,
Dr J Rosenkranz

1976: R W Bates, L Cohen, Dr R H Katz, J Mohan,
Dr J Rosenkranz

1977: M M Becker, M E Blumenthal, F Hamilton,
M S Lawrence, R D Rubin, J C Swanson Jr

1978: M K Brachman, R Goldman, E B Kantar,
W Eisenberg, M Passell, P Soloway

1979: L E Bluhm, R A Freeman, M Lair, C Russell,
T K Sanders, E M Wold

1980: R D Arnold, R J Levin, J J Meckstroth,
A E Reinhold, E V Rodwell

1981: B J Becker, M M Becker, E Kaplan, N Kay, R D Rubin

1982: J Jacoby, J J Meckstroth, M Passell, E V Rodwell,
Dr J Rosenkranz, E M Wold

1983: W S Root, R Pavlicek, N Kay, E Kaplan

1984: C U Martel, L Stansby, H L Ross, P A Pender

1985: E V Rodwell, J J Meckstroth, R D Rubin,
M S Lawrence, M M Becker, P M Weichsel

1986: E Kaplan, N Kay, W S Root, R Pavlicek

1987: P A Pender, P A Boyd, L Stansby, H L Ross,
S W Robinson, C U Martel

1988:   E B Kantar, A Sontag, J Mohan, R W Bates
1989:   R D Rubin, M M Becker, B Bramley, R J Levin,
               L E Bluhm, P M Weichsel
1990:   D Morse, J Sutherlin, M J Kamil, R Gerard,
               T K Sanders, W L Pollack
1991:   S W Robinson, P A Boyd, C R Woolsey, E A Manfield;
1992:   A Goodman, J Mohan, R W Bates, J Schermer,
               N Chambers
1993:   H M Weinstein, P I Nagy, D Morse, J Sutherlin,
               T K Sanders, R D Arnold
1994:   S Deutsch, G Kasle, M Rosenberg, Z Mahmood,
               C U Martel, L Stansby
1995:   W S Root, R Pavlicek, M Polowan, M S Jacobus
1996:   Z Mahmood, S Deutsch, L Stansby, C U Martel
1997:   R Schwartz, S W Robinson, P A Boyd, P Soloway,
               R Goldman, M Lair
1998:   R Schwartz, P Soloway, R Goldman, M Lair,
               C U Martel, L Stansby
1999:   G Jacobs, R Katz, P M Weichsel, A Sontag,
               L Lauria, A Versace

The Spingold Master Knockout Teams

Contested annually at the Summer NABC. The event was first known as the Challenge Knockout Teams for the Asbury Park Trophy. The runner-up in the regularly scheduled portion of the event had the right to challenge the winners to a playoff, but that right was never exercised. In 1934, 36 & 37, the Asbury Park Trophy and the Masters Teams-of Four were separate events, and thus provided two sets of winners. The event adopted its current name in 1938.

From 1938 until 1965 the Spingold was a double elimination knockout teams. From 1966 until 1969 qualifying rounds were followed by knockout, and since 1970 it has been a straight knockout competition.

The Asbury Park Trophy
1930:   E Culbertson, Mrs J Culbertson, T A Lightner,
               W K von Zedtwitz
1931:   D Burnstine, O Jacoby, W S Karn, P H Sims

1932:	M T Gottlieb, O Jacoby, T A Lightner, L H. Watson
1933:	D Burnstine, O Jacoby, R L Frey, H Schenken
1934:	A Frank, J Glick, W Hopkins, C H Porter
1935:	S Fry Jr, E Hymes, T A Lightner, M D Maier, L H Watson
1936:	L A Bernard, L J Haddad, A Landy, M S Reilly, P Steiner
1937:	D Burnstine, C H Goren, O Jacoby, M D Maier, H Schenken

The Masters Teams-of-Four

1934:	D Burnstine, R L Frey, M T Gottlieb, O Jacoby, H Schenken
1936:	B J Becker, D Burnstine, O Jacoby, H Schenken
1937:	S Fry Jr, E Hymes, T A Lightner, W K von Zedtwitz

The Spingold Knockout Teams

1938:	B J Becker, D Burnstine, O Jacoby, M D Maier, H Schenken
1939:	O Jacoby, T A Lightner, M D Maier, R A McPherran, H Schenken
1940:	O J Brotman, B Lebhar, S Katz, A I Roth
1941:	A M Barnes, S Fry Jr, E Hymes, W K von Zedtwitz
1942:	S Dornbusch, R L Frey, L Hazen, S M Stayman
1943:	J R Crawford, C H Goren, E Hymes, H Schenken, S Silodor
1944:	B J Becker, G Rapee, Mrs H Sobel, S M Stayman
1945:	S Fry Jr, E Hymes, O Jacoby, T A Lightner, H Schenken
1946:	W Christian, M Hodges, S Mogal, Mrs M Wagar
1947:	B J Becker, C H Goren, L Hazen, Mrs H Sobel, W K von Zedtwitz
1948:	J R Crawford, G Rapee, H Schenken, S M Stayman, Mrs M Wagar
1949:	J Glick, A S Goldsmith, B Gowdy, A Landy, S Mogal
1950:	J R Crawford, O Jacoby, G Rapee, H Schenken, S M Stayman
1951:	M Field, C H Goren, S Silodor, Mrs H Sobel
1952:	B J Becker, J R Crawford, G Rapee, H Schenken, S M Stayman
1953:	C Bishop, M Q Ellenby, D A Oakie, W Rosen, D Steen
1954:	C Bishop, M Q Ellenby, L L Mathe, J Moran, W Rosen

1955:   M Field, L Hazen, R Kahn, C J Solomon,
                 S M Stayman

1956:   1= H Harkavy, V Mitchell, A I Roth, I S Rubin, T Stone
                 R Abeles, Dr K Apfel, F P Begley, L Kelner,
                 R Rosenberg
                 C H Goren, P A Leventritt, B Koytchou,
                 H A Ogust, W E Seamon, Mrs H Sobel

1957:   B J Becker, J R Crawford, G Rapee, A I Roth,
                 S Silodor, T Stone

1958:   P Allinger, W Hanna, S H Lazard, C Neuman, R Rothlein

1959:   W P Grieve, O Jacoby, V Mitchell, I S Rubin,
                 M Rubinow, S M Stayman

1960:   C H Goren, P A Leventritt, B Koytchou,
                 H A Ogust, H Schenken, Mrs H Sobel

1961:   A Gabrilovitch, E B Kantar, M Miles, W S Root

1962:   L B Harmon, E B Kantar, M Miles, I Stakgold

1963:   R D Arnold, H Harkavy, Mrs E Kemp, A I Roth,
                 C Russell, W E Seamon

1964:   B C Elliott, S R Kehela, E R Murray, P Sheardown

1965:   B C Elliott, S R Kehela, E R Murray, P Sheardown

1966:   W S Root, A I Roth, I S Rubin, C K Smith

1967:   E Kaplan, N Kay, W S Root, A I Roth

1968:   S R Kehela, E Kaplan, N Kay, S H Lazard,
                 E R Murray, G Rapee

1969:   W Eisenberg, R Goldman, R D Hamman,
                 M S Lawrence, J Jacoby, R S Wolff

1970:   S B Altman, T M Smith, D I Strasberg, J Stuart,
                 P M Weichsel

1971:   S B Altman, E Neiger, T M Smith, J Stuart,
                 P M Weichsel

1972:   B J Becker, M M Becker, A Bernstein, J Rubens

1973:   L Cohen, W Eisenberg, E B Kantar, R H Katz,
                 A E Reinhold

1974:   L E Bluhm, L E Gould, S Goldberg, R Shepherd

1975:   G S Baze, J Fejervary, L Stansby, P Vakil,
                 R von der Porten

1976:   R W Bates, L Cohen, R H Katz, J Mohan,
                 Dr J Rosenkranz

1977:   L E Bluhm, D Morse, C Russell, C K Smith,
                 T K Sanders, E M Wold

1978: M K Brachman, R Goldman, E B Kantar,
M Passell, P Soloway

1979: F Hamilton, R D Hamman, I S Rubin, R S Wolff

1980: M M Becker, K Larsen, R D Rubin, A Sontag,
R Von der Porten, P M Weichsel

1981: L N Cohen, R Gerard, R Katz, W Rosener,
A Stauber, J Sutherlin

1982: R D Rubin, M M Becker, R D Hamman, R S Wolff,
A Sontag, P M Weichsel

1983: M K Brachman, R S Wolff, R Goldman,
R D Hamman, P Soloway, R E Andersen

1984: J J Meckstroth, E V Rodwell, M A Bergen,
L N Cohen, Dr J Rosenkranz, E M Wold

1985: T Mahaffey, J Denny, B Passell, R D Arnold,
I S Rubin, C F Burger

1986: M K Brachman, R Goldman, R E Andersen,
M Passell, M Lair, P Soloway

1987: B Glubok, D Rotman, H Stappenbeck, J Shivdasani

1988: J Mahaffey, R E Andersen, P Soloway, R Goldman,
E V Rodwell, J J Meckstroth

1989: J Cayne, C F Burger, R D Hamman, R S Wolff,
M Passell, M Lair

1990: J Cayne, C F Burger, C U Martel, L Stansby,
R D Hamman, R S Wolff

1991: Z Mahmood, M Rosenberg, S Deutsch,
J J Meckstroth, E V Rodwell

1992: R D Rubin, R A Ekeblad, M M Becker,
R Sukoneck, R J Levin, P M Weichsel

1993: R A Freeman, F T Nickell, E V Rodwell,
J J Meckstroth, R S Wolff, R D Hamman

1994: R A Freeman, F T Nickell, R D Hamman,
R S Wolff, J J Meckstroth, E V Rodwell

1995: R A Freeman, F T Nickell, R D Hamman,
R S Wolff, J J Meckstroth, E V Rodwell

1996: R A Freeman, F T Nickell, R D Hamman,
R S Wolff, J J Meckstroth, E V Rodwell

1997: G S Baze, T Golias, A Zmudzinski,
M Szymanowski, M Lesniewski, C Balicki

1998: F T Nickell, R A Freeman, R D Hamman,
P Soloway, J J Meckstroth, E V Rodwell

1999:   F T Nickell, R A Freeman, R D Hamman,
            P Soloway, J J Meckstroth, E V Rodwell

The Grand National Teams

The winners of this event receive the Albert Morehead Trophy. The early stages are contested over several months at local and regional level, until each of the US districts produces a single representative. Those 23 teams then meet at the Summer NABC.

1973:   R D Arnold, J Beery, J Jaeger, R Pavlicek,
            W E Seamon, R G. Sharp
1974:   L N Cohen, W Eisenberg, E B Kantar, R Katz,
            P Soloway, J C Swanson Jr
1975:   J Fisher, C P Gabriel, R D Hamman, J L Hooker,
            C E Weed, R S Wolff
1976:   W Eisenberg, E B Kantar, P Soloway, J C Swanson Jr
1977:   R D Hamman, D Morse, C K Smith, E M Wold, R S Wolff
1978:   G A Caravelli, C Peres, W A Rosen, M Rosenberg,
            D Rotman
1979:   G DeFotis, J R Goldfein, A Leavitt, L Robbins, C Vogel
1980:   J Bitman, J P Janitschke, V C Janitschke, R Lesko
1981:   I Chorush, J Jacoby, M Passell, Dr J Rosenkranz,
            E M Wold
1982:   R Von der Porten, H L Ross, C U Martel,
            L Stansby, K Larsen, P A Pender
1983:   C U Martel, H L Ross, P A Pender, L Stansby
1984:   C R Woolsey, E A Manfield, P A Boyd,
            R H Lipsitz, S W Robinson
1985:   C U Martel, H L Ross, L Stansby, P A Pender,
            A Sheinwold (npc)
1986:   S Deutsch, R S Wolff, R D Hamman, J Jacoby
1987:   C U Martel, H L Ross, P A Pender, L Stansby,
            M S Lawrence
1988:   S W Robinson, E A Manfield, P A Boyd, R H Lipsitz
1989:   S Sion, R Barr, H Stengel, B A Miller
1990:   D Simpson, W Johnson, J J Meckstroth,
            E V Rodwell, D Clerkin
1991:   L Robbins, J H Goldfein, J N Oest, P I Nagy,
            S Garner, H M Weinstein
1992:   S W Robinson, P A Boyd, R H Lipsitz, kE A Manfield

1993:	R Murthy, M B Moss, L Stansby, C U Martel, H L Ross, J Ferro
1994:	J Cayne, A Sontag, D Berkowitz, L N Cohen
1995:	S Garner, J N Oest, L Robbins, J H Goldfein, G A Caravelli, G Cohler
1996:	R Buchalter, H L Ross, K Larsen, R Smith, C U Martel, L Stansby
1997:	J Wolfson, R J Levin, J J Meckstroth, N Silverman, R Pavlicek, M E Seamon

The North American Life Masters Pairs

Contested annually at the Summer NABC, this six-session event is divided equally into qualifying, semi-final and final. The winners receive the Von Zedwitz Gold Cup.

1930:	P H Sims, W K von Zedtwitz
1931:	D Burnstine, H Schenken
1932:	M T Gottlieb, T A Lightner
1933:	D Burnstine, H Schenken
1934:	R L Frey, H Schenken
1935:	B J Becker, T A Lightner
1936:	D Burnstine, O Jacoby
1937:	S.G Churchill, C S Lockridge
1938:	M Elis, S Stearns
1939:	R Appleyard, H J Fishbein
1940:	H J Fishbein, M Elis
1941:	M D Maier, H Schenken
1942:	C H Goren, Mrs H Sobel
1943:	J R Crawford, H Schenken
1944:	S Katz, P A Leventritt
1945:	R Appleyard, M A Lightman
1946:	S Silodor, C J Solomon
1947:	A P Harvey, F Weisbach
1948:	S G Churchill, C Head
1949:	Mrs R Gilbert, L Roet
1950:	M Sherwin, C W Yorke
1951:	R Kahn, P A Leventritt
1952:	W W Jackson, W Joseph
1953:	M Q Ellenby, W A Rosen
1954:	D C Carter, J W Hubbell

1955:	Ben Fain, P H Hodge
1956:	A I Roth, T Stone
1957:	H S Brown, M Cohn
1958:	1= C H Goren, Mrs H Sobel
	W Landley, L Levy
1959:	E Rosen, D Rotman
1960:	Mrs H Portugal, M Portugal
1961:	P Feldsman, M Miles
1962:	P Feldsman, I S Rubin
1963:	L L Mathe, E O Taylor
1964:	B J Becker, Mrs D Hayden
1965:	V Mitchell, S M Stayman
1966:	H Baron, M Schleifer
1967:	P Feldsman, L L Mathe
1968:	W Eisenberg, R Goldman
1969:	S R Kehela, E R Murray
1970:	P Heitner, M Moss
1971:	A I Roth, Mrs B Rappaport
1972:	A I Roth, Mrs B Rappaport
1973:	J Blair, P Swanson
1974:	G L Michaud, G R Nail
1975:	R Fox, E O'Neill
1976:	R H Lipsitz, N Silverman
1977:	A Sontag, P M Weichsel
1978:	Mrs M J Farell, Mrs M Johnson
1979:	R Katz, K Schutze
1980:	R D Hamman, E V Rodwell
1981:	F M Stewart, S M Weinstein
1982:	T K Sanders, R E Andersen
1983:	R D Hamman, E B Kantar
1984:	M S Lawrence, P M Weichsel
1985:	G Steiner, D Pedersen
1986:	E V Rodwell, D Simson
1987:	L N Cohen, D Berkowitz
1988:	M A Bergen, L N Cohen
1989:	R H Katz, R J Levin
1990:	R D Rubin, M M Becker
1991:	D Simson, E V Rodwell
1992:	R D Hamman, H Lall
1993:	D Morse, J Sutherlin

1994:	R J Levin, J Wolfson
1995:	J Knivel, A P Siebert
1996:	D Berkowitz, L N Cohen
1997:	S Garner, H M Weinstein
1998:	E A Greco, G Hampson

MASTERPOINTS

The various masterpoint systems around the world come in for a great deal of derision, particularly from the better players, but this is a misguided attitude. There can be little doubt that some form of masterpoint ranking system is a good thing for the game. Firstly, organizing bodies charge clubs for the masterpoint certificates, making the system a primary source of income for the Federation/League/Union. (In the early days, the ACBL charged players for registering points, but this was found to be far less beneficial financially.) When players go to their local club, the extra 20p (or something like that) that they pay towards the cost of masterpoint certificates is easily overlooked. Thousands of players regularly contributing small amounts is an ideal way to fund the game. If that money did not come from masterpoints, then it would have to come from elsewhere. Perhaps an alternative source of funding would be higher annual subscriptions, although it is an uphill battle at current rates to persuade fringe players to join the Union. Another option would be higher tournament entry fees, but there are plenty of players, and particularly young players, whose continued interest is vital to the survival of the game, who already think entry fees are too high now. A third alternative would be a reduction or abolition of prizes and, again, there are plenty of players who think they are already far too low. Perhaps a masterpoint system is not such a bad idea after all...

It is also vital to realize that for the majority of players setting out on the voyage of discovery into the unknown world of bridge, masterpoints really do mean something. We can all surely remember the excitement of winning our first masterpoints, or receiving our first ranking certificate. For many novices, who might otherwise lose interest and be lost to the game forever, the masterpoint system offers an incentive to play regularly and to take those first steps into the tournament world.

Becoming a Life Master in the UK, and in many European countries, is a long struggle. For some, it is a realistic goal, but for the majority it is nothing more than the pot of gold at the end of a rainbow, and equally unattainable. The target is so far off that it does not act as incentive to attend a few extra tournaments every year. Not so in the US, where Life Mastership is a goal to which any player can aspire, and realistically hope to achieve. There are many players who attend regional tournaments only because they need gold or red points to become a Life Master. Eventually, most will achieve that goal. The addition of the silver point requirement for becoming a Life Master has meant a significant increase in attendance at Sectional tournaments – again, a good thing for the grass roots game. The ACBL has also made it a big deal to win the Barry Crane 500 (formerly McKenney Trophy) and its lesser equivalents, and this also adds kudos to the masterpoint system there. Ask American players how good they are or how good they think someone else is, and many of them will tell you their masterpoint rank. Reaching certain masterpoint plateaus may be little more than a long-service award in reality, but if the system encourages players to attend more tournaments and to play at their local clubs more often, then it can only be good for the game as a whole.

Achieving Life Master (and, in England, Grand Master) status in the early days, when there were only a handful of major events annually, was much harder than it is today. The proliferation of nationally rated events has made it easier to collect those vital coloured points today. Those very first Life and Grand Masters truly were the best players of their day, and to commemorate their achievement we list here the first 50 players to achieve Life Master status in the US, and the first 50 Life and Grand Masters in the England.

The First 50 North American Life Masters:

The rank of Life Master was introduced in 1936 (although, curiously, the first Life Masters Pairs for the Von Zedwitz Gold Cup was staged in 1930). The selection of the first Life Masters was made based on tournament successes up until then. Initially, the rank of Life Master was conferred on ten players, ranked in order of the number and importance of their victories in national events. Nine years after the designation of the first Life Masters there were 50 (six of whom were women). Three years later, in 1948, the number of Life Masters reached the 100 mark (including 14 women). Fifty years later, in 1998, that number had passed the 60,000 plateau. In 1961, the first Life Masters Women's Pairs for the Helen Sobel Smith Trophy was contested.

LM no.	Year	Name
1	1936	Bruce, David
2		Jacoby, Oswald
3		Schenken, Howard
4		von Zedwitz, Waldemar K
5		Sims, P Hal
6		Becker, B Jay
7		Lightner, Theodore A
8		Frey, Richard L
9		Gottlieb, Michael T
10		Fry, Sam Jr
11		Maier, Merwin D
12	1937	Lochridge, Charles S
13	1938	Goren, Charles H
14		Barnes, A Mitchell
15	1939	Fishbein, Harry J
16		Solomon, Charles J
17		Young, Mrs Sally (*1st woman LM*)
18		Kaplan, Fred D
19		Crawford, John R
20		Jacobs, Walter
21		Elis, Morrie
22	1940	Abramsohn, Phil
23		Hymes, Edward Jr
24		Landy, Alvin
25	1941	Smith, Mrs Helen Sobel (*2nd woman LM*)
26		Stearns, Sherman
27		McPherran, Robert A
28	1942	Glick, Jeff
29		Glatt, Arthor
30		Ecker, Dr Richard Jr
31		Weiss, Albert
32		Hazen, Lee
33		Solomon, Mrs Peggy (*3rd woman LM*)
34		Roth, Alvin I
35	1943	Silodor, Sidney
36		Peterson, Mrs Olive (*4th woman LM*)
37		Wagar, Mrs Margaret (*5th woman LM*)
38		Leventritt, Peter A
39	1944	Wood, Edson T

LM no.	Year	Name
40		Kempner, Ralph
41		Goldsmith, Arthur S
42		Becker, Simon
43		Fenkel, Stanley O
44		Rapee, George
45		Sherman, Mrs Ruth (*6th woman LM*)
46	1945	Appleyard, Robert
47		Lightman, M A
48		Stayman, Samuel M
49		Marcus, Edward N
50		Hall, Charles A

The First 50 English Life Masters

The English Bridge Union's masterpoint scheme was established in 1956. In England, five of the first 50 Life Masters were women, and 17 of the first 100. Ten years after the inception of the scheme, in 1966, with 75 players having attained Life Master status, the EBU introduced the Life Masters Pairs for the Waddington Cup.

LM no.	Name
1	Sharples, James
2	Sharples, Robert
3	Gordon, Mrs Fritzi (*1st woman LM*)
4	Harrison-Gray, Maurice
5	Nunes, Jack
6	Franks, B H
7	Lazarus, Joseph
8	Rose, Albert
9	Spurway, E John
10	Spurway, Paul F
11	Schapiro, Boris
12	Booker, S
13	Rodrigue, Claude
14	Flint, M Jeremy
15	Lee, Dr Sidney
16	Shanahan, Miss Dorothy (*2nd woman LM*)
17	Rimington, Derek C W

LM no.	Name
18	Tarlo, Louis
19	Fleming, Mrs A Leslie (*3rd woman LM*)
20	Rockfelt, Dr Melvin
21	Wolach, Michael
22	Markus, Mrs Rixi (*4th woman LM*)
23	Swimer, Ralph
24	Hochwald, Joe
25	Manning, Irving
26	Priday, R Anthony
27	Reese, J Terence
28	Farrington, Franklin
29	Konstam, Kenneth W
30	Finlay, Alf
31	Truscott, Alan F
32	North, Frederick
33	Griffiths, Graham C
34	Oldroyd, Mrs Rita (*5th woman LM*)
35	Franklin, Harold
36	Dormer, Albert
37	Swinnerton-Dyer, H Peter F
38	Preston, Richard
39	Crown, Ronald
40	Topley, B Philip
41	Barbour, Kenneth C
42	Vickerman, C
43	Brock, Raymond S
44	Higson, Roy T
45	Pugh, John
46	Collings, John D R
47	Milnes, Eric C
48	Hiron Alan M
49	Jamieson, Eric
50	Miezies, John

The First 50 British Grand Masters:

Grand Master is the highest masterpoint ranking a player can
achieve in England. The requirements for Grand Master are
equivalent to becoming a Life Master four times over. The rank was
introduced in 1966, and two EBU members reached the target the

following year. In 1983, some 17 years later, the 50th Grand Master
card was issued, nine of them having been claimed by women. Five
years later, in 1988, there were 100 Grand Masters (including 11
women). By the end of 1998, 252 players had achieved Grand
Master status. The Grand Masters Pairs for the Harrison Gray
Salver was introduced in the late 1970s, although in those early
days pairs could be made up of a Grand Master playing with a Life
Master. Nowadays, both members of each partnership have to be
Grand Masters.

GM no.	Name
1	Sharples, James
2	Sharples, Robert
3	Harrison-Gray, Maurice
4	Priday, R Anthony
5	Oldroyd, Mrs Rita (*1st woman GM*)
6	Amsbury, Joe
7	Rockfelt, Dr Melvin
8	Flint, M Jeremy
9	Spurway, Paul F
10	Rimington, Derek C W
11	Rowlands, Robert J
12	Stanley, Keith E
13	Crowhurst, Eric W
14	Finlay, Alf
15	Collings, John D R
16	Priday, Mrs A Jane (*2nd woman GM*)
17	Brock, Raymond S.
18	Smerdon, Douglas J
19	Nunes, Jack
20	Williams, Mrs Phyllis M (*3rd woman GM*)
21	Jourdain, Patrick D
22	Hiron, Alan M
23	Topley, B Philip
24	Fox, Mrs Betty (*4th woman GM*)
25	Dilks, Michael E
26	Rose, Irving N
27	Franses, Robert
28	Thomas, Mrs Nina (*5th woman GM*)
29	Sowter, Dr Anthony P

GM no.	Name
30	Thomas, Stephen W
31	Gardener, Miss Nicola P (*6th woman GM*)
32	Hamilton, David L
33	Bretherton, R David
34	Hirst, Mike
35	Fleming, Mrs A Leslie (*7th woman GM*)
36	Landy, Mrs Sandra (*8th woman GM*)
37	Fox, G C H
38	Reese, J Terence
39	Pomfrey, Michael R
40	Thompson, Andrew M G
41	Forrester, Anthony R
42	Airey, Michael H
43	Huggett, David F
44	Goldenfield, Bernard N
45	Panto, Ian M
46	Horton, Mrs Sally (*9th woman GM*)
47	Buck, John
48	Semp, Raymond
49	Collins, D N
50	Ferrari, Robert C

The WBF Masterpoint Scheme:

The World Bridge Federation masterpoint system works slightly differently from those in the individual countries. For a start, the value of some WBF masterpoints diminish with age, in keeping with the stated aim of the WBF system to indicate the current standing of a player.

Just as the systems in individual countries award different coloured points for various events, so the WBF system has two categories of award – Master Points (MPs) and Placing Points (PPs). Master Points are awarded to approximately the top third of the field and for matches won in World Championship events. These points reduce by 15% in value each year and, if not added to, eventually disappear. Placing Points are awarded only for very high finishes, and those retain their value indefinitely with the objective of representing the career of a player.

There are only three WBF ranks – World Grand Master, World Life Master and World Master. The requirements are:

World Grand Master (WGM) 10 PPs and at least one World
Championship title;
World Life Master (WLM) 5 PPs; and,
World Master (WM) 150 MPs.

Having achieved either of the higher two rankings, a player retains
those for life. The World Master rank lasts only until the MPs
diminish to the extent that the total falls below 150.

MPs won in Open events and those won in events reserved for
women are subject to different rankings, and appear in two separate
lists. If a women player wins sufficient MPs or PPs in an Open
event, then her name appears on both ranking lists. However, only
those points won in Open events determine her ranking in the Open
list, whereas points won in both Open and Restricted events
determine her position in the Women's ranking list.

Below is the listing of all living players who have achieved the
rank of World Grand Master as of the start of the 1999 season,
together with their total MPs and PPs. Note that since these lists
were produced, two players have subsequently died (Goldman and
Rapee), but their names still appear in the official 1999 rankings.

1999 WORLD GRAND MASTER RANKINGS – OPEN

Rank	Name	Country	MPs	PPs
1	Hamman, Bob	USA	4202	79.5
2	Rodwell, Eric	USA	3837	31
3	Meckstroth, Jeff	USA	3769	29.5
4	Wolff, Robert	USA	3448	68.5
5	Mouiel, Hervé	France	3078	21
6	Chagas, Gabriel	Brazil	2856	32
7	Levy, Alain	France	2652	15
8	Martel, Charles	USA	2495	25
9	Stansby, Lewis	USA	2480	26
10	Branco, Marcelo	Brazil	2381	30
11	Martens, Krzysztof	Poland	2330	14.5
12	Chemla, Paul	France	2309	25
13	Perron, Michel	France	2301	23
14	Mari, Christian	France	1969	19.5
15	Lauria, Lorenzo	Italy	1968	12.5
16	Multon, Frank	France	1788	10
17	Gawrys, Piotr	Poland	1698	12

Rank	Name	Country	MPs	PPs
18	Rosenberg, Michael	USA	1667	13
19	Weichsel, Peter	USA	1625	10
20	Szwarc, Henri	France	1610	19.5
21	Ross, Hugh	USA	1316	22
22	Forquet, Pietro	Italy	1182	58
23	Pabis Ticci, Camillo	Italy	1171	36
24	Bourchtoff, Gérard	France	1169	7.5
25	Siniscalco, Guglielmo	Italy	1163	4
26	Mello, Roberto	Brazil	1119	12
27	Lawrence, Michael	USA	1066	23.5
28	Branco, Pedro Paulo	Brazil	999	11.5
29	Deutsch, Seymon	USA	995	10
30	Lebel, Michel	France	988	18.5
31	Passell, Michael	USA	752	13
32	Soloway, Paul	USA	702	25.5
33	Garozzo, Benito	USA	669	75.5
34	Delmouly, Claude	France	571	7.5
35	Hamilton, Fred	USA	441	13.5
36	Goldman, Robert	USA	340	26
37	Franco, Arturo	Italy	320	18
38	Kantar, Edwin	USA	293	14
39	Cintra, Gabino	Brazil	245	17
40	Schapiro, Boris	GB	228	14
41	Eisenberg, William	USA	197	25.5
42	Rapee, George	USA	162	6.5
43	Kreijns, Hans	Neth	150	9.5
44	Fonseca, Christiano	Brazil	135	10
45	Assumpcao, Pedro Paulo	Brazil	116	14.5
46	Ghestem, Pierre	France	22	10.5
47	Rubin, Ira	USA	19	16.5

1999 WORLD GRAND MASTER RANKINGS – WOMEN

Rank	Name	Country	MPs	PPs
1	Auken, Sabine	Ger	2732	20
2	von Arnim, Daniela	Ger	2426	19
3	Deas, Lynn	USA	2320	24.5
4	Meyers, Jill	USA	2256	17.5
5	Vriend, Bep	Neth	1855	11
6	Sanborn, Kerri	USA	1828	21.5

Rank	Name	Country	MPs	PPs
7	Chambers, Juanita	USA	1794	16
8	Wei-Sender, Katherine	USA	1674	19.5
9	Greenberg, Gail	USA	1654	20.5
10	Quinn, Shawn	USA	1652	11.5
11	Landy, Sandra	GB	1519	24
12	Palmer, Beth	USA	1516	15.5
13	Nehmert, Beate	Ger	1500	12
14	Smith, Nicola	GB	1443	23
15	Davies, Pat	GB	1433	18
16	Picus, Sue	USA	1380	17.5
17=	Fischer, Doris	Austria	1338	14
	Weigkricht, Terry	Austria	1338	14
19	McCallum, Karen	USA	1325	17
20	Erhart, Maria	Austria	1247	14
21	Radin, Judi	USA	1240	21.5
22	McGowan, Elizabeth	GB	1216	10
23	Letizia, Marinesa	USA	1145	10
24	Sanders, Carol	USA	1098	15.5
25	Mitchell, Jacqui	USA	1058	21
26	Osberg, Sharon	USA	822	10
27	Kennedy, Betty-Ann	USA	791	14.5
28	Brock, Sally	GB	765	13.5
29	Truscott, Dorothy	USA	561	17
30	d'Andrea, Marisa	Italy	540	10.5
31	Capodanno, Luciana	Italy	466	10.5
32=	Bianchi, Marisa	Italy	128	11.5
	Valenti, Anna	Italy	128	11.5
34	Farell, Mary-Jane	USA	105	15
35	Johnson, Marilyn	USA	0	11.5

To provide interested readers with some point of reference for the figures in the tables above, the following charts show the number of MPs and PPs awards in each of the various World Championship events.

Olympiad Open Teams

	MPs		MPs
1	1000	6	300
2	700	7	250
3	500	8	200
4	400	9	160
5	350	10	120

From 11th to last of the first third: 50 MPs

In the Round Robin:
Each match won by the team:
6 MPs (accumulative)
Each tied match: 3 MPs
(accumulative)

Olympiad Women's Teams

	MPs		MPs
1	700	5	210
2	500	6	170
3	350	7	130
4	250	8	90

From 9th to last of the first third: 50 MPs

In the Round Robin:
Each match won by the team:
6 MPs (accumulative)
Each tied match: 3 MPs
(accumulative)

Placing Points:
In both events placing points are awarded to the first five finishers on a 5, 4, 3, 2, 1 basis. In addition, where there have been quarter-finals, semi-finals and a final, 1 PP is awarded to all losing quarter-finalists.

Bermuda Bowl

	MPs		MPs
1	800	5	150
2	500	6	120
3	300	7	90
4	200	8	60

In the Round Robin:
Each match won by the team:
6 MPs (accumulative)
Each tied match: 3 MPs
(accumulative)

Venice Cup

	MPs		MPs
1	800	5	150
2	500	6	120
3	300	7	90
4	200	8	60

In the Round Robin:
Each match won by the team:
6 MPs (accumulative)
Each tied match: 3 MPs
(accumulative)

Placing Points:
Again, in both events placing points are awarded to the first five finishers on a 5, 4, 3, 2, 1 basis.

World Open Pairs

	MPs		MPs
1	800	17	240
2	750	18	230
3	700	19	220
4	650	20	210
5	600	21	200
6	550	22	190
7	500	23	180
8	450	24	170
9	400	25	160
10	350	26	150
11	300	27	140
12	290	28	130
13	280	29	120
14	270	30	110
15	260	31	100
16	250		

From 32nd to last of the first third: 50 MPs

World Women's Pairs

	MPs		MPs
1	600	11	180
2	550	12	170
3	500	13	160
4	450	14	150
5	400	15	140
6	350	16	130
7	300	17	120
8	250	18	110
9	200	19	100
10	190		

From 20th to last of the first 50 MPs

Placing Points:

In both events placing points are awarded to the first four finishers on a 4, 3, 2, 1 basis.

Mixed Pairs

	MPs		MPs
1	200	6	70
2	160	7	60
3	130	8	50
4	110	9	40
5	90	10	30

From 11th to last of the best placed 5% of participants: 10 MPs

Placing points:
2 to winners; 1 to runners-up

Rosenblum Cup

	MPs		MPs
1	600	5-8	160
2	450	9-16	100
3	350	17-32	60
4	300	33-64	40

McConnell Cup

	MPs		MPs
1	450	5-8	120
2	340	9-16	80
3	270	17-32	50
4	230	33-64	30

In both events placing points are awarded to the first four finishers on a 4, 3, 2, 1 basis.

Seniors Pairs

	MPs		MPs
1	200	4	50
2	150	5-10	30
3	100	11-15	20

Seniors Swiss Teams

	MPs		MPs
1	150	4	30
2	100	5-16	20
3	50		

Placing Points:
In both events 1 placing point will be awarded to the winners and ½ to the runners-up.

WBF Simultaneous Pairs Events

	MPs		MPs		MPs		MPs
1	120	4	80	7	50	10	20
2	100	5	70	8	40	11	10
3	90	6	60	9	30		

Approved Zonal Championships

OPEN
More than 100,000 members

	MPs	PPs
1	150	1
2	100	½
3	80	
4	50	
5	30	

WOMEN'S
More than 100,000 members

	MPs	PPs
1	150	1
2	100	½
3	80	
4	50	
5	30	

Other Zones with at least 8 participants

	MPs	PPs
1	80	½
2	50	
3	30	

Other Zones with at least 8 participants

	MPs	PPs
1	80	½
2	50	
3	30	

With less than 8 participants

	MPs	PPs
1	50	½
2	30	

With less than 8 participants

	MPs	PPs
1	50	½
2	30	

World Junior Bridge Team Championship

	MPs	PPs
1	150	1
2	100	
3	50	

World Transnational Open Teams Championship

	MPs	PPs
1	300	2
2	240	1
3	180	$\frac{1}{2}$
4	150	
5	100	
6	50	

WORLD BRIDGE ORGANIZATIONS

Are you planning an overseas vacation and wondering if you can find a bridge game while you are away? Perhaps you have always wanted to visit a particular part of the world, and feel that going there to a tournament would be a good excuse? Alternatively, maybe you have an old bridge-playing friend with whom you have lost contact, and all you know is which country he/she is in.

The guide that follows tells you how to contact the associations responsible for organizing Tournament Bridge in countries throughout the world. In most cases, you will find a postal address, plus telephone and fax numbers. In some cases, we also list their email address and the URL for their web page.

Whether you are seeking an answer to a specific query or just general information on bridge in a country, the national association is the logical place to start.

The "Membership" figure given for each association gives some clue as to how big tournament bridge is in each country. For example, with 150,000 the ACBL has more members than any other national association. The Nederlandse Bridge Bond has just over 100,000 members, but that is quite incredible when you remember that Holland's total population is about half that of Alabama.

World Bridge Federation (WBF)
Web site: www.bridge.gr

Address: 40 rue François 1er
              75008 Paris
              France
Tel: (33)-1-53 23 03 15
Fax: (33)-1-40-70-14-51
Email: cfrancin@worldbridgefed.com

Zone One – Europe – 370,000 members
European Bridge League (EBL)
Web site: www.ebl.gr

Austria:	Österreichischer Bridgesport Verband
Address:	Reischachstrasse 3, A-1010 Wien
Telephone:	(43)-1-713 1017
Fax:	same
Email:	bridgel@mail.austria.eu.net
	d.schiller@xpoint.at
Membership:	2,100

Belarus:	Byelorussian Bridge Union
Address:	K.Marks Str. 21-28, 220050 Minsk
Telephone:	(375)-172-277617
Fax:	(375)-172-202353
Contact:	Ilya Feranchuk
Email:	ilya@fer.minsk.by
Membership:	200

Belgium:	Fédération Belge De Bridge
Address:	Rue N.D. du Sommeil 28/1
	B-1000 Brussels
Telephone:	(32)-2-514 5457
Fax:	(32)-2-514 1727
Membership:	8,400

Bulgaria:	Bulgarian Bridge Federation
Address:	Aprilov Street 18, BG-1504 Sofia
Telephone:	(359)-2-843121
Fax:	(359)-2-802042
Membership:	550

Croatia:	Croatian Bridge Federation
Address:	Kraiiska 19, 41000 Zagreb
Telephone:	(385)-1-610 2608
Fax:	(385)-1-611 5741
Contact:	Aleksandar Ivancic
Email:	aivancic@as4ll.tel.hr
Membership:	400

Cyprus: The Cyprus Bridge Association
Address: 6 Mykonos Street, P O Box 5467, Nicosia
Telephone: (357)-2-459220
Fax: (357)-2-360716
Membership: 150

Czech Republic: The Bridge Federation of Czech Republic
Address: Lublanska 23, CS-120 00 Praha 2
Telephone: (42)-02-7211 2162
Fax: (42)-02-7211 2410
Membership: 500

Denmark: Danmarks Bridgeforbund
Address: Asminderødgade 53, DK-3480 Fredensborg
Telephone: (45)-48-475213
Fax: (45)-48-476213
Web site: www.bridge.dk/
Email: dbf@bridge.dk
Membership: 20,000

Eire: Contract Bridge Association of Ireland (CBAI)
Address: CBAI Central Office, 41 Gledswood Avenue,
     Clonskeagh, Dublin 14
Telephone: (353)-1-269 7275
Contact: Paul Porteous
Web site: indigo.ie/~irebridg/
Email: irebridg@indigo.ie
Membership: 3,250

England: English Bridge Union (E.B.U.)
Address: Broadfields, Bicester Road, Aylesbury,
     Buckinghamshire HP19 3BG
Telephone: (44)-1296-317203
Fax: (44)-1296-317220
Web site: www.ebu.co.uk/
Email: postmaster@ebu.co.uk

Estonia: Estonian Tournament Bridge League
Address: P O Box 14, EE-10502 Tallinn
Telephone: (372)-2-448503
Fax: (372)-2-434172
Contact: Aavo Heinlo
Web site: www.lai.ut.ee/~ulfa/bridge/
Email: ulfa@lai.ut.ee
Membership: 500

Finland: Suomen Bridgelitto
Address: Vatintie 19, SF-20300 Turku
Telephone: (358)-212-393600
Fax: (358)-212-394322
Web site: personal.eunet.fi/pp/lneimo/
Email: finbridge@lneimo.pp.fi
Membership: 1,800

France: Fédération Française De Bridge
Address: 73 Avenue Charles de Gaulle, F-92200 Neuilly
Telephone: (33)-1-41-437700
Fax: (33)-1-47-386674
Web site: www.lebridgeur.fr/
Email: webmaster@ffbridge.asso.fr
               ffb.direction@wanadoo.fr
Membership: 81,400

Germany: Deutscher Bridge-Verband
Address: Wolframs-Eschenbacher-Straße 60,
               D-90449 Nürnberg
Telephone: (49)-911-672 3113
Fax: (49)-911-672 2125
Web site: www.bridge-verband.de/index.htm
Email: www@bridge-verband.de
Membership: 24,500

Great Britain: British Bridge League (BBL)
Address: The Old Railway Station, Long Melford,
Sudbury, Suffolk CO10 9HN
Telephone: (44)-1787-881920
Fax: (44)-1787-881339
Contact: Anna Gudge (Secretary)
Web site: www.britishbridge.org/
Email: anna@ecats.co.uk
Membership: 37,400

Greece: Hellenic Bridge Federation
Address: 30 Phidippidou Street, GR-115 27 Athens
Telephone: (30)-1-748 0400
Fax: (30)-1-748 0403
Web site: users.hol.gr/~eom
Email: eom@hol.gr
Membership: 1,700

Hungary A Magyar Bridzs Szövetség
Address: Bartók Béla út 15/d, H-1114 Budapest
Telephone: (36)-1-269 5181
Fax: (36)-1-269 5184
Web site: www.ecosoft.hu/bridge/
Email: gmarjai@freemail.c3.hu
Membership: 970

Iceland: Bridgesamband Íslands
Address: °önglabakka 1, Pósthólf 9238, 129 Reykjavík
Telephone: (354)-587 9360
Fax: (354)-587 9361
Web site: www.islandia.is/~isbridge/
Email: isbridge@islandia.is
Membership: 3,340

Israel: Israel Bridge Federation (IBF)
Address: P O Box 9671, Haifa 31096
Telephone: (972)-4-833 5333
Fax: (972)-4-833 6343
Contact: Zvi Ben-Tovim (General Manager)
Web site: www.bridge.co.il/
Email: ibf@netvision.net.il
Membership: 6,530

Italy: Federazione Italiana Gioco Bridge (FIGB)
Address: Via Ciro Merotti 11/C, 20129 Milano
Telephone: (39)-02-7000 0483
Fax: (39)-02-7000 1398
Web site: www.federbridge.it/
Email: fedbridge@galactica.it
Membership: 28,830

Lebanon: Fédération Libanaise de Bridge
Address: P O Box 54, Beirut
Telephone: (961)-1-201023
Fax: (961)-1-647947
Web site: web.cyberia.net.lb/BRIDGECL/flb.htm
Email: etsa@cyberia.net.lb
Membership: 200

Liechtenstein: Liechtensteinische Bridge Vereinigung
Address: Postfach 183, FL-9490 Vaduz
Telephone: (41)-75-237 0607
Fax: (41)-75-237 0666
Contact: P Sprenger
Membership: 100

Lithuania: Lietuvos Sportinio Bridzo Asociacija
Address: Paménkalnio Street 14, 2001 Vilnius
Telephone: (370)-2-627015
Fax: (370)-2-628281
Membership: 80

Luxembourg: Fédération Luxembourgeoise de Bridge
Address: 12 rue Massarett, L-2137 Luxembourg
Telephone: (352)-432962
Membership: 150

Malta: Malta Bridge Association
Address: Palm Street, St Julians STJ 12
Telephone: (356)-380333
Fax: (356)-380555
Contact: Mario Dix
Web site: www.bridge.org.mt
Email: mario@bridge.org.mt
Membership: 100

Monaco: Fédération Monegasque de Bridge
Address: Centre de Congress, Auditorium de Monaco,
                     Monte Carlo
Telephone: (33)-93-300 4030
Membership: 120

Netherlands: Nederlandse Bridge Bond (NBB)
Address: Willem Dreeslaan 55, 3515 GB Utrecht
Telephone: (030)-275 9999
Fax: (030)-275 9900
Web site: www.bridge.nl/nbb.htm
Email: NBB@bridge.nl
Membership: 102,530

Northern Ireland: Northern Ireland Bridge Union (NIBU)
Web site: www.nibu.co.uk/
Email: tjod@bfsni.dnet.co.uk

Norway: Norsk Bridgeforbund
Address: Postboks 2828 Solli, N-0204 Oslo
Telephone: (47)-22-431356
Fax: (47)-22-551701
Web site: nettvik.no/foreningsgaarden/bridge/
                     www.bridgefederation.no/
Email: kontoret@bridgefederation.no
Membership: 12,850

Poland: Polski Zwiazek Brydza Sportowego (P.Z.B.S.)
Address: ul. Zlota 9/4, 00-019 Warszawa
Telephone: (48) 22-827 2429
Fax: (48) 22-827 3488
Contact: Andrzej Orlow
Web site: www.polbridge.pl/
Email: biuro@polbridge.pl
Membership: 7,820

Portugal: Federação Portuguesa de Bridge
Address: Avenida António Augusto de Aguiar
                  163 - 4° Esq°, P-1050 Lisboa
Telephone: (351)-1-388 4844
Fax: (351)-1-383 2156
Web site: www.fpbridge.pt/
Email: nmatos@mail.telepac.pt
Membership: 950

Romania: Federatia Romana de Bridge
Address: Vasile Conta 16, Postal Office 37,
                  R-70139 Bucharest 2
Telephone: (40)-1-222 7675
Fax: same
Membership: 1,000

Russia: Russian Bridge League
Address: Starokoniushennyj 19-64, 121002 Moscow
Telephone: (7)-095-205 0115
Fax: (7)-095-241 7300
Contact: Michael Rosenblum
Email: alia@lebedev.msk.ru
Membership: 1,070

San Marino   The Bridge Federation of San Marino
Address: Via G Giacomoni 73, I-47031 San Marino
Telephone: (378)-992114
Fax: (378)-990434
Membership: 60

Scotland: Scottish Bridge Union (SBU)
Address: 7 Whitehaugh Drive, Paisley PA1 3PJ
Telephone: (44)-141-887 1903
Contact: Tom Workman (Secretary)
Web site: www.sbu.dircon.co.uk
Email: liz.mcgowan@cableinet.co.uk
    (c/o Liz McGowan)

Serbia: Bridge Savez Srbije
Web site: members.xoom.com/B_S_S/
email: fascicod@eunet.yu

Slovenia: Bridge Zveza Slovenije
Address: Grampovcanova 7, SLO-1000 Ljubljana
Telephone: (386)-61-123 1393
Membership: 130

Spain: Federacion Espanola de Bridge
Address: C/ Juan Hurtado de Mendoza 17
    E-28036 Madrid
Telephone: (34)-1-350 4700
Fax: (34)-1-350 5453
Email: Javalma@arrakis.es
Membership: 3,240

Sweden: Sveriges Bridgeförbund (SBF)
Address: Kungsgatan 36, 111 35 Stockholm
Telephone: (46)-8-220056
Fax: (46)-8-220057
Web site: www.bridgefederation.se/
email: micke.melander@bridgefederation.se
Membership: 15,000

Switzerland: Fédération Suisse de Bridge
Address: Klarastr. 3, 8008 Zurich
Telephone: (41)-1-262 5655
Fax: (41)-1-262 5645
Web site: home.worldcom.ch/~fsb/
Email: fsb@worldcom.ch
Membership: 3,610

Turkey: Turkiye Bric Federasyonu
Address: Iller Sokak No. 6/5, 06580 Tandogan, Ankara
Telephone: (90)-312-223 1142
Fax: (90)-312-222 6087
Membership: 1,500

Ukraine: Ukranian Bridge Federation
Address: Mikhailovskaya 1/3 (office 302), 252001 Kiev
Telephone: (380)-44-229 2510
Fax: (380)-44-265 0034
Email: ctret@dixi.carrier.kiev.ua
Membership: 120

Wales: Welsh Bridge Union (W.B.U.)
Web site: web.ukonline.co.uk/wbu/
email: wbu@ukonline.co.uk

Zone Two – North America – 167,500 members

Bermuda: Bermuda Contract Bridge League
Address: P O Box HM 2753, HMLX Hamilton
Telephone: (1)-441-293 0531
Fax: (1)-441-293 1351
Membership: 150

Canada: Canadian Bridge Federation
Address: 2719 E Jolly Place, S4V OX8 Regina,
                       Saskatchewan
Telephone: (1)-306-761 1311
Fax: (1)-306-789 4919
Web site: www.cbf.ca/
Email: query@cbf.ca
                       can.bridge.fed@sk.sympatico.ca
Membership: 16,790

Mexico:	Federacion Mexicana de Bridge
Address:	Andador 7, 25, Lomas de Sotelo
	DF 11200 Mexico
Telephone:	(525)-395 7260
Fax:	(525)-395 7211
Web site:	www.txdirect.net/users/biigal/u173HomE.htm
Email:	mchauvet@mail.internet.com.mx
Membership:	350

USA:	American Contract Bridge League (ACBL)
Address:	2990 Airways Blvd, Memphis TN 38116-3847
Telephone:	(1)-901-332 5586
Fax:	(1)-901-398 7754
Web site:	www.acbl.org/
email:	ceo@acbl.org
	acbl@compuserve.com
Membership:	150,150

Zone Three – South America – 5,860 members
Confederacion Sudamericana de Bridge

Address:	Estados Unidos 951
	Asuncion
	Paraguay
Telephone:	(595)-21-213 813
Contact:	Pascal Burró

Argentina:	Asociation del Bridge Argentino
Address:	Maipu 934 1 Piso, 1006 Buenos Aires
Telephone:	(54)-1-315 4544
Fax:	(54)-1-314 2238
Email:	aba@sminter.com.ar
Membership:	1,200

Bolivia:	Federacion Boliviana de Bridge
Address:	P O Box 635, La Paz
Telephone:	(591)-278 2050
Fax:	(591)-277 1656
email:	dgl@datacom.bo.net
Membership:	120

Brazil: Confederacao Brasileira de Bridge
Address: Av Brigadeiro Faria Lima, 1685 conj. 1B,
01452-001 Sao Paulo
Telephone: (55)-11-212 7904
Fax: (55)-11-814 1518
email: ernestdorsi@compuserve.com
Membership: 2,980

Chile: Federacion Chilena de Bridge
Address: P O Box 635,
Av Monsenor Escriva de Balaguer 5428,
Vitacura, Santiago
Telephone: (52)-206 4030
Fax: (52)-22-336516
Membership: 970

Ecuador: Asociation de Bridge Ecuatoriana
Address: Casilla 17.21.01260
Edificio Albatros, 6to Piso, Suite 603
Av de los Shyris 1240 y Portugal, Quito
Fax: (593)-2-432997
Membership: 80

Paraguay: Asociation Paraguaya de Bridge
Address: Chaco Boreal 381, Asuncion
Telephone: (595)-21-611302
Fax: (595)-21-601168
Membership: 55

Peru: Comision National de Bridge
Address: Av Jorge Basadre 475, 27 Lima
Telephone: (51)-14-419995
Fax: (51)-14-423138
email: busimega@amauta.rcp.net.pe
Membership: 250

Uruguay: Asociation Uruguaya de Bridge
Address: Sarandi 584, 11000 Montevideo
Telephone: (598)-2-957820
Fax: (598)-2-951247
Membership: 225

Zone Four – Africa, Asia & Middle East – 17,700 members
Bridge Federation of Africa, Asia & the Middle East (BFAAME)
Address: 217-218 Central Hotel Annexe
                      Abdullah Haroon Road, Karachi, Pakistan
Telephone: (92)-21-568 1495
Fax: (92)-21-568 6223
Contact: Mazhar Jafri (President)

Bangladesh: Bangladesh Bridge Federation
Address: Dhaka Club, Ramna Dhaka 2
Fax: (880)-2-863625
Membership: 90

Botswana: Botswana Bridge Federation
Address: P O Box 802, Gaborone
Fax: (267)-352490
Membership: 100

Egypt: Egyptian Bridge Federation
Address: P O Box 231, 32 Tawfik City, Nasser City,
                      Cairo
Telephone: (20)-2-403 9941
Fax: (20)-2-262 3549
Web site: www.egybf.com/mainpage.html
email: ebf@eis.egnet.net
                      ebf@egybf.com
Membership: 440

India: Bridge Federation of India
Address: 23, VPR Road, 625 014 Madurai
Telephone: (91)-452-532397
Fax: (91)-452-531737
Membership: 11,000

Jordan: Jordanian Bridge Association
Address: P O Box 922498, Amman
Telephone: (962)-655-26990
Fax: (962)-655-25340
Membership: 220

Kenya: Kenya Bridge Association
Address: P O Box 42914, Nairobi
Telephone: (254)-2-228994
Fax: (254)-2-318931
Membership: 110

Kuwait: Kuwait Bridge Committee
Address: P O Box 9226, 61003 Ahmadi
Telephone: (965)-361 2101
Fax: (965)-398 1585
Membership: 80

Mauritius: Mauritius Bridge League
Address: Old Moka Road, Sain-Jeean Quatre Bornes
Telephone: (230)-454 3810
Fax: (230)-636 8695
Membership: 100

Morocco: Fédération Royale Marocaine de Bridge
Address: 10 Rue Bendahan, Casablanca
Telephone: (212)-222 3875
Fax: same
Membership: 200

Nepal: Nepal Bridge Association
Address: Dasarath Sports Complex, Trepwreswore
Telephone: (977)-1-521283
Fax: (977)-1-526283
Email: praveen@mt.wlink.com.np
Membership: 100

Pakistan: Pakistan Bridge Association
Address: PIDC House, 2nd floor
          Dr Ziauddin Ahmed Road, 75530 Karachi
Telephone: (92)-21-568 9237
Fax: (92)-21-568 5506
Membership: 1,300

Palestine: Palestine Bridge Federation
Address: P O Box 3598, Al-Bireh, Ramallah
Telephone: (972)-2-995 1285
Fax: (972)-2-627 1285
Email: zeev.k@netvision.net.il
Membership: 110

Reunion: Comité de Bridge de la Reunion
Address: 1, rue Rico Carpaye, 97420 Le Port
Telephone: (262)-298380
Fax: (262)-211425
Membership: 310

Saudi Arabia: Arabian Bridge Federation
Address: P O Box 5660, 31311 Dhahran
Telephone: (966)-3-874 3617
Fax: (966)-3-878 4783
Membership: 110

South Africa: South Africa Bridge Federation
Address: P O Box 890347, 2106 Lyndhurst
Telephone: (27)-11-440 6435
Fax: (27)-11-333 6698
Membership: 2,440

Sri Lanka: Bridge Federation of Sri Lanka
Address: 97 Castle Street, 8 Colombo
Telephone: (94)-1-691823
Fax: (94)-1-686670
Membership: 100

Syria: Syrian Bridge Association
Address: Al Assad Village area, Dimas-Damascus
Fax: (963)-11-224 9507
Membership: 100

Tanzania: Tanzania Bridge Association
Address: P O Box 5104, Dar-Es-Salaam
Telephone: (255)-51-38375
Fax: (255)-51-112949
Membership: 25

Tunisia: Federation Tunisienne de Bridge
Address: Laboratoire Médical, Centre Cial Jemil
              El Menzah 6, 1002 Tunis
Telephone: (216)-1-751050
Fax: (216)-1-750858
Membership: 200

Uzbekistan: Uzbekistan Bridge Federation
Address: P O Box 4501, Tashkent 700000
Telephone: (737)-1-162 6360
Email: coval@saturn.silk.org
Membership: 100

Zimbabwe: Zimbabwe Bridge Union
Address: 11 Bookless Road, Khumalo-Bulawayo
Telephone: (263)-9-63145
Fax: (263)-9-78425
Membership: 500

Zone Five – Central America – 2,130 members
Central American & Caribbean Bridge Federation (CACBF)

Address:	54 Duke Street, Kingston, Jamaica
Telephone:	(876)-967 1194
Fax:	(876)-924 9120
Contact:	Felicity Reid (President)
Web site:	www.geocities.com/TheTropics/Paradise/2245/index.html
Email:	cacbf@geocities.com

Antigua:	Antigua Contract Bridge Association
Address:	P O Box 384, St Johns
Telephone:	(268)-461 1208
Fax:	(268)-462 1444
Contact:	Merna Norde (Secretary)
Email:	jamesp@candw.ag
Membership:	80

Aruba:	Aruba Bridge Federation
Address:	17 Beaujonstraat, Oranjestad
Telephone:	(297)-824953
Fax:	same
Contact:	Adeline Eiler (Secretary)
Membership:	60

Bahamas:	Bahamas Bridge League
Address:	P O Box N-1184, Nassau
Telephone:	(242)-323 6593
Fax:	(242)-328 0622
Contact:	Bill Weeks (Secretary)
Email:	dcsands@bahamas.net.bs
Membership:	75

Barbados:	Barbados Bridge League
Address:	23 Pine Road, Belleville, St Michael
Telephone:	(246)-427 4839
Fax:	(246)-431 0510
Contact:	Adelle Spring (Secretary)
Email:	tonyw@caribsurf.com
Membership:	65

Colombia: Federacion Colombiana de Bridge
Address: Carrera no 92-92 – Apt 401, Bogota
Telephone: (57)-1-256 1728
Fax: (57)-1-256 6368
Contact: Hoover Hena (Secretary)
Email: romanlee@axesnet.com
Membership: 400

Costa Rica: Asociacion Nacional de Bridge de C.R.
Address: Apartado Postal 3075-1000, San Jose
Telephone: (506)-232 9154
Fax: (506)-220 1741
Contact: John Crance (Secretary)
Email: amelsa@sol.racsa.co.cr
Membership: 100

Dominica: Commonwealth of Dominica Bridge Association
Address: 37 King George V Street, Roseau
Telephone: (809)-448 4839
Fax: (809)-448 1762
Contact: Peter Israel (Secretary)
Email: shillingfordd@tod.dm
Membership: 25

French Guyana: Comité de Bridge de Guiana
Address: P O Box 599, Cayenne
Telephone: (594)-313271
Fax: (594)-316368
Contact: Jean Jacque (President)
email: ffbguyan@citeweb.net
Membership: 80

Grenada: Grenada Bridge Club
Address: P O Box 221, St Georges
Telephone: (473)-443 5328
Fax: (473)-440 4113
Contact: Brenda Williams (Secretary)
Email: brenwil@caribsurf.com

Guadeloupe:	Comité de Bridge de Guadeloupe
Address:	16 Residence Presqu'ile – Marina,
	97110 Pointe-a-Pitre
Telephone:	(590)-908368
Fax:	same
Contract:	G Bourgouir (President)
Email:	derivery@outremer.com
Membership:	150

Guatemala:	Asociacion Guatemalteca de Bridge
Address:	1ra Calle,18-83, Zona 15, Vista Hermosa II
Telephone:	(502)-369 1025
Fax:	(502)-369 6850
Email:	kaleido@guate.net
Membership:	55

Guyana:	Guyana Bridge League
Address:	101 Regent Street, Lacytown, Georgetown
Telephone:	(592)-2-60543
Fax:	(592)-2-61939
Contact:	Amina Beepat (Secretary)
Email:	mbeepat@networksgy.com
Membership:	20

Haiti:	Association Haitienne de Bridge
Address:	P O Box 273, Port au Prince
Telephone:	(509)-463558
Fax:	(509)-460699
Email:	jeroy@acn2.net
Membership:	50

Jamaica:	Jamaica Bridge Association
Address:	57a East Queen Street, Kingston
Telephone:	(876)-922 5283
Fax:	(876)-922 7874
Contact:	Betty Williams (Secretary)
Email:	russian@n5.com.jm
Membership:	75

Martinique: District de Bridge de la Martinique
Address: c/o Bamex SA, BP 423
                     97292 Lamentin Cedex 2
Telephone: (596)-640011
Fax: (596)-502071
email: bamex@cgit.com
Membership: 80

**Netherlands
Antilles:**   Bridge Bond Nederlandse Antillen
Address: Kaya Roi Katochi 93, Curaçao
Telephone: (599)-9-733 3311
Fax: (599)-9-737 0176
Contact: Peter Hendriks (Secretary)
Email: hendriks@cura.net
Membership: 100

Panama: Asociacion Panamena de Bridge
Address: P O Box 10520, Panama 4
Telephone: (507)-263 2558
Fax: (507)-263 2059
Contact: Manuel Hern (President)
email: mhc@sinfo.net
Membership: 105

St Kitts & Nevis: St.Kitts Bridge Association
Address: c/o Ian Slack, P O Box 282, Basseterre
Telephone: (869)-465 2074
Fax: (869)-465 1201
Contact: David Rawlings (President)
Email: skbc@caribsurf.com
Membership: 50

St Lucia: St Lucia Bridge Association
Address: P O Box 105, Castries
Telephone: (758)-452 0027
Fax: (758)-453 6168
Email: Genla@candw.lc

Suriname: De Surinaamse Bridgebond
Address: P O Box 635, Paramaribo
Telephone: (597)-476810
Fax: (597)-410344
Contact: Piem Reizige (President)
Email: Jimloor@sr.net
Membership: 80

Trinidad &
Tobago: Trinidad & Tobago Contract Bridge League
Address: P O Box 1328, Port of Spain, Trinidad
Telephone: (868)-633 8577
Fax: (868)-674 0145
Contact: Denis Josa (Secretary)
Email: aml@trinidad.net
Membership: 90

Venezuela: Federacion Venezolana de Bridge
Address: Centro de Bridge de Caracas
                       Quinto Ekeko, 2a Calle de Campo,
                       Alegre, Caracas
Telephone: (58)-2-262 1160
Fax: (58)-2-241 3076
Contact: Lillian Morgan (Secretary)
Email: ccaponi@marnr.gov.ve
Membership: 285

Virgin Islands: Virgin Islands Bridge Federation
Address: 1B King Street, P O Box 3485
                       Christianstedt, St Croix
Telephone: (809)-773 0096
Fax: (809)-778 8640
Membership: 150

Zone Six – Pacific Asia – 69,350 members
Pacific Asia Bridge Federation (PABF)
Address:	33 Silom Road, #1508, Bangkok, Thailand
Telephone:	(66)-2-236 8984
Fax:	(66)-2-259 2248
Contact:	Khunying Ester Sophonpanich (President)
Email:	chodhoy@mozart.inet.co.th

China:
	Chinese Bridge Association
Address:	c/o All-China Sports Federation
	9 Tiyukuan Road, 100763 Beijing
Telephone:	(86)-10-6504 4062
Fax:	(86)-10-6504 3842
Email:	cbridge@sport.go.cn
Membership:	55,000

Chinese Taipei:
	Chinese Taipei Bridge Association
Address:	71 Kuan Chien Road, Taipei
Telephone:	(886)-2-772 4510
Fax:	(886)-2-771 4493
Membership:	2,300

Hong Kong
	Hong Kong Contract Bridge Association (HKCBA)
Address:	GPO Box 1445, Hong Kong
Telephone:	(813)-33-573741
Fax:	(813)-33-577444
Web site:	http://imsnispc01.netvigator.com/~hkcba/
Membership:	275

Indonesia:
	Gabungan Bridge Seluruh Indonesia (Indonesian CBA)
Address:	GABSI Secretariat, Stadion Utama Senayan
	Pintu I Plaza Barat, Jakarta 10270
Telephone:	(62)-21-574 1288
Fax:	(62)-21-856 9118
Email:	pbgabsi@vision.net.id
Membership:	5,070

Japan: Japan Contract Bridge League
Address: 4th Floor Toranomon Kitsuqvo Kaikan
                  Yotsuya 1-13, Shijuku-Ku, 160 Tokyo
Telephone: (81)-3-3357 3741
Fax: (81)-3-3357 7444
Web site: www2h.biglobe.ne.jp/~jcbl/index.html
Email: info@jcbl.or.jp
                  jccl@mxd.meshnet.or.jp
Membership: 5,900

Macau: Macau Contract Bridge Association
Address: Apt. 13 A, Edif, Ka Vo, No 30
                  Praca Lobo d' Avila, Macau
Telephone: (853)-312085
Fax: (853)-312180
Membership: 70

Malaysia: Malaysia Contract Bridge Association
Address: 9.06 Wisma Inai, 241 Jalan Tun Razah
                  50400 Kuala Lumpur
Telephone: (60)-3-245 4882
Fax: (60)-3-248 7868
Membership: 95

Philippines: Philippine Contract Bridge League
Address: 5338 Amorsolo Street, Dasmarinas Village,
                  Makati
Telephone: (632)-844 2337
Fax: same
Contact: Allen Tan
Web site: user.qinet.net/altan/index.html
Email: altan@qinet.net
Membership: 170

Singapore: Singapore Contract Bridge Association
Address: P O Box 47, Newton Post Office,
                  9122 Singapore
Telephone: (65)-446 2084
Fax: (65)-443 6603
Membership: 175

Thailand: Contract Bridge League of Thailand
Address: 319/1 Sukhumvit 31, Bangkok 10110
Telephone: (66)-2-230 1884
Fax: (66)-2-236 8984
Membership: 285

Zone Seven – South Pacific – 45,450 members
South Pacific Bridge Federation (SPBF)
Address: P O Box 2335, Christchurch 1, New Zealand
Telephone: (64)-3-379 2600
Fax: (64)-3-379 1196
Contact: John Wignall (President)
Email: ewco@clear.net/nz

Australia: Australian Bridge Federation
Address: P O Box 397
ACT 2609 Fyshwick
Telephone: (61)-6-239 2265
Fax: (61)-6-239 1816
Web site: www.abf.com.au/
Email: abf@abf.com.au
abf@netinfo.com.au
Membership: 27,320

French Polynesia: Federation de Bridge de Polynésie Française
Address: P O Box 524, 98713 Papeete
Membership: 145

New Caledonia: New Caledonian Bridge Federation
Address: P O Box 9615, Noumea
Telephone: (687)-269249
Fax: (687)-252570
Membership: 115

New Zealand: New Zealand Contract Bridge
Address: P O Box 12.116, Wellington
Telephone: (64)-4-473 7748
Fax: same
Email: fran@nzcba.co.nz
Membership: 17,880

WHO'S WHO
The great names of the past, present and future

ÅA, Terje of Norway. (b.1961). Represented Norway in two Bermuda Bowls. 3rd in European Championships in 1993 & 97. Won the Schiphol International Teams in 1993.

ABECASSIS, Michel of Paris, France. (b.1952). Won the European Pairs in 1991 and 1993. Has represented France in one European Championship.

ABEDI, Nishat M H of Karachi, Pakistan. (b.1939 in Allahabad, India). 2nd in the 1981 Bermuda Bowl and the 1986 Rosenblum. Has also won the BFAAME Championship twice.

AHMED, Nisar of Karachi, Pakistan. (b.1936). 2nd in the 1981 Bermuda Bowl and the 1986 Rosenblum. Won the BFAAME Championship four times. 2nd in the 1979 Far East Championship.

ALBARRAN, Pierre of Paris, France. (b.1894 in the West Indies; d.1960). Won the first European Championship, in 1935, and represented France in the first World Championship that same year. Represented France on more than 30 occasions and won 19 national titles. Authored nine books and was responsible for developing the canapé principle. He also represented France in Davis Cup tennis.

ALDER, Phillip D of New York City, New York, USA. (b.1951). Formerly of London, England. Bridge journalist, who succeeded Jim Jacoby as bridge columnist with Newspaper Enterprise Association. Life Master in England and the US. When he became a Life Master in England, he was the second youngest to attain that rank. Author of *You Can Play Bridge* and *Get Smarter at Bridge*, and principal analyst for the many World Championship books. Editor of *Bridge Magazine* (1980-85) in London. Bulletin Editor at many World and Zonal Championships. Winner of BOLS brilliancy prize for journalism in 1979. Represented England in the 1980 Camrose, and 1971 & 72 Junior Camrose. Represented Great Britain in the 1972 Junior European Championships and 1974 & 76 Junior Common Market Championships. Has won two US national titles.

ALLISON, Karen R of Jersey City, New Jersey, USA. Formerly of Toronto, Canada. Represented Canada at the 1980 Women's Team

Olympiad and the 1976 World Open Team Olympiad, becoming the first woman to represent Canada in an Open Team Championship. Placed 8th in the 1990 World Women's Pairs, and 2nd in the inaugural World Women's Teams in 1994. National titles include the Women's Teams in 1968 & 69 and the 1983 Master Mixed Teams.

ALTMAN, Steven B of Tenafly, New Jersey, USA. (b.1943). An original member of the Precision Team and coach to the US Bermuda Bowl teams in 1973 & 77. Won the *Sunday Times* Invitational Pairs in 1973. National wins include the Spingold twice and the Vanderbilt.

ANDERSEN, Ronald E "Ron" of Chicago, Illinois, USA. (b.1941; d.1997). Professional bridge writer, player, commentator and teacher. A WBF World Master and ACBL Grand Life Master who was number three on the ACBL total lifetime masterpoints list at the time of his death. He was a regular commentator on Vu-Graph at NABCs, European and World Championships. Finished 6th in the 1978 World Pairs, and 8th in 1982. 5th in 1984 World Teams Olympiad. 3rd in the 1990 *Sunday Times* Invitational Pairs. Won the London *Times* Charity Pro-Am in 1991, and the 1990 Proton Invitational Teams in Taipei. He edited four books on the Precision Club system, was associate editor of the *International Precision Newsletter*, and regularly wrote articles for the ACBL Bulletin and other bridge periodicals. He authored two books, *Where and How High* and *Lebensold*, and co-wrote many more. He was twice coach of the US Women's team. He was a four-time winner of the McKenney Trophy, the first three times with a record total. He won eleven national titles.

ANDERSON, A T Rex of Coleraine, Northern Ireland. (b.1945). Solicitor. WBF World Master. 3rd in 1979 European Teams, and represented Ireland in three other Zonal Championships and two World Championships. Represented Northern Ireland regularly in Camrose Trophy matches since 1971. National titles include the Open Teams 11 times and the Open Pairs eight times.

ANDERSSON, Pia of Sweden. Represented Sweden in the 1997 European Championships. Won the 1998 European Mixed Pairs.

ARMSTRONG, John M of Formby, England. (b.1952). Actuary and systems analyst. WBF World Master. British Grand Master #54. 2nd in the 1987 Bermuda Bowl. Won the 1991 European Teams, and finished 2nd in 1987. Has represented Great Britain in five

European Championships and four World Championships. Also played 25 Camrose matches for England. Won the Schiphol International Teams in The Netherlands in 1996. Many national wins.

ARNARSON, Gudmundur P of Reykjavik, Iceland. (b.1954). Publisher, teacher and writer. Won the Bermuda Bowl in 1991, and represented Iceland in two other World, five European and two Nordic Championships. National wins include the Open Teams twice and the Open Pairs once. He is the Publisher and Editor of *Icelandic Bridge* magazine, writer of a daily column for *Morgunbladid*, and the author of bridge books. He also owns Iceland's only bridge school.

ARNOLDS, Carla of Tilburg, The Netherlands. (b.1960). Bridge teacher and journalist. WBF World Master. Finished 2nd in the 1989 Venice Cup. Won the 1994 World Women's Pairs. Also finished 3rd in 1990, and 5th in 1998. Represented the Netherlands in three other World Championships and two European Championships. National titles include the Dutch Women's Pairs in 1991.

ARNTHORSSON, Orn of Reykjavik, Iceland. (b.1945). Pension funds manager. WBF World Master. Won the 1991 Bermuda Bowl. Represented Iceland in six other World, six European and one Nordic Championship. National titles include the Icelandic Teams five times and the Open Pairs twice

ASSUMPÇÃO, Pedro-Paulo P of São Paulo, Brazil. (b.1935). Retired company director. WBF Grand Master and #41 in the world rankings in 1999. Won the World Team Olympiad in 1976. Finished 2nd in the 1978 Rosenblum. Represented Brazil in 13 other World Championships. Won the South American Teams 17 times. Many national titles.

ATTAGUILE, Luis of Buenos Aires, Argentina. (b. 1926). World Life Master. Won the South American Championships eight times. Represented Argentina at the Bermuda Bowl five times, and in two World Team Olympiads. Many national titles.

AUKEN, Jens of Charlottenlund, Denmark. (b.1949). Lawyer. WBF World Master. Finished 3rd at the 1984 World Team Olympiad and 3rd in the 1998 World Mixed Pairs. Represented Denmark in one other World Championship and four European Championships. Many national titles. Top Danish masterpoint winner five times. Won the Nordic Club Cup and the European

Club Cup, both in 1990. EBL Executive Committee member and a specialist in bridge law.

AUKEN, Sabine (née Zenkel) of Charlottenlund, Denmark. (b.1965). Formerly of Germany and Chicago, IL, USA. WBF Grand Master and #1 in the world women's rankings in 1999. She has represented Germany in five Venice Cups, reaching the final in 1993, and winning in 1995. Won the 1989 European Women's Teams, and finished 2nd in 1991 & 95. Won the 1985 European Union Women's Pairs. In 1994, she won the European Mixed Pairs and collected 2nd place in the World Mixed Pairs. 2nd in the European Mixed Teams in 1996. Finished 2nd in both the World Women's Teams and the World Women's Pairs and 3rd in the World Mixed Pairs in 1998. Won the European Women's Pairs in 1995 & 97. Finished 3rd in the 1998 Macallan Invitational Pairs. National titles include the German Women's Pairs in 1988, the Grand National Open Teams in 1989 and the 1992 German Open Teams. Became the fastest ever US Life Master (8 weeks) in 1989.

AVARELLI, Walter of Rome, Italy. (b.1912; d.1987) Judge. WBF Grand Master and 5th in the world career rankings at the time of his death. Won the World Team Olympiad three times and the Bermuda Bowl nine times. Won four European Teams Championships. Many national titles. He was a co-inventor of the Roman Club system.

BABSCH, Andreas of Vienna, Austria. (b.1961). Bridge teacher. Represented Austria in three World Championships, two European Championships and seven other European events. National titles include the Austrian Teams twice, the Life Master Individual twice, and the Open Pairs. Was Austria's youngest ever Life Master.

BACHERICH, René of Lille, France. (b.1906). Retired merchant. WBF Grand Master. Won the World Teams in 1956 & 60. Represented France in six World Championships. Won the European Teams three times.

BALDURSSON, Jon of Reykjavik, Iceland. (b.1954). Airline manager. Iceland's most successful player in recent years. WBF World Master. Won the 1991 Bermuda Bowl and the 1988 Nordic Teams. Has represented Iceland in six other World, seven European, four other Nordic and one European Junior Championship. Won the Generali World Individual in 1994. Many national titles.

BALICKI, Cezary of Wroclaw, Poland. (b.1958). Bridge professional and chess instructor. WBF World Life Master. Has finished 2nd in two World Championships – the 1991 Bermuda Bowl and the 1994 Rosenblum. 3rd in the 1990 World Pairs. 4th in the 1998 World Par Contest. Won the European Teams in 1989, and has represented Poland in three other World and two other European Championships. Has won numerous Polish national titles. Won his first US national title in 1997, the Spingold.

BAMBERGER, Gabrielle "Gabi" of Vienna, Austria. (b.1953). Bridge teacher. WBF World Master. 2nd in the Venice Cup in 1991. Won the European Women's Teams in 1991, and 2nd in 1999. Represented Austria in two World Team Olympiads and five other European Championships. Many national titles.

BARAN, Boris of Montreal, Canada. (b.1945 in Switzerland). Professor of computer information systems. 3rd on the lifetime masterpoint list amongst Canadians. 2nd in the 1995 Bermuda Bowl. 3rd in the Rosenblum Teams and has represented Canada in six other World Championships. 2nd in the 1992 Pan-American Open Teams. Won the Icelandic Invitational Pairs in 1991. Many national titles.

BARBOSA, Sergio M P of Rio de Janeiro, Brazil. (b.1942). Engineer and economist. WBF World Life Master. Won 1976 World Team Olympiad. Finished 2nd in the 1978 Rosenblum. Represented Brazil in six other World Championships. Many national titles.

BATES, Roger W of Mesa, Arizona, USA. (b.1947). Won the Rosenblum Teams in 1994. 3rd in the 1978 World Open Pairs. Won the Cavendish Invitational Pairs in 1980. Fifteen national titles.

BAZE, Grant S of San Francisco, California, USA. (b.1943). A leading professional player and an expert rubber bridge player. He recently sold his interest in a major Internet online Bridge Club to OKBridge. Winner of the Barry Crane Top 500 three times. Became the first player to break the 3,000 masterpoint mark in a year in 1984 and ranks 6th on the all-time masterpoint list. Many national titles.

BECKER, B Jay of New York City, New York, USA. (b.1904; d.1987). Attorney, bridge teacher and columnist. He also managed three New York clubs including the Cavendish (1942–47). One of the greatest players of all time. ACBL Life Master #6. Won the Bermuda Bowl twice. Thirty national titles. His final victory in the Vanderbilt at the age of 76 was a record at the time, but was later surpassed by Oswald Jacoby. He is the father of Steve and Michael Becker.

BECKER, James W "Jim" of New York City, New York, USA. (b.1937; d.1994). Owner/manager of the Beverly Bridge Club. Won the Barry Crane Top 500 in 1991 and is ranked 15th on the all-time masterpoint list.

BECKER, Michael M of Tenafly, New Jersey, USA. (b.1943). Options trader. Became a Life Master at the age of 19. In 1973, Michael and father B Jay Becker became the first father-son combination to play as teammates in a World Championship (and the only ones until Paul, Jason and Justin Hackett represented Great Britain at the 1996 Olympiad). Won the 1983 Bermuda Bowl. Thirteen national titles. He is B Jay Becker's son, and Steve Becker's brother.

BELLADONNA, Giorgio of Rome, Italy. (b.1923; d.1996). Public official. WBF Grand Master and #1 in the 1992 world career rankings. He was the primary inventor (with Walter Avarelli) of the Roman Club system, and a contributor to the Super Precision system. He co-wrote books on various aspects of bidding theory with Walter Avarelli, Benito Garozzo and C C Wei. He was the only ever-present member of the 16 Italian World Championship victories during the great Blue Team era – winning the World Team Olympiad three times and the Bermuda Bowl thirteen times. Won the European Teams Championship a record ten times – four more victories than anyone else. Many Italian national titles.

BENJAMIN, Albert L of Glasgow, Scotland. (b.1909). Company director, bridge writer, and former club owner. He is the inventor of Benjaminized Acol and the co-author (with Ewart Kempson) of *Tournament Bridge for Everyone*. He represented Scotland 17 times in the Camrose Trophy, winning in 1964. National titles include the Scottish Open Teams six times.

BERGEN, Marty A of Farmingdale, New York, USA. (b.1948). Bridge teacher, writer and professional player. A regular contributor to the *ACBL Bulletin* and to *Bridge Today*. The author of *Better Bidding with Bergen Volumes I & II* and *Points Schmoints*. Assisted in the development of the Law of Total Tricks, and invented many of today's common conventional gadgets such as Support Doubles and a Semi-Forcing 1NT response to Major-suit openings, as well as Bergen Raises. Won the Cavendish Invitational Pairs twice. Many national titles. He is also a former high school and collegiate tennis champion.

BERKOWITZ, David of Old Tappan, New Jersey, USA. (b.1949). Accountant. 2nd in the 1998 World Open Pairs. Won the Open Teams and placed 3rd in the Pairs at the 1992 Pan-American Championships. More than a dozen national titles.

BERKOWITZ, Lisa H of Old Tappan, New Jersey, USA. (b.1952). Former Accountant. Won the 1997 Venice Cup. Won the Women's Teams and finished 3rd in the Women's Pairs at the 1992 Pan-American Championships. Many national titles.

BERNASCONI, Pietro of Geneva, Switzerland. (b.1932). Bridge club manager and teacher. Best known for creating the hands for the Par contest at the 1990, 94 & 98 World Championships. These electronic tests for world-class players are generally acknowledged to be the most difficult playing challenge ever devised. Represented Switzerland in five World and 15 European Championships. Many national titles.

BESSE, Jean of Geneva, Switzerland. (b.1914; d.1998). Bridge writer and theorist. He was the first Vice-President of the International Bridge Press Association. The originator of the Swiss Acol system, he was a VuGraph commentator at numerous major championships. Played for Europe in the 1954 Bermuda Bowl. Represented Switzerland in 10 World and 17 European Championships. Won the *Sunday Times* Invitational Pairs in 1969. Won the 1976 BOLS Bridge Tip contest. National titles in both Switzerland and France include the Open Teams numerous times.

BESSIS, Veronique of Paris, France. (b.1950). Bridge teacher and former mathematics teacher. Finished 2nd in the 1987 Venice Cup, 3rd in 1985, and 4th in 1997. 2nd in the World Women's Pairs in 1994, and 3rd in 1998. Won the European Women's Teams four times. She has represented France in three other World and four other European Championships. .

BETHE, Henry of Ithica, New York, USA. (b.1944). Formerly of London, England. Senior financial officer, and a regular contributor to numerous bridge magazines. Wrote the original computer program for scoring IMP Pairs. Coach of the winning North American Venice Cup team in 1993. National wins include the Life Masters Pairs in 1968. Away from bridge, he won the New York Triathlon in 1979 & 80.

BIANCHI, Benito of Leghorn, Italy. (b.1924; d.1979). Furrier. WBF Grand Master. Co-developer of the Leghorn Diamond system. Won the Bermuda Bowl twice and European Teams four times.

Represented Italy in nine European Championships. National titles include the Italian Cup once.

BIANCHI, Marisa of Leghorn, Italy. (b.1928). WBF Grand Master and #32 in the world women's rankings in 1999. Won the World Women's Team Olympiad twice (in 1972 & 76). Won the European Women's Championship five times (in 1970, 71, 73, 74 & 77) and represented Italy in two other European Championship. Won the EC Women's Teams in 1971 & 73. National titles include the Italian Mixed Teams twice. She also won one British national title – the 1973 Women's Teams.

BIRD, David L of Eastleigh, England. (b.1945). Retired IBM systems analyst. The leading living writer of bridge humour, and perhaps of all time. The author of more than 40 books, his famous "Abbot" series featuring the Monks of St Titus began as a collaboration with Terence Reese, but have remained as popular as ever since the latter's death. British Grand Master #230. Lost in the final of the Spring Fours twice, both by less than 3 IMPs. National titles include the Pachabo a record four times (1974, 89, 90 & 99) and the Tollemache four times.

BIRMAN, David of Tel Aviv, Israel. (b.1948 in Poland). Engineer. The Editor of Israel's *Bridge Magazine* since 1983. 3rd in the 1985 Bermuda Bowl. 2nd in the 1985 European Teams. 2nd in the 1972 European Junior Teams. He has represented Israel regularly in World and European Championships. Won the Cavendish Teams in 1991. National titles include the Israeli Teams five times and the Open Pairs three times.

BLACKWOOD, Easley R of Indianapolis, Indiana, USA. (b.1903; d.1992). Insurance manager. One of the most famous names in bridge and yet he never won a North American national title. He is best known for the ace-asking convention that he invented and which bears his name. He was honoured with the IBPA's Charles Goren Award as the "Bridge Personality of the Year" in 1983. He was honoured by the Mayor of Indianapolis, who proclaimed 28 October 28 1977 as "Easley Blackwood Day". He was the author of many books, including *Blackwood on Slams* and *The Play of the Hand with Blackwood*.

BLAKSET, Knut of Copenhagen, Denmark. (b.1960 in Norway). Financial consultant. He was a member of the Danish team that lost the 1992 World Team Olympiad quarter-final by just 2 IMPs to the eventual French winners. Won the 1986 Open Teams and the 1983

Junior Teams at Nordic Championships. National titles include the Danish Teams three times and the Open Pairs twice.

BLAKSET, Lars of Copenhagen, Denmark. (b.1961 in Norway). Bridge teacher. A bidding theorist, he is the author of the official Danish system book. He is the bridge columnist for *Berlingske Tidende* and a regular magazine contributor. 3rd in the 1988 World Team Olympiad. Like his brother, he was also a member of the narrowly defeated Danish team at the 1992 Olympiad. Represented Denmark on many other occasions including three European Championships. Won the 1986 Open Teams and the 1983 Junior Teams at Nordic Championships. Won the Hoechst Invitational Teams in The Netherlands in 1991. National titles include the Danish Teams four times and the Open Pairs three times.

BLANCHARD, Jillian Shane "Jill" of New York City, New York, USA. (b.1961). Attorney. Instituted a lawsuit to force the ACBL to allow women to compete in major Men's events, as a result of which the ACBL now run Women's events and Open events, but no Men's events. Won the World Women's Teams in 1994. 2nd in the 1989 Reisinger. Her mother is Gail Greenberg.

BLOUQUIT, Claude "Mamie" of Paris, France. (b.1941). Bridge professional and teacher. Placed 2nd in the World Mixed Pairs in 1998. Finished 3rd in both the 1978 World Women's Pairs and the 1984 World Women's Team Olympiad. Won the European Women's Teams in 1995, and 2nd in 1993. She has represented France in four other European Championships. 2nd in the European Women's Pairs in 1989. Many national titles, including women's, mixed and open.

BLUHM, Louis E "Lou" of Atlanta, Georgia, USA. (b.1940; d.1990). Professional bridge player, and poker & gin expert. 3rd in the 1978 World Mixed Pairs. Won the Cavendish Invitational Pairs in 1981. Many national titles.

BLUMENTHAL, Mark E of Chicago, Illinois, USA. (b.1942). A member of the Dallas Aces from 1972-74. Twice 2nd in the Bermuda Bowl. National titles include the Vanderbilt twice. Ill health forced his retirement from competitive bridge in 1977.

BOCCHI, Norberto of Naples, Italy. (b.1959). Won the European Teams twice. 2nd in the 1999 European Pairs. 2nd in the 1984 European Junior Teams. Won the 1992 Schiphol International Teams and the 1997 Forbo Invitational Teams, both in The Netherlands.

BOMPIS, Marc of France. Won the World Team Olympiad in 1996. Placed 2nd in the World Mixed Pairs in 1998.

BOYD, Peter A of Silver Springs, Maryland, USA. (b.1950). Systems analyst. Harvard graduate. Won the Rosenblum Teams in 1986. Won the Cavendish Teams in 1997. Many national titles.

BRACHMAN, Malcolm K of Dallas, Texas, USA. (b.1926). Oil company president. Graduate of Yale and Harvard. Won the 1979 Bermuda Bowl. Many national titles.

BRAMLEY, Bart of Chicago, Illinois, USA. (b.1948). Stock options trader. Die-hard NY Yankee and Grateful Dead fan. 2nd in the 1998 World Par Contest. 5th in the 1991 Bermuda Bowl. Many national titles.

BRANCO, Marcelo C of Rio de Janeiro, Brazil. (b.1945). Computer engineer and government official. WBF Grand Master and #10 in the 1999 world ranking. Won the 1976 World Team Olympiad, the 1978 & 90 World Open Pairs, and the 1989 Bermuda Bowl. He is the only player to have won the World Pairs twice, and one of only eight to have won the Triple Crown (World Teams, World Pairs and Bermuda Bowl). Twice finished 2nd in the Rosenblum Teams (in 1978 & 98). He has also represented Brazil in many other World Championships. Won the South American Teams 13 times. He won his first North American national title in 1992 (the Reisinger). Won the 1992 *Sunday Times* Invitational Pairs, and the Cap Gemini Invitational Pairs twice. National titles include the Open Teams ten times.

BRANCO, Pedro-Paulo C of Rio de Janeiro, Brazil. (b.1940). Insurance executive. WBF Grand Master and #24 in the world rankings in 1999. Won the 1989 Bermuda Bowl. Won the South American Teams nine times. He has represented Brazil in nine World Championships. Fifteen national titles include the Open Teams four times.

BROCK, Raymond S of Buckinghamshire, England. (b.1940). Computer consultant. British Life Master #43 and Grand Master #17. 2nd in both the Bermuda Bowl and the European Teams in 1987. He has represented England in more than 25 Camrose matches. Many national titles. Coach and npc of British Junior teams since 1983, including two World Junior Championship winning teams. President of the British Bridge League 1986–88 and 1990–92.

BROCK, Sally of Buckinghamshire, England. (b.1953). Formerly Sally Sowter and Sally Horton. WBF Grand Master and #28 in the

1999 world women's ranking. British Grand Master #46. Won the Venice Cup twice, the European Women's Teams twice and the EC Women's Teams three times. Many national titles including the Gold Cup three times. Assistant Editor of *Bridge Magazine*. Former Executive Editor of *International Popular Bridge Monthly*. Author of several bridge books.

BROGELAND, Boye of Bergen, Norway. (b.1973). Editor of *Bridge i Norge*. Won World Junior Pairs in 1995. 2nd in World Junior Teams in 1997. Won the European Junior Teams in 1996. 3rd in the 1997 European Open Teams on his first appearance in the Open team, and subsequently reached the semi-final of the 1997 Bermuda Bowl. 2nd in the 1999 European Teams. Won the Nordic Under-20 Teams in 1993, the Nordic Junior Teams in 1995, and the Nordic Open Teams in 1998. Won the 1998 Young Chelsea Marathon in England. Several national titles.

BRUNNER, Michelle of Manchester, England. (b.1953). Won the Venice Cup in 1985. 2nd in the 1988 World Women's Teams. Won the European Women's Teams in 1979 and finished 2nd in 1977. National titles include the Pachabo in 1986.

BRUNZELL, Anders of Gothenburg, Sweden. (b.1938). Math/physics teacher. 3rd in the Bermuda Bowl in 1977 and represented Sweden in four other World Championships. Won the 1977 European Teams and the 1968 Nordic Teams.

BURATTI, Andrea of Genoa, Italy. (b.1950). Computer broker. Won the 1998 Rosenblum Teams. Won the European Teams twice. Quarter-finalist in the 1997 Bermuda Bowl. Won the EC Teams three times. Won the 1997 Forbo International Teams in the Netherlands. Many national titles.

BURGESS, Stephen of Sydney, Australia. (b.1956 in New Zealand). Options trader. 3rd in the 1986 World Pairs. He has represented Australia in four World and four Zonal Championships. Has won numerous national titles both in Australia and in New Zealand. Along with Paul Marston, he was the originator of the Moscito relay system.

BURN, David A L of London, England. (b.1956). Computer analyst. Coach of numerous British teams and a regular contributor to British magazines. National titles include the Spring Fours (South) in 1985.

BURNSTINE, David (aka David Bruce) of Los Angeles, California, USA. (b.1900; d.1965). ACBL Life Master #1. He invented the concept of opening Two Clubs with all strong hands, thus releasing the other two-level suit openings for other purposes. One of the "Four Horsemen" (along with Jacoby, Schenken and Sims). He wrote *Four Horsemen's One Over One*, the team's system book, and later *Four Aces System of Contract Bridge*. He was a member of the American team that won the first official World Championship, in 1935. Twenty-five national titles.

CAESAR, Karin of Germany. Won the Venice Cup in 1995 and finished 2nd in 1993. Won the European Women's Teams in 1989, and 2nd twice. 2nd in the European Women's Pairs in 1993.

CALDERWOOD, "Gus" Angus I of London, England. (b.in South Africa). British national titles include the Gold Cup in 1992, Crockfords in 1986 and the Spring Fours four times.

CAMPBELL, Hastings of Belfast, Northern Ireland. (b.1949). Company director and lecturer. He has made more than 40 appearances for Northern Ireland in the Camrose Trophy, and has also represented all-Ireland in one European Championship.

CAMPOS, João P of São Paulo, Brazil. (b.1968). Bridge teacher. Won the IOC in Lausanne in 1998. 2nd in the 1998 Rosenblum Cup. Won the 1998 South American Teams. Two national titles.

CANNELL, Drew of Winnipeg, Canada. (b.1952). Computer operations manager, bridge club manager and bridge teacher. He has represented both Canada and Panama in World Championships, and he was the youngest competitor in 1974. He has also been the coach and npc for both countries. Won the CAC Zonal Championship in 1978. North American titles include the North American Swiss twice and the 1986 Grand National Pairs, which no Canadian had previously won. Won the Canadian National Teams Championship in 1984, and was npc of the 1985 winners. He was also responsible for developing the Panama Relay system.

CANSINO, Jonathan of London, England. (b.1939). Stockbroker. British Life Master #54. Represented Britain in two European Championships and England in numerous Camrose matches. Won the inaugural English Life Master's Pairs in 1966. Many national titles. Was forced through illness to retire from competitive bridge in the early 1970s.

CAPODANNO, Luciana of Naples, Italy. Won the 1976 World Women's Team Olympiad. 2nd in the 1978 Venice Cup. Won the European Women's Teams twice.

CARRUTHERS, John of Toronto, Canada. (b.1947 in England). Research chemist and systems analyst. The Editor of the *Ontario Kibitzer* since 1990 and a regular contributor to bridge magazines worldwide. He has been the coach and npc for numerous Canadian teams at Open, Women's and Junior levels. He has also represented Canada in five World Championships. North American titles include the 1991 Master Mixed Teams. Won the Canadian National Teams Championship twice. Won the Canadian Open Pairs Championship in 1990.

CASEY, Jill of Newport, Wales. (b.1948). Teacher. Represented Britain in one Venice Cup and three EC Championships. She has represented Wales in both the Open Camrose series as well as numerous appearances in the Women's equivalent, the Lady Milne, including one victory.

CHAGAS, Gabriel P of Rio de Janeiro, Brazil. (b.1944). Financier and investment consultant. WBF Grand Master and #6 in the world rankings in 1999. Won the 1976 World Teams Olympiad, the 1989 Bermuda Bowl, and the 1990 World Open Pairs. He is one of only eight players to have won the Triple Crown (World Teams, World Pairs and Bermuda Bowl). Winner of the IOC in Lausanne in 1998. He has represented Brazil in 34 other World Championships, a record. Won the South American Teams a record 22 times in 28 attempts during the period 1967–98. Won 28 national titles, and is the top-ranked South American player. North American national titles include the Reisinger in 1992. Won the *Sunday Times* Invitational Pairs twice, and the Cap Gemini twice. Magazine contributor. Created the term intra-finesse.

CHAMBERS, Juanita of Schenectady New York, USA. WBF World Grand Master and #7 in the 1999 world rankings. Won the Venice Cup in 1987, the World Mixed Pairs in 1990, and the Pan-American Women's Pairs in 1992. Many national titles.

CHEMLA, Paul of Paris, France. (b.1944 in Tunis). Bridge professional. WBF Grand Master and #12 in the world rankings in 1999. Won the 1997 Bermuda Bowl. Won the World Teams Olympiad twice, and finished 2nd in 1984. Won the 1998 Generali World Individual. Won the European Pairs three times. Won the European Mixed Teams and finished 2nd in the European Mixed Pairs in 1998. 2nd in the European Seniors Teams in 1999. Won the *Sunday Times* Invitational Pairs in 1991. Was named IBPA's "Bridge Personality of the Year" in 1998. Numerous French national titles.

CHUA, Cathy of Sydney, Australia. (b.1959). Historian. Won the Far East Women's Teams in 1990. Also won the South Pacific Junior Teams and Pairs. National titles include the Open Teams and the Grand National Teams

CHIARADIA, Eugenio of Naples, Italy. (b.1917; d.1977). Professor of Philosophy. (aka The Professor). Won the Bermuda Bowl six times. Won the European Teams five times. National titles include the Italian Open Teams five times. He was instrumental in the development of The Neapolitan Club system. After retirement, he lived in Brazil, where he coached the national team.

CINTRA, Gabino of Rio de Janeiro, Brazil. (b.1942). WBF Grand Master and #35 in thc world rankings in 1999. Won the World Pairs in 1978. Won the World Team Olympiad in 1976. Represented Brazil in 14 World Championships. Won the South American Teams nine times. National titles include the Brazilian Open Teams seven times.

CINTRA, Lia of Rio de Janeiro, Brazil. Won the South American Women's Teams eight times. Represented Brazil in three World Championships.

COHEN, Larry N of Boca Raton, Florida, USA. (b.1959). Bridge professional and writer. Former options trader. He is *not* the Larry Cohen involved in the Houston Affair cheating scandal in 1977. 2nd in the 1998 World Pairs. Semi-finalist in the 1993 Bermuda Bowl. Won the Cavendish Invitational Pairs twice. Won the Cap Gemini Invitational Pairs in 1999. Many national titles including the Blue Ribbon Pairs a record four times. He is the author of *To Bid or Not to Bid*, winner of the ABTA Book of the Year award and the world's best-selling bridge book in 1992-93. He is also a regular conductor of *The Bridge World*'s "Master Solver's Club".

COHEN, Nadine of France. Won the European Women's Pairs in 1999. Won the European Seniors Pairs in 1997. 3rd in the European Seniors Teams in 1999. Numerous French national titles.

COHEN, Stasha of Glen Ridge New Jersey, USA. (b.1945). Civil trial attorney. Won the Venice Cup in 1990. Many national titles.

COLLINGS, John D R of Surrey, England. (b.1933). Retired banker. British Life Master #46 and Grand Master #15. Represented Great Britain in one Bermuda Bowl. 2nd in the 1981 European Teams. Won the *Sunday Times* Invitational Pairs in 1969, finished 2nd in 1971, and 3rd in 1970. In 1965, he won both the Pairs and the Teams at the Juan-les-Pins tournament in France. He won the first English Life Masters Pairs in 1966. Many other national titles.

CORN, Ira Jr of Dallas, Texas, USA. (b.1921; d.1982). Businessman, writer and historian. Organizer, financier and captain of the Dallas Aces team. In 1970, he led the first American team to win a World Championship since 1954. His team repeated in 1971, and again in 1983, shortly after his death. National titles include the Vanderbilt in 1973, the Men's Pairs in 1963 and the 1968 Men's Teams.

COTTER, E Patrick C of London, England. (b.1904). Bridge columnist and schoolteacher. 2nd in the European Teams in 1938. National wins include the Gold Cup twice, Crockfords in 1951 and the 1953 Hubert Phillips Bowl.

COYLE, Willie of Renfrew, Scotland. (b.1937) School teacher. 3rd in the World Teams Olympiad in 1976. Represented Scotland in 14 Camrose matches. National titles include the Gold Cup five times and the Scottish Open Teams twice.

CRANE, Barry (originally Barry Cohen) of Studio City, California, USA. (b.1927 in Detroit, MI; d.July 5, 1985). Television producer and director. Considered by many to be the top matchpoint player of all time. He became the ACBL's top lifetime masterpoint holder in 1968, and held that position until 1991, six years after his untimely death (he was the victim of a brutal murder that has never been solved). Won the World Mixed Pairs in 1978. Many national titles. He also won the McKenney Trophy (awarded for gaining most masterpoints in a calendar year) a record six times and finished 2nd a further six times. In recognition of his domination of the event, it was renamed the Barry Crane Top 500 after his death. He was honoured with the IBPA's Charles Goren Award as the "Bridge Personality of the Year" in 1984.

CRAWFORD, John R of New York City, New York, USA. (b.1915; d.1976). Bridge teacher and writer. ACBL Life Master #19. Won the first three Bermuda Bowls, and also represented the US in the 1958 Bowl and the first World Team Olympiad in 1960. He won the first of his record 37 national titles at the age of 22. His ten victories in the Chicago (renamed the Reisinger in 1965) still stand as a record. In 1957, he achieved a unique grand slam of the major tournaments, winning the Chicago, the Vanderbilt, the Spingold, as well as the Men's and Mixed Teams. Many other national titles.

CRONIER, Benedicte of Paris, France. (b.1961). Bridge professional and teacher. Won the European Junior Teams in 1984. 2nd in the Venice Cup in 1987. Won the European Women's Teams twice. She plays in the French Open Premier League.

CRONIER, Philippe of Paris, France. (b.1953). Bridge teacher and writer. Finished 3rd in the Bermuda Bowl and won the European Teams, both in 1983. 2nd in the 1987 European Pairs.

CROUCH, Peter J of London, England. (b.1960). Won the EC Junior Teams in 1985. National titles include the Gold Cup twice.

CROWHURST, Eric W of Reading, England. (b.1935). Accountant and bridge writer. British Life Master #83 and Grand Master #13. He contributed the section on "Suit Combinations" to the ACBL *Bridge Encyclopedia*. He was the inventor of the Crowhurst Convention that is popular in the UK for use over a wide-range 1NT rebid. His books on British bidding include *Acol in Competition* and *Precision Bidding in Acol*. National titles include the Gold Cup in 1971 and the Spring Fours twice.

CULBERTSON, Ely of New York City, New York, USA. (b.July 22, 1891 in Rumania; d.Dec 27, 1955 in Brattleboro, Vermont). America's earliest authority on contract bridge, Culbertson is credited with making the game an internationally popular pastime. A scholar in many fields, he was a skilled linguist, conversing fluently in Russian, English, French, German, Czech, Spanish and Italian, and capable of reading Slavic, Polish, Swedish and Danish-Norwegian, as well as classical Latin and Greek.

After the 1917 Russian Revolution wiped out his family's fortune, Culbertson exploited his skill as a card player throughout Europe. In 1921, he returned to the US almost penniless, and continued earning a living from card games. In 1923, having acquired some reputation as a bridge player, he married Mrs Josephine Murphy Dillon, a respected bridge teacher in New York City. Together they became a successful pair as tournament players and bridge authorities.

As contract began replacing auction bridge in the late 1920s, Culbertson planned a campaign that included the construction of a bidding system, the publication of a magazine, the authorship of a textbook, and the organization of professional bridge teachers. The first step was the founding of his magazine, *The Bridge World*, in 1929, and the publication of the first of his bridge books, all of which were best sellers.

Through his growing business empire, he maintained an organization of bridge teachers, which at its peak had 6,000 members, and he ran bridge competitions under the banners of the United States Bridge Association, the World Bridge Olympics, and the American Bridge Olympics. In its best year, 1937, The Bridge World Inc grossed in excess of $1 million, of which $220,000 were royalties payable to Culbertson before profits were calculated.

In 1930, Culbertson won the Vanderbilt, the American Bridge League Knock-Out and BAM Team events, and finished second in the Master Pairs. He also led a team that played the first international match, in England, and defeated several teams there.

The success of Culbertson's *Blue Book* in 1930 caused the auction bridge authorities to join together to combat his domination of contract bridge. Culbertson countered by challenging the leading player amongst his opposition, Sidney Lenz, to a match, offering 5-1 odds. Culbertson's victory in this match, played in 1931-32, fortified his position. Thanks to the publicity accorded the match, Culbertson and his wife each acquired contracts for syndicated newspaper columns. He also made a series of movie shorts, and received $10,000 a week for radio broadcasts.

After 1934, Culbertson played little tournament bridge, but he continued to play high-stake rubber bridge until about two years before his death.

His contributions to contract bridge, both practical and theoretical, were basic and timeless. He devised the markings on duplicate boards for vulnerability, and the bonuses for games and part scores. He was the first authority to treat distribution as equal or superior to high cards in formulating the requirements for bids. Forcing bids, including the one-over-one, were original Culbertson concepts, as were four-card suit bids, limited no-trump bids, the strong Two-bid, and the ace-showing 4NT slam try named after him. These were all presented in the historic lesson sheets on the Approach-Forcing system published in 1927, and in numerous magazine articles.

In 1938, with war imminent in Europe, Culbertson lost interest in bridge and devoted his time to political science. After the formation of the United Nations, to which Culbertson's ideas made a discernible contribution, he persisted in a campaign to give it adequate power. His principal works on political science were *Total Peace*, 1943, and *Must We Fight Russia?* in 1947.

As a result of these activities, Culbertson lost his position as the leading bridge authority. By 1950, Charles Goren had surpassed him in the sale of books and in the adherence of bridge teachers and players. However, when a Bridge Hall of Fame was inaugurated in 1964, nine years after his death, Culbertson was the first person elected. Although he never became an ACBL Life Master, he was named an Honorary Member in 1938.

CULBERTSON, Josephine M (née Dillon) of New York City, New York, USA. (b.Feb 2, 1898 in Bayside, New York; d.Mar. 23, 1956). Bridge teacher, player and writer. The first woman who was acknowledged to play a high-level championship standard. Won the Schwab Cup twice. She was a member of the teams that won the first internationals against England and France, as well as the victorious team in the Culbertson-Lenz Match. Won the ABL Open Teams and the Vanderbilt in 1930. She finished 2nd in the first Life Masters Pairs (in 1930) and the first North American Open Pairs in 1928. 2nd in the 1935 Reisinger. She also authored numerous books and wrote a regular column in *The Bridge World*, which she continued to co-own even after her divorce.

CUMMINGS, Richard John "Dick" of Sydney, Australia. (b.1932). Bridge writer and teacher. One of Australia's greatest players, he had a long and successful partnership with Tim Seres. 3rd in the Bermuda Bowl in 1971 & 79, he also represented Australia many other times. He has won more than 20 Australian national titles. The bridge columnist for the *Sydney Morning Herald* and the *Sydney Sun-Herald*, Cummings also edits the *World Bridge Federation News*. Won a BOLS Brilliancy Prize as a player in 1980.

D'ALELIO, Massimo "Mimmo" of Rome, Italy. (b.1916). Lawyer. WBF Grand Master. Won the World Teams Olympiad three times and the Bermuda Bowl ten times. Won the European Teams three times. Italian national titles include the Open Teams six times.

D'ANDREA, Marisa of Naples, Italy. WBF Grand Master and #30 in the world women's rankings in 1999. Won the World Women's Teams in 1976 and finished 2nd in 1978. Won the European Women's Teams twice.

D'OVIDIO, Catherine (née Saul) of Paris, France. (b.1959). Bridge club manager. 2nd in the World Women's Pairs in 1994, and 3rd in 1998. Won the European Women's Teams twice. Won the

European Mixed Pairs in 1993. Won the EC Women's Pairs in 1993.

DAMIANI, José of Paris, France. (b.1939). Industrialist. President of the World Bridge Federation since 1994. President of the European Bridge League 1987-94. He was responsible for originating the Philip Morris Mixed Team and Pairs, Generali European Teams Championships and World Individual Championship (Generali Masters). President of the French Bridge Federation 1978-83. 3rd in the European Mixed Pairs in 1998. 2nd in the European Seniors Teams in 1999. Non-playing captain of the French World Champion team in 1992. Numerous French national titles. He was honoured with the IBPA's Charles Goren Award as the "Bridge Personality of the Year" in 1985.

DARVAS, Robert of Budapest, Hungary. (b.1906; d.1957). Bridge journalist. Wrote or collaborated on numerous books including the bridge fairy tale classic co-written with Norman de V Hart, *Right Through the Pack*.

DAVIES, Patricia "Pat" of Bath, England. (b.1947). University lecturer. WBF Grand Master and #15 in the world women's rankings in 1999. Won the Venice Cup twice. 2nd in the World Women's Team Olympiad three times. Won the European Women's Teams three times. Won the EC Women's Teams twice. National titles include the Spring Fours, the Pachabo and the Gold Cup.

DE BOER, Wubbo of Amsterdam, The Netherlands. (b.1963). Computer systems manager. Won the 1993 Bermuda Bowl. 3rd in the 1992 World Team Olympiad. Won the European Junior Teams in 1986, and the World Junior Teams in 1987. Won the 1998 Cavendish Teams. Several national titles.

DE FALCO, Soldano "Dano" of Padua, Italy. Won the 1974 Bermuda Bowl. Won the 1997 World Transnational Teams. Won the European Teams three times. Won the EC Teams twice. Represented Italy on many other occasions.

DE V HART, Norman of London, England. (b.1888). Bridge writer. Systems pioneer who was partially responsible for control-showing responses to Strong Two Club openings (CAB). He wrote or collaborated on numerous books including the bridge fairy-tale classic co-written with Robert Darvas, *Right Through the Pack*.

DEAS, Lynn of Newport News, Virginia, USA. (b.1953). Professional bridge player and teacher. Coin collector and dog lover. WBF Grand Master and #3 in the 1999 world women's ranking. Won the Venice Cup three times. 2nd in the World Women's Pairs in 1982, 3rd in 1994, and 4th in 1990. 3rd in the 1992 Pan-American Women's Teams. Many national titles.

DELMOULY, Claude of Paris, France. (b.1927). Bridge teacher and writer. WBF Grand Master and #30 in the world rankings in 1999. Won the World Team Olympiad in 1960, and also represented France in the 1968 & 72 Olympiad and in three European Championships. Won the European Seniors Teams in 1999. Won the 1968 *Sunday Times* Invitational Pairs. Won the British Masters Pairs in 1960. National wins include the French Open Pairs in 1959 and the French Open Teams twice. Author of six books and a regular contributor to various bridge periodicals.

DEUTSCH, Seymon of Laredo, Texas, USA. (b.1935). Rancher and merchant. WBF Grand Master and #25 in the world rankings in 1999. Won the 1988 World Team Olympiad. Several national titles.

DHONDY, Heather of London, England. Quarter-finalist in the 1997 Venice Cup. Won the World Mixed Teams in 1996. Won the European Women's Teams twice (1997 & 99). Represented England in the Lady Milne Trophy. National titles include the Pachabo twice.

DIXON, Chris of Somerset, England. (b.1944). Computer consultant. 2nd in the 1971 European Teams. Represented Great Britain in one World Championship and England in numerous Camrose Trophy matches. National titles include the Gold Cup three times.

DODDS, Leslie W of London, England. (b.1903; d.1975). Import/export merchant. Won the Bermuda Bowl in 1955. Won the European Teams four times. Represented Great Britain in seven European Championships. Many national titles. One of the originators of the CAB system. He was named as an Honorary EBU Member in 1956.

DORMER, Albert G of London, England. (b.1925). Bridge journalist and retired surveyor. British Life Master #36. Won the first World Senior Pairs in 1990. National titles include the Gold Cup twice. He was the Editor of *The British Bridge World* 1962–64, associate editor of the ACBL Bulletin 1965, Editor of the *IBPA Bulletin* 1972–82, and Editor of *World Bridge News* 1971–87. He was honoured with the IBPA's Charles Goren Award as "Bridge Personality of the Year" in 1981. Author of ten books including *The Complete Book of Bridge*, co-written with Terence Reese.

DUBOIN, Giorgio of Turin, Italy. (b.1959). Computer programmer and bridge teacher. Won the European Teams twice. 2nd in the European Pairs in 1999. Won the European Junior Pairs in 1980. 2nd in the 1984 European Junior Teams. Won the EC Pairs in 1985, and the Teams in 1985 & 87. Won the Schiphol International Teams in The Netherlands in 1992. Numerous national titles.

DURRAN, Joan of Welwyn Garden City, England. Won the World Women's Pairs in 1966. 2nd in the 1966 World Mixed Pairs. Won the European Women's Teams twice. Represented Britain in four World and five European Championships. Represented England in the Lady Milne Trophy several times. Numerous national titles. Placed 2nd in the 1966 Life Masters Pairs playing with Jane Juan (later Priday), the highest position achieved by a women's pair in the event.

EISENBERG, William "Billy" of Boca Raton, Florida, USA. (b.1937). Bridge professional, teacher, coach and Vu-Graph commentator. Former professional backgammon player. WBF Grand Master and #37 in the 1999 world rankings. Won the Bermuda Bowl five times (with four different partners). Won the Staten Bank Invitational Pairs (now the Cap Gemini) in 1991. Numerous national titles. He won the World Backgammon Championships in 1974.

EKEBLAD, Russell A of Providence, Rhode Island, USA. (b.1946). Co-owner (with wife Sheila) of a jewellery distributing firm. 3rd in the 1990 Rosenblum Teams . Won the 1998 World IMP Pairs. Won the Canadian Invitational Pairs Calcutta in 1990, and placed second in 1991. National titles include the Spingold in 1992 and the 1993 Vanderbilt.

ELLENBY, Milton Q of Skokie, Illinois, USA. (b.1923). Actuary and physicist. Worked on the Manhattan Project. Won the 1954 Bermuda Bowl. National titles include the Spingold twice and the Life Masters Pairs.

ERDOS, Ivan of Los Angeles, California, USA. (b.1924 in Budapest, Rumania; d.1967). Formerly of London, England. Won the 1966 World Mixed Pairs. Represented North America in the 1965 Bermuda Bowl. National titles include the 1959 Men's Teams and the Men's Pairs in 1962. A regular contributor to numerous American bridge magazines.

ERHART, Maria of Rattenberg, Austria. (b.1944). WBF World Grand Master and #20 in the 1999 world women's ranking. Won the

World Women's Teams (the McConnell Cup) in 1998. Won the 1992 World Women's Team Olympiad. Finalist in the 1991 Venice Cup. Won the European Women's Individual in 1992 and the Generali World Women's Individual in 1996. Won the European Women's Teams in 1991. Won the European Mixed Pairs in 1996. She also represented Austria in numerous European Open Championships. Many national and European titles include the St Moritz teams and pairs.

EWEN, Robert B "Bob" of Miami, Florida, USA. (b.1940). The creator of Two-Way Game Tries. A regular contributor to the *ACBL Bulletin* and other publications. His books include *Doubles for Takeout, Penalties and Profit* and *Opening Leads*.

FALLENIUS, Björn of Malmo, Sweden. (b.1957). Twice finished 3rd in the Bermuda Bowl. 3rd in the Rosenblum Teams in 1998. Won the 1987 European Teams, and 2nd in 1999. Numerous Swedish national titles. Several North American national wins.

FARELL, Mary-Jane of Los Angeles, California, USA. Bridge teacher. WBF World Grand Master and #34 in the 1999 world women's ranking. She was named *Los Angeles Times* "Woman of the Year" in recognition of her achievement in overtaking Helen Sobel as the ACBL's leading woman masterpoint winner of all time. Won the 1978 Venice Cup and the World Women's Team Olympiad in 1980. Won the World Women's Pairs in 1970 and the World Mixed Pairs in 1976. Many national titles.

FERRO, Jeff of San Francisco, California, USA. (b.1968). ACBL Life Master at the age of 15. Won the 1991 World Junior Teams. Quarter-finalist in the 1991 Bermuda Bowl. National titles include the 1993 Grand National Teams and the 1991 Junior Pairs.

FISCHER, Doris of Vienna, Austria. (b.1959). WBF World Grand Master and #17 in the 1999 world women's ranking. Won the World Women's Teams (the McConnell Cup) in 1998. Won the 1992 World Women's Team Olympiad. Finalist in the 1991 Venice Cup. Won the European Women's Teams in 1991. Numerous national titles.

FISHBEIN, Harold J of New York City, New York, USA. (b.1898; d.1976) President of the Mayfair Club. Inventor of the Fishbein defence to pre-empts. ACBL Life Master #15. Represented the US in the 1959 Bermuda Bowl and was npc of the North American team at the 1960 Olympiad. Seventeen national titles.

FLINT, M Jeremy of London, England. (b.1928; d.1990). Bridge writer. British Life Master #14 and Grand Master #8. Losing finalist in the 1960 Olympiad and the 1987 Bermuda Bowl. Won the European Teams in 1963. Represented Great Britain in seven other World and five other European Championships. Won the Far East Open Pairs in 1973. In 1966, whilst on tour in the US, he set a new record of 11 weeks for achieving Life Master status, and he also finished 2nd in the McKenney race that year. Co-inventor of the Multi Two Diamonds and of the Little Major system, and responsible for the convention bearing his name that was popular in Britain in the 1970s. Bridge columnist for the London *Times* 1980-90, he was also responsible for numerous televised bridge programmes in the UK. Many national titles.

FLODQVIST, Sven-Olov "Tjolpe" of Stockholm, Sweden. Computer analyst. 3rd in two Bermuda Bowls and one World Team Olympiad. Won the European Championship 1977 & 87. He has represented Sweden in five other World and six other European Championships. Won the *Sunday Times* Invitational Pairs twice. He also wrote the definitive book on the Carrot Club system. National titles include the Swedish Open Teams six times. In 1984, he shared (with Anders Morath) the IBPA's C C Wei Award for the year's best article on the topic of bidding.

FONSECA, Christiano of Rio de Janeiro, Brazil. (b.1940), Financial executive. WBF World Grand Master and #40 in the 1999 world ranking. Won the 1976 World Teams Olympiad and represented Brazil in four other World Championships. Won the South American Teams six times. National titles include the Open Teams six times.

FORQUET, Pietro of Naples, Italy. (b.1925). Retired banker. WBF World Grand Master and #44 in the 1999 world ranking. Winner of 15 World Championships – the Bermuda Bowl twelve times and the World Team Olympiad three times. Won the European Championship five times. Numerous national titles include the Italian Open Teams five times. He is the author of *Bridge with the Blue Team*.

FORRESTER, Anthony R "Tony" of Yorkshire, England. (b.1953). Chartered accountant and bridge professional. British Grand Master #41. He is the current bridge columnist for the *Daily Telegraph*. 2nd in the 1987 Bermuda Bowl. Won the European Teams in 1991. Won the 1978 European Junior Teams.

Won the EC Open Teams twice (1981 & 83). Represented Britain in five other World and three other European Championships. His 41 appearances for England in the Camrose Trophy is a record. Won the *Sunday Times* Invitational Pairs in 1990, and the Cap Gemini Invitational Pairs in 1990 & 98. After a string of near misses he collected his first North American national title in 1998, winning both the Reisinger and the Open Pairs. Many British national titles.

FOX, G C H of Hove, England. (b.1914; d.1999). Bridge writer and teacher. British Life Master #79 and Grand Master #37. Bridge columnist for the *Daily Telegraph* 1957-93. Represented England in one Camrose Trophy match. National titles include the Pachabo twice.

FRANCO, Arturo of Milan, Italy. (b.1946). WBF World Grand Master and #33 in the 1999 world ranking. Won the Bermuda Bowl twice and lost in three finals. Won the European Teams three times. Numerous national titles.

FREDIN, Peter of Stockholm, Sweden. (b.1970). 3rd in the World Pairs and the Rosenblum Teams in 1998. 3rd in the 1997 European Pairs and a finalist in 1999. 2nd in the European Teams in 1999. Won the 1996 Nordic Teams, and previously won the Nordic Junior Teams. National titles include the Junior Teams.

FREEMAN Richard A "Dick" of Atlanta, Georgia, USA. (b.1933). Senior executive. Became the ACBL's youngest Life Master at the age of 18 in 1952. Won the Bermuda Bowl in 1995. Many national titles.

FREY, Richard L of New York City, New York, USA. (b.1905; d.1988). Editor of the *ACBL Bulletin* 1958-70, and earlier of *The Bridge World*. Also co-edited the first three editions of The ACBL's *Official Encyclopedia of Bridge* and 12 World Championship books. President of IBPA 1970-81. ACBL Life Master #8. He was one of the Four Aces team (with Burnstine, Jacoby and Schenken). Numerous national titles.

FRY, Sam Jr of New York City, New York, USA. (b.1909; d.1991). Secretary of the Regency Whist Club. Contributing Editor of *The Bridge World* 1932-66. ACBL Life Master #10 and was the youngest (at 26). Represented North America in the 1959 Bermuda Bowl. Many national titles.

FUCIK, Jan of Vienna, Austria. (b.1956 in Czechoslovakia). Austria's leading masterpoint winner. Finalist in the 1985 Bermuda

Bowl and the 1988 World Team Olympiad. Won the European Teams in 1985 and the European Junior Teams in 1976. 2nd in the 1985 European Pairs and the 1992 European Individual. Won the Statenbank Invitational Pairs twice. National titles include the Austrian Open Teams nine times.

GARDENER, Nico of London, England. (Originally Nico Goldfinger). (b.1908 in Latvia; d.1989). Bridge teacher and writer. Founder and proprietor of the London School of Bridge. He was the inventor of the Gardener No-Trump Overcall. Won the World Mixed Teams in 1962. 2nd in the 1960 World Team Olympiad. Won the European Teams twice, 2nd in 1953. Represented Great Britain in two other World and two other European Championships. Won the *Sunday Times* Invitational Pairs in 1970. Many national titles.

GAROZZO, Benito of Palm Beach, Florida, USA. (b.1927). Formerly of Rome, Italy. Retired jeweller. Considered by many as the best player in the world during the Italian domination of world bridge. His partnership with Pietro Forquet is acknowledged as one of the all-time greats. WBF World Grand Master and #29 in the 1999 world rankings. Won the Bermuda Bowl ten times and finished 2nd three times. Won the World Team Olympiad three times. Won the PAMP World Individual in 1990. Finished 2nd in the 1970 World Pairs, and was 4th in 1966. 2nd in the 1998 World Seniors Pairs. Won the European Teams five times. Many Italian and North American national titles. He was the co-creator (with Belladonna) of Super Precision, and he co-wrote (with Leon Yallouze) the definitive book on the Blue Club system. He has twice (1974 & 79) won the IBPA's Charles J Solomon Award for the year's best-played hand.

GAWRYS, Piotr of Warsaw, Poland. (b.1955). Architect. WBF World Grand Master and #17 in the 1999 world rankings. Won the World Team Olympiad in 1984. Finished 2nd in the 1991 Bermuda Bowl and the 1996 Rosenblum Teams. Won the 1995 European Pairs, the 1994 European Cup, and the 1992 European Individual. Won the Cavendish Invitational Pairs in 1990. Numerous Polish national titles.

GERBER, John of Houston, Texas, USA. (b.1906; d.1981). Best known as the inventor of the Gerber ace-asking convention. 2nd in the 1961 Bermuda Bowl. He was npc of several North American Bermuda Bowl teams. National titles include the 1964 Chicago (now the Reisinger), the 1953 Men's Teams, the Men's Pairs in 1959 and the Master Mixed Teams in 1964.

GHESTEM, Pierre of Lille, France. (b.1929). WBF World Grand Master and #42 in the 1999 world rankings. Best known as the inventor of Ghestem two-suited overcalls. He also developed the complex Monaco Relay System that he played in World Championships with René Bacherich. Won the Bermuda Bowl in 1956 and the World Team Olympiad in 1960. Represented France in five World Championships. Finished 3rd in the 1990 PAMP Pairs. Won the European Teams three times, and finished 2nd twice. Numerous national titles. He is also a former World checkers champion and French chess champion.

GITELMAN, Fred A of Toronto, Canada. (b.1965). Computer programmer specializing in bridge software. Creator of the Internet's *Bridgeplaza* and the *Bridge Base* hand-generation software. 2nd in the 1995 Bermuda Bowl. 2nd in the World Junior Teams in 1991. 3rd in the Cavendish Invitational Pairs in 1998. National titles include the Canadian National Teams in 1994 and the National Swiss Teams twice. North American national titles include the 1998 Open BAM Teams.

GLUBOK, Brian of Florida, USA. (b.1959). Formerly of New York City. Rubber bridge professional and novelist. Became a Life Master at 15 and reached the final of the Reisinger partnering Oswald Jacoby at the age of 17. 4th in the 1990 World Pairs. Won a gold medal at the 1983 Maccabean Games. National titles include the 1987 Spingold, the Reisinger in 1991, and the Open Swiss Teams three times. Won the Australian Open Teams in 1990. Won the IBPA Romex Award in 1991.

GOLDBERG, Victor of Glasgow, Scotland. (b.1923). Company director. Represented Scotland in the Camrose Trophy numerous times including the rare Scottish victories of 1964 & 65. National titles include the Gold Cup four times and the English Spring Fours in 1979.

GOLDMAN, Robert "Bobby" of Highland Village, Texas, USA. (b.1938; d.1999). WBF World Grand Master and #32 in the world rankings at the time of his death. Television company vice-president and bridge professional. An original member of the Dallas Aces team, he wrote the definitive book on their bidding methods – *Aces Scientific*. He was also responsible for numerous bidding innovations including Exclusion Blackwood and

Kickback/Super Gerber. Won the Bermuda Bowl three times. Won the World Mixed Teams in 1972. Won the Pairs and the Teams at the 1977 Pan-American Championships. Numerous national titles.

GORDON, Dianna M of Toronto, Canada. (b.1944). Travel agent. Won the World Mixed Pairs in 1982. 3rd in the 1989 Venice Cup. 4th in the World Women's Team Olympiad in 1976. 6th in the World Women's Pairs in 1986. North American national titles include the Women's Swiss in 1985.

GORDON, Fritzi of London, England. (b.1916; d.1992). British Life Master #3 and the first woman Life Master. Her partnership with Rixi Markus is acknowledged as one of the best women's pairs of all time. Won the World Women's Pairs twice. Won the World Women's Team Olympiad in 1964. Won the World Mixed Teams in 1962. Won the European Women's Teams eight times – only Gordon and Markus (who has nine victories) have won this event more than five times. Represented England numerous times in the Lady Milne Trophy. Many national titles including the British Gold Cup twice.

GORDON, Irving P "Haggis" of London, England. Won the World Seniors Pairs in 1998. National titles include the Spring Fours twice and the British Gold Cup twice.

GOREN, Charles H of New York City, New York, USA. (b.1901; d.1991) Lawyer. ACBL Life Master #13. Goren was the world's foremost bridge authority during the middle part of the 20th century. Known to millions as Mr Bridge, they brought his books, attended his lectures, took lessons from his accredited teachers, "travelled with Goren" on bridge cruises, and read his columns. He won his first major events in 1933 – the US Bridge Association and the American Bridge League's Open Teams. In 1936, he published his first book, *Winning Bridge Made Easy*. The *Chicago Tribune* and the *New York Daily News* replaced Culbertson's syndicated columns with Goren's. As a player, he won the McKenney Trophy for accruing the most masterpoints in a calendar year eight times, a record that still stands. Soon he became the ACBL's #1 all-time masterpoint winner, a position he held from 1944–62. His Point-Count Bidding methods revolutionized bidding to the extent that "Goren" became the basis for Standard American, and Culbertson's honour-trick valuation died overnight. It is estimated that Goren books have sold more than 10 million copies. His television show, *Championship Bridge* *with Charles Goren*, ran from 1959–64. It was the first successful bridge programme on television and won an award as one of the best new television features.

Goren became a World Champion in Bermuda, in 1950, when the first Bermuda Bowl was held. He later finished 2nd twice in the Bermuda Bowl.

Goren won the equivalent of 34 North American national titles and finished 2nd in a further 21. Before retiring from active competition in 1966, he won virtually every major tournament bridge trophy in the US. He became an ACBL Honorary Member in 1959 and was one of the first three players elected to the Bridge Hall of Fame in 1963.

In 1973, he was awarded the IBPA's C C Wei Award for the year's best article on the topic of bidding.

GÖTHE, Hans G of Spånga, Sweden. (b.1937). Computer expert. 3rd in the 1987 Bermuda Bowl and the 1988 World Team Olympiad. Won the European Teams twice and finished 3rd in 1989. Won the Nordic Teams three times. Numerous Swedish national titles.

GOWDY, Bruce D of Toronto, Canada. (b.1930). Accountant. 3rd in the 1972 World Team Olympiad. At the age of 19, he won the 1949 Spingold, and became the youngest ever player to win a major North American knockout team events, a record that still stands today. National titles include the Canadian National Open Teams five times.

GRANOVETTER, Matthew of Netanya, Israel. (b.1950). Formerly of Ballston Lake, New York. Bridge writer/publisher. He has also written two children's musicals and several books including *Murder at the Bridge Table*, *I Shot My Bridge Partner*, and *The Bridge Team Murders*. Together with his wife, Pam, he is the co-editor of *Bridge Today* magazine. He was a member of the New York team that defeated the Lancia Team in 1975. In 1981, he appeared in *Grand Slam*, a challenge match televized by the BBC. 2nd in the 1974 World Mixed Teams. Won the Cavendish Invitational Pairs and the Cavendish Teams in 1993. Won the New Orleans Money Tournament and the *Bridge Today* All-Star Game, both in 1982. North American national titles include the Open Pairs in 1972 and the Men's Teams twice (1975 & 82). Israeli national titles include the Open Pairs, Mixed Pairs and Open Teams, all in 1993.

GRANOVETTER, Pam of Netanya, Israel. (b.1953). Formerly of Ballston Lake, New York. Bridge writer/publisher. Together with her husband, Matt, she is the co-editor of *Bridge Today* magazine. She has played in three World Championship events, once representing the US and twice under the Canadian flag. Won the Cavendish Teams in 1993. Won the New Orleans Money Tournament in 1982. Israeli national titles include the Mixed Pairs and Open Teams, both in 1993.

GRANT, Audrey of Toronto, Canada. (b.1940). Bridge teacher and writer and she is the educational consultant for the ACBL. She wrote the official ACBL teaching series. She is the author or co-author of numerous other teaching books. She also produced numerous ACBL television teaching series including *The Bridge Class*, *Play Bridge with Audrey Grant I* and *II*.

GRECO, Eric A of Annandale, Virginia, USA. (b.1975). Became a Life Master aged 15. Former ACBL King of Bridge. He won the ACBL Youth Player of the Year title (for players under 20) five years in a row. North American national titles include the Life Masters Pairs in 1998 and the Open Pairs I in 1997.

GREENBERG, Gail H of New York City, New York, USA. (b.1938). Bridge teacher and professional. WBF World Grand Master and #9 in the 1999 world rankings. Won the Venice Cup twice. Won the World Women's Team Olympiad twice. 2nd in the 1972 World Mixed Teams. 4th in the 1974 World Mixed Pairs. 4th in the 1998 World Women's Pairs. Won the first Pan-American Women's Teams in 1992. Many national titles. Greenberg has been married to three top-level bridge players including World Champion Mike Moss. Her son Brad Moss and daughter Jillian Blanchard are also top-class players.

GROETHEIM, Glen of Trondheim, Norway. (b.1959). 2nd in the 1993 Bermuda Bowl, and 3rd in 1997. Finished 3rd in the European Teams three times. Won the Schiphol International Teams in 1993. Numerous national titles.

GU, Ling of Guangzhao, China. (b.1959). 2nd in the Venice Cup in 1997, 3rd in 1991. Won the Far East Women's Teams twice. Numerous national titles.

GUDGE, Anna of Suffolk, England. (b.1946). Secretary of the British Bridge League since 1986. National titles include the 1986 Women's Teams.

GULLBERG, S Tommy of Solna, Sweden. (b.1943). 3rd in the 1988 World Team Olympiad. Twice 3rd in the Bermuda Bowl. Won the European Teams in 1987. Won the European Junior Teams in 1968. Won the Nordic Teams twice. Bridge columnist and the author of two teaching books. Numerous national titles.

HACKETT, Jason P of Manchester, England. (b.1970). Jason is the elder of the two twins by ten minutes. British Grand Master #187. At 25 he became the youngest ever to achieve that rank, and the only one to do so while still a junior. Playing with his brother, Justin, Jason won the *Daily Mail* Schools Cup in 1988 and in 1990 won the first of five Junior Camrose Trophy victories representing England. Won the European Junior Teams and reached the final of the World Open Pairs in 1994, and then won the World Junior Teams in 1995. They made their debut for the British Open team at the 1996 World Team Olympiad, establishing another record at that time as father, Paul, was also on that team. They have a host of international successes including the Tunisian Open Teams in 1992 & 93, the Estoril Pairs and Teams in Portugal in 1994, the Schiphol International Teams, the Singapore National Open Pairs and Teams, and the Djarum Cup in Indonesia in 1995. They repeated their Indonesian victory, added the Trinidad National Pairs, and finished 2nd in two North American Nationals (the Open Swiss and the BAM Teams) in 1996. In 1997 they won the Argentine National Teams and reached the final of the Reisinger. In 1998, they reached the quarter-final of the Rosenblum Teams, finished 15th in the World Pairs, and won the NEC Cup in Japan and the Chilean Invitational. Many national titles.

HACKETT, Justin T of Manchester, England. (b.1970). British Grand Master #216. Justin's record is virtually the same as Jason's. He also won the British Life Masters Pairs in 1994.

HACKETT, Paul D of Manchester, England. (b.1941). British Grand Master #137. 2nd in the 1981 European Teams, the EC Pairs in 1981 and the 1995 European Pairs. Has represented Great Britain in three World Championships. Numerous national and international victories, including many of those listed above for Jason.

HAMILTON, Fred of Encino, California, USA. (b.1936). Bridge teacher and professional. WBF World Grand Master and #31 in the 1999 world rankings. Won the 1976 Bermuda Bowl, 2nd in 1977. Won the World Seniors Pairs in 1996. 2nd in the 1980 World Team Olympiad. 4th in the 1982 Rosenblum Teams. Many national titles.

HAMMAN, Robert D "Bob" of Dallas, Texas, USA. (b.1938). Formerly of Van Nuys, CA. Company president and professional bridge player. WBF World Grand Master and #1 in the world rankings since 1985. Has appeared in 16 World Team Championship finals, just two short of Belladonna's record. Hamman has won the Bermuda Bowl seven times and finished 2nd four times. Won the World Team Olympiad once, in 1988, and reached four other finals. Won the World Open Pairs 1974, 2nd in 1994. Twice 2nd in the World Mixed Pairs. 2nd in the 1990 PAMP World Par Contest. Won the Cavendish Invitational Pairs in 1998. ACBL Player of Year twice. He was named an Honorary Member in 1991. Hamman holds a record 39 North American nationals titles. These include a remarkable 23 wins in the three major teams events – the Reisinger eight times, the Vanderbilt four times and the Spingold a record 11 times. He has twice won the IBPA's C C Wei Award for the year's best defensive play.

HAMPSON, Geoff of Toronto, Canada. (b.1968). Bridge professional. 2nd in the World Junior Teams in 1991. 2nd in the Pan-American Open Teams in 1992. Canadian national titles include the 1991 CNTC. North American national titles include the 1992 Open Swiss Teams, the Mixed Pairs in 1994, the 1997 Open Pairs I, and the Life Master Pairs in 1998.

HANDLEY, Michele V of London, England. (b.1964). 2nd in the World Women's Team Olympiad in 1982. Won the European Women's Teams in 1997. Won the ECand the Teams in 1993. When she won her first North American national title (the 1992 Women's Swiss) she became, with Sandra Landy, the first non-North American winner of a major ACBL team championship. She co-presented the British television programme *Play Bridge with Zia* in 1991.

HARRISON-GRAY, Maurice of London, England. (b.1900; d.1968). Bridge writer. British Life Master #4 and Grand Master #3. Won the European Teams four times. Represented Great Britain in three World Championships. Many national titles. Gray was the bridge correspondent for the *Evening Standard* and *Country Life* magazine. He was a member of the group that developed the Acol system in the 1930s. He was also a vocal advocate of the Losing Trick Count.

HAZEN, Lee of New York City, New York, USA. (b.1905; d.1991). Attorney. Played professional baseball for the Brooklyn Dodgers.

Twice finished 2nd in the Bermuda Bowl, and was twice the US team's npc. Honorary member in 1958. Many national titles.

HELGEMO, Geir of Trondheim, Norway. (b.1970). Bridge professional. Won the World Junior Pairs in 1995. 2nd in the 1993 Bermuda Bowl, 3rd in 1997. 2nd in the 1993 World Junior Teams. Won the European Junior Teams in 1990. Won the 1996 Generali World Individual. 3rd in the European Open Teams in 1993 & 97. Won the Cap Gemini Invitational Pairs twice, and the Macallan Invitational Pairs twice. Won the British Spring Fours in 1999, and the 1993 Schiphol International Teams in The Netherlands. Several North American national titles. Numerous Norwegian national titles. In 1990, he won the IBPA's C C Wei Award for the year's best defensive play.

HELNESS, Tor of Oslo, Norway. (b.1957). Stockbroker. 2nd in the 1993 Bermuda Bowl, 3rd in 1997. 3rd in the 1980 World Team Olympiad. Won the 1980 European Junior Teams. 2nd in the European Teams in 1999, and 3rd twice. Won the Cap Gemini Invitational Pairs twice, and the Macallan Invitational Pairs twice. Won the 1993 Schiphol International Teams in The Netherlands. Numerous national titles.

HIRON, Alan M of Marbella, Spain. (b.1933; d.1999). Formerly of London, England. Computer and games consultant. British Life Master #48 and Grand Master #22. Won the first World Senior Pairs in 1990. Represented Britain in one European Championship. National titles include the Gold Cup in 1963, Crockfords twice, and the Pachabo twice. Editor of *Bridge Magazine* (1985–90), and bridge correspondent for the *London Independent* until his death.

HOFFMAN, Martin of London, England. (b.1932). Bridge writer and professional. British Grand Master #76. Winner of many European tournaments and one of the fastest analysts in the game. Author of *Hoffman on Pairs Play*. National titles include Crockfords in 1981 and the National Pairs in 1966. He is a survivor of Auschwitz.

HORTON, Mark H of London, England. Editor of *Bridge Magazine*. Won silver medal in the 1996 EC Mixed Teams. Captain of Great Britain Women's team that finished second in the 1992 Olympiad. Represented Great Britain and England. National titles include the Life and Grandmasters' Pairs. Chief bulletin editor of the World Bridge Federation; editor of Batsford Bridge Books; author of numerous books.

JACOBY, James O "Jim" of Richardson, Texas, USA. (b.1933; d.1991) Stock broker. Notre Dame graduate. Won the Bermuda Bowl twice, and finished 2nd twice. Won the 1972 World Mixed Teams. Won the World Team Olympiad in 1988, and was 2nd in 1972. 2nd in the 1966 World Pairs and the 1978 World Mixed Pairs. Won the McKenney Trophy in 1968. Many national titles. Co-author, with his father (Oswald), of Jacoby Transfer Bid, Jacoby 2NT and a syndicated bridge column.

JACOBY, Oswald of Dallas, Texas, USA. (b.Dec. 8, 1902 in Brooklyn, New York; d.1984). Bridge columnist. Played in the Lenz-Culbertson match, and later became a member of the Four Horsemen and Four Aces teams. ACBL Life Master #2. He won the first major contract bridge tournament, the Goldman Pairs in February, 1929. He was a member of the winning American team in the first official World Championship, against France in 1935. He missed the first Bermuda Bowl because of the Korean War. Between 1959 and 1963, he won the McKenney Trophy four times in five years, becoming the first player aged over 50 to win it, and claiming his fourth victory aged 61. He was the ACBL's top all-time masterpoint holder from 1962–68, claiming that position from Goren and conceding it to Barry Crane. He was elected to the Bridge Hall of Fame in 1965 and became an Honorary ACBL member in 1967. In 1982, the IBPA honoured him with the Charles Goren Award as "Bridge Personality of the Year". He was npc of the US teams in 1969, 70 & 71. He is the father of Jim Jacoby. He won 27 ACBL North American titles, but he also won championships sponsored by the USBA and the ABL, taking his grand total to 38, one more than John Crawford's official pre-Hamman record.

Jacoby pioneered many bidding innovations, notably Jacoby transfer bids over no-trump openings, the Jacoby 2NT response to major-suit openings, and weak jump overcalls.

In addition to many books, he was the co-author, with his son (Jim), of *Jacoby Transfer Bid*, *Jacoby 2NT* and a syndicated bridge column. Jacoby also wrote books on poker, canasta, gin rummy and mathematical odds. In 1973 he won the World Backgammon Championship.

JAÏS, Pierre of Paris, France, (b.1913; d.1988). Physician. Jaïs was the first player (there are now eight) to win the Triple Crown – Bermuda Bowl in 1956, World Team Olympiad in 1960, and the

World Pairs in 1962. Won the European Teams twice and finished 2nd three times. Won the *Sunday Times* Invitational Pairs in 1963. Numerous French national titles. His 20-year partnership with Roger Trézel was acknowledged as one of the world's strongest, and they were one of the first to champion canapé methods. He was a regular magazine contributor, and wrote several books, many of them in tandem with Terence Reese.

JANNERSTEN, Eric of Stockholm, Sweden. (b.1912; d.1982). Editor and publisher. Represented Sweden numerous times and won many national titles, but it is as a writer that Jannersten made his contribution to the bridge world. He founded *Bridgetidningen* in 1939, now the world's second oldest bridge magazine. In 1958, he founded the European Bridge Press Association, which two years later became International and changed name to its present-day IBPA. The bidding box was another of Jannersten's innovations.

JANSMA, Jan of Nijmegen, The Netherlands. (b.1962). Won the European Junior Teams in 1986 and the World Junior Teams in 1987. Won the Cavendish Invitational Teams in 1998. Numerous national titles include the Meesterklasse Teams in 1997.

JONES, Martin A of Coventry, England. (b.1965). Represented England in three Junior Camrose Trophies. Represented Great Britain at Junior level and made his Open team debut in the 1999 European Teams while still a junior. National titles include Crockfords in 1994 and the Gold Cup in 1997.

JONSSON, Thorlakur of Kopavogur, Iceland. (b.1956). Mechanical engineer. Won the Bermuda Bowl in 1991. Won the Nordic Teams in 1988. National titles include the Icelandic Teams twice and the Open Pairs once.

JORDAN, Robert F of Cincinnati, Ohio, USA. (b.1927). Twice finished 2nd in the World Team Olympiad. 2nd in the 1963 Bermuda Bowl. Won the McKenney Trophy in 1960. National titles include the Vanderbilt twice and the Reisinger twice. Jordan's partnership with Arthur Robinson is widely considered to have been America's best in the 1960s.

JORGENSEN, Adalsteinn of Reykjavik, Iceland. (b.1959). Shopkeeper. Won the Bermuda Bowl in 1991. Won the Cavendish Invitational Pairs in 1990. National titles include the Icelandic Teams five times and the Open Pairs twice.

JOURDAIN, Patrick D of Cardiff, Wales. (b.1942). Journalist and bridge teacher/club owner. British Grand Master #21. He has represented Wales in more than 50 Camrose Trophy matches, easily a record. National titles include the Gold Cup in 1976, the Spring Fours in 1990, and hundreds of Welsh titles. President of the WBU 1984–85 and Vice-President of the BBL since 1993. He is the Editor of the *IBPA Bulletin* and the bridge correspondent for the *Daily Telegraph*.

KANTAR, Edwin B "Eddie" of Santa Monica, California, USA. (b.1932). Bridge teacher, writer and professional player. WBF World Grand Master and #34 in the 1999 world ranking. Author of numerous bridge books, many of them already classics such as *Introduction to Declarer's Play*, *Introduction to Defender's Play*, *Roman Key-Card Blackwood*, *Bridge Humor* and *The Best of Eddie Kantar*. He is also a regular columnist for the *ACBL Bulletin* and *The Bridge World*. In 1980, he was awarded the IBPA's C C Wei Award for the year's best article on the topic of bidding. Kantar learned to play bridge at 11 and taught his first class at 17. Won the Bermuda Bowl twice, 2nd in 1975 and 3rd in 1969. Won the 1981 Maccabean Games. Won the Pan-American Teams in 1977. Many national titles. He was Minnesota state table-tennis champion in 1948, and represented the USA at the 1957 World Championships.

KAPLAN, Edgar of New York City, New York, USA. (b.1925; d.1998). Bridge writer and teacher. Editor and publisher of *The Bridge World* from 1967 until his death. Commentator at WBF events, he was known for his analysis and his wit. He was the world's leading authority on the laws of the game. He became an Honorary ACBL member in 1993. In 1978, he was named as IBPA's Bridge Personality of the Year. His 40-year partnership with Norman Kay was one of the most enduring and successful of all time.

He represented the US in World Championships many times. 2nd in the 1967 Bermuda Bowl and the 1968 World Team Olympiad. 4th in the 1990 World Pairs, 5th in 1982. Won the McKenney Trophy in 1957.

Kaplan won numerous national titles over five decades. He was the co-inventor of the Kaplan-Sheinwold system and the author of several books including *Winning Contract Bridge Complete*.

KASLE, Gaylor of Boca Raton, Florida, USA. (b.1941). Bridge professional. Kasle was a driving force behind the growth of professional bridge in the 1960s and early 1970s. Won the Rosenblum Teams in 1994. National titles include the 1994 Vanderbilt, the Men's Teams in 1973, and the Open Swiss three times.

KATZ, Ralph of Burr Ridge, Illinois, USA. (b.1957). Options trader. He has reached four World Pairs finals, finishing 2nd in 1978, 8th in 1994, 11th in 1986 and 13th in 1982. National titles include the Spingold in 1981 and the Life Masters Pairs in 1979.

KAY, Norman of Narberth, Pennsylvania, USA. (b.1927). Retired accountant. His 40-year partnership with Edgar Kaplan was one of the most enduring and successful of all time. Twice 2nd in the Bermuda Bowl. 2nd in the 1968 World Team Olympiad, and 3rd in 1960. Won the McKenney Trophy in 1955. Numerous national titles.

KEARSE, Amalya L of New York City, New York, USA. (b.1937). US Court of Appeal judge. The first woman to sit on the Manhattan Federal Appeals Court. Named as IBPA's "Bridge Personality of the Year" in 1979. Won the World Women's Pairs in 1986. National titles include the Women's Pairs in 1971, the Life Masters Women's Pairs in 1972, the Women's Knock-Out Teams in 1987, the Women's BAM Teams in 1990 and the Women's Swiss in 1991. She is the author of *Bridge Conventions Complete*.

KEHELA, Sami R of Toronto, Canada. (b.1934 in Baghdad). Bridge teacher and journalist. Twice finished 3rd in the World Team Olympiad, and 4th in 1964. 3rd in the 1982 Rosenblum Teams, and 5th in 1978. Kehela was also coach of the North American Bermuda Bowl teams in 1962, 63 & 65. His 30-year partnership with Eric Murray is acknowledged as one of Canada's best ever. Many North American national titles. Won the Canadian National Teams Championship twice.

KELSEY, Hugh W of Edinburgh, Scotland. (b.1926; d.1995). Novelist and bridge writer. Represented Scotland 12 times in the Camrose Trophy. National titles include the British Gold Cup twice and every major Scottish titles many times. He was the bridge columnist for *The Scotsman*. Author of more than 45 bridge books including the classic *Killing Defence in Bridge*. He was named IBPA "Bridge Personality of the Year" in 1992.

KEMPSON, Ewart of Durham, England. (b.1895; d.1966). Bridge writer and army officer. The Editor of *Bridge Magazine* from 1949 until his death. He was a member of the first official teams to represent both England and Great Britain. A supporter of the method called British Bridge – direct bidding without forcing bids. He was the first, so far as is known, to invent and publish (in 1934) the idea of using a Two Club response to a 1NT opening as a way of locating a 4-4 major-suit fit. Along with Norman de V Hart, he pioneered control-showing responses to strong Two Club openings (CAB). He wrote more than 20 books including *Kempson on Contract* and *The Quintessence of CAB*. National titles include the National Pairs.

KENNEDY, Betty-Ann of Shreveport, Louisiana, USA. WBF World Grand Master and #27 in the 1999 world rankings. Recipient of the 1985 Image Award. Inducted into the Louisiana Sports Hall of Fame in 1993 (only the second woman to be so honoured). A world champion several times over, she won the Venice Cup twice and finished second twice. Won the 1982 World Women's Pairs, and was 2nd in 1978. Won the World Women's Team Olympiad in 1984. Won the Ambassador's Cup in China in 1988, the 1981 Hong Kong Open Teams, the 1993 International Bridge Team Championship in Beijing, and was 3rd in the first International Invitational Chinese Open Teams in 1981. Numerous national titles.

KIRBY, Graham T of Warrington, England. (b.1955). Researcher. British Grand Master #55. 2nd in the 1987 Bermuda Bowl. Won the 1991 European Teams, and 2nd in 1987. Played more than 25 Camrose Trophy matches for England. National titles include the Spring Fours three times, the Gold Cup seven times and Crockfords three times.

KLINGER, Ronald Denny "Ron" of Sydney, Australia. (b.1941 in Shanghai, China). Bridge writer and teacher. 3rd in the 1989 Bermuda Bowl, and 5th in 1976 when he won the BOLS prize for the Best Played Hand at the tournament. Won the Far East Teams in 1970. Won the Far East Pairs twice. Won the South Pacific Teams in 1993. He has represented Australia in numerous World and Zonal Championships. Many Australian national titles. He has authored more than 30 books including the 1991 "Book of the Year", *Guide to Better Card Play*. Before taking up bridge, he was Australian Junior Chess Champion.

KOKISH, Eric O of Montreal, Canada. (b.1947). Bridge professional, writer, teacher and coach. Collects rock & roll records and baseball cards. Frequent traveller in his work with international teams, preparing them for world events. He is the inventor of several conventions including Kokish (for use after Two Club

openings), Reject, and the Montreal Relay. In 1980 he won the
IBPA's Romex Award and a BOLS brilliancy prize. In 1974, he was
awarded the IBPA's C C Wei Award for the year's best article on the
topic of bidding.

Finished 2nd in the 1995 Bermuda Bowl and in the 1978 World
Pairs. He won the 1979 Deauville Tournament of Champions in
France, two World Inter-City Team tournaments in Tokyo, the 1985
Calcutta International Teams in India, the 1989 CDN International
Pairs, and has been a regular invitee to the Cap Gemini Invitational
Pairs and the London *Sunday Times*/Macallan Pairs. Many North
American and Canadian national titles.

Kokish has written large portions of the World Championship
books 1979–85 and 1988–91. He writes weekly bridge columns for
The Montreal Gazette, was an associate editor of *International
Popular Bridge Monthly*, directs the Master Solvers Club for *The
Bridge World*, is a regular columnist for the *ACBL Bulletin* and
many other bridge publications around the world.

KONSTAM, Kenneth W of London, England. (b.1906; d.1968).
Executive and journalist. British Life Master #29. Won the
Bermuda Bowl in 1955. Won the European Teams six times, a
record second only to Giorgio Belladonna. Represented Great
Britain in six World and twelve European Championships. Many
national titles. He was bridge editor of *The Sunday Times*.

KOWALSKI, Apolinary of Warsaw, Poland. (b.1948). Bridge
professional. Won the World Mixed Pairs in 1994. 2nd in the
Generali World Individual in 1998. 4th in the 1994 World Pairs. 3rd
in the 1999 European Pairs. 2nd 1997 European Teams. 4th in the
European Mixed Pairs in 1995. Numerous national titles.

KRAUSS, Don P of Los Angeles, California, USA. (b.1937).
Stockbroker. 2nd in the 1964 World Team Olympiad. Won the
1981 Maccabean Games. National tiles include the Vanderbilt in
1964, the Chicago in 1962, the Reisinger in 1971 and the 1970
Men's Pairs.

KUBAK, Fritz of Vienna, Austria. (b.1949). 2nd in the 1990 World
Team Olympiad, and represented Austria in numerous other World
and European Championships. National titles include the Austrian
Open Teams seven times and the Mixed Pairs twice.

KWIECIN, Michal of Warsaw, Poland. Won the 1998 World Pairs.
3rd in the 1997 World Transnational Teams. 2nd in the European
Teams in 1997.

LAIR, Mark of Canyon, Texas, USA. (b.1947). Bridge professional. 4th in the 1982 Rosenblum Teams. Won the 1990 Barry Crane Top 500, and finished 2nd in 1979. National titles include the Vanderbilt three times, the Spingold twice, the Reisinger twice, the Blue Ribbon Pairs, the Open Swiss Teams twice, and the Men's/Open BAM Teams three times.

LANDY, Alvin of New York City, New York, USA. (b.1905 in Cleveland, OH; d.1967). Executive Secretary of the ACBL and WBF Secretary/Treasurer. ACBL Life Master #24. He was named as an Honorary ACBL Member in 1957. He invented the Landy Defence to 1NT. National titles include the Spingold and Chicago (now the Reisinger) both in 1949, the Mixed Teams in 1939, and the Men's BAM Teams a record four times. He was also an expert whist player, finishing 2nd in the American Whist League's Open Teams in 1934.

LANDY, Sandra of Buckinghamshire, England. (b.1938). Formerly of Hove, England. Former university lecturer. Head of the EBU's *Bridge For All* youth development programme. British Grand Master #36. WBF World Grand Master and #11 in the 1999 world rankings. Won the Venice Cup twice. 2nd in the World Women's Teams Olympiad four times, and 3rd in 1980. 3rd in the World Women's Pairs twice. Won the European Women's Teams five times, and 2nd three times. Won five EC titles. Represented Britain in one other World and six other European Championships. National titles include the Gold Cup in 1984 and the Spring Fours in 1988. When she won her first North American national title (the 1992 Women's Swiss) she became, with Michele Handley, the first non-North American winner of a major ACBL team championship.

LANZAROTTI, Massimo of Voghera, Italy. (b.1959). Garage owner. Won the 1998 Rosenblum Teams. Won the European Championship in 1995 & 97. Quarter-finalist in the 1997 Bermuda Bowl. Won the 1997 Forbo International Teams in The Netherlands. Three national titles include the Italian Cup once.

LASOCKI, Krzysztof of Warsaw, Poland. (b.1940). Bridge professional. Finished 2nd in the 1991 Bermuda Bowl. 3rd in the 1991 European Teams. Won the European Pairs in 1995. 2nd in the 1994 Rosenblum Teams. 3rd in the European Seniors Pairs in 1999. Won the Toronto Calcutta in 1993. 2nd in the Cavendish Invitational Pairs in 1993.

LASUT, Hengky of Manado, Indonesia. (b.1947). Finished 3rd in the 1996 World Team Olympiad. Won the Far East Teams nine times. Represented Indonesia in 12 World Championships. Won the English Four Stars Teams in 1996. Numerous Indonesian national titles.

LAURIA, Lorenzo of Rome, Italy. (b.1946). Insurance broker. WBF World Grand Master and #15 in the 1999 world rankings. Won the Rosenblum Cup in 1998. Twice lost a Bermuda Bowl final by 5 IMPs. Won the European Teams three times, also winning the Butler scoring at the latter two. Won the Schiphol International Teams in The Netherlands in 1992. Won the Macallan Invitational Pairs in 1997, and 2nd in 1999. Numerous Italian national titles. North American national titles include the Vanderbilt in 1999.

LAVINTHAL, Hy of Trenton, New Jersey, USA. (b.1894; d.1972). Retail storeowner. Inventor of the Suit Preference Signal, although it is commonly known in Europe as McKenney, after the journalist who first publicized it here. He was an associate editor of *The Bridge World* and the author of one book, *Defensive Tricks*.

LAWRENCE, Mike S of Berkeley, California, USA. (b.1940). Bridge professional and writer. WBF World Grand Master and #23 in the 1999 world rankings. Author of numerous acclaimed books, two of which, *How to Read Your Opponents' Cards* and *The Complete Book of Overcalls in Contract Bridge* were named "Book of the Year". Others, such as *Judgment at Bridge*, *The Complete Book on Balancing*, and *Play a Swiss Team of Four with Mike Lawrence*, are considered classics.

A member of the Dallas Aces team, he won the Bermuda Bowl three times and finished 2nd twice. 2nd in the 1972 World Team Olympiad. Numerous national titles.

LAZARD, Sidney H of New Orleans, Louisiana, USA. (b.1930). 2nd in the 1959 Bermuda Bowl, 3rd in 1969. Represented the US in four other World Championships. National titles include the Spingold twice, the Chicago, the Reisinger in 1997, the Vanderbilt in 1970, the 1990 Grand National Pairs, and the Masters Mixed Teams five times.

LEBEL, Michel of Nantes, France. (b.1944 in Romania). Bridge writer. WBF World Grand Master and #26 in the 1999 world rankings. Won the World Team Olympiad in 1982 and the Rosenblum Teams in 1980. Won the European Teams twice, and 2nd in 1973. Won the European Pairs in 1976. Numerous French national titles. He is the bridge columnist for *Le Point*, and the author of many books. In 1986, he won the IBPA's C C Wei Award for the year's best defensive play.

LEDERER, Rhoda (née Barrow) of Chalfont St Peter, England. (d.1990). Bridge writer and teacher. She was co-author (mainly with Ben Cohen) of numerous books outlining the Acol system for novices. Some have become classics, such as *Basic Acol*, *The Acolites Quiz Book*, and *Conventions Made Clear*. She was the Editor of the *IBPA Bulletin* from 1967–71. Secretary of the English Bridge Union Teachers' Association, which she helped to found with her husband (Tony).

LEDERER, Richard of London, England. (b.1894 in Hungary; d.1941). Club owner and writer. The first great figure of English bridge. He represented Great Britain in the 1934 Schwab Cup match. Lederer's Club was the breeding ground for many of Britain's top players such as Harrison-Gray, Konstam, Meredith and Reese. A prestigious annual invitational teams event is staged in London in his name, instigated by his son, Tony. National titles include the Gold Cup three times.

LEDERER, Anthony R "Tony" of England. (b.1919; d.1976). Bridge player and administrator. Won his first tournament at the age of 14, and played on most of the winning teams captained by his father (Richard). He instigated the Richard Lederer Memorial Trophy in his father's memory. With Jill Gatti, he founded the Charity Challenge Cup Simultaneous Pairs. Along with his wife (Rhoda) he founded the English Bridge Union Teachers' Association.

LENZ, Sidney S (b.July 12, 1873 in Chicago, Illinois d.1960). Lumber tycoon. Writer and an expert at whist and numerous other card games. He won many national titles at both whist and auction bridge. He was also a remarkable sportsman, performing to championship level in tennis, golf, table tennis, shooting and chess. He was also an accomplished magician, and he refrained from playing card games for money because of his ability to manipulate a pack of cards. He is best known in bridge circles as the captain of the team that lost the Lenz-Culbertson Match, although his contribution to technical advances is significant, including the high-low signal to show an even number of cards in a suit. He was elected to the Bridge Hall of Fame in 1965. National contract titles include the 1932 Eastern States Open Pairs.

LESNIEWSKI, Marcin of Zakopane, Poland. (b.1948). Mathematician and bridge professional. Won the World Pairs in 1996 and the World Transnational Teams in 1997. Won the 1984 European Cup, the 1989 European Pairs, and the 1992 European Mixed Pairs. Numerous Polish national titles. North American national titles include the Spingold in 1997.

LETIZIA, Marinesa of Bloomington, Indiana, USA. (b.1954). Bridge professional and former nurse. WBF World Grand Master and #23 in the 1999 world rankings. Won the World Women's Teams (the McConnell Cup) in 1994. Won the Venice Cup in 1997. National titles include the Masters Mixed Teams twice and the Women's Knock-Out Teams.

LEUFKENS, Enri of De Bilt, The Netherlands. (b.1963). Automation expert. Won the 1993 Bermuda Bowl. 3rd in the 1992 World Team Olympiad. Won the European Junior Teams in 1986 and the World Junior Teams in 1987. National titles include the Schiphol International Teams twice and the Meesterklasse Dutch Teams Championship twice.

LEV, Sam of Forest Hills, New York, USA. (b.1947). Twice finished 3rd in the Bermuda Bowl. National titles include the Reisinger twice (1989 & 91).

LEVENTRITT, Peter A of New York City, New York, USA. (b.1916; d.1997). Former ACBL President and co-founder of the Card School of New York. Finished 2nd in four Bermuda Bowls and was npc in 1955. National titles include the Spingold twice , the Chicago twice, the Vanderbilt twice, the Life Masters Pairs twice, and the Master Mixed Teams three times.

LEVIN, Robert J "Bobby" of Aventura, Florida, USA. (b.1957). Options trader and bridge professional. He became a Life Master in 1973, the youngest ever to do so at that time, and was the ACBL's King of Bridge in 1975. At the age of 13 he played in and won his first event, a sectional Men's Pairs. Won the Bermuda Bowl in 1981, becoming the youngest player ever to win an open World Championship. Won the 1992 Pan-American Teams. Won the Cavendish Invitational Pairs and the Cavendish Teams in 1999. Many national titles.

LEVY, Alain of Paris, France. (b.1948 in Morocco). WBF World Grand Master and #7 in the 1999 world rankings. Won the 1997 Bermuda Bowl. Won the World Teams Olympiad twice. Won the European Pairs in 1999. 3rd in the European Teams in 1981. 3rd in the European Individual in 1992. Won the EC Teams twice. Numerous French national titles.

LIGHTNER, Theodore A of New York City, New York, USA. (b.1893 in Grosse Pointe, Michigan; d.1981). Stockbroker. Harvard and Yale graduate. ACBL Life Master #7. He contributed to the development of the Culbertson system and invented the Lightner Double. He partnered Ely Culbertson during part of the Culbertson-Lenz match, and was a member of the Culbertson team that beat British teams in 1930, 33 & 34. Won the Bermuda Bowl in 1953.

LINDKVIST, C Magnus of Hoör, Sweden. (b.1958). Bridge writer, teacher and travel consultant. He has finished 3rd in six World Championship events – the Bermuda Bowl twice, the 1988 World Team Olympiad, the World Pairs in 1998, and the Rosenblum Teams twice. Won the European Teams in 1987, 2nd in 1999, and 3rd in 1989. Won the 1996 Nordic Teams. Won the Cavendish Invitational Pairs in 1988. Numerous Swedish national titles. He is the editor of the world's second-oldest bridge magazine – *Bridgetidningen*, and the co-author of four books.

LISE, Collette of Paris, France. (b.1944). Manager of *Le Bridgeur* Shop in Paris. Finished 3rd in the 1992 World Women's Team Olympiad. 2nd in the 1992 Generali World Individual. Won the European Women's Teams twice. Numerous French national titles.

LODGE, Steve J of London, England. (b.1957). Electronics engineer. Represented Great Britain in two World Championships. Won the European Junior Teams in 1978. 2nd in the 1981 European Teams. Won the Schiphol International Teams in The Netherlands in 1996. Numerous national titles.

McCALLUM, Karen (née Thomas) of Exeter, New Hampshire, USA. (b.1946). WBF World Grand Master and #19 in the 1999 world rankings. Author/publisher/editor of mystery novels, ghostwriter of bridge books, bridge professional and teacher. Won the Venice Cup twice. Won the 1990 World Women's Pairs. Placed 5th in the 1990 Rosenblum Open Teams. National titles include the Women's Swiss twice and the Women's Knock-Out Teams.

McGOWAN, Liz of Edinburgh, Scotland. Russian teacher and bridge journalist. WBF World Grand Master and #22 in the 1999 world rankings. Won the first World Transnational Mixed Teams in 1996. Twice 2nd in the World Women's Team Olympiad. Won the European Women's Teams twice. She has represented Great Britain in numerous world and European Championships. Represented Scotland numerous times in the Lady Milne Trophy. National titles include the Portland Mixed Pairs twice. She is the bridge correspondent for *The Scotsman*. In 1991, she won the IBPA's Charles J Solomon Award for the year's best played hand.

McKENNEY, William E (b.1891; d.1950). Philanthropist, administrator and writer. His daily syndicated bridge columns were so widely read that in Europe the Suit Preference Signal became known as the McKenney Signal, rather than being attributed to its inventor, Hy Lavinthal. He helped to found and to fund the fledgling ACBL and ABL organizations. The much sought-after McKenney Trophy (renamed The Barry Crane Top 500 in 1965) awarded to the winner of the most masterpoints in a calendar year was named in his honour.

MAAS, Anton of Amsterdam, The Netherlands. (b.1952). Bank manager. Finished 2nd in the 1982 World Pairs, and 3rd in 1994. 3rd in the 1980 Rosenblum Teams. National titles include the Schiphol International Teams in 1994, the Dutch Meesterklasse Teams seven times, and the Dutch Open Pairs three times.

MACKENZIE, Greer of Hillsborough, Northern Ireland. (b.1939). Software engineer. Represented Northern Ireland in more than 45 Camrose Trophy matches. He has represented All-Ireland in one World and two European Championships. Former President of the Irish Bridge Union, and Chairman of NIBU.

MADSEN, Lars Lund of Copenhagen, Denmark. (b.1972). Won World Junior Teams in 1997, 3rd in 1995. Finished 9th in the European Open Pairs in 1993, aged 20. Won the European Junior Teams in 1996, 2nd in 1994. Won the European University Teams in 1994, 3rd in 1996. 3rd in the European Union Junior Pairs in 1996. Won the Nordic Schools Teams in 1991. National titles include Junior Pairs three times and Junior Teams twice.

MADSEN, Morten Lund of Copenhagen, Denmark. (b.1974). Has the same achievements as his brother, Lars, above. He was 18 years old when they finished 9th in the 1993 European Open Pairs. In addition, after his brother was over-age, Morten finished 2nd in the European Junior Teams, EC Junior Teams, the EC Junior Pairs, and the Lipton Tea World Junior Teams in 1998. He also won the IBPA's Levendal Award (for best play by a junior) in 1998.

MAHMOOD, ZIA of New York City. New York, USA. (b.1946 in Pakistan). Formerly of London, England. Accountant, company executive, and rubber bridge player. One of the game's most popular characters. He finished 2nd in the 1981 Bermuda Bowl representing Pakistan. Won the BFAME Zonal Championship for Pakistan four times. 2nd in the Rosenblum Teams in 1986. He was named as "ACBL Player of the Year" in 1991 and 1995. Won the Cap Gemini Invitational Pairs twice. North American national titles include the Reisinger three times, the Spingold, the Life Masters Pairs twice, the Blue Ribbon Pairs, and the BAM Teams twice. He initiated the "Z Team" concept of star players partnering deserving players in the charity event that precedes NABCs. In 1981, he won the IBPA's Charles J Solomon Award for the year's best played hand.

MANFIELD, Edward A "Ed" of Hyattsville, Maryland, USA. (b.1943; d.1999). Economist. Won the Rosenblum Teams in 1986. Won the Cavendish Invitational Pairs in 1979. Many national titles. He was twice awarded the IBPA's C C Wei Award for the year's best article on the topic of bidding.

MANHARDT, Peter of Vienna, Austria. (b.1936). Won the World Pairs in 1970. Represented Austria in one other World and in eight European Championships. He dominated the European Grand Prix circuit in the 1970s, winning the Philip Morris European Cup four times, and finishing second twice. Many national titles. He led the Austrian all-time masterpoint rankings for more than 20 years.

MANNING-FOSTER, Alfred E of London, England. (b.1874; d.1939). One of England's leading pre-war bridge players. He founded *Bridge Magazine* and was its editor until his death. He was also the foreign correspondent for *The Bridge World* and bridge correspondent for the London *Times*. In 1931, he founded the British Bridge League and became its first President. He also wrote numerous bridge books.

MANOPPO, Eddy of Indonesia. Finished 3rd in the 1996 World Team Olympiad. Won the Far East Teams twice. Represented Indonesia in one other World Championship. Won the English Four Stars Teams in 1996. Numerous Indonesian national titles.

MARI, Christian of Paris, France, (b.1945). Bridge professional. WBF World Grand Master and #14 in the 1999 world rankings. Won the Bermuda Bowl in 1997. Won the World Team Olympiad twice. 3rd in the 1978 Rosenblum Teams. Won the European Teams in 1974. Won the EC Teams in 1973. Numerous French national titles.

MARKUS, Rika MBE **"Rixi"** of London, England. (b.1910 in Romania; d.1992). She was one of the greatest women players of all time, and the first to attain the rank of WBF Grand Master. She was the top woman in WBF rankings from the beginning (1974) until 1980. British Life Master #22.

She won 14 international titles, more than any other woman. These include a victory in the very first official Women's World Championship in 1937, representing European Champions, Austria. She also won the World Women's Team Olympiad in 1964, the World Mixed Teams in 1962, the World Women's Pairs twice, and the European Women's Teams a record nine times. Following her pre-war wins representing Austria, she fled to England in 1938. Her other wins, mainly partnering Fritzi Gordon, were for Great Britain, She also finished 2nd in both the World Mixed Pairs and the World Women's Pairs in 1970.

She was named "IBPA Personality of the Year" in 1975. In that same year, her contribution to bridge was acknowledged when she was awarded the MBE by Her Majesty Queen Elizabeth II.

She originated the idea of the annual matches between Britain's two Parliamentary houses, the House of Commons and the House of Lords. Numerous national titles include the Gold Cup in 1961, Crockfords in 1960 and the Masters Pairs in 1957.

She was the bridge editor for the *Guardian* from 1955 until her death, and the bridge columnist for the *Evening Standard* from 1975–80. She was a contributor to many magazines, and the author of seven books

MARSTON, Paul H of Sydney, Australia. (b.1949 in New Zealand). Club manager and bridge professional. Won the South Pacific Zone Playoff in 1991. Represented Australia and New Zealand eight times each in World and Zonal Championships. Australian national titles include the Open Teams five times. Along with Stephen Burgess, he was the originator of the Moscito relay system. He is the bridge correspondent for *Financial Review* and the author of five books.

MARTEL, Charles U "Chip" of Davis, California, USA. (b.1953). Professor of computer science. WBF World Grand Master and #8 in the 1999 world rankings. Won the World Open Pairs in 1982 (the youngest player to win this event, aged 29). Won the Bermuda Bowl twice. Won the Rosenblum Teams in 1994. 4th in the 1990 World Par Contest. 2nd in the 1990 EOE Optebeurs in The

Netherlands. Won the Cavendish Teams in 1999. Won the Rosenkranz Award for "Best Bid Hand" in 1979. Won the BOLS Tip competition in 1991. He was captain/coach of the winning US team at the 1991 World Junior Teams, and captain of the bronze medal team in 1993. Numerous national titles.

MARTENS, Krzysztof of Rzeszow, Poland. (b.1952). Chemical engineer and bridge professional. WBF World Grand Master and #11 in the 1999 world rankings. Won the 1997 World Transnational Teams. Won the World Team Olympiad in 1984. Finished 2nd in the 1991 Bermuda Bowl, and 3rd twice. Won the European Teams twice. Numerous Polish national titles.

MARX, John C H "Jack" of London, England. (b.1907 d.1991). Economist. One of the founding fathers of the Acol system, and an independent originator of the Stayman convention. Won the European Teams in 1950. Inventor of Byzantine Blackwood. Named as an Honorary Life Master in 1956. National titles include the Gold Cup three times.

MASOOD, Tahir of Karachi, Pakistan. (b.1956). Hotel executive. Finished 2nd in the 1991 Bermuda Bowl. Won the BFAME Zonal Teams in 1981, and the BFAME Pairs in 1985.

MATHE, Lewis L "Lew" of Canoga Park, California, USA. (b.1915. d.1986). Real estate broker. WBF Grand Master. Won the Bermuda Bowl in 1954. Represented North America in four other Bermuda Bowls. 22 national titles.

MECKSTROTH, Jeff J of Tampa, Florida, USA. (b.1956). Formerly of Reynoldsburg, Ohio, USA. Professional bridge player. WBF World Grand Master and #3 in the 1999 world rankings. His partnership with Eric Rodwell, known collectively as Meckwell, is widely acknowledged as the toughest in the world today.

The ACBL King of Bridge in 1974. He is one of only eight players to have won the Triple Crown – the Bermuda Bowl (twice, in 1981 & 95), the World Open Pairs in 1986, and the World Team Olympiad in 1988. Won the Macallan Invitational Pairs twice (1995 & 96).

Won the ACBL Player of the Year race in 1992. Won the McKenney Trophy in 1996. Numerous national titles. In 1998, he won the IBPA's Charles J Solomon Award for the year's best played hand.

MELLO, Roberto F de of Rio de Janeiro, Brazil. (b.1950). Engineer. WBF World Grand Master and #22 in the 1999 world rankings. Won the 1989 Bermuda Bowl and represented Brazil in six other World Championships. Won the South American Teams seven times. National titles include the Brazilian Open Teams three times.

MEREDITH, Adam "Plum" of London, England. (b.1913; d.1976). Rubber bridge professional. He became known for saying that "One Spade is always a good bid", and he had a reputation for opening and overcalling in spades with only a three-card suit, and sometimes even fewer. He was also known as a phenomenal dummy player, and was particularly adept at playing poor contracts!

Won the Bermuda Bowl in 1955. Won the European Teams twice. Represented Great Britain in five European Championships. British National titles include the National Pairs in 1951, the Masters Pairs in 1953, and the Gold Cup five times.

MESBUR, Adam of Dublin, Ireland. (b.1952). Accountant. 2nd in the 1974 European Junior Pairs and in the 1982 EC Pairs. He has represented Ireland regularly in World and European Championships since his debut in 1975. He has won more than 30 Irish national titles. He is the bridge columnist for the *Sunday Tribune*.

MEYER, Jean-Paul of Paris, France. (b.1936). Bridge writer. Won the European Pairs in 1987. Has represented France in two World and two European Championships. Bridge columnist for *L'Express* and a regular contributor to *Le Bridgeur*. He often edits the Daily Bulletin at EBL championships.

MEYERS, Jill J of Santa Monica, California, USA. (b,1950). Music supervisor in the movie industry. WBF World Grand Master and #4 in the 1999 world rankings. Won the Venice Cup twice. Won the World Women's Pairs in 1998. National titles include the Life Masters Women's Pairs in 1987, the Women's Knock-Out Teams twice , the Women's BAM Teams in 1991, and the Women's Swiss Teams twice.

MICHAELS, Michael N "Mike" of Miami Beach, Florida, USA. (b.1924; d.1966). Bridge writer and lecturer. Best known as the inventor of Michaels Cuebids, and for his association with Charles Goren in various journalistic enterprises. Never won a national title but reached the final of the 1959 Spingold.

MIDSKOG, Catarina "Cat" of Stockholm, Sweden. (b.1962). Bridge teacher. Won the European Women's Teams in 1993. Won the Nordic Women's Teams in 1992.

MILES, Marshall of San Bernadino, California, USA. (b.1926). Attorney and bridge writer. Prolific writer of books and articles. He is an expert member of magazine bidding panels around the world. National titles include the Spingold twice, the Life Masters Pairs in 1961, the Chicago in 1962, and the Reisinger in 1965.

MILNES, Eric C of Bradford, England. (b.1912; d.1984). Customs officer. Former editor of *Bridge Magazine*. National titles include the Hubert Phillips Mixed Knock-Out Teams twice (1958 & 63).

MITCHELL, Jacqueline M "Jacqui" of New York City, New York, USA. (b.1936). Bridge teacher. WBF World Grand Master and #25 in the 1999 world rankings. Won the Venice Cup twice, and 2nd in 1985. Won the World Women's Team Olympiad twice. Won the World Women's Pairs in 1986. Placed 2nd in both the World Mixed Pairs and the World Mixed Teams in 1974. Many national titles.

MITCHELL, Victor of New York City, New York, USA. (b.1923). Bridge teacher. 2nd in the 1964 World Team Olympiad. 2nd in the 1974 World Mixed Teams. Names as an Honorary ACBL Member in 1988. National titles include the Spingold twice, the Life Masters Men's Pairs, and the Men's Teams twice.

MITTELMAN, George of Toronto, Canada. Won the World Mixed Pairs in 1982. 2nd in the Bermuda Bowl in 1995. Twice placed 3rd in the Rosenblum Teams. North American titles include the Open Swiss Teams in 1986 and the BAM Teams in 1998. He has won the Canadian National Teams Championship six times.

MOEGEL, Marianne of Hanover, Germany. Won the Venice Cup in 1995, and finished 2nd in 1993. Won the European Women's Teams in 1989. 2nd in the 1993 European Women's Pairs. Six national titles.

MÖLLER, S Steen of Copenhagen, Denmark. (b.1939). Lawyer. Finished 2nd in the 1969 European Teams, and has represented Denmark in five World and 12 other European Championships. More than 30 Danish national titles including the Open Teams 11 times and the Open Pairs five times. He is a member of the EBL and WBF Appeals Panels. Former bridge columnist for *Berlingske Tidende*, and a regular contributor to magazines.

MOLLO, Victor of London, England. (b.1909 in St Petersburg, USSR; d.1987). Bridge writer. He wrote more than 25 books, but he is known and loved worldwide for those featuring the denizens of the Griffins Club, notably the Rueful Rabbit and the Hideous Hog.

He won four national titles including the Portland Mixed Pairs twice.

MOLSON, Markland "Mark" of Fenton, Michigan, USA. (b.1949). Formerly of Montreal, Canada. 2nd in the Bermuda Bowl in 1995. 3rd in the 1990 Rosenblum Teams. North American national titles include the Open Swiss Teams three times, the 1989 Reisinger, and the 1989 Blue Ribbon Pairs. He has also won the Canadian National Teams Championship six times, and the Canadian National Pairs in 1985.

MORATH, Anders "Carrot" of Järfälla, Sweden. (b.1944). Computer service manager. Twice finished 3rd in the Bermuda Bowl (1977 & 91). Won the European Teams in 1977, and 2nd in 1991. Won the European Junior Teams in 1968. Represented Sweden in numerous other World and European Championships. National titles include the Swedish Open Teams eight times, and he is the top all-time Swedish masterpoint holder. He is the co-inventor of the Swedish Carrot Club system. In 1984, he shared (with Sven-Olov Flodqvist) the IBPA's C C Wei Award for the year's best article on the topic of bidding.

MOREHEAD Albert H of New York City, New York, USA. (b.1909 in Glintstone, Georgia; d.1966). Bridge writer, editor and lexicographer. Harvard graduate. Ely Culbertson hired him because of his outstanding analytical ability and appointed him as technical editor of *The Bridge World* in 1933. In 1934, he became general manager of all Culbertson enterprises. He was only 25 when he played on the Culbertson team that defeated the British in the second international match for the Schwab Cup.

He was the first bridge columnist of the *New York Times*, with a Sunday column from 1935 and a daily column from 1959. He resigned in 1963 to devote his attention to writing, editing and publishing the dictionaries, encyclopedias and thesauruses that made him one of America's foremost lexicographers.

He became a governor of the newly formed ACBL and was President in 1943 and Chairman from 1943–45. He was also the author of the constitution of the World Bridge Federation – the first definition of the scope, structure, powers and duties of that organization. He was named as an ACBL Honorary Member in 1946, and was elected to the Bridge Hall of Fame in 1996.

He wrote many books including *Morehead on Bidding*, which was named "Book of the Year" in 1966.

MOSCA, Carlo of Milan, Italy. (b.1945). Bridge teacher. Formerly of Rome, Italy. Place 2nd in both the 1983 Bermuda Bowl and the 1976 World Team Olympiad. Won the European Teams in 1975. He was also npc of the winning Italian squad at the European Teams in 1995, 97 & 99. Won the EC Teams twice. National titles include the Italy Cup twice and the Italian Teams three times.

MOSS, M Brad of New York City, New York, USA. (b.1971). Bridge teacher. ACBL King of Bridge in 1989. In 1991, he became the youngest player ever to win the New York Player of the Year title. 4th in the World Junior Teams in 1991. National titles include the Master Mixed Teams in 1991, the Grand National Teams in 1993, the 1993 Life Masters Open Pairs, and the BAM Teams in 1998. His parents are Mike Moss and Gail Greenberg.

MOSS, Mike of New York City, New York, USA. (b.1935). Stockbroker. Placed 2nd in the World Mixed Teams in 1972. 2nd in the 1990 Rosenblum Teams. 4th in the 1972 World Mixed Pairs. National titles include the Master Mixed Teams twice, the Life Masters Pairs in 1970, the Mixed Pairs twice, the Men's Pairs in 1989, and the Open Pairs II in 1998.

MOUIEL, Hervé of Paris, France. (b.1949). Bridge professional. WBF World Grand Master and #5 in the 1999 world rankings. Won the World Team Olympiad twice. Won the Bermuda Bowl in 1997. Won the European Teams in 1983. Won the EC Teams twice. Won the EC Mixed Teams in 1992, and two other medals in European Mixed Pairs events. Numerous national titles.

MOYSE, Alphonse Jr "Sonny" of New York City, New York, USA. (b.1898 in Summit, Mississippi; d.1973). Formerly of Cincinnati, Ohio. Bridge writer. Publisher and editor of *The Bridge World* 1956–66. He first joined the Culbertson organization in the early 1930s as a writer of the syndicated columns that appeared under the Culbertson by-line. In 1973, just before his death, he became the first American to be named an IBPA Honorary Member. He is perhaps best known for his reputed love of 4-3 trump fits, which have henceforth been known simply as Moysian fits. National titles include the 1949 Men's Teams and the Men's Pairs in 1963.

MULLER, Bauke of Hoorn, The Netherlands. (b.1962). Psychologist. Won the 1993 Bermuda Bowl. 3rd in the 1992 World Team Olympiad. 2nd in the 1985 EC Junior Teams. Won the 1998 Cavendish Teams. National titles include the Schiphol International

Teams in 1994, the Dutch Open Pairs in 1991, and the Meesterklassc Dutch Teams Championship in 1992, 96 & 98.

MULTON, Franck of France. WBF World Grand Master and #16 in the 1999 world rankings. Won the World Team Olympiad in 1996. Won the Bermuda Bowl in 1997. Numerous national titles.

MUNSON, Kitty (formerly Bethe) of New York City, New York, USA. (b.1950). Systems analyst and bridge teacher. Harvard graduate. Won the Venice Cup in 1989. 4th in the 1986 World Mixed Pairs. 3rd in the European Women's Teams and won the EC Mixed Teams representing Great Britain. National titles include the Open Swiss Teams twice, the Women's Swiss Teams and the Mixed Pairs.

MURRAY, Eric R of Toronto, Canada. (b.1928). Barrister. His 30-year partnership with Sami Kehela is acknowledged as one of Canada's best ever. Finished 2nd in the Bermuda Bowl four times. 3rd in the World Team Olympiad twice, and 4th once. 3rd in the 1982 Rosenblum Teams. Won the Canadian Invitational Calcutta in 1993. Many North American and Canadian national titles.

NAGY, Peter I of Chicago, Illinois, USA. (b.1942 in Budapest, Hungary). Formerly of Montreal, Canada. Options trader and professional bridge player. Twice finished 2nd in the World Pairs (1978 & 90). 3rd in the 1982 Rosenblum Teams. Many North American and Canadian national titles. Won the IBPA Rosenkranz Award for Best Bid Hand in 1977, and a BOLS Brilliancy Prize for the Best Defensive Play at the 1980 World Team Olympiad.

NAIL, G Robert of Houston, Texas, USA. (b.1925). Bridge teacher and writer. Twice finished 2nd in the Bermuda Bowl. He invented the Big Diamond system. National titles include the Vanderbilt in 1967, the Men's Teams in 1965, and both the Life Masters Pairs and the Life Masters Men's Pairs in 1974.

NANDHABIWAT, Somboon of Bangkok, Thailand. (b.1922). Company president. Represented Thailand twice in the Bermuda Bowl and in five other World Championships. Won the Far East Teams three times. He invented the Bangkok Club system and is Thailand's top all-time masterpoint winner. He has won every major Thai national title, including the Open Teams ten times.

NEHMERT, Beate "Pony" of Wiesbaden, Germany. Bridge teacher. WBF World Grand Master and #13 in the 1999 world rankings. Won the Venice Cup in 1995. Twice finished 2nd in the European Teams. 2nd in the European Women's Pairs twice.

NICKELL, Frank T "Nick" of Raleigh, North Carolina, USA. (b.1947). Investment banker. Won the Bermuda Bowl in 1995, and finished 2nd in 1997. National titles include the Blue Ribbon Pairs in 1991, the Reisinger three times, and the Spingold five times.

NILSLAND, Mats of Malmo, Sweden. (b.1950). Flower wholesaler. He has finished 3rd in each of the major World Championship team events – the Bermuda Bowl in 1991, the Rosenblum Teams in 1998, and the World Team Olympiad in 1986. Twice finished 2nd in the European Teams. Numerous Swedish national titles. North American national titles include the 1996 Open Swiss Teams. He is the co-author of five books.

NIPPGEN, Georg of Karlsruhe, Germany. (b.1950). Businessman. Won the Rosenblum Teams in 1990. Won the European Mixed Pairs in 1994. Numerous German national titles.

NORDENSON, Britt (née Blom) of Norrköping, Sweden. (b.1925). Won the World Women's Team Olympiad in 1968. Won the European Women's Teams in 1967. Won the Nordic Women's Teams six times. Numerous national titles including the Swedish Women's Pairs 12 times.

NORRIS, Judy of Birkeröd, Denmark. (b.1940). Correspondent. Won the World Women's Team Olympiad in 1988 and the Nordic Women's Teams in 1988. Won the EC Mixed Teams in 1989. Represented Denmark in three World Team Championships, once in the Women's series and twice in the Open. Numerous national titles include the Danish Open Teams once.

NORTH, Frederick "Freddie" of Hove, England. Bridge writer and teacher. Represented Great Britain in two World Championships and England in the Camrose Trophy. National titles include the National Pairs, the Gold Cup and the Pachabo twice. Author of many books and a regular contributor to bridge magazines.

OGUST, Harold A of New York City, New York, USA. (b.1916; d.1978). Travel agent, and President/Founder of Goren International Inc, the company responsible for many bridge cruises. He was the inventor of Ogust Responses to Weak Two Bids. Finished 2nd in the 1957 Bermuda Bowl. Also represented the US in the 1960 World

Team Olympiad. National titles include the Spingold twice and the Reisinger twice. In 1976, he won the IBPA's Charles J Solomon Award for the year's best played hand.

OLDROYD, Rita of Yorkshire, England. Britain's first woman Grand Master (Grand Master #5) and Life Master #34. Finished 2nd in the 1976 Venice Cup. Won the European Women's Teams twice. Numerous national titles include the Pachabo twice.

OPPEN, Carol G J van of Amsterdam, The Netherlands. (b.1935). Bridge tour operator. Placed 3rd in the 1980 World Team Olympiad. Won the EC Teams, and represented The Netherlands in four other World and two European Championships. Numerous national titles include the Dutch Open Teams ten times and the Open Pairs twice. He is the author of four books.

ORTIZ-PATIÑO, Jaime of Marbella, Spain. (b.1928). Formerly of Switzerland. President of the WBF 1976–86 and President Emeritus since 1986. As WBF President he was responsible for forming two new zones (Central American & Caribbean, and Asia & Middle East), and for adding many new countries to the WBF roster, including China. He owns his own golf course – Valderrama, the venue for the 1997 Ryder Cup. He was the prime force behind the introduction of screens at major events, and was also a vocal supporter of bidding boxes. He represented Switzerland in four World and eight European Championships. Placed 5th in the World Par Contest in 1961. National titles include the Swiss Open Teams four times, and the Swiss Knock-Out Teams five times. In 1977 he was awarded the IBPA's Charles Goren Award as "Personality of the Year".

OSBERG, Sharon of San Francisco, California, USA. (b.1949). Bank executive. WBF World Grand Master and #26 in the 1999 world rankings. Won the Venice Cup twice. National titles include the Masters Mixed Teams in 1979, the Women's Knock-Out Teams twice, and the Women's BAM Teams in 1988.

OTTLIK, Géza of Budapest, Hungary. (b.1912; d.1990). Novelist and bridge writer. Co-author, with Hugh Kelsey, of *Adventures in Card Play*, which introduced many new, advanced card-play concepts such as the Entry-Shifting Squeeze and the Backwash Squeeze. He won the IBPA's first "Article of the Year" award in 1968. He represented Hungary in international matches in the 1930s and 1970s. His novel, *A School at the Frontier*, won the 1985 Kossuth Prize for Literature.

PABIS TICCI, Camillo of Florence, Italy. (b.1920). WBF World Grand Master and #45 in the 1999 world rankings. Won the World Team Olympiad three times. Won the Bermuda Bowl five times. Numerous national titles. A regular bridge columnist and magazine contributor.

PALMER, Beth of Silver Spring, Maryland, USA. (b.1952). Lawyer. WBF World Grand Master and #12 in the 1999 world rankings. Won the Venice Cup twice. Placed 2nd in the 1982 World Women's Pairs, 3rd in 1994, and 4th in 1990. Many national titles.

PASSELL, Michael "Mike" of Dallas, Texas, USA. (b.1947). Professional player and computer programmer. WBF World Grand Master and #27 in the 1999 world rankings. Ranks #2 behind Paul Soloway in the ACBL's all-time masterpoint list with more than 43,000 masterpoints. Won the Bermuda Bowl in 1979, 2nd in 1977, and 4th in 1983. Place 2nd in the 1980 World Team Olympiad. Won the McKenney Trophy (now the Barry Crane Top 500) in 1976. Numerous national titles. He and his wife, Nancy, are the only US couple to have won the Bermuda Bowl and the Venice Cup respectively. In 1991, he won the IBPA's C C Wei Award for the year's best defensive play.

PASSELL, Nancy L of Dallas, Texas, USA. (b.1949). Professional player and former teacher. Won the Venice Cup in 1991. National titles include the Life Masters Women's Pairs in 1988 and the 1991 Women's Knock-Out Teams.

PAULSEN, Erik of Upland, California, USA. (b.1926). Aerospace engineer. Won the Bermuda Bowl in 1976, and 2nd in 1977. 2nd in the 1970 World Pairs. 4th in the World Team Olympiad in 1976. National titles include the Reisinger four times and the Blue Ribbon Pairs.

PAVLICEK, Richard of Fort Lauderdale, Florida, USA. (b.1945). Bridge teacher and writer. Placed 6th in the 1986 Rosenblum Teams. Author of numerous teaching texts, and the co-author, with Bill Root, of *Modern Bridge Conventions*. National titles include the Grand National Teams twice, the Reisinger four times, the Vanderbilt twice and the Open Swiss Teams.

PAVLIDES, Jordanis T of London, England. (b.1903; d.1985). Company director. Won the Bermuda Bowl in 1955. Won the European Teams in 1954. National wins include the Gold Cup, Crockfords twice, the Master Pairs, and the Pachabo. He was made an Honorary EBU Member in 1956.

PENDER, Peter A of Forestville, California, USA. (b.1936; d.1990). Won the Bermuda Bowl in 1985, and 2nd in 1989. 2nd in the 1982 Rosenblum Teams. Won the Pan-American Invitational Pairs twice. He was coach for the US Women's team twice. Won the McKenney Trophy in 1966. Many national titles. In 1966, he helped Jeremy Flint become a US Life Master in 11 weeks. He was a US and Canadian figure-skating gold medallist and a former figure-skating coach.

PERRON, Michel of Paris, France. (b.1952). Bridge professional. WBF World Grand Master and #13 in the 1999 world rankings. Won the World Team Olympiad twice. Won the Bermuda Bowl in 1997. Won the *Sunday Times* Invitational Pairs in 1991. 2nd in the European Teams in 1995. Numerous French national titles.

PERROUX, Carl'Alberto of Italy. (b.1905; d.1977). Trial lawyer. The most famous non-playing captain in bridge history. He steered the legendary Blue Team to eight World Championships (1957–66) and five European Championships (1951–59).

PHILLIPS, Hubert of London, England. (b.1891; d.1964). Journalist and bridge writer. He was one of the pioneers of bridge organization in England, and the editor of the *British Bridge World* from 1936–39. He was also a noted author/compiler of intellectual and mathematical puzzles, and crosswords. He wrote more than 70 books on various subjects including general knowledge quiz books and detective novels. The English National Mixed Teams trophy is named after him.

PICUS, Susan J "Sue" of New York City, New York, USA. (b.1948). Computer scientist. WBF World Grand Master and #16 in the 1999 world rankings. Won the Venice Cup twice. Won the World Women's Teams (McConnell Cup) in 1994. National titles include the Master Mixed Teams, the Women's BAM twice, the Women's Swiss, and the Women's Knock-Out Teams. Formerly Mrs Ron Andersen, she is now married to Barry Rigal.

PIGOT, Peter of Dublin, Ireland. (b.1932). Economist. Represented Ireland in two World and eight European Championships. He has won all of Ireland's major national Championships at least once.

PITTALA, Vito of Turin, Italy. (b.1927). Mechanical engineer. Won the Bermuda Bowl twice, and 2nd twice. Won the European Teams in 1979. National titles include the Italian Open Teams six times.

POLLACK, Rozanne (née Marel) of Englewood Cliffs, New Jersey, USA. (b.1948). Sociologist. Won the World Women's Teams (McConnell Cup) in 1994. 2nd in the 1995 Venice Cup. 3rd in the 1986 World Mixed Pairs. National titles include the Masters Mixed Teams, the Women's BAM twice, the Women's Knock-Out Teams twice, and the Women's Swiss Teams.

POLLACK, William L "Bill" of Englewood Cliffs, New Jersey, USA. (b.1951). Software executive. 3rd in the 1986 World Mixed Pairs. National titles include the Vanderbilt in 1990 and the Masters Mixed Teams in 1985.

POTTAGE, John F of London, England. (b.1964). Accountant. Oxford graduate. Won the World Junior Teams in 1989. Won the EC Junior Teams twice. Represented England in numerous Camrose Trophy matches. Represented England five times in the Junior Camrose, winning on all five occasions. National titles include Crockfords in 1986. He is the co-inventor of the Pottage Defence to 1NT.

POTTAGE, Julian Y of Basingstoke, England. (b.1962). Pension plan manager. Cambridge graduate, and captained the winning Cambridge team in the 1983 Varsity match. Won the Junior Camrose in 1984. National titles include the Pachabo twice. He is the co-inventor of the Pottage Defence to 1NT. He also discovered the Compound Guard Squeeze. A regular columnist in bridge magazines, he is the co-author, with Terence Reese, of four books.

PRIDAY, Richard Anthony "Tony" of London, England. (b.1922). Hardwood company chairman. British Life Master #26 and Grand Master #4. WBF World Life Master. Finished 3rd in the 1962 Bermuda Bowl and the 1976 World Team Olympiad. Won the European Teams in 1961, and 2nd in 1971. Represented Great Britain in two other World and six other European Championships. Represented England 28 times in the Camrose Trophy. National titles include Crockfords in 1981, the Gold Cup seven times, and the Pachabo three times. Former Chairman of the British Bridge League and columnist for the *Daily Telegraph*.

PRZYBORA, Tomasz of Warsaw, Poland. (b.1949). Bridge professional. WBF World Life Master. Won the World Team Olympiad in 1984. Won the European Teams in 1981. Won the European Pairs in 1989. Represented Poland in five other World Championships. Numerous national titles.

PSZEZOLA, Jacek of Warsaw, Poland. Won the World Pairs in 1998. 3rd in the 1997 World Transnational Teams. 2nd in the 1997 European Teams. Won the 1990 Schiphol International Teams in The Netherlands. Numerous national titles.

QUANTIN, Jean-Christophe of Paris, France. (b.1966). Bridge trainer. WBF World Master. He is responsible for organizing and coaching the French Junior teams. Finished 2nd in the 1987 World Junior Teams, and 3rd in 1989. Won the 1988 European Junior Teams. Won the European Pairs twice. Finished 2nd in the European Teams in 1989. Numerous national titles.

QUINN, Shawn Y (née Womack) of Irvine, California, USA. (b.1961). Sales representative. WBF World Grand Master and #10 in the 1999 world rankings. Won the World Women's Team Olympiad in 1996. Won the World Women's Pairs in 1998. Many national titles.

RADIN, Judi (née Friedenberg) of New York City, New York, USA. (b.1950). Formerly Mrs John Solodar. Bridge teacher and professional player. WBF World Grand Master and #21 in the 1999 world rankings. Contributing editor to *The Precision Newsletter* and a co-author of *Precision Club*. Won the World Women's Pairs in 1978, 2nd in 1990. Won the World Women's Team Olympiad in 1984. Won the Venice Cup in 1987, and finished 2nd twice. Won the World Women's Teams (McConnell Cup) in 1994 to complete the Grand Slam of major Women's World Championship titles. She is the only player to have won all four (Venice, McConnell, Olympiad and World Pairs). Many national titles. She also finished 2nd in the 1974 Reisinger and the 1979 Vanderbilt.

RAPEE, George of New York City, New York, USA. (b.1915; d.1999). Attorney and real-estate investor. WBF World Grand Master and #38 in the world rankings at the time of his death. ACBL Life Master #44. He was the inventor of the Stayman convention. Won the Bermuda Bowl three times, and 2nd twice. Finished 3rd in the 1990 Rosenblum Teams at the age of 75. During the period 1942–80, Rapee had a better record in the three major North American Team Championships than anyone else, winning 21 titles and finishing second 18 times.

RAUSCHEID, Andrea of Germany. Won the Venice Cup in 1995. 2nd in the European Women's Teams and the European Women's Pairs in 1995. Numerous national titles.

REBATTU, Maximilliaan J "Max" of Amstelveen, The Netherlands. (b.1939). Bridge journalist and teacher. WBF World Life Master. Finished 2nd in the 1982 World Pairs. Represented The Netherlands in three World and six European Championships. National titles include Schiphol International Teams twice and the Dutch Open Teams ten times. He is the bridge correspondent for Holland's biggest newspaper, *Telegraaf*, and a contributor to numerous bridge magazines.

REESE, J Terence of Hove, England. (b.1913; d.1998). Bridge writer. British Life Master #27 and Grand Master #38. Won the Bermuda Bowl in 1955. Represented Great Britain in 1965, when he and Boris Schapiro were accused of cheating. Won the World Par Contest in 1961. Finished 2nd in the World Team Olympiad in 1960 and in the 1962 World Pairs. Won the European Teams four times. Represented Great Britain in five other European Championships. Won *Sunday Times* Invitational Pairs in 1964. National titles include the Gold Cup eight times and the Masters Pairs six times.

He was the first to write a book about the Acol system, which became standard in Britain. He conducted regular radio programmes about bridge, and acted as commentator at international championships. Bridge columnist of the *Observer*, the *London Evening News*, and many weekly/monthly periodicals. He was the editor of *The British Bridge World* from 1955–62. The author of more than 40 books of which two, *Reese on Play* and *The Expert Game*, are classics that made major contributions to the game. In his later life, he collaborated with David Bird to co-write the popular Abbot series.

REUS, Sharyn of St Laurent, Canada. (b.1950). At the 1972 World Women's Team Olympiad, she became the youngest player ever to represent Canada in a non-Junior event. A WBF World Master. 3rd in the 1989 Venice Cup. Twice finished 4th in the World Women's Team Olympiad (1976 & 88). 6th in the World Women's Pairs in 1986. In 1989, her team finished 2nd in the Canadian National (Open) Teams Championship.

RIGAL, Barry J of New York City, New York, USA. (b.1958). Formerly of London, England. Oil tax accountant. British Grand Master #97. WBF World Master. Won the EC Mixed Teams in 1987. 2nd in the European Junior Teams in 1981. British national titles include the Gold Cup and the Spring Fours five times. He is a regular commentator for VuGraph at WBF events. He is a regular contributor to numerous magazines and provides a column service in the *IBPA Bulletin*. He is also Chairman of the IBPA Awards Committee.

RIMINGTON, Derek C of Kent, England. (b.1927). Computer manager and bridge writer. British Life Master #17 and Grand Master #10. National titles include the Gold Cup in 1958 and the Pachabo in 1961. A regular contributor to bridge magazines.

ROBINSON, Steve W of Arlington, Virginia, USA. (b.1941). US Army computer specialist. Won the Rosenblum Teams in 1986. Won the World Mixed Teams in 1974. He is the co-inventor of the CRASH convention for defending against a strong club, and his book, *Washington Standard*, is the definitive work on modern East Coast style Standard American. Won the Cavendish Teams in 1997. Many national titles.

ROBSON, Andrew M of London, England. (b.1964). Bridge club owner, teacher and professional player. Won the World Junior Teams in 1989. Won the European Teams in 1991. Won the *Sunday Times* Invitational Pairs and the Statenbank Invitational Pairs, both in 1990. North American national titles include the 1998 Reisinger. He has co-authored one book.

RODRIGUE, Claude of London, England. (b.1930 in Egypt). Stockbroker. British Life Master #13. WBF World Life Master. Won the World Par Contest and the European Teams in 1961. Represented Great Britain in seven World and ten European Championships. Also represented Egypt in one Zonal Championship and England in numerous Camrose Trophy matches. Won the *Sunday Times* Invitational Pairs in 1967. National titles include the Gold Cup four times.

RODWELL, Eric V of West Lafayette, Indiana, USA. (b.1957). Professional bridge player and writer. WBF World Grand Master and #2 in the 1999 world rankings. One of only eight players to have achieved the Triple Crown of the Bermuda Bowl, Olympiad and World Pairs. Won the Bermuda Bowl twice. Won the World Pairs in 1986. Won the World Team Olympiad in 1988, and finished 2nd in 1992. Won the 1988 World Top Pairs in The Netherlands, and finished 2nd in 1994. Won the *Sunday Times*/Macallan Invitational Pairs twice, and finished 2nd in 1993. Won the Scientist vs Naturalist match in London. Won the Icelandic Pairs and Teams in 1992. Won the 1992 Pan-American Open Pairs. Won the Notrump Challenge Match in 1993. Numerous national titles.

Rodwell is acknowledged as an outstanding theoretician. He designed the Meckwell (Meckstroth/Rodwell) Precision System and invented Support Doubles. He has co-authored a number of books and is a major contributor to the ACBL Teaching Series authored by Audrey Grant.

ROHOWSKI, Roland of Stuttgart, Germany. (b.1967). Bridge teacher. WBF World Master. Won the Rosenblum Cup in 1990, aged 22, becoming the youngest ever World champion in the game's history.

ROMANSKI, Jacek of Lublin, Poland. (b.1950). Bridge professional. WBF World Life Master. Won the World Team Olympiad in 1984. 4th in the World Pairs in 1994. Numerous national titles.

ROOT, William S "Bill" of Boca Raton, Florida, USA. (b.1923). Bridge teacher and writer. Finished 2nd in the 1967 Bermuda Bowl and the 1968 World Team Olympiad. National titles include the Reisinger five times, the Spingold three times, the Vanderbilt three times. Root is acknowledged as one of America's most prolific teachers, holding an average of seven classes a week, each for over 100 students. His books include *Modern Bridge Conventions*, co-written with Richard Pavlicek. He has also produced numerous videos, notably the *Bill Root Teaches Bridge Volume 1-5* series.

ROSANO, Enza of Turin, Italy. Sales representative. Won the World Mixed Pairs in 1998. Won the EC Mixed Pairs in 1996. Won the European Mixed Teams in 1998. Numerous national titles.

ROSE, Albert of London, England. (b.1908; d.1970). Finished 2nd in the first World Team Olympiad in 1960. 3rd in the 1962 Bermuda Bowl. Won the 1961 European Teams, and finished 2nd in 1953. Represented Great Britain in four World and three European Championships. Many national titles include Crockfords three times and the Gold Cup seven times.

ROSE, Irving N of London, England. (b.1938 in Scotland; d.1996). Bridge club manager and rubber bridge player. British Grand Master #26. WBF World Master. Finished 3rd in the World Team Olympiad in 1976. 2nd in the 1981 European Teams. Represented Great Britain in three World and six European Championships. National titles include Crockfords in 1966, the Gold Cup in 1985, and the 1985 Pachabo.

ROSENBERG, Michael of New York City, New York, USA. (b.1954 in Scotland). Formerly of Glasgow, Scotland. Options trader. WBF World Grand Master and #18 in the 1999 world rankings. Won the World Par Contest in 1998. Won the Rosenblum Teams in 1994. Finished 2nd in both the 1992 World Team Olympiad and the 1994 World Pairs. Won the 1978 European Junior Teams. Represented Scotland numerous times in the Camrose Trophy, including three rare wins in 1974, 76 & 77. Also represented Scotland three times in the Junior Camrose Trophy. Won the *Sunday Times* Invitational Pairs in 1976, aged 21, becoming the youngest person ever to win this event. Won the Cap Gemini Invitational Pairs twice. Won the Cavendish Invitational Pairs in 1992, and finished 2nd in 1978.

British national titles include the Scottish Rayne Trophy in 1972, and the Gold Cup in 1976 (aged 21, and again the youngest ever winner). Many North American national titles.

Rosenberg also represented Scotland four times in the 1969–80 period in the World Student Chess Olympiad.

ROSENBERG, Mortimer "Monty" of Belfast, Northern Ireland. (b.1923). Retired furniture dealer. In the course of a 36-year international career, he represented Northern Ireland in the Camrose Trophy more often than any other player in history. He also represented all-Ireland many times in both World and European Championships. National titles include both the Open Pairs and the Open Teams many times. Former President of the Irish Bridge Union.

ROSENBLUM, Julius of New Orleans, Louisiana, USA. (b.1906; d.1978). Formerly of Memphis, Tennessee. President of the WBF from 1970–76 (an unprecedented three terms), and also a former ACBL President. He was captain of the US team that defeated Italy in the 1951 Bermuda Bowl, and also played briefly in that event, thus becoming the only person to have both captained and played on a team that defeated the Italians.

The IBPA bestowed the Charles Goren "Personality of the Year" award on Rosenblum in 1974. In 1977, the Australian Bridge Federation made him an Honorary member – the first non-Australian to be so honoured. He was named an Honorary ACBL Member in 1970. When the Rosenblum World Teams Cup was introduced in 1978, the event was named in his honour.

ROSENKRANZ, Edith of Mexico. (b.1924 in Austria). Represented Mexico in 11 World Championships in the period 1962–90. Mexico's leading female masterpoint holder of all time.

She was Mexico's first female Life Master. She has won the John Pike Memorial Trophy, awarded for the best performance in the Mexican nationals, four times. North American titles include the Women's Swiss Teams and the Masters Mixed Teams, both in 1990. She was famously kidnapped for three days during the Summer Nationals in Boston in 1984. The team on which her husband, George, was playing went on to win the Spingold without him.

ROSENKRANZ, Dr Jorge "George" of Mexico. (b.1916). Scientist and founding Chairman of the Syntex Corporation. His scientific contributions include the development of cortisone and birth control pills. Mexico's leading player and theorist, he has represented that country in World Championship events almost continuously since 1962. He was Mexico's first Life Master. He was named as an Honorary ACBL Member in 1990. In 1975, he won the IBPA's C C Wei Precision Award for the best article/series on systems or conventions. In 1975, he established a new IBPA award, the Rosenkranz Award, to be given for the "Best Bid Hand of the Year".

Finished 3rd in the 1983 Bermuda Bowl representing North America. Many North American national titles.

Rosenkranz is the inventor of Rosenkranz Doubles/Redoubles, and the author/developer of the Romex system. He has written more than ten books, and is a regular contributor to numerous magazines.

ROSS, Hugh L of Oakland, California, USA. (b.1937 in Montreal, Canada). Systems analyst. WBF World Grand Master and #21 in the 1999 world rankings. Won the Bermuda Bowl three times, and finished 2nd twice. 2nd in the 1982 Rosenblum Teams. Many national titles.

ROTH, Alvin I "Al" of Boca Raton, Florida, USA. (b.1914). Formerly of New York City, New York. Stockbroker and owner/manager of the Mayfair Club in New York City. ACBL Life Master #34 and WBF Life Master.

Roth is generally considered the most original bidding theorist of his bridge generation, and as one of the great players of all time. He is the co-inventor of the Roth-Stone system, and his contributions to bidding theory include the Unusual No-Trump, Weak Two bids, the Forcing 1NT response and Negative Doubles.

He finished 2nd in the Bermuda Bowl three times. 2nd in the 1968 World Team Olympiad. Numerous national titles.

Roth has written a handful of books and numerous articles for *The Bridge World*, mostly on bidding theory.

ROUDINESCU, Jean-Marc of Paris, France. (b.1932). Bridge writer, translator and theoretician. WBF World Life Master. Finished 2nd in the 1971 Bermuda Bowl, and 3rd in 1967. Won the European Teams twice. Won the European Seniors Teams in 1999. National titles include the French Open Teams four times. He has written books and is a regular contributor to French bridge magazines.

RUBENS, Jeff of Scarsdale, New York, USA. (b.1941). Mathematician and bridge writer. Co-editor of *The Bridge World* since 1967, and the editor since the death of Edgar Kaplan. He won the BOLS Tip competition in 1977. He has won the IBPA's C C Wei Precision award for articles on bidding three times. Rubens' contributions to modern bidding theory include Transfer Advances of Overcalls, and Rubensohl (for use when the opponents intervene over 1NT openings and overcalls). He has also written numerous books.

Finished 4th in the Bermuda Bowl in 1973. National titles include the Spingold in 1972, and the Men's Pairs and Men's Teams, both in 1965. Won the North American Intercollegiate Championship in 1958.

RUBIN, Ira S "The Beast" of Paramus, New Jersey, USA. (b.1930). Retired mathematician. WBF World Grand Master and #43 in the 1999 world rankings. Won the Bermuda Bowl in 1976, and finished 2nd twice. Placed 2nd in the 1980 World Team Olympiad. 4th in the 1970 World Pairs. Many national titles.

His contributions to bidding theory include Rubin Transfers, Two-Way Two-Bids, Gladiator Responses to No-Trump, and Extended Landy.

RUBIN, Ronald D "Ron" of Miami Beach, Florida, USA. (b.1948). Options trader. Won the Bermuda Bowl in 1983. 5th in the 1986 Rosenblum Teams. Many national titles. He won the "Challenge the Champs" feature in *The Bridge World* for a record ten consecutive months. Won the IBPA's Rosenkranz Award for the "Best Bid Hand of the Year" in 1976. He is the author and inventor of the Ultimate Club system.

He won the World Backgammon Championship in 1983, and finished 2nd twice. He is the only person to have held both the World Backgammon and Bridge titles simultaneously.

SAELENSMINDE, Erik "Silla" of Bergen, Norway. (b.1964). Student. Finished 3rd in the 1997 Bermuda Bowl. 2nd in the 1999

European Teams, and 3rd in 1997. Won the 1998 Nordic Teams. Numerous national titles.

SANBORN, Kerri (formerly Shuman) of New York City, New York, USA. (b.1946). Options trader and professional player. WBF World Grand Master and #6 in the 1999 world rankings. Ranks third in the ACBL lists of women all-time masterpoint winners. Won the World Mixed Pairs in 1978, and 2nd in 1986. Won the Venice Cup twice. Won the World Women's Pairs in 1990. She was the only female player invited to the World PAMP Par Contest in 1990. She won the McKenney Trophy in 1974, one of only three women ever to have done so (Helen Sobel Smith and Hermine Baron being the other two). In 1988, she won the IBPA's Charles J Solomon Award for the year's best played hand, the first woman to have done so. Many national titles.

SANDERS, Carol of Nashville, Tennessee, USA. (b.1932). WBF World Grand Master and #24 in the 1999 world rankings. Won the Venice Cup twice, finished 2nd twice, and was the npc of the winning team in 1987. Won the World Women's Pairs in 1982, finished 2nd in 1978. Won the World Women's Team Olympiad in 1984. Her 3rd place in the World Women's Teams (McConnell Cup) meant that Sanders narrowly missed out on becoming the second player to join Judi Radin in achieving the Grand Slam of Women's World titles. 3rd in the World Mixed Pairs in 1978.

She won both the Israel national Swiss Teams and the Beijing International Friendship Cup in 1986, and the Ambassador's Cup in 1987. Many national titles. She also finished 2nd in the 1961 Chicago (now the Reisinger).

SANDERS, Thomas K of Nashville, Tennessee, USA. (b.1932). Investor. He was npc of the winning Bermuda Bowl team in 1981. Finished 6th in the 1974 World Mixed Teams. National titles include the Spingold, the Vanderbilt three times, the Life Masters Pairs, the Blue Ribbon Pairs, the Men's BAM Teams, the Mixed Pairs, the Masters Mixed Teams, and the Men's Teams twice. He is the only graduate of Vanderbilt University to have won the Vanderbilt Trophy.

SANTAMARINA, Agustin of Buenos Aires, Argentina. (b.1934). Landowner. WBF World Life Master. Represented Argentina in four Bermuda Bowls and six World Team Olympiads. Won the South American Teams six times. National titles include the Open Teams 13 times, the Open Pairs twice, and the Gabarret Cup four times.

SCHALTZ, Dorthe of Odense, Denmark. (b.1956). Medical secretary. WBF World Master. Won the World Women's Team Olympiad in 1988. Reached the quarter-final of the 1992 World Team Olympiad (losing by just 2 IMPs) as a member of the Danish Open team, which is the best ever performance in the event by a female player. Numerous national titles.

SCHALTZ, Peter of Odense, Denmark. (b.1950). Wine company manager. WBF World Life Master. Finished 3rd in the 1984 World Team Olympiad, and was also on the Danish team that lost narrowly in the 1992 quarter-final. Won the European Junior Teams in 1970. 2nd in the 1979 European Teams. Won the Nordic Teams in 1986. Numerous national titles include the Danish Open Teams seven times and the Open Pairs three times. In 1992, he won the IBPA's Charles J Solomon Award for the year's best played hand.

SCHAPIRO, Boris of London, England. (b.1909). Retired company director. British Life Master #11 and Grand Master #63. WBF World Grand Master and #36 in the 1999 world rankings. Won the Bermuda Bowl in 1955. Won the first World Mixed Teams in 1962. Won the 1998 World Seniors Pairs at the age of 89, becoming the oldest person ever to win a World Championship at any sport. Finished 2nd in the inaugural World Team Olympiad in 1960, and in the first World Pairs in 1962. Won the European Teams four times. He represented Great Britain in seven World and ten European Championships. One of these was the notorious 1965 Bermuda Bowl, when Schapiro and Terence Reese were accused of cheating.

Won the *Sunday Times* Invitational Pairs in 1964, and finished 2nd in 1991 at the age of 81. Numerous national titles include the Gold Cup a record 11 times in a 50-year span between 1946 and 1998. He in the author of two books, and the bridge columnist for *The Sunday Times*.

SCHENKEN, Howard of New York City, New York, USA. (b.1905; d.1979). Real estate investor, bridge author and columnist. ACBL Life Master #3. Considered by many to have been the best player of all time. He is credited with discovering many aspects of card-play technique and deceptive play that are now considered standard. His bidding innovations include the Weak Two Bid, the Forcing Two-over-One response, and the concept of a "prepared" opening bid to facilitate a rebid. His own system, the Big Club, was one of the first artificial systems.

After occasional appearances with the Four Horsemen and the Bid-Rite teams, Schenken founded the Four Aces and stayed with them through numerous successes including victory over the French European champions in the first official World Championship in 1935. He won the Bermuda Bowl three times, and finished 2nd three times. He also represented the US in the first World Team Olympiad in 1960.

His 32 national titles is not a record in itself, but he has won two of North America's major events (the Life Masters Pairs and the Vanderbilt) more often than any other player. His record of ten victories in the Spingold stood for more than 35 years, until equalled in 1996 and then beaten in 1998 by Bob Hamman. He was second in another 19 national events.

He was named as an Honorary Member of the IBPA in 1973. His books include three classics, *The Four Aces System of Contract Bridge*, *Howard Schenken's Big Club* and *Education of a Bridge Player*. He took over the Four Aces syndicated bridge column in 1943, and in 1957 he merged it with Richard L Frey's to become co-author of the longest continuously published nationally syndicated bridge feature. In 1970, he became the sole author of the column, continuing until his death.

SCHIPPERS, Elly of Amstelveen, The Netherlands. (b.1943). Systems analyst. WBF World Life Master. Finished 2nd in the Venice Cup in 1989. 3rd in the World Women's Team Olympiad in 1984. Won the 1980 European Women's Pairs, and finished 2nd in 1987. Twice finished 2nd in the European Women's Teams. Numerous national titles include the Dutch Women's Pairs four times.

SCHROEDER, Dirk of Wiesbaden, Germany. (b.1943). Bridge teacher, journalist and theorist. WBF World Master. Won three EC Championship titles and more than 30 German national titles. He has led the all-time German masterpoint rankings since 1974. He developed the concept of the European Youth Camp, and organized the first one in 1975. He is a member of the IBPA Executive Committee and has been a columnist for *Deutsches Bridge Verbands-Blatt* since 1969.

SCHULLE, Kay of Santa Monica, California, USA. (b.1950). Bridge professional. Won the Venice Cup in 1993, and finished 4th in 1991. Won the South African National Pairs once and the National Teams twice. Several North American national titles.

SEAMON, Janice of North Miami, Florida, USA. Attorney and bridge teacher. Won the ACBL's Junior Master of the Year in 1976, in her first year playing. National titles include the Life Masters Women's Pairs twice, the Women's Pairs and the Women's Knock-Out Teams twice. She is the daughter of Bill Seamon and the sister of Michael.

SEAMON, Michael E of Miami Beach, Florida, USA. (b.1960). Bridge professional and teacher. WBF World Master. Won the World IMP Pairs in 1998. 2nd in the 1990 Rosenblum Teams. Won the Cavendish Invitational Pairs in 1997. National titles include the Open Teams twice, the Grand National Teams and the Open Pairs I. He is the son of Bill Seamon and the brother of Janice.

SEMENTA, Antonio of Salsomaggiore, Italy. (b.1968). Business consultant. Won the European Teams in 1995. Won the EC Teams in 1993. Won the European Junior Teams in 1992. 3rd in the European Pairs in 1995.

SENIOR, Brian R of Nottingham, England. (b.1953). Bridge writer and teacher. The editor of *IPBM* until its demise in 1999. British Grand Master #58. WBF World Master. He has represented both Great Britain and Ireland in both World and European Championships. He has also appeared for both England and Northern Ireland in the Camrose Trophy. National titles include the Gold Cup in 1993 and Crockfords in 1982. He has written numerous books and articles.

SENIOR, Nevena (née Deleva) of Nottingham, England. (b.1959). Mathematician. Formerly of Sofia, Bulgaria. WBF World Master. Won the European Women's Pairs in 1987, and finished 3rd twice, latterly in 1999 in Malta. 3rd in the World Women's Team Olympiad in 1988. She represented Bulgaria in several World and European Championships before becoming eligible to represent Great Britain in 1997.

SERES, Thomas Peter "Tim" of Randwick, New South Wales, Australia. (b.1925 in Austria). Horse-racing investor. WBF World Life Master. Twice finished 3rd in the Bermuda Bowl. Won the Far East Teams twice. Represented Australia in 12 World and ten Far Eastern Championships. More than 40 National titles include the Australian Inter-State Teams 21 times, and the National Open Pairs eight times.

He discovered a play subsequently named after him – the Seres Squeeze. He is a regular contributor to bridge magazines. He is an

Honorary ABF Member, and he was awarded the Order of Australia for his contributions to the game. In 1975, he won the IBPA's Charles J Solomon Award for the year's best played hand.

SHANAHAN, Dorothy of London, England. Statistician. Won the World Women's Team Olympiad in 1964. Won the European Women's Teams three times. Represented Great Britain in nine European Championships. She won the inaugural British Portland Mixed Pairs in 1956, playing with Maurice Harrison-Gray. Other National titles include Crockfords, the Women's Teams twice, the National Pairs, and the Hubert Phillips Mixed Knock-Out Teams twice.

SHARIF, Omar of Paris, France. (b.1932). Motion picture star. Formerly of Egypt. He represented the UAR in the 1964 & 68 World Team Olympiads. 2nd in the European Seniors Teams in 1999. He is one of the most active, and high-profile, promoters of bridge. The one thing that most non-bridge players know about the game is that Omar Sharif plays. He organized the Sharif Bridge Circus and was responsible for the Lancia Tournaments in the 1970s. In 1974 he received the IBPA's John E Simon Award as "Sportsman of the Year". Numerous national titles include the Interclubs Teams four times in the early 1960s. He is the bridge columnist for the *Observer*.

SHARPLES, James "Jim" of Kent, England. (b.1908; d.1985). Bank officer. British Life Master #1 and Grand Master #1. All his major achievements were accomplished playing with his twin brother, Bob. Finished 2nd in the 1958 European Teams. Represented Great Britain in three European Championships. Played 20 Camrose Trophy matches for England between 1950–77. National titles include the Gold Cup six times, Crockfords twice, the National Pairs, the Masters Pairs, the Hubert Phillips Mixed Knock-Out Teams twice, and the Pachabo.

SHARPLES, Robert "Bob" of Kent, England. (b.1908). Bank officer. British Life Master #2 and Grand Master #2. His playing record is identical to that of his twin brother, Jim.

SHEEHAN, Robert M of London, England. (b.1939). Spread betting bookmaker. Placed 2nd in the 1987 Bermuda Bowl, and 5th in 1981. Finished 2nd in the European Teams three times. Represented Great Britain in five World and six European Championships. Fifth in the World Pairs in 1974. National titles include the National Pairs and the Gold Cup five times. He is the bridge columnist for *The Times* and a regular contributor to several magazines.

SHEINWOLD, Alfred "Freddie" of Beverly Hills, California, USA. (b.1912 in London, England; d.1997). Bridge author and columnist. Formerly of New York City, New York. He is widely acknowledged as one of the greatest bridge writers in history. He is a member of the Bridge Hall of Fame. He was always fascinated by puzzles, and during World War II it was his job to break German codes, and he was so successful at this that he became America's chief code and cipher expert.

When the Kaplan-Sheinwold system that he co-developed with Edgar Kaplan came on the scene, the bridge world was ready to try weak no-trumps and controlled psychics. The system was widely used for several years, and there are still many players who are confirmed K-S advocates.

His daily bridge column in *The Los Angeles Times* was widely syndicated, and many would say it was consistently the best column in the world. He was also an editor of *The Bridge World* from 1934–63, the editor of the *ACBL Bulletin* from 1953–58, and the editor-in-chief of *Autobridge* from 1938 until his death. He was also games editor for *Argosy* and a contributing editor for *Popular Bridge*.

In 1963, he pioneered bridge lessons on Pay-television. He was also a major authority on backgammon, frequently serving as chief director for backgammon tournaments in Las Vegas. His 13 books include the most commercially successful bridge book ever written, *Five Weeks to Winning Bridge*, which sold more than a million copies.

He was the npc of numerous American teams in World Championships. One of these was the 1975 Bermuda Bowl, at which he threatened to withdraw the American team if the WBF allowed an Italian pair, who had been caught cheating, to continue playing. Sheinwold was overruled by ACBL directors who were present, and his team went on to lose a close final. The incident caused a rift between Sheinwold and the ACBL that lasted for many years.

He was named ACBL Honorary Member of the Year in 1983. He won two national titles, the Chicago in 1958 and the 1964 Men's Pairs.

SHENKIN, Barnet J of Florida, USA. (b.1950 in Scotland). Formerly of London, England. Carpet importer. Represented Great Britain in one World, three European and three EC Championships.

Played more than 40 Camrose Trophy matches for Scotland between 1974–92. Won the *Sunday Times* Invitational Pairs twice (1976 & 80). British national titles include the Spring Fours and the Gold Cup three times. North American national titles include the Open Swiss Teams in 1999.

SHIVDASANI, Jaggy of Bombay, India. (b.1958). Accountant. WBF World Master. Placed 4th in the World Team Olympiad in 1988. Twice finished 2nd in the BFAME Teams. Represented India in four World and numerous BFAME Championships. National titles include the Indian Open Teams four times and the Open Pairs twice, the first at the age of 18, a record. North American national titles include the Spingold in 1987 (the first non-American to win the event) and the Reisinger in 1988.

SILBORN, Gunborg of Norrkoping, Sweden. (b.1924). WBF Life Master. Won the World Women's Team Olympiad in 1968. Won the European Women's Teams in 1967. Won the Nordic Women's Teams six times. Numerous national titles.

SILODOR, Sidney of Havertown, Pennsylvania, USA. (b.1906; d.1963). Lawyer and bridge lecturer. Won the first Bermuda Bowl in 1950, and finished 2nd twice. 5th in the first World Team Olympiad in 1960. He won the McKenney Trophy in 1946. National titles include the Vanderbilt eight times, the Spingold three times, the Mixed Pairs three times, the Masters Mixed Teams four times and the Life Masters Pairs.

SILVER, Joseph "Joey" of Montreal, Canada. (b.1941). Trial attorney. Placed 2nd in the Bermuda Bowl in 1995. Represented Canada in five World Team Olympiads. Won the Cavendish Invitational Pairs in 1985 playing with Irving Litvack. They did not get to defend because they withdrew when an extra overseas pair arrived after an invitational mix-up – for this they received the IBPA's John E Simon Award for "Sportsman of the Year". North American national titles include the Vanderbilt, the Men's BAM Teams, the Open Pairs and the Open Swiss Teams.

SILVERMAN, Neil of Fort Lauderdale, Florida, USA. (b.1949). Options trader. WBF World Master. Won the Rosenblum Teams in 1986. Won the Maccabean Games in 1981. National titles include the Grand National Teams in 1997, the Life Masters Pairs in 1976 and the Men's Pairs in 1980.

SILVERSTONE, Victor A of London, England. (b.1940). Accountant. Formerly of Glasgow, Scotland. British Grand Master

#65. Represented Scotland in 25 Camrose Trophy matches, winning the event once. National titles include the Gold Cup three times and the Spring Fours.

SIMON, S J "Skid" of London, England. (b.1904; d.1948). Novelist and bridge writer. One of the originators of the Acol system. Won the European Teams in 1948, and represented Great Britain in one other European Championship. National titles include the Gold Cup twice.

He wrote numerous successful novels and a handful of bridge books, including one of the all-time classics, *Why You Lose at Bridge*. He was also a regular contributor to *The Bridge World*.

SIMS, P Hal of Deal, New Jersey, USA. (b.1886 in Selma, Alabama; d.1949). ACBL Life Master #5. He was one of the great players of his era, and his bidding system was the one favoured by most pre-war experts. He was captain of the Four Horsemen team that dominated early American contract tournaments, and also of America's highest-ranked auction bridge team. National titles include the Vanderbilt twice, the Spingold and the first Life Masters Pairs in 1930.

SLAVENBURG, Cornelius "Bob" of Rotterdam, The Netherlands. (b.1917; d.1981). Merchant. WBF Grand Master. Won the World Pairs in 1966. Represented The Netherlands in three World and five European Championships. Won the *Sunday Times* Invitational Pairs in 1971. National titles include the Open Teams four times and the Open Pairs three times.

SMITH, Marc of Southampton, England. (b.1960). Bridge writer. British Grand Master #228. Won the EC Junior Teams in 1985. Represented England in the Junior Camrose three times, winning on all three occasions. Represented Great Britain in one World and five European Championships. National titles include the Four Stars Teams in 1984, the Two Stars Pairs in 1995, and the Pachabo in 1999. He is the author of five books and a regular contributor to numerous bridge magazines. His book, co-written with Barbara Seagram from Canada, won the ABTA "Book of the Year" award in 1999.

SMITH, Nicola P (née Gardener) of London, England. (b.1949). Bridge teacher and former Director of the London School of Bridge. British Grand Master #31. WBF Grand Master and #14 in the 1999 world rankings. Won the Venice Cup twice. Placed 2nd in the World Women's Team Olympiad four times. Won the European

Women's Teams five times and finished 2nd three times. Won the Generali World Individual. Won five EC Championship titles. Represented Britain in nine World, 14 European and five EC Championships. National titles include the Gold Cup three times, the Spring Fours four times and the Pachabo twice.

SMOLEN, Michael of Alamo, California, USA. (b.1940; d.1992). Commodity trader. WBF World Master. He was #16 on the ACBL all-time masterpoints list at the time of his death. He invented the popular Smolen convention, for use with 5-4 major-suit hands facing a 1NT opening. National titles include the Reisinger in 1984, the Men's Teams in 1976, the Open Swiss Teams in 1978, the 1979 Mixed Pairs and the Men's Swiss Teams twice (1982 & 84).

SMOLSKI, Roman of Bermuda. (b.1950). Formerly of Bradford, England. Computer programmer. British Grand Master #53. Won the European Teams and the EC Teams in 1981. Represented Great Britain in five World and three European Championships. Played 15 Camrose Trophy matches for England. National titles include the Spring Fours three times,

SOBEL, Helen M (formerly White and later Smith) of Detroit, Michigan, USA. (b.1910 in Philadelphia, Pennsylvania; d.1969). ACBL Life Master #25. Formerly of New York City, Philadelphia, and Miami Beach. She is universally regarded as the greatest woman player of all time. Edgar Kaplan wrote of her, "In my lifetime, she is the only women bridge player who was considered the best player in the world." She was the first woman elected to the Bridge Hall of Fame.

Her brief stage career included a spell in the chorus of *Animal Crackers* with the Marx Brothers, and it was there that another chorus girl taught her to play bridge.

In 1948, she became the ACBL's highest-ranked women (taking over the top spot from Sally Young), and she held that position until 1964. She is one of only three women to have won the McKenney Trophy, and she did so three times.

Smith and frequent partner, Charles Goren, won the De La Rue International Invitational Pairs Tournament in London in 1956 (billed as a World Championship). She represented North America in the Bermuda Bowl in 1957 (one of only two women, Dorothy Truscott being the other, to have done so), and the United States in the World Team Olympiad in 1960.

The last of her 35 national titles came in the Masters Mixed Teams in 1968. This was her sixth win in the event, tying a record held by her former partner, Goren. Other national titles include the Spingold four times, the Chicago (now the Reisinger) four times, the Vanderbilt twice, the Life Masters Pairs twice, the Masters Mixed Teams a record six times, the Mixed Pairs twice, the Women's Teams four times, and the Women's Pairs twice.

SOKOLOW, Tobi (née Deutsch) of Austin, Texas, USA. Real-estate broker. Won the Venice Cup in 1997. Twice finished 3rd in the World Women's Teams (McConnell Cup). 5th in the World Women's Pairs in 1994. National titles include the Women's Knock-Out Teams in 1997, the Life Masters Women's Pairs in 1991, and the Women's Pairs twice (1987 & 90).

SOLODAR, John of New York City, New York, USA. (b.1940), Systems programmer. Won the Bermuda Bowl in 1981. Placed 3rd in the 1990 Rosenblum Teams. National titles include the Vanderbilt in 1980 and the Life Masters Men's Pairs in 1968. He was the New York manager for the Omar Sharif Bridge Circus in 1968.

SOLOWAY, Paul of Bothell, Washington, USA. (b.1941). Bridge professional. WBF World Grand Master and #28 in the 1999 world rankings. He has more masterpoints than any other ACBL member. Won the Bermuda Bowl three times. Twice finished 2nd in the World Team Olympiad. Won the Pan-American Invitational Championship in 1977. Won the McKenney Trophy twice. Many national titles.

SONTAG, Alan M of Gaithersburg, Maryland, USA. (b.1946). Bridge professional. WBF Life Master. Won the Bermuda Bowl in 1983. Won the Cavendish Invitational Pairs twice. Won the *Sunday Times* Invitational Pairs twice. Many national titles.

He was a member of the Precision Team and, with regular partner, Peter Weichsel, co-developed Power Precision. He is the author of two books, both classics in their fields – *Power Precision* and *The Bridge Bum*. He was given the IBPA John E Simon Award as "Sportsman of the Year" in 1974.

SOULET, Philippe of Paris, France. (b.1954). Bridge teacher. WBF World Master. Won the World Team Olympiad in 1982 and the Rosenblum Teams in 1980. Won the European Teams in 1983. Represented France in five World and two European Championships. Numerous national titles.

SOWTER, Dr Anthony P "Tony" of Nottingham, England. (b.1946). Bridge writer. Former editor of *IPBM*. British Grand Master #29. WBF World Master. Won the European Teams in 1991, and finished 2nd in 1981. Represented Great Britain in eight World Championships. National titles include the Spring Fours, the Gold Cup three times, Crockfords twice and the Pachabo.

SQUIRE, Norman of London, England. (b.1907; d.1991). Bridge writer. Won De La Rue International Par Contest in 1957. His contributions to bidding theory include Fourth-Suit Forcing and the Out-of-the-Blue Cuebid. He wrote 12 books and was a regular contributor to numerous magazines. National titles include Crockfords twice and the Gold Cup three times.

STANSBY, Lewis "Lew" of Castro Valley, California, USA. (b.1940). Commodities trader. WBF World Grand Master and #9 in the 1999 world rankings. Won the World Pairs in 1982. Won the Bermuda Bowl twice. Won the Rosenblum Teams in 1994. Won the Cavendish Teams in 1999. Many national titles. He won the IBPA Rosenkranz Award for the "Best Bid Hand of the Year" in 1979.

STAYMAN, Samuel M "Sam" of Palm Beach, Florida, USA. (b.1909; d.1993). Retired portfolio manager. WBF Grand Master. ACBL Life Master #48. In the June 1945 issue of *The Bridge World*, he described a convention, invented by his then partner George Rapee, which subsequently became known as the Stayman convention. His other contribution to bidding theory was Namyats opening four-level bids (called South African Texas in Europe), so named because it was Stayman spelled backwards.

Won the Bermuda Bowl three times. Finished 2nd in the World Team Olympiad in 1964. He won 20 national titles.

He was a former President of the Cavendish Club in New York City. He was named as an ACBL Honorary Member in 1969, and received the same honour from the American Bridge Teachers Association in 1979. He is the author of *Expert Bidding, The Complete Stayman System of Contract Bidding*, and *Do You Play Stayman?*

STEWART, Frederick M of Andes, New York, USA. (b.1948). Stockbroker. Placed 5th in the Bermuda Bowl in 1991. 14th in the 1986 World Pairs. Won the Pan-American Pairs in 1991. Won the Cavendish Invitational Pairs in 1993. National titles include the Reisinger in 1984, the Life Masters Pairs in 1981, the Blue Ribbon

Pairs in 1987, and the 1992 Open Swiss Teams. He is the step-father of Steve Weinstein.

STONE, Tobias of New York City, New York, USA. (b.1921). Bridge writer. WBF Life Master. ACBL Life Master #85. Finished 2nd in the Bermuda Bowl in 1958. 3rd in the 1960 World Team Olympiad. He and Al Roth became the first Americans to win the Deauville Invitational Pairs in France, and they did so with an incredible 82%. As the co-inventor of the Roth-Stone system, he has made numerous contributions to bidding theory. He won the McKenney Trophy in 1956. Many national titles.

He was also an international backgammon champion.

STOPPA, Dr Jean-Louis of Paris, France. (b.1932). Physician. WBF World Life Master. Finished 2nd in the Bermuda Bowl in 1971. Won the 1970 European Teams. 2nd in the European Seniors Teams in 1999. Represented France in seven World and four European Championships. Numerous national titles.

SUN, Ming of Beijing, China. (b.1955). WBF World Master. Won the World Women's Team Olympiad in 1996. 2nd in the Venice Cup in 1997, and finished 3rd twice (1991 & 95). Won the Far East Women's Teams five times, and finished 2nd twice. Numerous national titles.

SUNDELIN, Per-Olof "P-O" of Stockholm, Sweden. (b.1937). Computer consultant. Twice finished 3rd in the Bermuda Bowl. 3rd in the World Team Olympiad in 1988. Won the European Teams twice. Represented Sweden in ten World and 13 European Championships. Won the *Sunday Times* Invitational Pairs twice. Numerous national titles include the Swedish Open Teams seven times. North American national titles include the Life Masters Pairs in 1984 and the Seniors Swiss Teams in 1998. He is a regular contributor to bridge magazines. When he is either not selected or has not qualified to play, he also commentates for the VuGraph show at European and World Championships.

SVEINDAL, Jan of Bergen, Norway. (b.1946). Bridge journalist and teacher. Finished 2nd in the 1993 Bermuda Bowl. 2nd in the 1999 European Teams. Won the Nordic Teams in 1998. Represented Norway in numerous European Championships. Many national titles.

SWANSON, John C Jr of Mission Viejo, California, USA. (b.1937). Computer programmer. WBF Life Master. Won the Bermuda Bowl in 1977, and finished 2nd in 1975 and 4th in 1973

Placed 5th in the 1978 World Pairs. Many national titles. He is the author of *Inside the Bermuda Bowl*, and a regular contributor to bridge magazines. He is also the co-inventor of the Walsh system.

SWIMER, Ralph of London, England. (b.1914; d.1998). Company director. Finished 2nd in the first World Team Olympiad in 1960. He was the npc of the Great Britain team involved in cheating allegations during the 1965 Bermuda Bowl in Buenos Aires. National titles include Crockfords three times, the National Pairs, the Masters Pairs three times and the Gold Cup.

SZWARC, Henri of Paris, France. (b.1930 in Poland). Textile company director. WBF World Grand Master and #20 in the 1999 world rankings. Won the World Team Olympiad twice. Won the European Teams four times. 2nd in the European Seniors Teams in 1999. Represented France in eight World and 12 European Championships. Won the *Sunday Times* Invitational Pairs in 1977. Numerous national titles. In 1985, he won the IBPA's Charles J Solomon Award for the year's best played hand.

SZYMANOWSKI, Marek of Warsaw, Poland. (b.1955). Economist and bridge professional. Won the World Pairs in 1994. Finished 2nd in the Bermuda Bowl in 1991, and 3rd in 1989. Won the European Teams in 1989, and 3rd in 1991. Represented Poland in six World Championships. Numerous Polish national titles. North American national titles include the Spingold in 1997.

TAMMENS, Kees of Amsterdam, The Netherlands. (b.1950). Bridge journalist. WBF World Master. Coach of the Dutch Junior team. Contributor to numerous magazines. Represented The Netherlands in three World and three European Championships. National titles include the Schiphol International Teams in 1987, the Dutch National Teams three times, and the Open Pairs once.

TARLO, Joel of Marbella, Spain. (b.1905; d.1991). Retired solicitor. Formerly of London, England. Won the European Teams in 1963, when his brother Louis was npc. Represented Great Britain in two World and four European Championships. Represented Spain in the 1987 European Championship at the age of 82, a record. British national titles include the Gold cup twice and the Hubert Phillips Mixed Knock-Out Teams twice.

TARLO, Louis of Hove, England. (b.1905). Retired solicitor. Won the European Teams in 1950. Represented Great Britain in one World and six European Championships. He was also npc of the

British teams in two World and four European Championships. Won the Philippine National Pairs and Teams in 1960. British national titles include the Gold Cup six times, the Spring Fours, Crockfords twice, the National Pairs, the Masters Pairs, and the Pachabo twice.

TERRANEO, Franz of Vienna, Austria. (b.1953). Project manager. WBF World Life Master. Finished 2nd in both the 1985 Bermuda Bowl and the 1988 World Team Olympiad. Won the European Teams and finished 2nd in the European Pairs, both in 1985. Won the European Mixed Pairs in 1990. Won the Statenbank Invitational Pairs twice. Numerous national titles including the Austrian Teams six times and the National Mixed Pairs twice.

TERRANEO, Sylvia of Vienna, Austria. Won the World Women's Teams (McConnell Cup) in 1998. Finished 2nd in the European Women's Teams in 1999.

THOMPSON, Benjamin John Polya "Ben" of Melbourne, Australia. (b.1965 in California, USA). Computer scientist. Finished 3rd in the World Junior Teams in 1991. Won the Far East Junior Teams in 1990.

TINTNER, Leon of Paris, France. (b.1910 in Austria). Publisher. WBF Life Master. Finished 3rd in the Bermuda Bowl twice. Won the European Teams twice. Won the *Sunday Times* Invitational Pairs in 1971. National titles include the French Open Teams twice and the Interclubs twice.

TOIBIN, Niall of Dublin, Ireland. (b.1959). Administrator. Won the EC Open Pairs and Junior Teams, both in 1981. Represented Ireland in three World and two European Championships. Numerous national titles.

TOWNSEND, Tom G of Berkshire, England. (b.1970). Rubber bridge professional and bridge writer. Won the World Junior Teams in 1995. Won the European Junior Teams in 1994. National titles include the Spring Fours and Crockfords twice. He is a regular contributor to numerous magazines.

TREDINNICK, Gerald A of Kent, England. (b.1963). Actuary. Most of his victories have been achieved playing with his twin brother, Stuart. Won the World Junior Teams in 1989. Represented Great Britain in four European Championships, national titles include the Spring Fours twice, Crockfords, the Gold Cup twice, and the Pachabo.

TREDINNICK, Stuart P of Kent, England. (b.1963). Computer programmer. His playing record is the same as that of his twin brother, Gerald.

TRÉZEL, Roger of Paris, France. (b.1918; d.1986). Journalist. WBF Grand Master. He was the first player to win the Triple Crown – won the Bermuda Bowl in 1956, the first World Team Olympiad in 1960, and the first World Pairs in 1962. Won the European Teams twice, and finished 2nd three times. Won the *Sunday Times* Invitational Pairs in 1963. His partnership with Pierre Jaïs was acknowledged to be one of the world's strongest, and they were one of the first pairs to play canapé methods at the top level. He was the author of a series of booklets.

TRUSCOTT, Alan F of New York City, New York, USA. (b.April 16, 1925 in England). Bridge journalist. British Life Master #31. He has been the bridge columnist for *The New York Times* since 1964. He was President of the IBPA from 1981–86, and Secretary of the British Bridge League from 1957–62. He is a frequent contributor to numerous magazines, and he has been the Executive Editor of all five editions of the ACBL's Official *Encyclopedia of Bridge*. He has written many books.

As a player, he finished 3rd in the 1962 Bermuda Bowl. Won the European Teams in 1961. Represented Great Britain in one World and three European Championships, and represented the USA in eight World Championships. He has also coached both the Brazilian and the Bermudan teams in World Championships.

His innovations have included the Truscott Card, now widely used to prevent seating errors in team play. He has also invented numerous bidding conventions such as the Truscott Defence to Strong Club, Two-way Stayman, and the Truscott 2NT Response (which is commonly used after a major-suit opening is doubled). His contributions to theory include the Principle of Restricted Choice.

British national titles include the Masters Individual twice and the Pachabo in 1961. North American national titles include the Master Mixed Teams in 1985, the Open Swiss Teams in 1987 and the Mixed Pairs in 1989.

Truscott completed the 1986 New York Marathon at the age of 61.

TRUSCOTT, Dorothy (formerly Hayden) of New York City, New York, USA. (b.1925). Bridge teacher, writer and mathematician. WBF Grand Master and #29 on the 1999 world women's rankings. In 1980, she overtook Rixi Markus to become the world's #1-ranked woman player.

Won the Venice Cup three times, and was npc of the winning team in 1989. Won the World Women's Team Olympiad in 1980, and finished 3rd three times. Twice finished 3rd in the World Women's Pairs. She is one of only two women ever to represent North America in the Bermuda Bowl, in 1965 (Helen Sobel Smith being the other). She also finished 3rd in the 1966 World Pairs – the only female player ever to finish in the top ten.

Four of her 25 national titles have been won with partners she had never played with before. She won the inaugural Blue Ribbon Pairs playing with B Jay Becker in 1963, and is still the only women to have won the event.

Her contributions to bidding theory include the Splintcr Bid and DOPI. She has written several books and is a regular contributor to bridge magazines. She is currently writing a historical novel about New Amsterdam.

VAN CLEEFF, Jan of The Hague, The Netherlands. Bridge writer. The Editor/Publisher of *IMP Magazine*. Represented The Netherlands in numerous events. Won the Cavendish Teams in 1998. National titles include the Dutch Meesterklasse Teams in 1997.

VAN DER PAS, Marijke of Utrecht, The Netherlands. (b.1949). Bridge journalist. WBF World Life Master. A regular member of the Dutch Women's team since 1979. Finished 2nd in the Venice Cup in 1989, and 3rd in the 1984 World Women's Team Olympiad. Won the European Women's Pairs in 1980. Twice finished 2nd in the European Women's Teams. Numerous national titles including the Dutch Women's Pairs four times. A regular contributor to bridge magazines.

VANDERBILT, Harold S of Newport, Rhode Island, USA. (b.July 6, 1884 in Oakdale, New York; d.July 4, 1970). Harvard graduate. A bridge authority whose revisions of auction bridge scoring principles created modern contract bridge. He was also an innovator of bidding methods and a champion player.

He was born into the richest and most famous American family of the time. His father left him an estate of some $54.5 million including the family business, New York Central Railroad, founded by his great-grandfather, Cornelius Vanderbilt. He became a famed yachtsman, and his revisions of "right-of-way" rules are still known as the Vanderbilt Rules.

He took up bridge seriously in 1906, and although principles of contract bridge – counting only bid tricks toward game – were often proposed, they were rejected continuously by the auction bridge authorities. Experimenting with the new game while on a cruise in 1925, Vanderbilt originated the factors of vulnerability and inflated slam bonuses. He produced a scoring table so balanced as to make nearly every aggressive or sacrifice bid an approximately even bet, allowing just enough differential to permit the exercise of judgment. The rapid spread of contract bridge from 1926 to 1929 is largely attributable to Vanderbilt's efforts, and his social standing made the game fashionable.

Vanderbilt's technical contribution was even greater. He devised the first unified system of bidding, and was solely responsible for the use of an artificial One Club bid to show a strong hand and the negative One Diamond response, the strong (16-18 point) no-trump on balanced hands only, and the Weak Two-bid opening. These and other principles were presented in his many books.

He was a member of the Laws Committee of the Whist Club of New York that made the American Contract Bridge Laws (1927 & 31) and the first international code in 1932. He personally drafted the American and International laws through and including the 1963 revision.

In 1928, he presented the Harold S Vanderbilt Cup for the national team-of-four championship now known as the Vanderbilt. This became, and still is, the most coveted American team trophy, mainly because until his death Vanderbilt presented the replicas to the winners personally. In 1960, Vanderbilt supplied the permanent trophy for the World Bridge Federation's Olympiad Team tournaments, again adopting the policy of giving replicas to the winners.

He was also an expert player, and in 1932 and 1940 he won his own Vanderbilt Cup. He played by choice only in the strongest money games, and was a consistent winner. His regular partnership with Waldemar von Zedwitz was among the strongest and most successful in the US. In 1941 he retired from tournament bridge, but he continued to play in the most expert rubber bridge games, in clubs and at home.

In 1968, Vanderbilt spent more than $50,000 to re-create the lost moulds for the replicas of both trophies sufficient to last for the next 40 years. To perpetuate the practice of awarding individual replicas, Vanderbilt further bequeathed to the ACBL a trust fund of

$100,000, a gift that wisely foresaw the possibility of inflation. When last purchased, replicas of the American trophy cost $600; of the Olympiad trophy $500.

In 1969, the World Bridge Federation made Vanderbilt its first Honorary Member. When the Bridge Hall of Fame was inaugurated in 1964, Vanderbilt was one of the first three people elected.

VERSACE, Alfredo of Rome, Italy. (b.1969 in Turin, Italy). Professional player and teacher. Won the Rosenblum Teams in 1998. Won the European Junior Teams in 1992. Won the European Teams twice. Won the *Sunday Times* Invitational Pairs in 1997. Won the Forbo International Teams in The Netherlands in 1997. North American titles include the Vanderbilt in 1999. He also finished 2nd in the 1998 Reisinger. Italian national titles include the Open Teams five times (the first at the age of 15) and the Italy Cup three times.

VILLAS BOAS, Miguel of Salvador, Brazil. (b.1968). Economist. Won the 1998 IOC in Lausanne. 2nd in the Rosenblum Cup in 1998. Represented Brazil in three World Team events. Won the South American Teams three times. Won two national titles.

VIVALDI, Antonio of Turin, Italy. Bridge writer. WBF World Life Master. Finished 2nd in the Bermuda Bowl in 1976. Represented Italy twice in World Team Olympiads. Won the World Mixed Pairs in 1998. Won the European Teams in 1973. Won the EC Mixed Pairs in 1996. Won the European Mixed Teams in 1998. National titles include the Open Teams eight times.

VOGT, Waltraud of Kassel, Germany. Lawyer. WBF World Master. Finished 2nd in the Venice Cup in 1993. Won the European Women's Teams in 1989, and finished 2nd in 1991. 2nd in the European Women's Pairs in 1991. Represented Germany in three World Championships.

VON ARNIM, Daniela of Wiesbaden, Germany. (b.1964). WBF Grand Master and #2 in the world women's rankings in 1999. Has represented Germany in five Venice Cups, reaching the final in 1993, and winning in 1995. Won the 1989 European Women's Teams, and finished 2nd in 1991 & 95. Finished 2nd in both the World Women's Teams and the World Women's Pairs in 1998. Won the European Women's Pairs in 1995 & 97. Finished 3rd in the 1998 Macallan Invitational Pairs. Won her first North American national in 1990 – the Women's Swiss Teams.

VON DER PORTEN, Ronald P of Orinda, California, USA. (b.1936). Computer programmer. WBF Life Master. Twice finished

2nd in the Bermuda Bowl. National titles include the Chicago, the Vanderbilt, the Spingold twice, the Grand National Teams, and the Blue Ribbon Pairs. He regularly commentates on VuGraph at major events.

VON ZEDWITZ, Waldemar K (b.May 8, 1896 in Berlin, Germany; d.Oct.5, 1984). Linguist and lexicographer. ACBL Life Master #4. Former President Emeritus of the ACBL, he was one of the driving forces behind the founding of the WBF. He was an early contributor to the Culbertson system, and a member of both the Four Aces team and the *Bridge World* team that won the first international matches, in England and France, in 1930. His partnership with Harold Vanderbilt was one of the most successful of all time.

In 1930, he donated the Von Zedwitz Gold Cup for Master Pairs (now the Life Masters Pairs), and he then proceeded to win it in the first year.

He won the World Mixed Pairs in 1970, at the age of 74, becoming the oldest player at that time ever to have won a World Championship event. He won 20 national titles.

VRIEND, Bep of Amstelveen, The Netherlands, (b.1946). Secretary and bridge teacher. WBF World Grand Master and #5 in the 1999 world rankings. She has the best record of any Dutch women player. Won the World Women's Pairs in 1994, and finished 3rd in 1990. Placed 2nd in the Venice Cup and in the European Women's Teams, both in 1989. 3rd in the World Women's Team Olympiad in 1984. Won the European Women's Pairs in 1993. Won the European Mixed Teams in 1994, and finished 3rd in 1992. 2nd in the 1983 European Women's Teams, and 3rd twice. She has been a regular member of the Dutch Women's team since 1979. Numerous national titles include the Dutch Open Pairs three times, and the Women's Pairs seven times. She is married to Anton Maas.

WALSH, Rhoda of Los Angeles, California, USA. Attorney. WBF World Master. Finished 3rd in the 1968 World Women's Team Olympiad. In 1968, Walsh won all three major ACBL Women's events (Teams, Pairs and Life Masters Women's Pairs). Many national titles, including the Open Swiss Teams twice.

WALSHE, Pat of Dublin, Ireland. (b.1954). Computer analyst. WBF World Master. Won the EC Pairs in 1981. 2nd in the European

Junior Teams in 1974. 2nd in the EC Teams in 1983 and the Mixed Teams in 1989. A regular member of the Irish team in World and European Championships. He has more than 30 national titles to his name.

WANG, Wen Fei of Shanghai, China. (b.1968). Finished 2nd in the 1997 Venice Cup. Won the Far East Teams in 1997, and 2nd in 1993.

WATSON, Louis H of New York City, New York, USA. (b.1907; d.1936). A leading player in the early days of contract, Watson won the Asbury Park Cup (now the Spingold) in 1932 and the Cavendish Individual in 1933. It is as a writer that he is best known though. He was the bridge columnist for the *New York Post* and one of his books, Watson's *Play of the Hand*, was the definitive work on declarer play for many years, and is one of the classics.

WEI, Chung Ching "C C" of New York City, New York, USA. (b.1914 in Shanghai, China; d.1987). Shipping magnate. He was responsible for devising the Precision Club system used successfully by the Taiwan teams in the 1969 & 70 Bermuda Bowls and by the Precision Team in winning the Spingold twice and the Vanderbilt. The Italian team also used the system to win the Bermuda Bowl twice (1973 & 74) and the 1972 World Team Olympiad.

Wei was npc of the Taiwan teams in 1964 & 69 and of the US team in the 1981 Venice Cup. He also wrote many books on the Precision and Super Precision systems.

WEI-SENDER, Kathie of Nashville, Tennessee, USA. (b.Peking, China). Formerly of New York City, New York. Writer and lecturer on the Precision Club system. She is the official advisor to the Chinese Bridge League and is the only United States citizen to hold minister rank in China. She is also Ambassador of Bridge for the World Bridge Federation. She was named ACBL Honorary Member in 1987. She was honoured with the IBPA's Charles Goren Award as the "Bridge Personality of the Year" in 1986. Elected to the Bridge Hall of Fame in 1999.

WBF World Grand Master and #8 in the 1999 world rankings. Won the World Women's Pairs in 1978, and finished 2nd in 1990. Won the World Women's Team Olympiad in 1984. Won the Venice Cup in 1987, and finished 2nd twice (1981 & 85). She was co-captain and manager of the Taiwan team in the 1971 Bermuda Bowl (placed 2nd) and the 1972 World Team Olympiad. Many North American national titles.

WEICHSEL, Peter M of Encinitas, California, USA. (b.1943). Professional player. WBF World Grand Master and #19 in the 1999 world rankings. Won the Bermuda Bowl in 1983. Won the World Mixed Pairs in 1990. Won the Pan-American Teams in 1982. Won the Cavendish Invitational Pairs twice. Won the *Sunday Times* Invitational Pairs in 1975, and finished 2nd in 1973. He has won 20 national titles. He was a member of the Precision Team, and co-developed, with his regular partner Alan Sontag, Power Precision.

WEIGKRICHT, Terry of Vienna, Austria. (b.1958). Mathematics and French teacher. WBF World Grand Master and #17 in the 1999 world women's ranking. Won the World Women's Teams (the McConnell Cup) in 1998. Won the 1992 World Women's Team Olympiad. Finished 2nd in the 1991 Venice Cup. Won the European Women's Teams in 1991, and 2nd in 1999. Numerous national titles.

WEINSTEIN, Howard M of Chicago, Illinois, USA. (b.1953). Options trader. WBF World Master. Finished 5th in the Rosenblum Teams in 1990. National titles include the Grand National Teams in 1991, the Blue Ribbon Pairs in 1998, the Vanderbilt in 1993, the 1997 Life Masters Pairs, the Open Pairs I in 1996, the Reisinger in 1997.

WEINSTEIN, Steven M of Montclair, New Jersey, USA. (b.1964). Options trader. WBF World Master. He was the ACBL King of Bridge in 1982, and also played in the Rosenblum Teams that year at the age of 18, becoming the youngest player ever to represent the US in a World Championship event. One year earlier, he had become the youngest player ever to win a North American championship (the Life Masters Pairs, playing with his stepfather, Fred Stewart, with whom he has since won numerous other events). He was the ACBL Player of the Year in 1995.

Finished 5th in the Bermuda Bowl in 1991. Won the Cavendish Invitational Pairs twice. Won the Cavendish Teams in 1999. National titles include the Life Masters Pairs, the Blue Ribbon Pairs twice, the Reisinger and the Open Swiss Teams in 1992.

WERDELIN, Stig of Copenhagen, Denmark. (b.1937). Supreme Court lawyer. Denmark's most capped player. WBF World Master. Finished 3rd in the World Team Olympiad in 1984. Placed 2nd in the 1979 European Teams, and 3rd in 1961. Represented Denmark in four World and 12 European Championships. More than 40 national titles include the Danish Open Teams 16 times and the Open pairs eight times.

WESTERHOF, Jan of The Netherlands. (b.1954). Economics teacher. Won the Bermuda Bowl in 1993. Numerous national titles include the Dutch Meesterklasse Teams in 1997.

WESTRA, Berry of Rotterdam, The Netherlands. (b.1961). Bridge teacher. WBF World Master. Won the Bermuda Bowl in 1993. 3rd in the 1992 World Team Olympiad. Won the European Junior Teams in 1986 and the World Junior Teams in 1987. 2nd in the 1985 EC Junior Teams. Won the Cavendish Teams. Many national titles.

WIDENGREN, Britta of Kitzbühl, Austria. (b.1913 in Sweden). Retired managing director. WBF World Master. Finished 2nd in the Venice Cup in 1991 at the age of 78, making her the oldest person to have won a gold or silver medal in a World Championship event. Boris Schapiro's win in the Seniors Pairs in 1998 broke that record, but it still stands for non-Seniors events. Won the Nordic Women's Teams in 1948.

WIGNALL, John of Christchurch, New Zealand. (b.1932 in England). Sharebroker. WBF World Master. Represented New Zealand in six World and many Far East and South Pacific Championships. He has won numerous national titles. He has been the bridge columnist for the *Christchurch Press* and the *Otago Daily Times* since 1966.

WILLARD, Sylvie of Paris, France. (b.1952). Bridge organizer. WBF World Life Master. Finished 2nd in the Venice Cup in 1987, and 3rd in 1985. Won the European Women's Teams four times. Won the EC Mixed Teams in 1992, and two other medals in European Mixed Pairs events. Numerous national titles.

WIRGREN, Anders of Lund, Sweden. (b.1951). Bridge writer. WBF World Master. Finished 3rd in the Rosenblum Teams in 1986. Placed 2nd in the 1976 European Junior Teams, the 1973 Nordic Junior Teams, and the 1988 Nordic Open Teams. National titles include the Swedish Open Teams twice. He is a regular contributor to numerous magazines, and has twice won the IBPA award for the "Best Article of the Year". He has written eight bridge books and two chess books. He was Swedish Junior Chess Champion in 1968.

WOHLIN, Jan of Stockholm, Sweden, (b.1924). WBF Life Master. Represented Sweden in the Bermuda Bowls of 1950 & 53. Won the European Teams in 1952, and finished 2nd three times. Numerous national titles. He was the co-inventor of the EFOS system.

WOLD, Edward M "Eddie" of Houston, Texas, USA. (b.1951). Bridge professional. WBF World Master. Finished 4th in the Bermuda Bowl in 1983. 3rd in the Rosenblum Teams in 1978. 4th in the 1986 World Pairs. Won the McKenney Trophy in 1982. Many national titles.

WOLFF, Robert S "Bobby" of Dallas, Texas, USA. Business consultant, professional player, and syndicated bridge columnist. WBF World Grand Master and #4 in the 1999 world rankings. He was an original member of the Dallas Aces team. Wolff is the only player to have won four different World titles. Won the Bermuda Bowl seven times, and finished 2nd three times. Won the World Team Olympiad in 1988, and finished 2nd three times. Won the World Mixed Teams in 1972 and the World Pairs in 1974. He has twice finished 3rd in the Rosenblum Teams. Won the Pam-American Invitational three times. Many national titles.

His contribution to bidding theory is the Wolff Sign-Off convention. He has been on three televized bridge programmes. He has also contributed to numerous bridge videos.

WOOLSEY, Christopher R "Kit" of Kensington, California, USA. (b.1943), Systems analyst. WBF Life Master. Won the Rosenblum Teams in 1986, and finished 2nd in 1982. Finished 2nd in the Bermuda Bowl in 1989. Won the Cavendish Invitational Pairs in 1979. Won the Cavendish Teams in 1997. Many national titles. He has written a handful of books including the classic, *Matchpoints*. He won the IBPA's C C Wei Award for the best article about bidding conventions in 1977.

YOUNG, Sally of Narberth, Pennsylvania, USA. (b.1906; d.1970). One of the greatest ever women players. ACBL Life Master #17, and the first woman to earn that rank. In 1947, Young was the leader of the only all-woman team to win the Chicago (now the Reisinger). National titles include the Chicago four times, the Women's Team's a record seven times, the Women's Pairs four times, and the Masters Mixed Teams five times.

ZHANG, Ya Lan of Guangzhou, China. (b.1957). WBF Life Master. Finished 2nd in the Venice Cup in 1997, 3rd in 1991 and 4th in 1995. 2nd in the World Women's Team Olympiad in 1996. Won PABF Women's Teams seven times. Represented China in 12 World Championships. Numerous national titles.

ZMUDZINSKI, Adam of Katowice, Poland. (b.1956). Electronic engineer and bridge coach. WBF World Master. Finished 2nd in the Bermuda Bowl in 1991, and in the Rosenblum Teams in 1994. Won the European Teams in 1989. Represented Poland in six World Championships and two European Championships. Numerous Polish national titles. North American titles include the Spingold in 1997.

ZUCKERBERG, Debbie of New York City, New York, USA. (b.1968). Won the World Junior Teams in 1991, and finished 3rd in 1993. Won the Cavendish Teams in 1993. She was NYC Player of the Year in 1992. Married to Michael Rosenberg.

KEY WORDS

Above the line All scores other than for tricks bid and made are entered above the line on the score sheet.

Auction The phase during which the bidding takes place.

Balanced A hand with even distribution such as 4-3-3-3.

Bid A proposal to win a number of tricks in the denomination stated.

Bidding system The agreements between partners as to the meaning of their bids.

Blocked A suit that cannot be cashed because of the location of a high card.

Cash Playing a winning card.

Communications The ability to go from one hand to the other.

Contract The last bid of the auction, possibly doubled or redoubled.

Convention A bid or play that has a particular, frequently artificial, meaning.

Counting Calculating the location of the cards in the unseen hands from the bidding and play.

Cross-ruff Using the trumps from both hands to ruff losers rather than draw trumps.

Cuebid A control in a suit.

Deal The distribution of the cards to the players. Also used to signify the layout of the four hands and the bidding and play.

Dealer The player who deals and bids first.

Declarer The player who first bid the denomination of the final contract.

Defender The players opposing the declarer are the defenders.

Discarding Playing a card that is not of the suit led and not a trump.

Distribution The division of the suits in one hand or the way in which a suit is divided around the table.

Double A call that increases the penalties if a contract fails or increases the score if it makes. It may also be a conventional bid.

Doubleton A holding of two cards in a suit.

Double finesse A finesse against two missing honours.

Draw trumps Playing successive rounds of trumps to remove the opponents trumps.

Drop The play of a high card that collects a missing high card.

Ducking play Declining to take a trick that could have been won for tactical reasons.

Dummy The partner of the declarer; the exposed hand on the table.

Echo A defensive signal where a high card is followed by a lower one in the same suit.

Elimination Removing cards from a defenders hand to leave them with no safe exit when they are thrown in.

Encouraging A bid or play of a card suggesting partner continues.

Endplay The situation, usually towards the end of a deal, where a defender has to make a disadvantageous lead.

Entry A card that can be used to gain access to a particular hand.

Establish To set up winners in a suit; to create an entry.

Exit To give up the lead

Face down The standard way of making the opening lead in duplicate bridge.

False card The deceptive play of a card hoping to mislead the opponents.

Final contract The last bid before three consecutive passes end the auction.

Finesse An attempt to win a trick relying on the favourable location of a missing honour.

Fit The combined holding in a suit; the combination of two hands.

Following suit The obligation on a player to play a card in the suit led to the trick.

Forcing A bid that compels partner to reply; making a player ruff.

Forcing defence Trying to exhaust declarer of trumps by making him ruff a side suit.

Game A score of 100 points below the line.

Grand slam The winning of all thirteen tricks by one side.

Hand A players thirteen cards; the four hands and the bidding and play.

High-card points (HCP) The numerical strength of a hand.

Hold-up Declining to win a trick for tactical reasons.

Honour An ace, king, queen, jack or ten.

Honours A bonus score in rubber bridge for holding four or five honours in the trump suit or all four aces at no-trumps.

Interior sequence A sequence of honour cards, that may incorporate the nine, consisting of two or more touching cards and one higher honour, e.g. A-J-10-9

Jump bid Any bid made at a higher level than necessary.

Leading The first card played to a trick.

Lead out of turn A lead from the wrong hand.

Long cards The cards left in a suit when all the others in that suit have been played.

Major suit Spades or hearts.

Master The highest outstanding card in a suit.

Minor suit Diamonds or clubs.

Negative A response denying values.

Negative double A bid showing values as opposed to being for penalties.

No bid The traditional term for Pass in Great Britain.

No-trumps The highest denomination signifying there is no trump suit.

Opening lead The initial lead to trick one, before dummy is exposed.

Open the bidding The first positive bid during the auction.

Overbid A bid not justified by the strength of the hand held.

Overcalling A bid by the side that did not open the bidding.

Overruff Ruffing a trick that has already been ruffed with a higher trump.

Overtake Playing a higher card from one hand when the trick is already being won by the other.

Partscore A score below the line insufficient for game.

Pass The way a player indicates he does not wish to make a positive bid.

Passed hand A hand that has already passed.

Penalty The score arising from the failure to make a contract.

Penalty card A card exposed by a defender other than in the normal course of play.

Peter A defensive signal where a high card is followed by a lower one in the same suit.

Point count Evaluating a hand by assigning values to the high cards.

Positive A constructive bid implying an agreed number of points.

Pre-empt A high-level bid hoping to make the opponents bidding difficult.

Promotion Playing one card to ensure another achieves winning status.

Psychic bid A deliberate attempt to mislead as to the strength and distribution of a hand.

Rebid A bid in the same suit as the previous one; any bid on the second round by the opening bidder.

Redouble A bid that increase the score if a contract that has been doubled makes but increases the penalties if it fails.

Reopen A bid or double in a position where a pass would have ended the auction.

Responder The player who replies to a bid, usually the partner of the opening bidder.

Response The reply to a bid.

Revoke Failing to follow suit when able to do so.

Running Trying to escape from a poor contract.

Rubber The best of three games.

Ruff Playing a trump when another suit has been led.

Sacrifice A contract that is not expected to be made.

Safety play A line of play giving the best chance of making the required number of tricks, sometimes involving the surrender of a trick that need not have been lost.

Sequence A number of consecutive cards, e.g. A-K-Q-J-10.

Shape The way a hand is distributed.

Shows out Reveals a void by being unable to follow suit.

Side-suit A suit other than trumps.

Signal The way defenders convey information to each other.

Sign-off An invitation to partner to pass.

Singleton A holding of one card in a suit.

Slam A contract to make twelve or thirteen tricks.

Spot cards The two to nine inclusive.

Stopper A card that prevents the run of a suit.

Switch Leading a different suit from the one played to the previous trick.

Take-out double A double asking partner to bid.

Tempo The general rhythm of a players actions; the initiative in play or defence.

Tenace A combination of cards, e.g. AQ, that may be worth extra tricks depending on the location of the missing cards.

Three-suiter A hand that is either 4-4-4-1 or 5-4-4-0.

Trial bid A bid in a new suit inviting partner to bid game.

Trick The lead and the three subsequent cards.

Trump A card in the suit named in the contract.

Trump fit The number of trumps held by declarer and dummy.

Trump suit The suit named in the final contract.

Two-suiter A hand with at least five cards in two suits.

Unbalanced Generally a hand with a singleton or void.

Unbid suit A suit not bid during the auction.

Unblock Playing a card that would prevent the run of a suit.

Underbid A bid that understates the value of a hand.

Underruff An unusual play where a small trump is played under the ruffing card of an opponent, usually to avoid being endplayed or squeezed.

Undertrick Each trick by which declarer fails in his contract.

Void A holding of no cards in a suit.

Vulnerable A side that has made a game.

Yarborough A hand with no card higher than a nine. It is named after Lord Yarborough who offered odds of 1000-1 against holding such a hand. The real odds are 1827-1!